The Human Measure

SOCIAL THOUGHT IN THE WESTERN LEGAL TRADITION

DONALD R. KELLEY

HARVARD UNIVERSITY PRESS

CAMBRIDGE, MASSACHUSETTS

LONDON, ENGLAND

1990

LIBRARY OF CONGRESS CATALOGING-IN-PUBLICATION DATA

Kelley, Donald R.
The human measure : social thought in the western legal tradition
/ Donald R. Kelley.
p.   cm.
ISBN 0-674-41500-0
1. Sociological jurisprudence—History.
2. Law—Europe—History and criticism.
I. Title.
K370.K45   1990
K370.K45   1990
340'.115—dc20   89-71724
CIP

Contents

Preface

La coutume est une second nature qui détruit la première.

Pascal, *Pensées*

.

An ancient topos, "Custom is second nature," best locates the theme of this book, and a comment by Pascal gives it further definition. Although an admirer and intellectual beneficiary of Montaigne, Pascal differed from him on one point, which was the attempt to justify the idea of custom on the basis of reason. "Montaigne is wrong," wrote Pascal. "Custom should be followed only because it is custom, and not because it is reasonable or just."[1] People "believe that truth can be found, and that it exists in law and custom . . . and take their antiquity as a proof of their truth"; but in fact and humanly, Pascal wrote, "there is neither truth nor justice to introduce into them." Custom formed its own ground and established its own rationale and legitimacy.

Elsewhere, in defense of this view, Pascal performed his own variation on the ancient canon. "Custom is a second nature which destroys the former," he wrote. "For is custom not natural? I am very much afraid that nature itself is only a first custom, as custom is a second nature." In this locus modernus of ethical relativism, skeptical humanism, and inadvertent historicism, Pascal took the side of Thrasymachus against Socrates, of the Sophists against Plato (of Nietzsche against Kant), and asserted his doubts about the cosmic powers of human reason. For, as he wrote, "When I commenced the study of man, I saw that these abstract sciences are not suited to man," although on the grounds of religion rather than sophism he concluded, "True nature being lost, everything becomes its own nature; as the true good being lost, everything becomes its own true good."[2]

In this way Pascal, even though he himself was a devotee of mathematics and natural philosophy and was living in an age of "scientific revolution," reaffirmed the autonomy of the human sciences, as Vico was to do more elaborately in the next century, and denied that they needed a transcendent foundation in a First Nature. This has not been an uncommon reaction to the complexities of the human condition and an awareness of the ocean of language in which we all, conceptually, must swim. In Nietzschean—and Heraclitean—hyperbole, "The 'apparent' world is the only one: the 'real' world has been *lyingly added* . . ."[3] By its own lights and in its own terms, humanity is the name-giver, the myth-maker, the source of law, the creator of meaning. Whatever religion or philosophy may propose, self-knowledge requires man—humankind—to create its own measure, within its own horizons, under its own conditions, and through its own imperfections. This age-old search for a human self-measure, within the confines of language, is the theme of this work.

"Nomos" is the name I have associated with the present project for a dozen years. Of course I might have called the book *The Idea of Law* (on the analogy of, and with borrowed lustre from, R. G. Collingwood's *Idea of Nature* and *Idea of History*), except for the restrictive connotations of this word "law." For the polyvalent root term Nomos has had—across many cultures, ancient and modern, pagan and Christian—many meanings: not only law but also custom, pasturage, a familiar place, even "history" (*etiam dicitur historia,* says an editor of Suidas).[4] In my late, perhaps postmodern, usage it is intended to designate a fairly coherent set of problems which have been part of the perennial effort to understand and to cope with human society, culture, and collective experience over time. This of course begs more than one question—what are human "society," "culture," and other such metahistorical categories?—but then the naming process is itself a seminal part of social and "nomical" thought. Nomos implies the recognition of repetitions or regularities, the communication of common experiences, the establishing of rules, and the defining of "laws"— the discovery, in a phrase, of a human measure—which constitute the premises and "forejudgments" of more systematic thinking about (if not management of) collective human behavior.

The present work is in part an extension of, in part an atonement for, some of the interpretations offered in my first book, *Foundations of Modern Historical Scholarship.* That work was devoted almost exclusively to expressions of early modern historical, even proto-historicist, attitudes. So it neglected some of the larger and more traditional views of human culture, and it tended to undervalue the roles of imitation and myth in historical scholarship. Here I should like to redress the balance somewhat by inquiring into other, perhaps more fundamental, characteristics of Western self-understanding, and by considering the longer reach of intellectual and linguistic tradition opened up by this same search for cultural self-understanding. A proper understanding of any aspect of this history ought to go back (as Renaissance scholars tried to go back) to the earliest usages and textual evidence; and in a modest way I have followed this old philological precept.

Yet I am not much interested in the "history of ideas" in the sense of retrospective mind-reading. Mine is not a quest only for the original meaning, the pure authorial intention, of texts—not a quest for the "historical"

Gaius, in other words, or even for the historical Weber, as he lived, breathed, and thought. Rather, it is a quest for the changing expressions and interpretations of social and cultural thought—the forms of Nomos— through the *longue durée* of discourse, argument, criticism, formulation, and reformulation that comes down to us in largely textual terms. For the history of thought is a history of misinterpretation—a "map of misreading" and misappropriation—rather than a "perennial philosophy." Not that this "semantic autonomy of the text"(as Paul Ricoeur has called it)[5] is an invitation to miscommunication or to a neglect of context (necessarily inferred from other texts); rather, it is the very condition of communication, understanding, and the medium of language that permits, if not a meeting of minds, at least plausible interpretation over an expanse of time.

Culture, or custom, is always being paired with nature—Nomos with Physis—and therefore, in studying the history of social thought and writing, I have tried to keep in mind recent work in the history of natural science, which is at least a generation ahead of the history of social science in terms of breadth, depth, critical methods, and certainly control of source materials. (There is no George Sarton for any of the human sciences, nor a Thomas Kuhn.) I am not persuaded that talk of paradigms or fixed epistemes is appropriate for the history of the human sciences; but I do believe that the historian must attend to continuities of premises, vocabulary, styles of interpretation, and professional conduct. It is more notoriously difficult to carry this out for social thought than for the canon of natural philosophy, which has been given formal, or nominal, definition by the Aristotelian corpus. My solution to this problem is the hypothesis of a rough analogy to the Aristotelian tradition. A central premise of this book is that, historically, the principal questions, terminology, and lines of investigation of the study of humanity have been, over two millennia and more, the "science of law"—not the large universe of Physis, but the more familiar pasturage of Nomos, especially in the western legal tradition. (Nomos was in fact an Aristotelian term, but never a central category on the level of Physis.)

One of the fundamental differences between Nomos and Physis has to do with what I call the structure of reality. "Reality" in the land of Nomos, as Aristotle understood, is tied to practical knowledge (*phronesis*); for purposes of discrimination, judgment, and action it cannot hope to rise above the horizons of human experience and the sequence of human time to gain a universal and transcendent perspective or an imaginary Archimedean point of control. The "Socratic revolution" stemmed in part from this realization; but in Platonic philosophy the cosmic urge was preserved and those "sophists" who maintained a practical perspective—the "horizon-structure of experience," as it has been called—were denounced as mean and mercenary. Plato, as Nietzsche put it, "severed the instincts from the *polis*."[6] By contrast, the human standpoint, entangled as it has been with sex, the family, labor, language, community, commerce, politics, and war, led to an understanding of philosophical and epistemological questions long before "science" developed its "metaphysical foundations." By the time Descartes formulated his dualism—the subjective *res cogitans* and the objective *res extensa*—the legal tradition had long since installed the free subject ("person") at the very center of its framework, surrounded by a "reality" given a wide range of social meanings, such as possessions, commodities, and property (*res* that was not merely *extensa* but *corporalis* or *incorporalis, privata* or *publica, mobilis* or *immobilis,* and so on).[7] The difference was that in the Cartesian context the field of experience was thought or consciousness, while in the legal framework it was action, or freedom—not "I think," but rather (though implied instead of stated), "I act, therefore I am."

I am of course aware that in our day the dominance of natural-science models, affiliated with and in part descended from Aristotelian natural philosophy, have made this perspective unfashionable. Indeed, within the legal tradition itself—the headquarters and homeland of Nomos—the forces of Physis have made significant inroads and have seemed at times in the ascendant, especially since the seventeenth century. In this century too, legal positivism, the "pure theory of law," and a renewed natural law have reinforced this tendency.[8] Nevertheless, what I classify under the rubric of Nomos has preserved some vitality, integrity, and utility; and I have tried to restrict my horizons to those traditions of investigation and interpretation which view human social and cultural life in its own terms, largely to the exclusion of the analytical and often reductionist systems of "modernist" social science which, in one way or another, seek to unmask culture and to find an underlying (objective, behaviorist, quantifiable, and perhaps predictable) "nature." It may not be wise to neglect Mother Nature, but I believe that enough homage and historical attention has already been paid to Physis, certainly in comparison with its perennial rival, and shadow, Nomos—which has been neither deified nor mythologized, nor matrified, nor even vouchsafed significant conceptual status.

The story of Nomos is a subplot in the history of Western thought; and if the larger patterns are familiar, the cast of characters is probably not. Yet the tradition of Nomos, in all of its configurations, disguises, and transformations, is in many ways closer to human experience than that of physical science; for it shares a common structure (and "fore-structure") with Western languages as a whole. The conceptual model that seems most appropriate is what Hans Blumenberg calls "work on myth," especially in connection with the legal tradition.[9] In general the structures of social experience, like those of language, provide a continuing framework for human judgment and action and the formation of "social meaning" (which is one of the functions of myth). Most fundamentally, the language of the law has been preserved—through intellectual habits, professional conventions, technical terms, proverbs, maxims, and the like—across many centuries and has ostensibly permitted an endless and fairly continuous dialogue which has formed the canon and shaped the scholastic character of western jurisprudence.

This suggests another basic contrast between nomical and physical science, which in simplest terms is the problem of "ideology."[10] Social context, the situation of the individual within horizons defined by a particular community at a particular time, sets and shapes assumptions, values, and goals quite apart from cultural or intellectual tradition; and in the land of Nomos "meaning" is always and irretrievably "social." This is not to accept the naive view that natural science is not culture bound, that the meaning of scientific terms is not determined by theory, or that scientific language is not in its own way metaphorical; it is only to insist that social thought is doubly, and deliberately, bound to social context by requirements of participation, judgment, and action—"objectivist" posturing and "scientific" disclaimers notwithstanding. To some extent, indeed, it is the predicament of social thought that underlies the modern criticism of ideology and theoretical accommodations to it, including the "sociology of knowledge" and, more recently, the "anthropology of knowledge." I hope this study contributes something to the theoretical as well as the historical discussion of this most crucial of enterprises: to take the measure of humankind.

In what follows I draw in part on various investigations I have published over the past decade or so. Many of them were gathered in the collection *History, Law, and the Human Sciences* (London: Variorum Editions, 1984); others are "The Science of Anthropology: An Essay on the Very Old Marx," *Journal of the History of Ideas,* 45 (1984), 245–62; with Bonnie Smith, "What Was Property? Legal Dimensions of the Social Question in France," *Proceedings of the American Philosophical Society,* 128 (1984), 200–30; "Ancient Verses on New Ideas: Legal Tradition and the French Historical School," *History and Theory,* 26 (1987), 319–38; "Civil Science in the Renaissance: The Problem of Interpretation," *The Languages of Political Theory in Early-Modern Europe,* ed. Anthony Pagden (Cambridge, Eng., 1987), 57–78; "Jurisconsultus Perfectus: The Lawyer as Renaissance Man," *Journal of the Warburg and Courtauld Institutes,* 51 (1988), 84–102; and "*Altera Natura:* The Idea of Custom in Historical Perspective," *Science, Education and Philosophy: Studies in Intellectual History in Honour of Charles Schmitt* (London, 1989).

Like so many others, I owe more to Paul Oskar Kristeller than I can hope to repay, although I cannot be sure that he will approve of the direction taken by my own *Iter.* I am also bound to express gratitude to colleagues at the Institute for Advanced Study (especially Felix Gilbert, John Elliott, and Clifford Geertz) and the National Humanities Center (especially Charles Blitzer and Kent Mullikin), to the Folger Institute of the Folger Shakespeare Library (especially J. G. A. Pocock and Lena Orlin), to the Davis Center of Princeton University (especially Lawrence Stone and Anthony Grafton), as well as to the John Simon Guggenheim Foundation and the National Endowment for the Humanities for support of this project (and related studies) at various stages over the past decade and more. The last phases of this project were illuminated by discussions with colleagues at the conference on *Naturrecht* held at Göttingen under the leadership of Hans Erich Bödeker and Istvan Hont. I should also thank Hans Erich Troje and especially Paolo Grossi (whose scholarship and insight on matters legal I cannot hope to match) for comments on the manuscript; my coeditors on the *Journal of the History of Ideas,* above all Lewis Beck, Perez Zagorin, and Robin Ladrach, and colleagues at the University of Rochester for assistance, indulgence, and forbearance.

Most essential of all has been the support of Bonnie Smith, who has her own view of the "human measure"—to the boundless enhancement of my own *Lebenswelt.*

Rochester, N. Y.
24 August 1989

ONE

Introduction: The Idea of Nomos

Das Vergehen ist . . . die Versammlung des Währenden . . . die uns
als Botengänger *braucht*.

Heidegger, "Aus einem Gespräch von der Sprache"

·

Nature and Law

A posthumous work of R. G. Collingwood traces the idea of nature from
ancient Greek thought down to the present century;[1] among other things
this book offers a similar study of the parallel and in some ways analogous
idea of law. The analogy is heightened by the consideration that custom,
the most rudimentary but also most fundamental form of law, came to be
regarded as "second nature" over this same span of time. Nature and law,
physis and *nomos,* these twin concepts, sibling rivals for the legacy of
human wisdom, have interacted with each other across some twenty-four
centuries of Western intellectual tradition; and indeed, in modern versions
of the old contest, they are still interacting. C. P. Snow's "two cultures,"
Heinrich Rickert's "natural sciences" and "cultural sciences," Immanuel
Kant's "starry heavens above and moral law within," the "war between
naturalism and historicism" located by Ernst Troeltsch in the seventeenth
century, Descartes's distinction between *res extensa* and *res cogitans,* the
Renaissance conflict between scholasticism and humanism, the medieval
dispute between medicine and law, and the age-old debate between philosophy and rhetoric—all of these and more reflect, and in a sense are remote
descendants of, the antique polarity formulated by fifth-century Sophists
and protested by Plato, and embedded in language going back to the pre-
Socratics.[2]

In pursuing this inquiry it is not necessary to be invidious—contrasting
"hard" with "soft" sciences, for example, materialism with idealism, or
objectivity with subjectivity—but it will be useful in the following pages to
maintain a distinction between the attitudes and assumptions associated
with these two terms: that is, between a view focused on the universe at
large, its structure, texture, and transformations, and a view turned toward
humanity, its creations, predicaments, and fate. The distinction is not absolute, but it does correspond to certain fundamental intellectual priorities,
and it does imply different ways of posing questions and formulating

answers. It also corresponds to various binary patterns in Western languages which determine the form of such questions and answers.

Following the trail of Nomos—so let this amorphous subject be designated from now on—is considerably more difficult than following that of Physis, despite the multiplicity of faces which "nature" has displayed since the speculations of the *physiologoi*. Certainly the path is less clearly marked and is traveled by less familiar figures than the great system-builders and legislators of natural philosophy. Indeed, there are no "major authors" before Vico (and his credentials are widely suspect), none at least who can be invoked to illustrate the richness and imperial status of social philosophy in the way that Newton or Leibniz, or Aristotle, illuminates the richness and graces the canon of natural philosophy. The result is that there is no historiographical tradition of "nomical" science corresponding to the recognizable canon of physical science, nothing comparable to Collingwood's *Idea of Nature*, except to the extent that political theory (as expressed in the most general, usually neo-Aristotelian terms) has been vouchsafed a marginal position in the histories of philosophy or of thought more generally conceived.[3]

Yet the trail of Nomos can be charted, I think; and it does pass through territories which, though appearing on no large-scale maps, deserve exploration for any comprehensive understanding of Western thought. For at least as long as natural philosophers have inquired into the secrets of the cosmos, observers of human behavior have sought analogous insights into social life—and likewise, in various ways, have sought to control it. In this tradition, too, there are "major authors," although not always the names familiar to those conversant with the standard canons of the history of thought; and I hope their later, retrospective marginalization may be corrected in my account. On the most concrete and practical level the pioneers in this effort have been not the cosmologists who belatedly shifted their gaze from the heavens to the human community but rather, I believe, the law-makers who were confronted by the predicaments of human society. My first premise, in short, is that the primary vehicle of Nomos is the grand tradition of Western jurisprudence, which (like natural philosophy but in many ways independent of it) is rooted in Greek consciousness and was formalized and canonized by the Romans, elaborated along different lines by European interpreters and adapters, and—through a complex process of sublimation and increasingly liberating and even destructive criticism—transmuted into recognizably "modern" sciences of society and culture. In any case this project of understanding humanity in terms not of a primordial physical or socio-biological existence but of its own self-created "second nature" is the main story-line of this book.

Where to start? "In the beginning was the Word" is a formula valid only for theologians and certain kinds of philosophers; for historians the

"Word," the Logos, comes only at the end, and even then imperfectly. What comes first is the pre-logical, the pre-conscious, which is to say the mythical; and in fact one classic study treats these beginnings specifically as a development "from mythos to logos."[4] But of course myth is an even more confusing and controversial maze than Nomos. "Very deep is the well of the past," Thomas Mann wrote at the outset of one of the most imaginative contemporary efforts to seek out origins. "Should we not call it bottomless?" This is surely the case for the origin of law, which is implicit in any society, however "primitive" or apparently unstructured; and so, it seems to me, are attendant concepts of social and cultural behavior, however inarticulate or apparently undecipherable.

We begin, then, with presuppositions as fundamental as language itself—with "prejudices" in Heidegger's sense of a certain logically inaccessible "fore-structure" of knowledge that is the condition of linguistic communication. "Humanly," too, certain questions have always demanded assumptions if not reasoned answers: the status and role of the individual; the interplay of the sexes; the character and limits of the family; relations with other groups; problems of possession, ownership, and inheritance; norms of behavior; and larger puzzles concerning the origins and destiny of the community. Eventually, ancient jurisprudence gave formal classification to these questions through the categories of person, place, and action; but in the first instance (and as language suggests) answers were given in terms of myth or religion. Prehistorically, we may say, law was but one face of religious behavior, one meaning of myth; and so social thought must also be extracted from the all-but-undecipherable, pre-logical contexts.

In the longest perspective, legal terms and ideas and the social consciousness they bespeak cannot be separated from views of life and the natural world in general. As Henri Frankfort has written, "The realm of nature and the realm of man were not distinguished" in ancient Near Eastern speculative thought.[5] Indo-European culture, which despite the criticism of the past century remains (in Toynbee's famous phrase) the "intelligible field of study" for myth, was expressed first in response to nature. Consciousness first found expression in physical, and especially physiological, terms, the psyche being conceived as a form of breath which bestowed divinity on the head above other parts of the body, as was the case with the Roman counterpart, the *anima*.[6]

Similarly, ideas of law were often homologous with, if not indistinguishable from, ideas of natural order or disorder. As a consequence, social thought seems at first to be a function of a cosmological (or cosmogonical) view of the world. Creation myths are in a sense law-giving myths, "the way things are" being construed in one form or another as the way things ought to be, and the process of change as the proper operation of forces beyond human will. In general, speculative answers to the largest questions about the universe serve to condition and to interpret the most immediate and unreflective social behavior, as language again illustrates. In this sense Nomos can be seen as deriving from nature and indeed, as Aristotle put it, as "second nature."[7]

How far, even with the assistance of comparative linguistics and mythology, can we peer into the deep "well of the past"? "All wisdom comes from the East," declared one Renaissance pioneer of oriental studies; and this belief has itself had a mythic force in Western thought from at least the time of Herodotus.[8] Long before Homer, Near Eastern civilization had formulated sophisticated ideas of "righteousness" and "justice," most notably in poetic books of wisdom, such as the *Egyptian Book of the Dead,* which listed a wide range of social acts to be avoided and which displayed a moral vision similar to (if less grandiosely presented than) the Ten Commandments of the Hebrews and the teachings of such charismatic models as Gautama and Zoroaster.

A certain level of legal science (as distinguished from moral thought) is reflected in the codes of the Assyrians, of the Hittites, and especially of Hammurabi, whose lofty pronouncements prefigured the authoritarian aims and rhetoric of Justinian and Napoleon. Hammurabi's "code" was a purely secular assemblage of disparate customs dating back many generations and treating many commonplace matters of property and succession, and yet this "king of righteousness" had his legislative sights set on an eternal rather than a merely human creation. "Let him not," Hammurabi warned his successor, "alter the judgments of the laws which I pronounced, the decisions of the country which I have rendered."[9] Still more ambitious and elaborate, though inclined to religious and moral instruction, were the sacred books of Indian law (Sanskrit, *dharma*), especially the *Code of Manu,* which gathered a millennium of Hindu customs and taboos and which (so believed many nineteenth-century scholars) reflected a seminal stage in the development of Indo-European legal culture and social thinking.

More recent scholars have sought the roots of Western myth, religious patterns, and legal concepts in Indian, Mycenaean, and even Hittite cultures. Was there, for example, an "Indo-European god of exchange and reciprocity" traceable back, linguistically, to the figure of Hermes, god of thieves (before he became, by association with *hermeneia,* the god of critics)?[10] For the most part, precise channels remain mysterious, which is to say metalinguistic and a matter for anthropological speculation, if not cultural "prejudice." Too many questions remain and resist final answers— diffusion? influence? osmosis? constants of human nature? coincidence?— for scholars to reach any significant interdisciplinary consensus, except perhaps to incline to what G. S. Kirk (begging the question) has called a "phenomenological approach."[11]

For these reasons the traces of ancient Near Eastern social thought must remain peripheral to the career of Western Nomos as envisioned here. My starting point must be the mythical and social legacy of the Greek polis, and my second major focus the more concrete constructions of republican and imperial Rome, which was the principal beneficiary of the Greek legacy. Only after examining these ancient roots and foundations will it be possible to move into the derivative and divergent complexities of the European legal tradition, ending with what must at first seem the barely recognizable as well as remote intellectual descendants of the early forms of Nomos.

Chronologically, then, the story sweeps over two millennia and more, from the conceptions of Solon down to those of Marx and Maine, and perhaps Weber and Durkheim. Within this panoramic scope, I attend to selected aspects of Western intellectual history, including the formative Romano-Byzantine efforts in systematic jurisprudence, conceptions of law in the Judeo-Christian and early Germanic tradition, the revival of Roman legal science in the twelfth and thirteenth centuries, a number of national variations on the Roman theme, the emergence of the philosophical (natural-law) and historical schools, and the significance of the legal tradition in the rise of the modern sciences of society and culture in the eighteenth and nineteenth centuries.

There will, however, be no attempt to chronicle Western legal thought in a professional or a disciplinary way, nor do I intend to follow a strictly historical method in discussing legal authorities. There are plenty of surveys and a massive monographic literature devoted to the "external history" of the law and aimed at uncovering the "original" meaning of legal texts beneath successive layers of interpretation. I am more concerned with messages received by readers than with those intended by authors, and what I propose is not the examination of legal antiquities but rather an exploration of the legal canon as it unfolded and was interpreted and transformed. My purpose is to seek what Hans-Georg Gadamer (in trying to define the goal of hermeneutics) has called an "experience of tradition" and to explore the meaning of such tradition as it changes over a long span of time. For present purposes this "experience of tradition," and the tracing of interpretations and of course misinterpretations, requires a critical review of a very long intellectual continuum centering on the canon of Western jurisprudence created in classical antiquity and preserved by an intellectual tradition encompassing several cultures and many generations. In some ways the Western legal tradition represents a gigantic "map of misreading" which the historian must appreciate in its entirety as well as in its discrete textual segments.

The jurists were in general pioneers in that intellectual project which Stephen Toulmin has called "concept-formation" and which is the product in the first instance of "the exigencies of practical affairs [which] have provided the material for subsequent theoretical analysis."[12] In Toulmin's view, "lawyers, judges, and professors of jurisprudence have repeatedly dealt with questions of practical procedure which came up for philosophical analysis only later"—Solon preceding Socrates is his primary example—and this insight supplies another premise for my interpretations.

In another important way it is essential to view this tradition apart from particular historical moments and environments, for the members of the "republic of jurisconsults" professed allegiance to the lofty ideals of their "science" rather than to particular clients.[13] They spoke (and still speak) to one another over many centuries and across national boundaries, invoking not only their intellectual forebears but also their posterity—not only their "pre-cursors," it might be said, but also their "post-cursors." From the Greek orators and Roman *honoratiores* to modern legal and social "scientists," certain assumptions, terms, concepts, authorities, "prejudices," and larger intellectual conventions have been preserved, developed, and modified in various ways which must be understood beyond, as well as within, specific historical contexts.

To this extent a critical variety of the "Whig view" is inescapable and even necessary. Yet, while the story of Nomos from a twentieth-century perspective is cumulative, it can hardly be represented as a simple advance toward enlightenment and improvement. An accumulation of erudition and criticism there certainly was; but there was also the addition of new prejudices and new cultural and ideological constructs, or fictions, that served the needs, interests, and illusions of society. Jurists have insisted on the "scientific" character of their enterprise, but in a long view it might be better understood in terms of what Hans Blumenberg has called "work on myth." Modern legal scholars have rejected the misconceptions of the medieval doctors of law, but then have gone on to substitute their own idealizations of the ancient phases of their common tradition, while the rational jurists of the seventeenth century affected, in quasi-Cartesian fashion, to extricate legal philosophy from antique learning altogether. Then, in the nineteenth century, the Historical School tried to restore all the old myths, this time in the guise of critical historical scholarship, if not conservative social policy. My own offering can itself be only further "work on myth," for this is the general predicament of all historians, and in any case (as Blumenberg suggests) the "end of myth" is the grandest, the most persistent, and (for historical understanding) the most illusory of all myths.[14]

Natural Science and Social Science

Like primary and "second" nature, natural science and social science display a fundamental analogy. "The history of science," A. C. Crombie has written, "is the history of systems of thought about the natural world."[15]

Such a view is an invitation to open the legal tradition up to just as large a perspective as Collingwood did in his survey of the idea of nature, and perhaps to draw law into, or back into, the orbit of Western philosophy. Thomas Kuhn, reflecting on his conception of scientific paradigms and endorsing a remark of M. I. Finley, has suggested that "the history of law would provide an even more revealing parallel"; and indeed Antonio de Gennaro has attempted to see legal history as a succession of "paradigms"—centering respectively on cosmology, theology, mechanism, and "historicism."[16]

I refrain from pursuing further this adaptation of Kuhn's overexploited thesis to the complex career of social science; but I would venture to extend Crombie's notion through a suggestive statement made by another historian of science, Marshall Claggett, who remarks: "It is an obvious fact to the historian of science that the physical concepts of a Galileo or a Descartes, or even a Newton, radical as they may seem, were conditioned in many ways by the ancient and medieval learning that survived into the early modern period. And anyone who is honestly interested in the enormously complex *historical* process of the formation of modern science must examine in detail the general concepts of the preceding period. This examination will give some insight into how a proto-scientific theory was criticized and emended until it was no longer a cogent whole. It will also show how the very points of criticism of the older system became points of departure for the new."[17] In broad outline this pattern seems to have been recapitulated in the history of Western science at least down to the nineteenth century— which, in conceptual and methodological terms, seems to have been (to paraphrase Whitehead's remark about Plato's relation to philosophy) in large part a series of footnotes to Aristotle.

My purpose here is to view the history of social science in a similar fashion, granted the absence of an Aristotle, or a Newton, or even "systems of thought" that were as clearly definable and as clearly commanding assent as those derived from, or reacting to, Aristotelian philosophy. Yet the skeleton of a "system," the vague shadow of a paradigm, did emerge in late antiquity (see Chapter 4); it was, to return to Claggett's comment, "criticized and emended" by a long tradition of interpreters (Chapters 5– 8); it developed widely accepted and practiced "scientific" methods and terminology as well as an agenda of research (especially Chapters 11–12; and by the Newtonian age it had become the starting point for later systems (Chapters 12 through 15). If there were no true "scientific revolutions," there was a rich tradition of "normal science," which underlay a vast amount of (in effect) collaborative investigation and which underwent a series of upheavals and transformations. Let me, by way of concluding this introduction, suggest some of the main features of the tradition of legal science from the point of view of modern social and cultural thought.

The first distinguishing feature of Nomos is its anthropocentric, in some ways anthropomorphic, orientation. It does not take a cosmic or astral view of creation but rather, in the concept of "person," follows a "horizon-structure of experience." Here again is a link with myth. "For modern scientific man the phenomenal world is primarily an 'it,'" remarked Frankfort; "for ancient—and also for primitive—man it is a 'Thou.'"[18] Consciousness, though inaccessible historically, is the prerequisite of law—part of the "fore-structure" of legal knowledge—as it is for language; and it is transformed by legal science into the primary category of personality, defined by certain attributes, including will, freedom, reason, responsibility, perhaps "conscience," and more modern forms of individuality and presumed "subjectivity," though these are tied always to family and kinship. Voluntarism is in effect built into the very structure of law, not only in its making but also in its practice; and the juridical premise of "free will" long preceded Christian conceptions of conscience.

Next, inseparable from the condition of self-consciousness, comes the relationship of the person to physical "reality," although this second legal category ("thing") refers not merely to objective nature but to the material means of subsistence: that is, a civil state (and "real estate") associated with labor and some form of property. Here fact joins with law, nature with culture, especially in the juridical concept of "possession," which (as Eugen Ehrlich has noted) "is the true law of the economic order"—and, one might add, of the "nomic" order.[19] In more elaborate legal terms, this second legal category produces what has been called the "classificatory genitive"—that is, property, possession, and prescription.

Here we can see the primordial dialectic of society—not only the distinction between "mine" and "thine" but also the source of human "alienation." This basic condition of social existence was implicit in the legal tradition long before being formulated philosophically by Hegel, Marx, and others. Perhaps no one has said it better than Emerson:

> There are two laws discrete
> Not reconciled—
> Law for man, and law for thing;
> The last builds town and fleet,
> But it runs wild,
> And doth the man unking.[20]

The third and final member of the basic legal triad is the category of "action"—fundamentally social interaction among persons in the context of economic "reality." *Actio* represents the theoretical point where self-consciousness becomes social consciousness and where the defining faculty of human will, as expressed in language as well as behavior, becomes essential both for social activity and for legal regulation. It is the point, too, where ethical, economic, and social norms, reinforced by religion, find communal sanction and institutional expression, and perhaps pass from oral to written form.

In spite of being a large and metahistorical idealization, this "trichotomy" does seem to correspond to the tripartite structure of civil law from the beginning down to the present: persons, things, actions—corresponding, in terms of modern ("value-free") social science, to social psychology, economics, and sociological "action theory."[21] More fundamentally, it suggests a homology with Indo-European languages—subject, object, verb—whether or not it is deeply embedded in Western consciousness or subconsciousness. In social terms the logic of human action and interaction is syntax; for the human condition as viewed within a "horizon-structure of experience" can be expressed only through language, or a conventional analogue thereof; and as Emile Beneveniste has tried to show, subjectivity, and with it some form of voluntarism, is an unavoidable premise of language.[22]

So, perhaps, is its obverse, "reality" (*realitas,* the collective "reification" of things, *res*). In his essay "The Nature of Things and the Language of Things," Gadamer makes the analogy between the linguistic and legal conceptions of "things," both of which acquire meaning in terms only of personal consciousness and discourse.[23] Once again a parallel appears between the ideas of law and nature; for in the history of natural philosophy, too, the term and concept *res* has been pivotal. Most notably, Descartes employed it in his reductive and dualistic metaphysics, which recapitulated in the most radical manner the distinction between person and thing—between *res cogitans* and *res extensa*—likewise made on the basis of the human attributes of individual consciousness and will.

What this legal and linguistic trichotomy suggests, finally, is the epistemological foundation of Nomos, which is subject-centered and in effect expands concentrically from the center through ever-widening actions and experiences accomplished in a complex social field defined by cultural (and eventually legal) boundaries. Out of this experience, or out of the interacting and interlocking experiences of numerous subjects, arise perceptions, conceptions, and formulations of social organization and community, from family, kinship, and tribe to various economic, military, civic, and political forms. It is a cultural convention, reinforced by myth and authority, that institutions and laws are created by legislative will—an original law-giver or political leader—taking inspiration from a divine source; but the substance of early laws testifies to the existence of accumulated usages which achieved legitimacy and a certain level of what Eugen Ehrlich calls "universalization" before receiving political sanction.[24] The Roman system of "consanguinity," for example, had social force long before receiving expression in civil law; and so it was with the conventions underlying feudalism and modern property law. "Law arises from fact" was a truism acknowledged by jurists even as they professed to believe in an ultimately divine origin.

What most closely approximates Nomos in modern terms, perhaps, is the concept of "positive law" adapted from medieval jurisprudence by Gustav Hugo and John Austin (without any connection to the views of Auguste Comte or indeed more recent "legal positivism"). In every society, even those beginning ostensibly with a "code," or perhaps especially these, law first takes the form of rules and norms preserved by oral culture and some expression of elderly wisdom invoked to resolve conflicts. In every society, too, law grows through "interpretation" when applied to new problems and conditions, whence again the centrality of hermeneutics in following the career of Nomos. For there is little in human organization that is taken directly from nature—not personal "liberty," though this has been a useful and widely accepted fiction; not kinship models, which have followed civil and canon law as well as "genetic" patterns; not property, though "occupation" and "possession" may seem to be universal starting points; and still less the more complex institutions up to and including the state. However useful for moral philosophy or depth psychology, the "state of nature" has no place in the human sciences—except to the extent that they constitute a "second nature."

In a sense Nature itself—herself—is one of those numberless myths devised by humans to give meaning to their social condition. The seminal, mythopoeic phase of Nomos came with the Greeks, for whom justice and other proto-legalistic concepts had a place in the pantheon; but the myth-making process has continued through all subsequent ages, including our own. The Romans personified and sanctified ideas of public order and their national "genius," while Christian tradition drew strength from the legal fictions of the "power of the keys" and an idealized "primitive church." Each nationality has likewise developed its own legal myths—Italy its dream of Romanitas, England its "immemorial custom," France its "Salic law," Germany its ancient "liberties." In more recent and more secular ages legal mythology has run more to universalist themes—social contract, natural rights, primitive communism, and a variety of sentimental or scientific utopias—but it has by no means subsided. Fascination about the mysterious past, anxiety about the still more mysterious future, and hopes of maintaining an orderly present have kept this aspect of Nomos alive.

Besides such products of the juristic imagination, the Western legal tradition has preserved a variety of categories, typologies, and polarities which have remained part of the substructure of social thought. Distinctions not only between nature and society and between arms and laws but also that between the private and public spheres are permanent features of Western thinking about the human condition, as are conventions concerning corporate structure, class divisions, ideas of inheritance, and fictions of succession—not to speak of the primal dialectic of sex (going far beyond what today are regarded as "natural" gender differences). What has most complicated these social patterns has been the chronic assumption about the divine origin of law. In various forms this idea was invoked not only in the long series of imperialist legislative enterprises from Theodosius to Napoleon and beyond but also in the Romanoid model of Western canon law, which elevated "law" to a sacramental system.

Yet the human face of Nomos has always managed to show through such transcendent facades, and social thought has continued to move through conventional channels. The Western legal tradition and its practitioners have always depended on what Clifford Geertz has called "local knowledge"—and what eighteenth-century German scholars called *Lokalvernunft*—even as they reach out for more universal expressions of that knowledge.[25] In order to reach particular judgments, jurists have always been constrained to understand humanity in particular geographical, historical, and cultural terms; and Western social thought has inherited both the limiting conditions and the universalist aspirations of jurisprudence.

In modern times (since the twelfth century) the old legal tradition has undergone profound modifications, while nonetheless preserving much of its structure and texture, including general categories, time-tested assumptions and "maxims," standards of judgment, and methods of analysis. Within the professional canon the texts have lost their absolute authority, having been subjected first to the criticism of juristic scholasticism, next to the philological and historical exegesis of legal humanists, then to various kinds of legal reform based on comparative and systematic jurisprudence, and finally to the rationalist analysis of seventeenth- and eighteenth-century "jusnaturalists." Yet Nomos has survived and transcended the mainstream of civil law, enjoying a sort of posthumous existence in various para-legal systems, beginning especially with Vico 's *Universal Law* and Montesquieu's *Spirit of the Laws,* and including, at least collaterally, certain pioneering efforts in the modern social and cultural sciences, such as that of Max Weber, which carried on the "scientific" and universal as well as the normative and "local" projects of the legal tradition.

Paralleling and in some ways presupposing the development of legal conventions has been that of language, ever the vehicle if not the model of legal tradition. Drawing especially on the resources of Greek rhetoric, Roman jurists developed an elaborate terminology which has sustained and nourished social thought in much the same way as Aristotelian terminology (and later mathematics) gave a continuous medium of expression to natural philosophy; and down to the present this terminology has invaded and shaped vernacular languages and national traditions as well. The substance or dress of Nomos, to the extent that it aspires to being legal and social science, is verbal discourse; and the determination of "meaning" has always had to begin by determining the "letter" of the law, whether defined as authorial "intention" or linguistic propriety. At first, customs were established by commonly recollected and accepted rules; but the later applications and "extensions" of such rules were necessarily matters of "interpretation," which eventually became a professional—a priestly and then a lawyerly—monopoly transcending reason and common sense, though both might be invoked to justify and to expand this monopoly. Finally, a terminology that was both professional and traditional came to support and to inform a structure of "normal" legal science, which combined judgments of fact and value with solicitude for the ideals (and prejudices) of a particular society, but which remained technical and alien to "lay" understanding.

The linguistic dimension is revealed in another enduring theme which for centuries has offered common ground for Physis and Nomos, and this is the metaphor of the book, especially the "book of nature." Ernst Robert Curtius and more recently Hans Blumenberg have traced the *fortuna* of this topos over many centuries, from its Biblical origins—(Heaven rolled as a scroll both in Isaiah (34:4) and in the Book of Revelation (5:1)—down to its modern elaborations (including, for Blumenberg, the deciphering of dreams and of the genetic code).[26] The notion of the book of the world (of nature, of history, of life) is of course fundamentally ambivalent—suggesting on the one hand the act of creation as having divine authorship and on the other hand the interpretation of God's work, which might range from theodicy to Galileo's "mathematical philosophy," approaching the Book of Nature in geometrical terms. The metaphor of the book, in short, could be taken from the standpoint either of its writer or of its reader. But in any case it illustrates another conventional way of expressing the distinction between Physis and Nomos—between nature and "second nature."

If the book of nature is "written in the language of mathematics" (as Galileo thought), the book of human nature in its social forms has been written, in the most practical contexts, in the language of the law. The specific connections between the old art of law and the modern sciences of society and culture remain to be shown, but it should be clear in general that from the beginning jurisprudence not only has depended on assumptions about a "second," a human, nature but has also found it necessary to inquire into questions of social roles, structures, actions, and their various "local" conditions. "By viewing law as a social phenomenon," Walter Ullmann has remarked, "medieval jurisprudence was forced to elucidate some basic principles about society, and was thus led to consider topics which, under modern conditions, would be dealt with, not by the lawyer, but by the sociologist."[27] My assumption (and the demonstrandum of my argument) is that this insight may properly be extended to the whole tradition of Western jurisprudence—to the entire intellectual career of Nomos—and to the human sciences (including economics, anthropology, and history as well as sociology), which inherited much of the intellectual project of the old legal tradition and which shared some of its language, methods, and goals—and of course struggled to escape from them.

Central to the development of social thought presupposed by professional jurisprudence was the practice and theory of "interpretation"—legal hermeneutics—which paralleled and in some ways outstripped the philological, philosophical, and theological varieties, though its significance has seldom been appreciated for the history of thought in general. One exception is Emilio Betti and another is Gadamer, who has remarked (but not elaborated) on the significance of legal hermeneutics for the human sciences.[28] Hermeneutics has seldom pretended to scientific status: bound to language and to literary texts, hence to human convention and empirical scholarship (if not myth), it has been content to be regarded as an art (*techne*), at most a form of practical wisdom (*phronesis, prudentia*) and in this sense "local knowledge." So, in its pragmatic form, has the law—whence the emphasis on "prudence" ("jurisprudence" rather than "jurisscience") and the designation of jurists as *prudentes* or, more significantly, *interpretes*. Like jurisprudence, too, hermeneutics has had to consider human "intention," context, accident, and perhaps bad faith; and this has contributed to its complexity and "double focus" as it developed from commonsense judgment and naive hopes of retrospective mind-reading to sophisticated and professionalized theories of interpretation, criticism, and reconstruction.

"To make one's own what was previously foreign remains the ultimate aim of hermeneutics," Paul Ricoeur has remarked.[29] This applies not only to the jurists who drew upon the ancient and medieval legal tradition but also to the modern historian who hopes to trace the story of Nomos back to our "Greek memory," if not to prehistory and myth. Yet the common ground of language, however treacherous and shifting, makes the effort at least plausible. "Longer than deeds liveth the word," Pindar chanted, and for the present venture we can only hope that there is some truth as well as poetry in this ancient tag.[30]

Greek Roots

... osper gar physis ede to ethos.

Aristotle, *De memoria*, II

•

The Awakening of Psyche

Let us begin by searching what Paul Ricoeur has called our "Greek memory," which is flickering and often faulty, but which still forms a necessary point of departure for this effort of conceptual anamnesis. Unfortunately, we cannot search this memory very far back into myth, hardly even into the semi-mythical speculation of the pre-Socratics. In order to begin taking the measure of man we begin not with the cosmos nor even with the human community but rather, following Socrates, with the human creature in his own habitats.[1]

Perhaps the most fundamental phenomenon, or epiphenomenon, of Western history has been the emergence of consciousness, the awareness of the soul, or mind. At the dawn of thought—to the extent that we are able to think back through the medium of language into prehistory—there appeared glimpses not only of a universal Logos but also of a personal Psyche, and in the social ferment of the sixth and fifth centuries the one seemed to widen as the other deepened. Pythagoras was among the first to treat the soul as morally significant, as Heraclitus was the first to include it in his cosmological program. "I searched out myself," said Heraclitus; and though like other cosmologists he sought also the underlying principles of the universe, the former effort was the more difficult. "You could not find the ends of the soul," he declared, "though you travelled every way, so deep is its logos."[2] Self does not exist in isolation, of course, and must receive definition in relation to some "other," which is society or culture in some form; but the primordial defining of self does represent the starting point for social thought in a most fundamental sense.

The emergence of what Conrad Aiken has called the "small bright circle of consciousness" is a mysterious process which can be traced only inferentially and speculatively through indirect, mainly linguistic, evidence. In the Homeric poems there was no sense of personality or soul (*psyche*) except as expressed in material and physiological terms.[3] As Plato himself speculated etymologically, Psyche was a power which was located in the chest or heart and which, through a primitive and naturalistic sort of metonymy, was associated with the breath and especially the blood. The Greek family, too, that primary locus of social solidarity, was a manifestation of the power of the blood; and early Greek law reflected and revered this elemental force, which informed religious practices and which received social expression especially in paternal authority.[4] In various ways ancestral legal traditions, traced back to heroic origins, continued to compete and to interact with newer civic constructions which seemed to presume a higher level of social consciousness.

There are other ways to interpret the link between nature and society. One may see it as a transition from a "shame-culture," in which the principal threat is external "pollution," to a "guilt-culture," in which pressures are internalized and moralized.[5] Shame (*aidos*) is in general "a vulnerability to an expressed norm of the society," according to a modern Homeric scholar, "and the affective or emotional foundation of virtue."[6] Individuality may be seen as arising from the ensuing conflict, which was accompanied by opposition to blood ties and loosening of old family bonds. It is expressed most conspicuously in lyric poetry (Solon's included) and the drama, which, though enlivened or threatened by the antics of the gods, was basically concerned "with people and what they do to one another";[7] and it was epitomized in the sophistic movement, which opposed pedagogical to paternal authority and which "corrupted youth" by setting a premium on verbal combat and iconoclastic inquiry—in effect on the liberation of the psyche. In this context old mythical constructs like justice (Dike) were not only conceptualized but also internalized as central virtues of civilized man. For Solon, Dike was in effect the "soul" of the city, having knowledge of present, past, and future; for Plato she became the central idea of his philosophic vision.[8] So it was that the Greeks substituted human justice for Olympian criminality.

Another dimension of this transition may be seen in the development of language, though again the shift from oral to scribal culture may be detected only indirectly. Eric Havelock has tried to follow it through a "history of the word ''to be,'" which amounts to a kind of archeology of philosophical thought.[9] In general this history concerns the logical or, more properly, syntactical foundations of conceptual reasoning, by which abstractions are fashioned and manipulated through identification, qualification, classification, and other kinds of mental ordering. This is the human story of the mythical and original bestowing of names, the conceptual colonization of the natural world, by which men began to lay the foundations of their own civilizing structure of Nomos. No longer do the gods or natural forces, including Dike, act or "come" unbidden; now they are required to follow the conventional rules of written language. In the world of myth and unreflective honor or shame, justice was an unpredictable consort of Zeus unconcerned with human will; in the bright land of Platonic ideas she, or it, was subject to irreverent analysis: "What *is* justice?" But this, the basic question of Plato's *Politeia,* was to be answered not by a survey of actual laws in effect since Solon but rather by logical and syntactical virtuosity in the manipulation of ideas, arguments, and language.

The Greeks were always, especially through the pressures of self-conscious urban life, fascinated with language, and in this connection with Hermes, messenger-god and priest of the Delphic oracle (whose motto, remember, was "know thyself"). A "wily and deceptive messenger" (according to Plato), Hermes was also the god of thieves and perhaps, according to a modern linguist, an Indo-European god of exchange.[10] "Hermeneutics," the theory and practice of interpretation, has preserved some of this deviousness. In general the basis of interpretation, expressed in classic form in Aristotle's *Per hermeneia,* was always grammar and syntax, although the emphasis shifted increasingly toward logic—from convention to nature, in the sense of reason. Yet there continued to be a powerful tradition of philological hermeneutics, starting especially with criticism of the Homeric poems. Techniques of figurative and allegorical as well as grammatical, historical, and dialectical criticism were developed in the effort to find the meaning—which Plato thought of as the reality—behind the letter of a text. It is partly through the tradition of interpretation and its techniques that we will try, in this and succeeding chapters, to gain access to ideas of nature and culture as they emerge in Western consciousness.[11]

The emergence of Psyche implies awareness—but awareness of what? Parents, family, community, alien people ("barbarians"), alien forces, the universe at large—surely all these, but awareness also of time, changing, aging, death, and a wide range of instabilities and unpredictabilities. The first question is how to make sense of these perceived shapes and forces outside the self, perhaps even to control them. It seems "natural" to group such perceptions concentrically, from the smallest family circle outward to the great cosmos reflected in earth and sky—perhaps because we belong to the same tradition, the same continuum of consciousness (if only via language, institutions, and "interpretation") as the ancient Greeks—whence "our Greek memory." From our perspective they were the first to define their own consciousness in terms of a fundamental distinction between physical environment and the world of man's making—between nature and society, between Physis and Nomos.

If the first might be explained in terms of a universal Logos, the second needed formulation, classification, and interpretation according to rather different rules, or so some observers preferred to believe. Ultimately, perhaps, humankind was part of nature and so subject to some universal principles; but this assumption, whether expressed as an ideal or a cynical and reductionist view of human nature, was in practice at odds with the immediate (and indeed reflective) perceptions of the psyche. For self-understanding a distinction had to be made, especially for purposes of social judgment and action. Under such conditions, as Mario Untersteiner has written, "Metaphysics is superseded by anthropology, which finds its ultimate meaning in the political act."[12] It was in the act of setting anthropology apart from cosmology that the Greeks gave definition to the realm of Nomos.

From Mythos to Nomos

"To whom do you ascribe the authorship of your legal arrangements?" asks the Athenian at the outset of Plato's *Laws* (*Nomoi*).[13] To a god, answered the Cretan (in this case truthfully), and more specifically to Zeus. From the beginning the notion of the divine character of law (*nomos*) was present in Greek speculation, justice itself (*dike*) being obedience to the commands of the gods. Among the many forms of Zeus, magical and intimidating, was that of the patriarchal guardian of the city and of its laws. Whether or not one may discern earlier Mycenaean or Indo-European overtones (as Martin Nilsson and Georges Dumézil have urged), there are surely proto-legal elements in Greek theogony, especially in the retribution wrought by Zeus upon Prometheus, when cunning (*metis*) gave way to reason, and arbitrary will to justice.[14] It is in this world of myth that we must look for the first glimmerings of that tradition of self-conscious social thought corresponding originally to the concept of Nomos.

Mythologically, the transition from force to law had a sexual as well as a rational aspect, for it was wifely influence that caused Zeus's changes of mood. Among his various marital unions, useful and lustful, the first was with Metis, whom Zeus, finding her a source of discord, devoured. His second mate was Themis, goddess of communal order and, less poetically, personification of the oracles of Zeus, those "themistes" by which the monarch of the gods advised subjects of his will.[15] In the Greek pantheon "Themis of the good counsel," as Pindar called her, ranked second only to Gaia (earth) and indeed is represented by Aeschylus as a form of Gaia, hence "the oracular power of earth." In Homer she convenes and dissolves the assembly and presides over the feast. Etymologically, she is perhaps related to the Anglo-Saxon "doom" (via the Sanskrit *dhaman*), which was a rule established by the gods over the family.

According to Jane Harrison, writing in the anthropological heyday of matriarchy and *Mutterrecht*, Themis was the ultimate symbol of motherhood. "She is the force that brings and binds men together, she is 'herd instinct,' the collective conscience, the social sanction. She is *fas*, the social imperative." Though not religion, she is "the stuff of which religion is made."[16] However plausible this sexualist construction, the polarity itself between an active and aggressive enforcement and an ideal of social stability and quiescence associated with law seems a permanent pattern of ancient social thought. To the Greek opposition of belligerent Zeus and pacific Themis there succeeds, however remotely and prosaically, the Roman image of sword and toga; and in fact the relative effeminacy of the law-making function was often a matter of masculine and especially of princely apologetics.

Left to his own devices, Zeus could be a terrible and uncivilized tyrant; domesticated, he took on an almost human appearance. Lying with Mnemosyne, he fathered the nine muses, whose sweet voices brought delight and understanding to mankind. Among the offspring he had with Themis were several guarantors of social order (not counting the *moirae,* the fates, who performed a more general regulatory function), most notably Dike, Eunomia, and Eirene. Dike, "divine daughter of Zeus," appeared to men as "just retaliation," personifying the ideal of justice—that is, familial rule as distinguished from the domestic order of Themis—which raised men above the animal world. "For those who practice violence and cruel deeds," declared Hesiod, "far-seeing Zeus, the son of Chronos, orders a punishment" (*dike*); and later *dike* would be the standard term for a law case.[17] In the *Iliad* the "dikaioi" were counselors who judged (perhaps threw, or pointed, from *dikein,* related etymologically to the Latin *dico*) between two disputants, and whose fairmindedness contrasted particularly with arrogant *hubris.*[18] The goddess Dike reflected the ethical and political as well as the religious aspect of this charge. She it was who made straight the "themistes" of Zeus (and later her name was applied to particular cases). Her sister Eunomia represented the social and legal harmony attendant on such straightness, and her example was followed by Eirene, the embodiment of peace. Together—despite the opposition of such representatives of discord as Eris and Dysnomia—they formed the basis for the social idea of *homonoia,* that harmony which Solon and later Pericles brought to Athens and which was celebrated idealistically and perhaps nostalgically in the works of Plato and Aristotle.

The fanciful hypotheses of mythology did not prevent a more down-to-earth realization of the human dimension of law. If justice was divine, Solon said, particular laws were made by men (God was the author of justice, medieval jurists would teach, and man the author of laws); and this more positive and prosaic conception depended on human, if partly legendary, law-givers. On this level the struggle against injustice (*adikia*) was carried on by specific legislation, especially by that of Draco and Solon (usually referred to as *thesmoi*) and, in the fifth century, of Cleisthenes (when the term *nomoi* was first used in a technical sense). At this point we leave divinity for humanity—leave the battlefields of the gods for those of aggressive and acquisitive men and leave the myths of origins for the discourse of history. We also leave the antique view of law as a cosmological principle, as "Nomos, king of all mortals and immortals alike," in the words of Pindar. This "King Nomos" (*Nomos Basileus; nomos despotes*), celebrated in the fifth century by Herodotus and by Pindar, was no mythical creation, nor was it ever personified; rather it was the living force of human laws, customs, and cultural achievements.[19]

Nomos, according to the most recent historian of the concept, "played a central role in Greek life and thought." What, in human terms, did it signify? Etymology links the word with the root *nem-*, which since Homer has suggested some sort of distribution, as in the power of Zeus, the great Nemetor, "to distribute fortune to men"; and by extension it came to imply domination.[20] A direct offspring is Nemesis, conceptually and mythologically related to fate and fortune (Moira and Tyche), a goddess who was perhaps the mother of Helen, ironically the source of so much disorder. From Hesiod through Herodotus the connotations of *nomos* multiplied, among them suggestions of division, partition, occupation, administration, and social order in general. At first the word seems to have referred to a browsing place for animals, then the human lot bestowed by providence or society; later it came to approach the idea of nature to the extent that it implied what was normal, regular, even universal, such as the *nomoi* of kinship and mating, or of grammar and music. Yet in another sense it was also opposed to nature, as in Hesiod's view of the *nomos* of Zeus, by which men were distinguished from the animals that lived without *dike* and devoured one another. Later, for instance in Pindar and Heraclitus, Nomos became the highest social and political value, the very Logos of the human community. Nonetheless, it preserved a certain arbitrary quality: "To obey the will of one man," said Heraclitus, "is also *nomos*."[21]

In a curious way, ostensibly the reverse of the pattern of linguistic development, the term *nomos* seemed to shift reference from the general to the particular—from a sort of natural regularity to specific mores and norms of particular peoples and cities. This is evident both in the anthropological (and authoritarian) usage of Herodotus and in the satirical usage of Aristophanes, reinforcing the contrast between custom and nature. So Nomos served to designate particular rites, customs, human rules and solutions, eventually "positive law," and in this sense convention. In the fifth century it was applied—and through the reforms of Cleisthenes in 507 officially applied—to written law and statutes; and in this political sense it was used by dramatists and philosophers, most notably in Plato's own treatise, *The Laws*.

The significant thing is that, for good or for ill and unlike any other apotheosis of Greek myth, Nomos was wholly man-made. Yet while created by man, Nomos was nonetheless set above particular men, requiring, above all, reverence to the gods and obedience to parents. Originally, these may have been matters of unwritten law (*agraphos nomos*), but they also had high priority in early written codes. Historically, it might be suggested that Nomos represented the process of socialization, marking the transition from clan to community, perhaps also from oral to scribal culture, since recording laws was a primary impulse to writing. In the place of that masculine pride for which Homeric heroes had fought, the building of communal order took precedence; and instead of existing as unreflective tribal taboo, Nomos became a way of enforcing this order and extending it in time. When asked what should be returned to the gods, the Delphic oracle is supposed to have replied, "Follow the nomos of your city." And as Heraclitus said, "The people must fight for their *nomoi* as for their city walls."[22] Such was the tradition, unprofessional as it was, which made possible the rule of "King Nomos." For this purpose, however, the requirement was no longer submission to the gods; rather, declared Solon, "Obey the magistrates, whether it be just or unjust."[23] Such was the Nomos—as well as the Logos—of the Greek polis.

Nomos and the Polis

The polis was the first home of Nomos, and in this context we can see another and less attractive aspect of the concept. In terms of social reality the ideal of justice underlying Nomos might seem to be just another of those Socratic "clouds" to be ridiculed by Aristophanes; for much of the experience of the Greek city-states of the fifth century seemed to show that not Law but rather, in the words of Heraclitus, "War [*polemos*] is the father of all and the king of all."[24] As always in Western tradition, law could be the object of resentment, contempt, or satire—the "bribe-devouring judges" lamented by Hesiod, for example, or the topos made famous by Isocrates (and Tacitus after him) identifying a multiplicity of laws with bad government.[25] Although Eunomia remained the prize, her sister Dysnomia also, unfortunately, had a place in the realm of Nomos; and order often seemed beyond human grasp.

If community superseded clan, in other words, it was soon divided by class—and needless to say the subordination of women was an ineradicable feature of Greek "civilization." Thus demythologized and institutionalized, Themis became "the epitome of the judicial supremacy of the early kings and nobles," according to Werner Jaeger, as Dike was "the war-cry of class conflict."[26] According to the Athenian constitution (sometimes attributed to Aristotle), "The poor, with their wives and children, were enslaved to the rich"; and in general the mutual progress of slavery and liberty illustrate what M. I. Finley has called the "final paradox" of Greek civilization.[27]

Anomaly and even antinomy were thus the offspring of both the root *nem-* and the concept Nomos, which indeed suggested not only order but also, as Jacqueline de Romilly remarked, a disturbing "tension" between the real and the ideal, between positive and normative values.[28] Yet this tension, and the accompanying awareness of the human social predicament, of the strengths as well as the weaknesses of the polis, may well have enhanced the value of Nomos as a basis of social analysis and understanding.

The Greek idea of law was by no means a purely rational construct even in Plato's time. In Athenian society law preserved much of its original religious character, as suggested by its association with the priestly office of *archon basileus* and by the activities of the so-called "exegetes," who were experts in interpreting civic ritual.[29] Though Greek legal codes were the creation of wise men, they were also submitted for approval to the Delphic oracle, and in general they were the object of almost religious veneration. The family continued to be a locus of religious tradition, and ancient beliefs continued to figure in the civic and legal ideology of the Greek polis.[30] Ancestor-worship was extended from the private to the public sphere, as was concern for posterity. Each city had its own patron gods and appropriate rites. Nor did the innovations of democracy imply rejection of religion, for even the drawing of lots was assumed to be a revelation of divine will. And so, we should keep in mind, was the formulation of law, not only as chanted orally but also as enacted in written codes. Ultimately, it was religion that formed the basis for legal and political integrity—that "autonomy," which was, perhaps paradoxically, another offspring of Nomos.

Until the fifth century the legal history of Athens was obscured by myth, even as reflected in the supposedly historical *Constitution of Athens* and in Aristotle's more speculative *Politics*. Not much is known of the laws of Draco (621-20?), except that they were (in Plutarch's words) "written in blood not ink."[31] No doubt the extensive recourse to capital punishment had a leveling if not a socializing effect. In general the pattern of Athenian legal development followed that of the constitution (*politeia*), which is to say from tribal to communal institutions and from king (*basileus,* retained only as a religious office) to archon. The chief judicial body was the Draconian Council of Areopagites, through which the state began to interfere in private life, starting with the right of blood feud. It was on this foundation that Solon built—by constitutional reforms, by instituting a court of appeal (*eliaia*) and popular jury system, and especially by his legendary laws (*Solonoi Nomoi*), which, like those of Draco, have been obscured by the passage of time.

Solon should be the eponymous hero of Greek (or at least Athenian) Nomos. A quasi-mythical figure who traced his lineage from Poseidon, this most pragmatic of "wise men" left solid achievements, legal as well as

literary, going beyond legend. Like many another law-giver, Solon first
made his reputation in war before turning to social reform in 594; but
(except for poetic effect) he was not inclined to look for direct divine
assistance. Success or failure, in peace as well as war, was the product of
collective will. Pray to Zeus, he urged, but "charge not the gods" with
misfortune, and remember that "on every side the mind of the immortals
is hidden from mankind." According to one of his legalistic lyrics, "If on
our city ruin comes, it will never be by the dispensation of Zeus and the
purpose of the blessed gods . . . It is the people themselves who in their
folly seek to destroy our great city."[32] Solon consciously evoked Eunomia
when he freed the land from the *horoi*, stone symbols of forced labor and
dependence; and he idealized "obedience to the law" as maintaining "all
things in order and harmony" and setting "shackles on the unjust." Yet
his prescriptions were eminently practical. His legislation was designed not
merely to placate the gods but also to give institutional expression to the
collective will: reinforcing the family by legislating natural obligations between generations but subordinating it to the communal order; easing class
tensions by abolishing the old debts but maintaining the severity of punishment
for theft, verbal abuse, and other threats to internal order; and invading
many areas of private life but insisting on the primacy of public authority.

Throughout the sixth century magistrates and juries preserved their allegiance to Solon's "established laws" (*keimenoi nomoi*). "I will judge
according to the laws and decrees of Athens" was the oath reported by
Demosthenes, "and matters about which there are no laws I will decide by
the justest opinion."[33] The laws themselves, though obscured by passage
of time since Draco and Solon, caused little confusion. They were displayed
for all to see on wooden and stone tablets (*axones* and *kyrbeis*) set up in
different parts of the city, a nice symbolic representation of the transition
from oral to scribal culture, from custom to law, and so of the public
appearance of Nomos, although that term also continued to designate
unwritten law, which itself continued to be invoked. Other terms were
applied to particular laws, especially *thesmos* (Solon's preferred word) and
psephisma; but *nomos,* which implied a more fundamental and permanent
rule, finally prevailed, especially in a legal and political sense. The socialization of the term *nomos* was complete by 507 B.C., when the democratic
reforms of Cleisthenes fixed it as the official designation for a statute.

In this way Nomos became "king" also in a linguistic sense. Under its
reign there came into prominence various etymological consorts, including
eunomia, dysnomia, anomia, and especially *isonomia.* It is clear that, for
the archon Solon, Dysnomia represented not Hesiod's mythical offspring
of Strife and Night but rather the disorderly conditions of Athens, just as
Eunomia represented the human remedy, the product of Dike in the sense
of organized justice. In this sense *eunomia,* the opposite of *anomia,*

appeared also in the *Athenian Constitution*. Ideologically even more evocative was the idea of *isonomia*, which became the legal aspect of the anti-tyrannical and democratic ideal celebrated in various writings of the fifth century. So, settled in the constitutional context established especially by Solon, this family of "nomical" terms lost their mythical aura and came to designate key concepts of social thought.[34]

After the founding of the Athenian democracy, new laws came to be added by vote of the Ecclesia of free citizens, with the approval of the Council (*boule*); and in this way Nomos became a changing and growing force in society. Late in the fifth century (410-03) efforts to collect the old laws were made by appointed "inscribers" (*anagrapheis*) and, after civil war and the restoration of democracy in 403, by legislators (*nomothetai*) acting in concert with the Council.[35] At the same time it became possible to limit arbitrary legislation by means of written proposals and prosecutions (*graphe paranomon*) charging illegality or "unsuitable laws," beyond the prosecution of particular cases, private or public (*dike idia; dike demosia*), which remained a part of oral legal culture. In these and other ways law was brought into line with social practice and made more responsive to the popular will; and the ideals associated with Nomos created a model and a legend that was reflected far beyond the cultural circle of Hellas, becoming allegedly the inspiration not only for Rome but also for modern Western communities such as Renaissance Florence.

The major victory of Nomos came, however, in the area of social and cultural thought, especially during that "tragic age" which Nietzsche associated with the rise of consciousness, the separation of nature and culture, and the pernicious effects of Plato, who "severed the instincts from the *polis*." It is clear that the contrast between nature and convention, so essential in the development of social conceptualization, was reinforced by city dwelling, especially because of the tension between private life in the family—the "economic" and "ethical sphere"—and the second sphere, or "political life" (*bios politikos*) of citizenship. Certainly the legal arrangements of Cleisthenes aimed at breaking down tribalism must have seemed unnatural in a most fundamental way, Aristotle's later rationalizations to the contrary notwithstanding. There have been fewer conceptions more influential than Aristotle's view of the polis as a "natural" creation and especially of man as a "political animal" (*zoon politikon*), but the assumption that the balance between the social and the biological had been attained was in no way borne out by experience or by subsequent history. Much more conspicuous—in the incidence of war, civil strife, and criminality— has been the antagonism between the natural and social sides of humanity. Indeed this interaction is perhaps the most important of all conditions of the so-called "enlightenment" of the fifth century in Athens (as Friedrich Solmsen has called it)—though often forgotten in the rosy reconstructions of some modern classicists.[36] Much of the light, and some accompanying heat, was provided by the conflict and interplay between the forces of Physis and those of Nomos.

Nomos and Physis

Let us look more directly at the fundamental polarity which has moved to the center of this inquiry, namely, that between the natural and the human worlds.[37] In mythical thinking this distinction was confused, avoided, or (some might say) transcended. Thus "cosmos," a pivotal term in Greek formulations of the structure of experience, was applied alternatively to notions of a well-ordered human community and to those of an intelligible universe (*eukosmia,* as opposed to *dyskosmia,* is Aristotle's term). It was impossible to preserve this homogeneous outlook in the conditions of rapid social change and conflict occurring in the crucible of civic (and intercivic) life. During the fifth century a new threshold of consciousness was attained through the increasingly sharp distinction made between private life, with its existential fears, rewards, and punishments, and public interaction, with its rights, duties, and altogether different set of priorities and expectations. Such, in any case, was the social pattern underlying the need to discriminate between nature and convention, or, more grandiosely, between nature and law.

Physis and Nomos: two intimidating forces—neither, however, associated with the ancient pantheon (though at one point Hesiod represented Themis as triumphing over Physis). Whence came this great dialectic of Western consciousness, this central topos and antithesis of Western thought? It seems a bit perfunctory to attribute it merely to "Greek national consciousness" (as do Felix Heinemann and G. S. Kirk), but as usual mythic and pre-conscious roots can be suggested only speculatively. Is it another expression of an instinctive "polarity" in Greek thought (analogous to earth-sky and male-female)? Or a reflection of an inherent duality of language (that is, subject-predicate)? Kirk wonders about some association with deep-seated binary patterns of human comprehension; but speculations about the relation of the binary brain to emergent social consciousness goes beyond even the "phenomenological approach" to myth endorsed by Kirk, as do modern geo-psychological insights into "territorial imperatives."

Is it possible to see a mythical analogy in the story of Prometheus, who defied Zeus to obtain a share of *dike* for mankind? Historic and anthropological theories of progress, W. K. C. Guthrie has written, "were obviously on the side of *nomos.*"[38] Prometheus brought culture but had to pay the penalty for such knowledge. "The truth," wrote Nietzsche, "is the vulture that gnaws at the liver of the Promethean promoter of Culture."[39] Moreover, through Prometheus's brother Epimetheus ("afterthought," Prometheus himself being "forethought"), Pandora was allowed to bestow upon men not only speech but countless evils attendant on awareness of the Logos. Among the consequences were portrayals of man's struggles with nature and divine fate and, in general, that "tragedy of the mind," as Untersteiner called it, underlying the paradoxes of consciousness and giving rise to sophism and skepticism.[40] The price of human consciousness and freedom was in a sense the separation of mind from life, of reason from reality, and the basic duplicity of thought in which the Sophists were supposed to have reveled and through which dramatists stirred their audiences. "'Twas nature that willed it," according to the famous Euripidean formula, "who cares naught for law."[41]

One root of the distinction may be seen dimly reflected in pre-Socratic thought, and here we encounter another portentous root-term with ambivalent connections with the idea of nature. *Ethos* originally suggested dwelling, or customary place, whether the world or more particularly "home." This is in any case the construction of Heidegger, who translates the famous fragment of Heraclitus (no. 119)—*ethos anthropo daimon*—as "man's familiar abode (there where man belongs most properly) is the region open for the daimon."[42] The more common rendering is "man's character is fate." However rendered, this cryptic insight illustrates another formula which was to have an extraordinary fortune in Western thought, especially legal and social thought: namely, the notion that individual character—and by extension social "custom"—is a kind of "second nature."[43]

This contrast between a primary physical and a secondary human nature is more apparent in Aristotle, for whom custom (*ethos*) appears as conceptually inferior to nature (*physis*) in at least two contexts. In his essay on memory and recollection, custom seems to approach or to take the place of nature, just as recalled experiences are gathered into general ideas. An analogous movement from the particular to the general can also be seen in the *Rhetoric,* discussing custom in the sense of habit. Here, defining pleasure as a movement of the soul to a natural state, Aristotle remarks that "that which becomes habitual becomes as it were natural; for the distance between 'often' [*pollakis*] and 'always' [*aeon*] is not great, and nature belongs to the idea of 'always,' custom to that of 'often.'"[44] These themes will reappear in many later philosophical and social contexts.

Another classical illustration of the polarity between nature and convention appears in Plato's *Cratylus,* where it is associated with one of the most fundamental of all epistemological problems, the origin of language.[45] Of course Plato—Socrates—opts for natural signification in opposition to the Attic equivalent of language philosophy. His interlocutor in this case is Hermogenes ("son of Hermes"), and this is where Plato takes the opportunity to criticize the god of interpretation (hermeneutics) as "wily and deceptive in speech and . . . oratorical" (*agorastikon*). Much of the dialogue, ironically enough, is taken up with the most fantastic word derivations in order to get at the "reality" behind names, setting the style for speculative etymologizing for centuries—through Isidore of Seville to Vico and even Heidegger.[46] For Plato this was another way of saying that philosophers were the true and sovereign "name-makers" (*onomastikoi*) or "law-givers" of society and so superior to the orators, who were purveyors of unenlightened opinion, custom, and convention (*doxa, ethos, nomos,* all used pejoratively), and blind to natural reality. It was also a way of dismissing custom as "second nature" in a naive and physicalist sense, implicity closing the door to less doctrinaire anthropological inquiry.

More important for European legal and social thought is the formulation in Aristotle's *Nicomachaean Ethics,* where the two varieties of "political justice" are distinguished—"natural" (*physikon dikaion*) and "conventional" (*nomikon dikaion*).[47] The first is immutable and the second mutable, and the two are related, Aristotle tells us, as universals to particulars. Later in this work Aristotle sets down what becomes the basic vocabulary of human as distinguished from natural—"practical" as distinguished from "theoretical"—science, beginning with the fundamental distinction between pure science (*episteme*), exemplified by mathematics, and "prudence" (*phronesis*), which must involve experience (*empierias*), as in the disciplines of economics (*oikonomia*), legislation (*nomothesia*), and several varieties of politics, all of which displayed "variety and fluctuation of opinion," as unfortunately did rhetoric, which Aristotle reduced to a rather trivial art (*techne*) and subordinated to dialectic in the process of interpretation. Beyond these terminological prescriptions concerning Nomos, Aristotle had little to say about law, or rather what he did say was probably in a lost section of the *Politics.* Nevertheless, his framework had an indelible influence on later Roman jurists and especially medieval commentators, and the inherent naturalistic bias of Aristotelian thought reinforced the philosophical eclipse of Nomos.

"Nature" itself conceals a paradox which has always been troubling to philosophy despite large efforts, at least since Aristotle, to argue it away. On the one hand, *physis* refers to physical reality, including animal instinct as well as material processes, and in this sense is related, at least genetically, to the idea of custom. Here we see the naturalistic mode of explanation—generation and corruption—employed by Aristotle, and we may recognize the nature "red in tooth and claw" seen by the poet. On the other hand, the term came to be identified with universal reason, perhaps with the ideal, the perfection, the "final cause," which Aristotle defined as the *telos* of natural objects; and in this sense it seems to be correlated exactly with the experience of custom. Mainstream philosophical tradition has preferred the second construction of Physis to the first, and of course to the irregularity of Nomos. The locus classicus of this invidious conception comes in the work of Plato, especially the *Republic* but also the *Laws,* where the beautiful rationality of Justice is contrasted with the instability and irregularity of custom.[48] In this rationalist sense Physis was the basis not only of an elevated conception of political science but also of the long and fascinating tradition of utopian thought.

Despite pretensions to rationality, the champions of Physis also helped in a sense to preserve the hegemony of the divine and the mythical over the human and the social. It may be that "the gods were laid low by philosophy," as Bruno Snell has remarked, but *mythos* in fact survived in Platonism and even in Aristotelianism.[49] Plato (or Socrates) often had resort to metaphor and parable to reach that remote truth lying behind appearance and opinion, that is, convention, while Aristotle likewise carried on the pre-Socratic cosmologists' search for a single *arche,* or *logos.* For him (and them) understanding could be achieved only through a language, a *logos,* that is, a logic expressible through propositions and amenable to a proof (*apodeixis*) that was certain and not merely probable. The subject of science in general was a nature that could be formulated through a system of causes (*aitia*) and principles (*archai*) and thus given rational and theoretical form. Causation and classification: these were the cornerstones of Aristotelian naturalism, at least as handed down (sometimes the worse for wear) in the most powerful and intimidating of all "philosophical" traditions.

Philologists say that, historically, the polarization of physis and nomos appeared first in cosmological and ontological speculation, notably in Parmenides and Empedocles, where it is analogous to the antithesis between opinion and truth (*doxa-aletheia*) and, even more fundamentally, between word and deed (*logos-ergos*). Torn by this opposition, Logos itself suggests not only words in stories (the original meaning of *logoi*) but also the idea behind terms. "Naturally," words were simply sounds; by convention they took on human meaning. (And so the terms were set for the endless Western debate about the origin of language.) "By convention color and taste exist," explained Democritus; "really there are only atoms and the void."[50] (And so the terms were set for the epistemological development of physical science, fairly continuous from the ancient atomists through the medieval nominalists down to Galileo's "new science" and after.) Again, according to Antiphon "Justice is to respect the laws when witnesses are present but otherwise to follow the precepts of nature"; for "Laws are artificial contracts, they lack the inevitability of natural growth."[51] (And so the terms were set for the theories of the "state of nature" and "state of society," which have been central to Western political thought, through scholastic interpreters of Aristotle down to modern champions of "antique-modern" natural law.)

For social thought the significant point was the identification of Nomos with what would later be known as positive law and its reliance on memory (*mnemon*), exemplified in particular (as Louis Gernet reminds us) by court experience.[52] The analogy with the Democritean formula is plain: by convention men behave according to certain customs and cultural imperatives; "really they are natural creatures driven by the same instincts and fears"— or united by the same reason and values. If naturalistic political and social "science" in an Aristotelian mold has tended to emphasize the second part of the formula, the underlying "reality," the fundamental investigations of human behavior, historical and anthropological, have been more concerned with the first.

The beginning of this tradition, the first settlement in the kingdom of Nomos, is characteristically an attitude of skepticism toward transcendent concerns, philosophical as well as mythological—though not toward the world of human judgment and action. "If physical philosophy began in wonder, ethics may be said to have begun in skepticism," Guthrie has observed, thus giving expression to another version of the distinction between a primary and a "second" nature.[53] This ironical connection is implied by the view attributed to Pyrrho, that "there is nothing really extant but custom and convention to govern action, for no single thing is in itself any more than that."[54] It remained for the Sophists to turn this critical insight into a positive conceptual program.

Sophism

From the beginning the kingdom of Nomos was the conceptual home of the Sophist movement; and indeed their philosophical, or anti-philosophical, enterprise can only be understood in terms of the fundamental divergence between nature and culture—and of the "privileging" of the latter. The distinction between *physis* and *nomos,* as Werner Jaeger has argued, "becomes of the greatest practical significance when it is used by sophists like Antiphon, Hippias, and the 'Callicles' of Plato's *Gorgias* to demonstrate that the prevailing laws and accepted social mores are a product of mere convention, and arbitrary decisions."[55]

But "mere" convention and "arbitrary" decisions bespeak the Platonist, and of course since (and largely because of) Plato the Sophists have had a very bad press. Aristotle has Gorgias define law as a convention, "a guarantee of mutual right"—"but not [adding in his own words] such as to make the citizen good and just."[56] We all know these charges, if only via the pejorative image of "sophistry": concern with probability rather than truth, willingness to argue either side of a question (probably for money), false promise of enlightenment, political duplicity, and an inclination to atheism. To be an orator was to "Gorgianize" in this most distasteful sense. Was not Protagoras banished from Athens for subversive teaching? And likewise Critias, the political intriguer who once suggested that law-makers "fabricate the deity" in order to impose order on disorderly subjects? And was not Antiphon, who argued that no human statement could have a single meaning, condemned for revolutionary activities? Not to mention the contempt for sophism expressed by Plato, Xenophon, Aristotle, and others of the more orthodox philosophical persuasion (forgetting, however, the fate of Socrates), and their disapproval of the apparently unprincipled pedagogical behavior of the Sophists.

Yet this was clearly a partisan view sustained by a variety of historical circumstances not related to the conceptual quality of the Sophist position. Jaeger himself has reminded us that these men were the "first humanists," and more recently Guthrie has compared them with the *philosophes* of another Western "enlightenment," who were likewise more concerned with social problems than with metaphysics. No doubt sophistics, like Socratics, could be misused; but "did not Herodotus call Solon a sophist?" asked Aristides, "and in turn Pythagoras?"[57] The term applies also to the seven wise men, he added, and to Socrates and even Plato. In their own way the Sophists also pursued the Logos; they were in fact the first language experts, and by virtue of this, as Plato acknowledged, the first practitioners of "civic science" (*ta politica techne*).[58]

The ground for defending sophism was above all the consideration that the arts of discourse, especially rhetoric, should never be divorced from philosophy. "I think it belongs to the same [man] and to the same art," wrote the author of the *Double Arguments (Dissoi logoi)*, "to discourse in their brief style and to understand [the] truth of things and to know how to make a right judgment in the law courts and to be able to make public speeches and to understand the art of rhetoric and to teach concerning the nature of all things, their state and how they came to be."[59]

The positive side of sophism has not gone unnoticed.[60] In antiquity few such defenses of the "first humanism" survived, at least among the Greeks; but in Renaissance humanism they were revived, most notably by Lorenzo Valla in his anti-Aristotelian tirades and by Ermolao Barbaro in his famous dispute with the Platonizing Pico della Mirandola. In the nineteenth century George Grote made another effort of rehabilitation, and the "new rhetoric" of recent times has brought attention to, if not enthusiastic acceptance of, the social values of rhetoric. Despite this a favorable estimate of their position still represents a minority opinion, especially in the sciences of society—another testimony, perhaps, to the superior forces of Physis in the recurrent struggles with Nomos. Yet the significance of sophism and the defenders of *phronesis* for social and anthropological thought can hardly be exaggerated, especially in view of the convergence and continuing close relations between rhetoric and law. Occurring in the first instance under the aegis of sophism, this collaboration constitutes another enduring theme in the story of Western social thought.

The appreciation of Nomos in the fifth century contributed to the rise

of a new skepticism and especially to that "tragic epistemology," as Untersteiner called it, which received classic expression in Protagoras, whose
accomplishments included drawing up a code of laws for the Athenian
colony of Thurii, where Herodotus lived for a while. Protagoras, too, was
something of a legend; and many stories were told about his arguments,
clever retorts, and large fees. He was perhaps the first philosopher of
language and was credited with the principal modes of speech (narration,
question, answer, command, report, entreaty, and invitation, according to
one recollection). He was also reportedly "the first to maintain that in
every experience there are two *logoi* opposed to each other."[61] For Protagoras direct knowledge of nature was impossible, since reason, the logos,
was present not in reality but in appearances. His rejection of natural
knowledge and of rational theology gave him a reputation as a skeptic and
atheist. Yet what he had in mind was something more positive, and this
was a linguistic philosophy. For this reason Protagoras—himself dubbed
"Logos" by some contemporaries—was also committed to the defense of
convention over nature. He believed, for example, that the wisdom of "our
fathers" could be proof against logical virtuosity, and that it was wrong to
"practice cleverness on divine things."

Not that rhetoric was committed to social conformity; on the contrary,
in contrast to their philosophical critics, the Sophists embraced change and
novelty. "Are you still saying the same old things, Socrates, that I heard
you saying long ago?" asked Hippias. "I always try to say something
new."[62] Antiphon made a more subtle point against philosophical orthodoxy when he defended the practice of coining new terms. Neology was
something else which would offend not only classicists but also rationalists,
for whom reality was essentially metalinguistic.

Such, "tragic" or not, was the epistemological basis of the new art (and
science) of rhetoric, and such the grounds for the centuries-long duel
between this discipline and formal "philosophy," monopolized by the progeny of Socrates. The old cliché, spread by Oliver Goldsmith and others,
that every man is born either a Platonist or an Aristotelian, has reinforced
this monopoly and the exclusion of rhetoric as a serious line of conceptualization. According to the dialectical vision of Aristotle the kingdom of
Nomos would be reduced to a province of nature and humankind to an
object of biological observation on one level or another. "First philosophy"
was not anthropology, nor self-knowledge even in a Socratic sense, it was
metaphysics; and so in the analysis of human discourse language gave way
to logic—again, in a sense, convention to nature—as, in the analysis of
behavior, psychology gave way to physiology. Even in political and social
investigation the intellectual structures erected on the basis of Aristotle's
dialectical blueprint have kept the naturalistic style of the original plan, as
indeed (for "pragmatic" interpreters like Polybius) has the study of his-

tory.[63] The significance of rhetoric has been above all to open up conceptual thought to concrete social experience and to the idea of a science of human culture on its own terms—the terms, that is to say, of human language. For rhetorical and sophistic interest in verbal dexterity and persuasion was not merely mercenary and demagogic ambition; it represented also primary access to an understanding of civilization in the fundamental terms of language, human wills, human creations, and human values.

What, in the face of this distorted record, has happened to the legacy of the "first humanists"? It survived tenuously, for example in the teachings of that renegade Socratic, Isocrates, who had been a pupil as well of Gorgias.[64] Writing in the fourth century, an age of social disintegration and disillusionment if ever there was one, Isocrates was highly critical of the "eristic" character of Platonic thought (and wrote also "against the Sophists," in the current vulgar and pejorative sense); and his remedy was to raise rhetoric to the level of philosophy. For Isocrates opinion was something to be shaped and transcended not by meta- or extra-linguistic logic and abstract categories but rather by positive knowledge, with the ultimate aim of unifying society, at least on a national basis. His ideal of culture was "not an accumulation of factual knowledge in any sphere," according to Jaeger, but rather it was "concerned with the forces which hold society together. These are summed up in the word *logos*."[65] Although it was vain to expect such an ideal of cultural unity in Isocrates' time, the notion did serve as a guide for a viable science of humanity, a way of giving conceptual form to the realm of Nomos which might be explored in a more propitious age.

Man the Measure

Here is the central topos of what we may call the nomic, or nomothetic, view: *metron anthropos*. "Man is the measure of all things," Protagoras declared cryptically, "of the things that are that they are, and of the things that are not that they are not."[66] Man is in effect the name-giver, the law-maker, the historian, critic, the philosopher—and of course the skeptical denier of all these.

In general this Protagorean aphorism (whatever its original "intention") seems to reflect the emergence of self-awareness—which is to say the afore-mentioned "awakening of Psyche," usually identified with Socrates, who indeed took the Delphic device "know thyself" as his motto, and thus (as Cicero said) "brought philosophy down from the heavens into the house-holds of men." But Protagoras went further in this interiorization and socialization of thought. For from our perspective "man the measure" implies both an epistemological principle, which is that the world receives its definition from human apprehension and judgment, and a plea for human values in philosophy. This was the true source of Protagoras's professed ignorance of the gods, since it was not they but man himself who created Nomos; and it was not Nature but Society which created man in recognizably rational, because "political," form. If this seemed to bind law to mere opinion, it was also a counsel of humility and moderation; and as Guthrie has argued, it accommodated a more secular and a more rational version of the Promethean myth, a more immediate and useful approach to the problems implied in it, and in general a more historical view of the human condition and the question of "meaning." Sophism involved not only the replacement of myth by human judgment but also the transcendence of that offspring of myth, metaphysics, by anthropology.

Myth continued to figure in Protagorean thinking about the human condition, most notably in the allegory of the beginnings of civilization related by Plato. No doubt the "atheist" Protagoras shaped this traditional story to his own sophistical ends, or so he is represented in Plato's dialogue. "Once upon a time there were gods only and no mortal creatures," he began.[67] After living beings had been fashioned by the gods out of earth and fire, it fell upon Epimetheus and his brother Prometheus to distribute natural qualities; but because of Epimetheus's short-sightedness (remember that his name means "afterthought") men were deprived of their natural advantages; and by way of recompense Prometheus ("forethought") stole fire and technical knowledge from the gods (Hephaestus and Athena) for subsistence, though unfortunately he was unable to seize as well the political wisdom possessed by Zeus. Prometheus received his punishment and man his reward, which was the exclusive privilege of knowing and worshiping the gods and, more practically, the ability to invent names and the arts of survival. Political understanding he still lacked, and so his social creations were constantly falling into disorder; but Zeus sent Hermes to bestow upon all men a sense of justice, hence a vision of social goals if not the means to achieve them. Needless to say, the skeptical and relativistic implications of this myth were not pleasing to Socrates (or Plato), but they are in keeping with the anthropocentric—and what we might call "anthroponomic"—orientation of sophism.

Yet this sophistical conception of the human condition challenged ethnocentricity as well as orthodoxy, and these implications were drawn out by others of Protagoras's persuasion, including the anonymous author of the *Double Arguments*. "Two-fold arguments concerning the good and the bad are put forward in Greece by those who philosophize," he declares. "Some say that the good is one thing and the bad another, but others say that they are the same, and that a thing might be good for some purposes but bad for others, or at one time good and at another time bad for the same purpose."[68] What is taken here from the universal Logos, the will of

Zeus, is given to human judgment; and so attention shifts from an abstract Nomos to particular *nomoi,* which Hippias defines as "covenants made by citizens whereby they have enacted in writing what ought to be done and what not."[69] And not only might justice "also be injustice," as Antiphon was prepared to argue, but also "there is no real distinction between Greek and barbarian."[70] Under such conditions the thrust of social thought had to be empirical and perhaps comparative, a lesson learned by Aristotle, if not Plato, at least in the empirical aspect of his political science.

The drift toward empiricism and interest in ethnography can be seen in a variety of historical, geographical, and medical works—the fields adjacent to "anthropology" in a modern sense. One example is the Hippocratic treatise *Airs, Waters, Places,* which employed directly the Nomos-Physis distinction in its description of the "ethos" of Asian and European peoples.[71] Seminal for the anthropological tradition, too, was the work of Democritus and of Posidonius, whom E. R. Dodds claimed as perhaps "the first true field anthropologist."[72] The most influential author was Herodotus, who transformed relativism into a methodological principle of "history," as he was the first to call it. If men were offered their choice of the best customs (*nomoi*) in the world, he remarked, "they would examine the whole number and end by preferring their own, so convinced are they that their own usages far surpass those of all others." Although Herodotus's own theme was the superiority of Greek law and liberty, his conception of "history" included accounts (*logoi*) of the origins, myths, religious practices, and customs of various peoples outside the magic circle of Hellenism.[73] He was by no means uncritical, and he distinguished, for example, between truth and myth ("the logos that is not"), between eyewitness and hearsay evidence, between cause (*aitia*) and pretext (*prophasis*); moreover, he was an original "name-giver" of early social thought—fate and fortune, change and growth, national character and "laws" are among his contributions. In this proto-sociological sense, too, Herodotus was a loyal subject of what he himself called "King Nomos."

But this empirical approach to anthropology represented a minor aspect of the major tradition defined by Nomos. The accomplishments of the Greeks were considerable. They discovered the conscious self and placed personality at the center of thought about society and culture; they made a fundamental distinction between private and public consciousness and behavior; they invented—devised or adapted—the terms for understanding the social and political order reflected in this distinction, centering on the idea of law; and they shaped language into a vehicle for interpreting the structure and processes of society and for its practical management. What they could not do was to create a science of law in a normal sense, partly because Greek oratory never developed into a full-fledged profession, partly because Greek ideas of social structure and change were elaborated for the most part in a naturalistic direction, at least on the level of theory, and partly because the centrifugal social experiences of the Greeks tended to discourage large aspirations to legal uniformity. It remained for a more determined and better organized, if less reflective and imaginative, people to shift the tradition of social thought from the secularized myth of Physis to the human construct of Nomos, and on this basis and in a systematic way to begin taking the earthly measure of man.

THREE

Roman Foundations

Consuetudo quasi altera quaedam natura.

Cicero, *De finibus*, V, 74

Consuetudo contra naturam.

Seneca, *Epistulae*, 122

·

From Fas to Ius

The Roman tradition of social thought seems to lead back in a rather different direction from that of the Greeks, and perhaps to be a bit more accessible.[1] Lacking the same impulse toward an abstract ideal, the Romans were apparently content mostly with rationalizing their own customs, conventions, and prejudices, and only eventually worked toward a kind of universality by accommodating, or absorbing, foreign culture by means of nativist "interpretation" (the so-called *interpretatio Romana*).[2] For the most part they seemed to be content with the creations of their own "second nature" rather than the primary nature of Greek speculation.

In general Roman culture was not reflective nor much given to cosmological speculation: the Romans had no Plato, no Aristotle, not even a tradition comparable to sophism. They had a Cicero, however—a lawyer even in his (mostly derivative) philosophizing—and Cicero's first ideal was ancestral wisdom (*mos maiorum*). The genius of Rome was thus directed toward "practical" rather than "theoretical" knowledge, and Cicero celebrated the ways in which "our ancestors excelled other nations in wisdom of this sort."[3] They concentrated above all on the preservation, organization, and extension of their community, and only later on the legitimation of their tradition. They were mostly committed, in other words, to convention rather than nature. (And so, for example, no Romans, not even Pliny, appear in Collingwood's survey of the "idea of nature".) Nor indeed did they feel obliged to distinguish between nature and convention until relatively late in their history, and then only under the tutorship of the Greeks. In general the Romans prized the faculty of memory over that of reason and practical over theoretical philosophy—reason enough, perhaps, to agree with the conclusion that "Roman ideology takes a historical form."[4]

The point of departure of Roman social consciousness seems to have been neither poetry nor cosmology, as it had been for the Greeks. Rather, as Henry Sumner Maine once observed, "Roman history begins, as it ends, with a code";[5] and the law of the Twelve Tables must indeed serve the historian as a substitute for the Homeric poems and for all of the pre-Socratic philosophers. Of philosophy there is little trace, but the poetic (oral and mnemonic) character of the collection is still reflected in the remaining fragments of this "fountain of all laws." Cicero remarked that the Twelve Tables were still chanted in his youth (though not afterward). The story was told by Livy and others, and is still widely believed, that in the mid-fifth century B.C. the Roman decemvirs who had been assigned to the task of codification traveled to Athens to consult with wise men, a tradition perhaps more consistent with ancient belief in the personal character of legislation than with the incidence of specific borrowings or affinities with Greek law.[6] In fact the major influx of Greek ideas came much later, as did analogies between the laws of Rome and those of Solon, including those pointed out by Cicero and later by Gaius. The major link may be simply the notion of codification itself, which was an extension of the practice of writing down and "publishing" laws, together with the corollary distinction between public and private law, which indeed was central to Roman as to Greek history.

In a long perspective Roman social thought, like that of Greece, arose in a religious context and must be seen against a background of Indo-European myth with various parallels to those of Hellas, whether through common provenance or osmosis.[7] Characteristically, Roman religion took a practical rather than a theoretical turn; and the Roman gods tended to personify not large natural principles but specific social values. Equity, Clemency, Virtue, Concord, Honor, Victory, Piety, Spirit or Mind (*mens*), and above all Faith (*fides*)—these were the tutelary powers of Roman character, the central figures in the legal pantheon, and honored, all of them, with temples.[8] The Romans had a businesslike, often contractual, relationship with their divinities, who in return were supposed to assist in the attainment of worldly objectives. Ideas of law, as of history, were products of religious tradition and were first formulated by the pontifical college, which was also the authority on questions of legal principle and procedure. Religious attitudes were preserved above all through the seminal and unceasing influence of the family, especially the extended form called the *gens* (equivalent to the Greek *genos*), described by Fustel de Coulanges as "at first the only form of society."[9] The "domestic religion" sheltered in this essentially patriarchal institution was in a sense the spiritual counterpart of the civic communities of families, which formed the nucleus of the Roman Republic.

In keeping with the general neglect of cosmology, Roman tradition rested on the myths not of creation but of foundation. Aside from Aeneas (who had Etruscan associations before being grafted by Virgil onto Greek legend), the central figure was of course the eponymous Romulus, who was "custodian of the law and ancestral customs" as well as regulator of Roman rites.[10] Although the city established on Latin-Sabine foundations actually emerged only after Etruscan domination and the famous "expulsion of the kings," Romulus came to symbolize the main traits of Roman character. As *conditor urbis,* he gathered to himself many lesser legends and images; and among other things he was credited with introducing the social ranks and that domestic focus of civil law, the paternal power (*patria potestas*). Above all it was Romulus who plowed the sacred *pomoerium,* the taboo zone around the city which provided divine protection for Roman territory.

This territorial symbolism was given legal force by Romulus's successor, Numa Pompilius, who (it was said) "decided that whoever dug up the boundary line would be offered up, along with his animals, to the gods of the underworld."[11] The Roman tendency to assimilate landed possessions to religious principle is well illustrated by the policy of this second (historically perhaps first) king of Rome. Although renowned for piety and active in the formulation of religious ritual which tied (*ligere*) man to the gods, Numa gave first priority to fixing the boundaries of the city—itself, of course, a "religious" act, carried out under the aegis of the multi-formed god Terminus. Ovid describes the festival of the terminalia and the invocation, "O Terminus, whether thou art a stone or post set in the ground, thou too hast been held divine from days of old." And further, "Thou dost fix the bound of the people and cities and huge kingdoms. Without thee every field would be a scene of wrangling." Again the contrast with Hellas is apparent. As Zeus issued his "themistes" to guide the Greeks, so Jupiter Terminus stood guard over Roman territory. This aspect of this father-god was reinforced by the image of the "killing god," whom Mommsen called "the central object not only of Roman but of Italian worship." Like Roman religion, then, Roman law was governed by an irresistible "territorial imperative."[12]

Such was the foundation of *fas*—a right which was also conceived to be a divine command, a holy principle in the name of which possessions were guarded and war, the original form of Roman imperialism, was declared. In general the emergence of Roman social thought, paralleling the transition from oral to written culture, was the product of a movement from an agrarian society ruled by unwritten custom (*mos*), sanctified by divine law (*fas*) and faith (*fides*), to an urban community organized by secular and super-familial law (*ius*), written down and extended beyond the old patrician families to the plebs and later to colonies and subject peoples.

Like *fas, ius* seemed originally to have referred to a spoken word, specifically an oath (from *iurare*) testifying to the truth of something. *Ius* was

parallel to *dike,* since it suggested a more general rule than *lex* (parallel to
the Greek *thesmos*), and had a special affinity with its Latin cousin *dico*
(as in *iudex* and *iurisdictio*). Like the term *nomos,* moreover, *ius* suggested
a norm derived from popular will, perhaps in contrast to *imperium,* as *lex*
(from *ligare,* to bind, or *legere,* to read) was contrasted with *rex* (from
regere, to rule). This was especially the case for "unwritten law," which
was distinguished, by Aristotle (*nomos agraphos*) as well as Cicero (*ius*
non scriptum), from written law. Although original etymologies might be
forgotten, some of the underlying implications were preserved throughout
the long career of Western social thought. In certain ways, then, Roman
ius—and indeed the whole family of *ius*-words (*iustitia, iurisprudentia,*
iurisdictio, and so forth)—represents the first intelligibly defined fulfillment
of Nomos, though in the rationalizations of jurists and philosophers it also
had aspirations to reach the universal level of Physis.[13]

Ius Civile

Over the course of generations Roman religion was secularized, diluted,
and subjected to foreign adulteration; but on the whole (so it appears in
retrospect) it was transformed by politicization rather than rationalization;
and it evolved not into philosophy but into the ideology of the Roman
state.[14] Grounded in *fas,* Roman civil law, as we can see it in fragmentary
remains, reflected the secular life of the Republic. The earliest legal formulations, including the more or less mythical royal statutes (*leges regiae*)
and the *ius Papiniarum* (named after the first presumed *pontifex*), were
made by the college of pontiffs; but the law of the Twelve Tables was not,
unlike so many other primitive "codes," presumed to be of divine origin.[15]
Indeed its principal justification seems to be indicated by its most famous
motto, "Let the welfare of the people be the supreme law" (*lex populi*
suprema lex esto), and by the last law of the last table, "Whatever the
people has last ordained shall be held as binding by law." Like the laws of
Solon, this "fount of all public and private law" (in Cicero's words) has
been called into question textually; but it had been similarly inscribed on
wooden and then bronze tablets, preserved in oral tradition, and alluded
to in literary and antiquarian works. To this nucleus of the original civil
law was added certain legislation, which passed in the third century from
the pontiffs to the secular magistrates and, as the plebeians began to enter
public life, was subjected to public discussion through juridical "responses."
In theory, however, the ultimate source of authority remained the same;
for as Gaius wrote in the second century A.D., "*Lex* is what the *Populus*
orders and determines."[16]

Civil law was an expression of Roman society in more than the technical
sense that it was defined by jurists as a product of popular will. More
fundamentally and concretely, it was formed by individual "actions of law"

initiated to resolve specific disputes. These *legis actiones* also had religious roots, as is obvious from the earliest type, the *legis actio sacramento;* and though the original significance was lost, the ritualistic formalism was preserved in later collections. Yet this basic legal process also became secularized. Pomponius tells the story of the scribe Gnaeus Flavius, minor emulator of Prometheus, who stole the books of civil law from the college of pontiffs around 300 B.C. and delivered them over to the People, thus ending the priestly monopoly.[17] The books in question concerned the fundamental forms of legal action, which were thus made available more widely; and a variety of types of *legis actiones* were defined by later statutes (*leges*). Despite the complexity of the formulas, all of these "actions of law" embodied the process by which contending parties resolved their differences according to the norms (and thus perhaps helping to shape the norms) of the *ius civile*. Under the Principate the *leges* were applied more directly to the public sphere, but for the most part they continued to be particular inferences from the Roman idea of *ius*.

The keystone of Roman society, even more conspicuously than that of the Greeks, was the family; and ultimately all of the elements of Roman social (and religious, economic, and political) thought derive from this private, prehistorical, and reputedly "natural" institution. In civil law, marriage was based not on religion but on agreement, that is, human will, although the joining of wills—consummation—was not required for a "just" union. And if the family was the keystone, the arch itself was the material wealth of the community, "property" in a general sense.[18]

The ruling principle of the Roman family, reflected in a wide range of Indo-European myths, was that of masculine supremacy—though, to be sure, this proposition has been challenged by matriarchalists at least since the time of J. J. Bachofen. Beginning with the customs reflected in the Twelve Tables, however, paternal power (*patria potestas*) was absolute, all-encompassing, and its purpose was specifically the preservation and perhaps the extension of property, landed and otherwise, in time as well as space. Concomitantly, it involved control of religious rites, which gave coherence to the family through pious attention to ancestors and progeny. The family was a small empire, then, the "hand" (*manus*) of the patriarch (*paterfamilias*) being equivalent, and more, to the sovereignty (*maiestas*) of the people, or emperor, and the private property (*res privata*) being equivalent to the Roman state (*Res Publica*). The *pater* had the power of life and death, of liberty and enslavement, over his children as well as his slaves. According to the Twelve Tables, even the wife had the technical status of property acquired by possession (*usucapio*) and so was subject to the paternal *imperium*. Father was thus priest and king as well as husband and progenitor and prototype of the male chauvinist who has dominated history—or at least the history of political and social thought.

The connection between the prehistorical but hardly mythical principle of paternal power and political authority was, and has long been, profound and mutually reinforcing. In effect the king—as later the *dictator* and *imperator*—was a kind of *paterfamilias* writ large, though to be sure political authority was technically delegated by land-possessing families, those lesser empires which made up the citizenry (the *Populus Romanus*). And as the father was virtually king and god to his household, so the "fathers" (*patres*) and the "patriciate" which they formed held ultimate authority (*auctoritas patrum,* the term always used for senatorial power) and thus the "majesty" of the Roman Republic.

In short, it was through a projection of private virtue (*virtus* being the appropriate masculine term) into public trust and service that the stability and expansiveness of the state were guaranteed. "Public faith" (*fides publica*) was the name given to this projection, and in the third century a temple was erected in its honor.[19] In these and other ways the pattern of Roman social development was (as historians have noted) marked by homologies between private and public law, between domestic and political institutions, between moral and legal philosophy. In a special sense this also represents a movement from nature to convention, that is, from a mostly biological to a man-made community—or so many later interpreters have envisaged this cultural process.

In the most fundamental sense the Romans were "realists"—concerned with *res*—and in both a public and a private way were devoted to "real estate." They had a great "hatred of thieves" (in the words of Gaius), and their state was based above all on respect for property—that is, their own property.[20] Yet this socio-economic institution, underlying both kinship relations and "gentile" succession, also lies at the roots of class divisions already evident in the Twelve Tables. There five social groupings were recognized, but the fundamental distinction was between the old patriciate and those excluded from it—plebeians, clients, and freedmen (all assimilated to citizenship in the course of urban growth) and slaves. A more direct reflection of social divisions is the "timocratic" distinction between possessors (*adsidui*) and the expropriated (*proletarii*). In combination with religion—for the Twelve Tables contained "sacred" as well as civil law—the control of land was a determinant of social patterning perhaps common to all Indo-European societies. According to Dumézil, the three principal Roman gods and their "kindling priests"—those of Jupiter, Mars, and Quirinus (*flamines Dialis, Martialis, Quirinalis*)—correspond to the three universal classes of priests, warriors, and owners. What is more, they correspond to certain "substructures of Roman history": the reverence and worship of the gods, the founding and protecting of the city, and subsequent building of the empire.[21] In material as well as spiritual terms Ius—the *ius civile* or *ius Quiritium*—was a product of Fas.

Yet the inclination of the Romans, especially in the republican period, was to socialize, to politicize, and thus to "popularize" their religious commitment, so as to elevate and to hypostasize the Populus, and with it the Senate, as a transcendent spiritual collectivity and source of authority. As Cicero remarked, "Cato used to say that the superiority of our city to others depended upon the fact that the latter almost always had their laws and institutions from a single legislator . . . whereas our republic was not created by the genius of any individual, nor in the lifetime of one man, but through countless centuries."[22] Caesarism may have undermined this conviction, but classical jurisprudence until perhaps the third century A.D. preserved this insight, so essential for the development of social thought.

Interpretatio Romana

As sacral law gave way to civil law, so civil law was superseded by juristic law, as a tradition of legal experts set about giving form and meaning to the bare texts of the Twelve Tables and other legislation in terms of particular issues and confrontations.[23] This vital process of "interpretation" was carried on first by the pontifical college, and the sacred commentaries and responses covered civil as well as religious matters.[24] The sacred phase of the legal tradition culminated in the work of the great members of the Mucian clan—P. Mucius Scaevola, P. Licinius Crassus Mucianus, and Q. Mucius Scaevola, all of them *pontifices maximi*. In the first century B.C. the task of legal interpretation passed for the most part to secular jurists, who contributed to civil law in various ways, whether as advocates, judges, or advisors to magistrates in the drawing up of edicts and "knowledge" of causes (*cognitio,* or cognizance, being equivalent to jurisdiction). From a priestly monopoly, legal interpretation became a public vocation; and through the members of this profession the so-called *ius honoratiorum,* practical incarnation of the *ius civile,* was given scientific form.

In the archaic age, *interpretatio* had been an act virtually of religious divination (like early modern "hermeneutics"); and to judge from fragmentary sources, mainly formularies and judicial responses, it remained literal and formalistic down to the Principate. Yet the task of the jurisconsult demanded skill and sensitivity as well as a knowledge of the world. In general, Cicero taught, three things were required of a jurisconsult: to be expert in judging, in providing pleas, and in prescribing forms: *respondere, agere, cavere*—these were the charges of the incipient legal profession. By Cicero's time such expertise was claimed by practicing lawyers, that is, "orators," as well as by magistrates and judges. None of these had formal training, though in his Platonizing idealism Cicero envisaged the orator as a paragon of encyclopedic learning and practical experience worthy of a Roman version of Plato's paradigm—in effect the "philosopher-magistrate." For the most part, however, it was the rhetorical not the philosophical vision of Greek *paideia* that was adopted by Roman jurisprudence. The difference was that these Roman heirs of the Sophists, likewise serving a "civic science," established a firmer professional base and, more important, forged lasting ties with economic interests and political authority.

By Cicero's time, then, the *ius honoratiorum* was coming under control of a tradition of legal experts whose contributions to social thought far surpassed those either of the Ciceronian windbags (*pragmatici*) or of the amateurish careerists who took temporary positions in the magistracy.[25] From the late republican period these professional jurists (*jurisconsulti, jurisprudentes, jurisscientes*) ranged socially from orators of humble origins to members of older families pursuing administrative careers up to the level of praetorship. When one of the three professional functions was given official recognition—*respondere* being formalized in the famous (though perhaps overrated) *ius respondendi*—the jurists attained in effect legislative as well as judicial authority; and they expressed this authority in a massive literature, especially in the form of commentaries on legislation (on *leges, senatusconsulta,* and *edicta*), treatises on particular topics (responses, questions, and disputations), and pedagogical works. They had their ideological differences—as in the alleged division between the conservative and republican "Proclian" and the more imperial-minded "Sabinian" schools—but they remained united by their "science" and, from the time of Vespasian, by their allegiance to the emperor and his causes.

In the classical period the most distinguished of the jurisconsults was Papinian, third-century praetorian prefect and author of various works in rhetorical style—characteristically classroom "questions" about abstract cases concerning "Titius" ("John Doe") intended to elicit correct "responses." Among his colleagues and commentators were Paul and Ulpian, perhaps the most philosophical of Roman jurists; Gaius, whose *Institutes* is the only surviving classical work of this tradition; and Modestinus, the last of the line, who died in 234.[26] These five "juristic evangelists," as Fritz Schulz called them, were given special authority by the famous "law of citations" (A.D. 426), declaring that the judgments of these authors were decisive, especially those of Papinian, which outweighed all the others in case of a tie. Through the post-classical collections of the "bureaucratic period," the views of these jurists remained a conduit of ancient social thought and so a shaping force, not only juristic and pedagogical but also political and philosophical, in Western culture.

Yet civil law and its honoratorial extension also had a less attractive side. They had been forged in the crucible of Roman history and never wholly lost the scars of class conflict, heedless imperial expansion, and war. They reflected not only "what the People ordered" but also what the People suffered. The legal tradition was filled with anachronisms: "for long lapse of time has rendered old works and customs obsolete," wrote Aulus Gellius, "and it is in the light of these words that the sense of laws is to be understood." In this spirit Gellius discussed the term "proletarian" (*proletarius civis*) as "ancient lore of the Twelve Tables put to sleep by the *lex Aebutia*,"[27] as Gaius did with the old forms of procedure (*legis actiones*), superseded by second-century law. Civil law was filled, too, with inequities, to the extent that more than one modern historian has tried to see it as essentially an "instrument of social control." Finally, civil law remained in disrepute because of associations with the supposed duplicity of rhetoric. Cicero himself warned people to distinguish between "the language of the cause" and "that of the man and orator," and he reminded readers "sophistically" that pleaders could always find arguments for either side of a case.[28] Like their sophistical forebears, lawyers have chronically and proverbially had a bad press. "The more laws, the worse the state" was a Greek topos adopted by Roman critics of their own society (*plurimae leges, pessima republica*); and popular opinion tended to reinforce suspicions about litigiousness as a sure sign of a decline from ancient virtue. "From this tomb," reads one of several like-minded inscriptions, "let all fraud and all lawyers be absent."[29]

The ambivalence of the legal tradition is well illustrated by the public life of Cicero himself, which seems almost to recapitulate that of civil law. Until the age of forty he was a practicing advocate, and this rough-and-tumble experience continued to inform his legal and social consciousness. He pleaded for factional causes even as he deplored factionalism. He urged the advantages of a "mixed constitution" even as he celebrated the utopian ideals of Platonic philosophy. In his own career, in short, Cicero combined the hardest realism, enhanced by contact with the lamentable corruption of pre-imperial society, politics, and law courts, with the most elevated conception of justice and the moral authority of law. Offering an idealization of Roman public values, Cicero in effect raised *Romanitas* to the level of universal *humanitas*. What Gaius would attribute to the consensus of the Roman Populus (and the "prudence" of the jurists) Cicero identified with human reason. This was his way of appropriating for Roman tradition the ideal splendor of Plato's Republic; and as he followed the Stoics in this regard, so he would later be followed by modern devotees of "natural law"—once again to the general discredit of Nomos.[30]

Professional jurists were more critical than Cicero of these conceptual gifts from the Greeks, but they were also happy to see the forces of Stoic Physis coming as it were to the assistance of Roman Nomos. This encounter between civil law and Greek conceptualizing, especially through the terminology and hermeneutical techniques associated with the Greek philosophy of language, made possible the transformation of the *ius honoratorium*—the "living voice of the *ius civile*," as it was regarded—into a full-fledged science. The *honoratiores*, a new order of the "priests of the law" (as Ulpian would call them), carried on a long-term intellectual effort which one historian has celebrated as a "scientific revolution" possessing vital implications for social thought as well as for jurisprudence.[31] From a perspective of over twenty centuries these *honoratiores* seemed to Max Weber, indeed, to stand at the very headwaters of Western social science.

Legal Science

Concerning the Roman legal tradition, one thing should always be kept in mind, and that is the parallel and sometimes intersecting fortunes of civil law and the art of oratory, or rhetoric, for which the Romans again went to school with the Greeks.[32] The crucial connection can be seen in the Roman adoption of the old notion of "custom" (*consuetudo*), the original form of law, as "second nature" (*altera natura*), and the association of this distinction with language. Aside from ordinary usage by authors such as Pliny, Sallust, and Tacitus, the term *consuetudo* was employed by both Cicero and Quintilian in the sense of a norm of the speech community, comparable to the terms *mos* and *usus*. Cicero deliberately contrasted everyday, customary life (*vitae consuetudo*) with the philosophical idealizations of Plato's *Republic;* and in general, convention was conceived by philologists such as Varro and Gellius, and argued by skeptics such as Sextus Empiricus, to be a social rather than a logical standard.[33] One of the most familiar of all topoi—repeated by Quintilian, Cicero, and Pliny—was that custom (*consuetudo, usus*) was the ruler (*magister, magistra*) of human speech and so more generally of human life, in terms both individual (in the sense of habit) and collective (in the sense of social usage). All of these assumptions had analogues in the law and served in some ways to set it apart from natural philosophy. Private law has itself been (in the words of Arnold Toynbee borrowed by Helmut Coing) an "intelligible field of study" for historians.

As usual, however, it was in formal philosophy that Greek influence was most conspicuous. In a long perspective, Roman legal science may be seen as the product of cross-fertilization between Roman Nomos and Greek Physis, "natural law" serving to give form and method to the substance of civil law. Romans professed contempt for some aspects of Greek cleverness, especially sophistry and notorious untrustworthiness (*graeca fides* is the ironic phrase), but they did not scruple to plunder the riches of Hellenism. Whatever its historicity, the legend of the Decemvirs' pilgrimage to Athens (repeated by Pomponius and many others until the time of Vico, and since) neatly symbolizes the fundamental borrowings from Greek thought.

Though the channels of transmission are obscure, Platonic ideals, Aristotelian categories, sophistic topoi, and dialectical method turned Rome's formalistic, quasi-religious legal doctrine into a rational and international discipline, a Hellenistic "science" (*legitima scientia,* as the jurists called their field).[34] The expansion of horizons is reflected again in the hyperbole of Cicero, who praised Socrates for bringing philosophy down from the heavens but who hoped himself to raise social thought once again to a cosmic level, the level indeed of universal Physis. Following the secular mythos of Platonism, Cicero turned back in effect to the old idea of the divine origin of law. In his view the "science of law" came "neither from the pretorian's edict, as the majority now think," nor "from the Twelve Tables, as people used to think," but rather "from the deepest mysteries of philosophy."[35]

Initially at least, the "scientific revolution" in civil law was accompanied by a radical shift in the direction of the naturalism associated with Greek political philosophy. For Cicero, law was defined as the highest reason (*summa ratio, recta ratio*), the ordering principle of the great commonwealth of nature as well as of human government rightly conceived. Yet even Cicero, in his Hellenizing enthusiasm, tried to give a Roman cast to the idea of law. He rejected, philosophically at least, the etymology which linked law (*nomos*) to the root *nemo-,* suggesting distribution or giving everyone his due; and he preferred instead the derivation of law (*lex*) from *lego,* implying a selection or choosing between good and evil.[36] To Cicero law was not a mathematical science but a form of prudence requiring moral judgment and "equity." Jurisprudence, in Ulpian's famous phrase, is "the art of the good and the just" (*ars boni et aequi*).[37]

It was not the orators, however, but the jurisconsults who, as their historian Pomponius put it, "laid the foundations of civil law."[38] Jurists tended to be distrustful of political theory, partly because it was controversial and partly because it was unprofessionally philosophical; and they had perforce to concentrate on the vast array of legal conventions accumulated over many generations of Roman history and on the level of private law and middle-range social questions. The depth and dimensions of their achievement in legal science are but imperfectly reflected in the fragmentary remains of Justinian's Digest. Perhaps the only way their intellectual "revolution" can be appreciated is in the transformation of language, the development of technical terminology and modes of argument, and the attempts to systematize legal knowledge and procedures. But this was an enterprise begun long before the time of Cicero, and we can only surmise the earliest patterns of linguistic and conceptual change.

Legal hermeneutics, unlike other varieties, involved judgment of fact as well as of law. In general the task of jurists was always to reason from experience, particular cases, causes, and questions, to valid and realistic conclusions: judgments (*res judicatae*) were extended, according to a specifically legal kind of empiricism, into general principles. In the context of an expanding Mediterranean economic, military, and political arena, jurists were forced to broaden their professional horizons accordingly. In their confrontations with urban and international problems, they began self-consciously to employ a wider range of conceptual devices, including axioms, hypotheses, analogies, and regular ideas of authority, precedence, classification, comparison, and cause. They made systematic distinctions (*divisiones, differentiae,* or, especially for medieval commentators, *distinctiones,* corresponding to Aristotelian *diairesis*); beginning as early as the elder (Q. Mucius) Scaevola they arranged legal materials into genera and species; they began the sophistic legitimation of the practice of arguing both sides of a case (*disputatio in utramque partem,* analogous to the Greek *dissoi logoi*); and they devoted themselves to the theory and practice of "equity" (*aequitas*). In these various ways was forged the long-standing, though often controversial, alliance between philosophy and jurisprudence.[39]

One of the most significant products of this union was the development of various definitions and rules (*definitiones* or *regulae iuris,* corresponding to Greek *horoi* or *kanones*). Originally suggesting model or pattern, the *regulae antiqui iuris,* fashioned in the Hellenistic and especially classical periods and collected by Justinian, evolved into general norms and "maxims" which for centuries served as the subject of commentary and interpretation.[40] Some of these are conservative ("the rights of blood cannot be annulled by civil law"; "in the claim of two persons the position of the possessor is preferable"), some are idealistic ("liberty is to be prized above all things," and "slavery is comparable to death"), some textual ("when words are ambiguous, the most probable or ordinary significance should be adopted"); but most seem to be the product of common sense, habit, or experience, and often to be beyond analysis. In any case they represent the bottom stratum of the legal wisdom accumulated through the Roman view of Nomos as shaped to some extent by Greek notions. Besides being in a sense the juridical ancestors of Durkheim's "rules of sociological method," they have survived as a set of norms inherent in civil law; the first rule, indeed, is that "the law is not derived from the rule, but on the contrary the rule is established by the law."

"All definition is dangerous" is another juristic rule, implying that jurists ought to subordinate independent reasoning to the conventions of their professional tradition and world of discourse, and remain in their own province of the kingdom of Nomos.[41] It should not be surprising that Roman jurists inclined more to Greek grammar and rhetoric than to formal philosophy in the Socratic mode. "Orators" of course employed all the resources of logic in their argumentation, but the conventional model of language was more important to legal science. The use of analogy and above all consensual ideas of "custom" and "authority" were essential to language as they were not to philosophy. Law was bound to language, especially written language, and depended on a similar theory of interpretation, especially on the classical problem of determining the meaning from the letter of a text, which in legal terms meant inferring the intention or will (*voluntas*) of the legislator from the words (*verba*) of the law. Here was another famous and endlessly repeated rule: "To know the laws is to grasp not merely the words but their force and significance" (*vis et potestas*).[42] So civil law may be regarded as an aboriginal context of the hermeneutical debate over intentionality (or what critics have called the "intentional fallacy"), and especially over liberal versus strict (analogous to figurative or rational versus literal or grammatical) interpretation. This is the original locus of the unending search carried on by jurists and social thinkers—from Celsus and Ulpian down to Montesquieu and Vico and beyond—for "the spirit of the law" (*mens legis, ratio legis*).

What gave shape and direction to the Roman idea of law from the late republican period was ultimately the grandiose idea of universal Nature, especially as distinguished from convention; and Roman views of the structure of law were basically translations of Greek concepts: the contrast between natural and civil law (*ius naturale, ius civile,* corresponding to *physei dikaion* and *thesei* or *nomon dikaion*), between the law of nations and civil law (*ius gentium, ius civile,* corresponding to *koinon dikaion* and *politikon dikaion*), and between written and unwritten law (*ius scriptum* and *non scriptum,* corresponding to *nomos gegrammenos* and *nomos agraphos*).[43] Civil law, natural law, law of nations, custom: here (with the addition of divine law) are the fundamental categories of Western legal and social thought as viewed over two millennia and more.

The last and perhaps most valuable of the conceptual gifts brought by the Greeks was the affection for systematic thought, together with some of the means for realizing it. The Stoics were of particular importance in attempting to universalize the idea of law, and eager Roman pupils responded by trying in effect to Romanize the natural law celebrated by Stoicism. The convergence of these two movements—the Roman legal tradition on its path to world conquest and universal order and the Greek obsession with establishing a ruling principle (*arche*) of natural order—prepared the ground for the classic effort to create a global legal system, and with it a comprehensive system of social thought. The idea of a legal system, a code, was already implied by the pretorian edict and in certain legal reforms envisaged by both Cicero and Caesar (*ius in artem redigere* was the formula); but the major intellectual work was accomplished by the new class of professionals, especially the teachers of law. The scholar most responsible, or at least given retrospective credit, for the systematization of civil law was the second-century (A.D.) jurist Gaius, whose *Institutes* (miraculously recovered in the early nineteenth century) affords the only extensive view of classical jurisprudence. With Gaius the Roman legal tradition achieved "scientific" form. Though not worked out for centuries, the implicit aim of "Gaianism" was to find, in Roman terms, fulfillment of the old Greek ideal installed in jurisprudence in the famous formula of the Stoic dialectician Chrysippus, celebrating the theme we have been following as "Nomos, ruler of all things divine and human."[44]

Gaius Noster

Of the jurisconsult Gaius little is known, not even his full name.[45] Nor is his doctrinal background clear, except that he seems to have inclined to the "Sabinian" school of jurisprudence, preferring liberal to literal interpretation of the law, and that he taught and lectured as well as consulted. Among his many works were commentaries on the Twelve Tables, on the pretorian and provincial edicts, on the rules of law, and on many cases and topics of civil law. The famous manuscript of Gaius's *Institutes of Civil Law*, discovered by B. G. Niebuhr (a palimpsest, overwritten by a copy of St. Jerome's letters), provides a unique view not only of an ancient jurist but also of the character of formal jurisprudence before the work, destructive as well as reconstructive, of the Emperor Justinian in the sixth century. Not that there was much novelty in the *Institutes,* which were apparently lecture notes, taken perhaps by a student. In effect Gaius was merely applying techniques made famous three centuries earlier by Q. M. Scaevola, who was probably the creator of "the first dialectical system of law in the grand manner"; and only paleographical fortune leads us to celebrate a Gaian rather than a Mucian tradition.[46]

In any case Gaius's *Institutes,* the only nearly complete pre-Justinianian text, became more influential than the books of more authoritative jurists such as Papinian and Ulpian. Distilling, simplifying, and organizing the resources of ancient legal wisdom, Gaius became the mentor not only of Rome but also of Byzantium and, through a wide range of modern codes, of Europe as a whole. To Justinian, and so to many jurists down to the present century, he was "Gaius noster"; he was or is, so to say, "our teacher."

As the first systematic expression of Roman social thought, Gaianism may be defined by three distinguishing features. The first is a basically historical approach, displayed most prominently in the famous second title of the Digest drawn from Pomponius's monograph "On the Origin of Law" but embodied more concretely in Gaius's *Institutes,* which was a veritable cornucopia of Roman social experience and legal wisdom. The second is the dialectical method by which Gaius generated essential divisions, distinctions, and methods of interpretation. Last and most important was his formulation of the classical juridical trinity, fixed forever under the rubric "On the Division of Law" (*De iuris divisione*): "All the law which we use pertains either to persons or to things or to actions" (*de personis, de rebus, de actionibus*). In other words, the social field was distributed exhaustively into the categories of "personality," "reality" (though for jurists the "things," *res*, of the "real" world could be intangible, *incorporealis*, as well as tangible), and the actions and interactions of persons and things, including commerce as well as conflicts over property.[47] This fundamental classification entailed not only moral priorities and a means of ordering reality but also a characteristic mode of perceiving, of construing, and potentially of controlling the social field.

What was the source of this fundamental threefold structure which permeated all of Roman (and much of modern) social and legal thinking? To some commentators on "subjectivity" and "personality" in law, homocentric organization seems hardly to require explanation; others have seen it as one manifestation of a more general Roman fixation on "trichotomy."[48] Though impossible to demonstrate (and therefore regarded as untenable by many jurists), the most reasonable suggestion would seem to be the analogy between this legal trinity and the structure of language—Latin, or perhaps Indo-European, grammar itself—which is to say, the relationship between subject and predicate, including object and verb. In any case the categories of person-thing-action constitute, first implicitly and later explicitly, what might be regarded as the metaphysical (or metanomical) foundations of Roman social thought. In view of later developments, they may also be regarded as a system rivaling the naturalistic construction of Aristotelianism, as another version of the many-faceted contrast between Physis and Nomos—of primary and second nature.

In the most fundamental way, then, Roman jurisprudence was anthropocentric. Awakened by the Greeks, Psyche became as it were the center and cynosure of Roman social thought; and the conscious "personality" (*personalitas*) remained the essential focus for perceiving the world of "reality" (*realitas*). (Latin corporate groups, too, would be granted a theoretical sort of "personality" to fit in with legal convention and be capable of legal "action.") The foundation of Roman law was and in many ways continued to be "custom" (*consuetudo, ius non scriptum*); and this realm of second nature, too, was interpreted in terms of the individual person, his force of will, and his responsible actions.[49] The transition from tribal to civic law (*ius gentilitatis* to *ius civitatis*) was accomplished through legal acts ranging from particular demands for private justice to public legislation. Statutory law began, in other words, as an "action" initiated by the proposal (*rogatio*) of a magistrate, while private law originated in the responses to particular claims realized through "actions of law" (*legis actiones*). Similarly, the basic meaning of laws determined by jurisconsults was established on the basis of the "intention" (*mens, intentio, sententia*) of the original law-maker, whether legislative or judicial.[50] Both law and judgment, in other words, both *ius* and *iudicium,* were human creations, and in that sense expressions of convention rather than nature. According to the Roman view, social order in general was not a natural phenomenon but rather the result of human effort, an act of "faith," which was a central social and political as well as moral and religious virtue; and legal science has never been able to escape this premise.

Another aspect of the indelible anthropocentrism of civil law was the emphasis placed on individual "liberty," since free will was in effect the defining characteristic of "personality."[51] Perhaps "status" is a better word, for there were degrees of *libertas,* ranging from the condition of those enjoying it from birth (*liberi,* or those under their own law, *sui iuris*), to those freed by manumission (*libertini*), to "peregrines" and still lesser breeds, including soldiers and colonial communities. All such "persons" had legal identity, human "will," and responsibility, and were eventually admitted to citizenship. All others besides propertied freemen (when they were not women, children, foreigners, or otherwise incapacitated) were slaves and for most purposes were transferred to the next category, that of things, property. Nor did the law grant rights to any who were unable to control their own fate, so that an "insane person," for example, "and one who is forbidden to manage his property, has no will." The liberty of citizens, those admitted to full humanity, was in effect the private counterpart of the public authority of the state; and it was so sanctified that the killing of a freeman was regarded as the worst of crimes—parricide—and slavery, proverbially, as a form of death.

Here again is a parallel with Greek views of humanity, which defined man in terms of rationality and participation in civic, or "political," life. Roman jurists elaborated this conception in more concrete, if parochial, social terms. But if the definition of the free "personality" become citizen began simply as a legalistic form of *Romanitas,* it was extended by legal science into a broader conception of *humanitas,* transcending (as well as incorporating) the Greek notion of a socialized Psyche—the "political animal," in Aristotle's words. In later ages the political character of this primary category of Roman law (the "condition of man") was drawn out further. Indeed, there is a direct link between this rubric and the Renaissance notion of the "dignity of man," as celebrated by Pico and other humanists, and, more remotely, the French "declaration of the rights of man," which achieved independent status in much later incarnations of civil law (the Romanoid Code of Napoleon and its many offspring).[52]

The second category—that of "things" (*res,* "reality" in a primordial sense)—introduced the endless problems of how to acquire, preserve, exchange, and bequeath material acquisitions and wealth, or rather how to legitimize such action.[53] It was also the primary link between person and society, centering on the hybrid (natural-social) institution of the family.

The material base of the Roman family was its landed property (technically, "possessions"), which was at once the source and embodiment in time of paterfamilial power and political status. Prehistorically or at any rate philosophically, the root of property (*dominium*) was simply consciousness of the difference between mine and thine (*meum et tuum*); but the complexity and variability of the human condition produced endless variations on this theme of the extended self—for given requirements for physical survival, property in a general sense was indeed a natural extension of liberty and personality.

Logically if not legally related to private property was the law of possession, a deceptively simple notion implying rights and "good faith" as well as physical occupation, which in later centuries became the subject of incredibly convoluted debates, especially in connection with ideas of communal property associated with the Roman institution of "public land" (*Ager publicus* or *Romanus*) distributed to citizens during republican expansion. Even more than Platonic speculation this was a locus classicus for later discussions of primitive communism or state collectivism.[54] For the most part, however, possessory edicts were designed as a remedy against violent seizure. A third related concept—completing what one historian has called the "classificatory genitive"—was "prescription," which introduced the factor of time into the legitimization of possession or property. The centerpiece of Roman social reality, however, remained the so-called *dominium ex iure Quiritum* of the original members of the civil community. Along with its public counterpart, such private dominion, an archetype of "possessive individualism," was the very essence of *Romanitas*.

The generative and dynamic principle of civil law was represented by the equally complex concept of action, itself divided into personal and real types.[55] Not only public but also private law was in a sense created by an original act (starting with the old *legis actio* and including later "possessory actions"), which provided legal remedy and (cumulatively) legal norms, and secondarily by the legal "exception," which referred to the counter-action of the defendant. Through such "acts of law," each corresponding to a particular "obligation," individuals, as agents, exercised not only their liberties but also their wills, so long as they had legal "cause" (for the *obligatio* in question) and good faith. The social arena of *actio*, despite its technical character, was a world of human values, by-products in a sense of attempts to regulate interactions in the field of criminal law. Through this third member of the juridical trinity, the ancient legal version of modern "action theory," individuals extended their wills and interests beyond the domestic sphere into the further reaches of society and, however inadvertently, helped to create the substance and forms of civil law.[56]

If Gaianism made use of Greek materials, it gave them Latin style and dress. Behind the pedagogical intent of the *Institutes* there are philosophical implications that seem distinctly Roman. Consider above all the significance of the anthropocentric, if not anthropomorphic, ordering of social categories (consistent, of course, with sophism as well). For Gaius, understanding began not with the cosmos but with Psyche—with the human subject, first of consciousness, that is, will, and then of rights—which formed the center of a sort of rudimentary sociology of knowledge; then, with the establishment of the field of vision, horizons could be expanded to encompass other individuals and natural objects, potentially property; and finally the social field could be completed by observing and judging human actions and interactions. Second, and correlative to this, the Gaian system was aimed not just at causal explanation—value-free science, so to speak—but also at human problems, the rendering of practical and normative judgments, and the determination of remedies and larger principles.

In general, social thought Roman style seems organized in concentric rings, moving outward from a private center to a remote, public, and even foreign and alien periphery, following the "horizon-structure of experience," as it is called in modern hermeneutics.[57] The person occupies the center, the first circumference of which is the family, that is the household, founded on the institution of marriage and forming a primary, interfamilial link with society in a more public sense. Although possessing its own religious ideology, the family had become a secular institution during the Republic, as had marriage. It was defined but not necessarily carried on by blood; for its life-principle was in fact, or rather in law, paternal power (*patria potestas*), the masculine will which controlled family members and determined inheritance, hence shaped the future and maintained the state.[58]

Here is a major cross-over between the private and public spheres, for the *Res Publica* always depended on the right ordering of the *res privatae*. Roman jurisprudence was centrally concerned with protecting and strengthening the governing class, still theoretically stemming from the community of *patresfamilias* symbolized, if not represented, by the Senate. The coming of empire did not fundamentally change social doctrine on this level, except by defining more carefully the outermost circle of personality, which was citizenship; by subordinating the private to the public sphere; and by making larger claims for the role of legal science. For jurists like Ulpian *legitima scientia* was not only an expression of Roman Nomos; it was *vera philosophia*—true (and more than merely Greek) philosophy. And so it would remain for many centuries.[59]

· F O U R ·

Byzantine Canon

Inveterata consuetudo pro lege non immerito custoditur.

Julianus

Consuetudo optima legum interpres.

Paulus

·

Corpus Juris Civilis

Having taken law from the Greeks, a Renaissance jurist once remarked, Rome in the end restored it to them—referring to the Emperor Justinian's appropriation of Roman legal tradition in his monumental effort of codification in the sixth century A.D.[1] The Romano-Byzantine Digest, and secondarily the Institutes, represented for jurisprudence the culmination of the Greek impulse to philosophical system. Preserved and sanctified in this collection were the old Gaian trinity, the basic distinction between private and public law, the idea of natural law as the ultimate standard of justice, and many other features of classical legal science. Justinian's system was an ambitious project designed both to fulfill the juridical ideal of "true philosophy" and to begin what was in effect the first system of social engineering; and it was the expressed intention of the emperor that his structure should "prevail for all time."[2]

If Roman law began and ended with a code, it also ended, as it began, with claims to be divine—moving in effect fom *fas* to *ius* and back again to *fas*. For not only did Justinian lay claim to the legacy of *Romanitas*, "almost 1400 years of it"; he insisted on recognition of the sanctity and divinity of civil law as well as of his imperial person. In Roman law the religious element had always been prominent—from the mythical origins noted by Justinian, to the boast of classical jurists to be "priests of the law," to the convergence with Christianity and imperial invocations of the Trinity as the basis of legitimation. A century earlier the Theodosian Code had been designed as a complete "guidance for life" for the Christian community of the West; and "Theodosianism in general not only softened the rigors of ancient Roman law and showed favor to the Barbarians but also marked, along with the demise of paganism, the beginning of religious uniformity." Justinian's enterprise was the culmination of this new legal religiosity, to the extent indeed that he "wished God to be the author and head of the whole work."[3] According to imperial intention, therefore, the Corpus Iuris Justiniani represented not only the dogmatic and terminal reformulation of the old *ius civile* but also a transcendent expression of universal Physis—the definitive and universal social base for the Christian Logos and its imperial incarnation.

Originating in priestly law, the *ius civile* had received new sanctification by Constantine's conversion and legalizing of Christianity, which completed and then subverted the old Roman pantheon. Like the obverse images of the unconquerable sun and the cross on Constantine's new coin, *Christianitas* and *Romanitas* became two sides of the same imperial currency. The new religion, which champions such as Eusebius insisted was really old, became a "licensed cult" (*religio licita*) and indeed an acquisitive corporation—a fictitious "person" with earthly needs as well as spiritual pretensions. Such was the result of the rescript of Milan—the "great charter of the New Republic," as Charles Norris Cochrane called it—giving to the devotees of Christ access to the things that had been Caesar's.[4] For the legal tradition, now almost wholly subject to imperial will, this meant the establishment of a new *telos,* a new source of unity and *eunomia;* and henceforth the Trinity (the Nicene not the Gaian trinity) became a dominant rubric of "Roman" jurisprudence. The Trinity was indeed, as Augustine remarked, "everywhere." The convergence of Christian morality and social teachings with classical traditions of order and political will reinforced the drive toward the systematic organization of the law under the aegis of "Caesaro-papism"—Constantine retaining the pagan title of Pontifex Maximus—and with the complex problem of combining two disparate traditions of positive law.

The impulse toward legal system had already been implied in the "revolution" of legal science inaugurated in the second century B.C., but carrying out such a utopian plan depended ultimately on strong central authority. On the ides of March in the very first year of his reign (13 February 528) Justinian began to transform the old aspiration of "reducing law to an art" into a quasi-religious mission. He appointed a committee of ten jurists, headed by the Quaestor Tribonian, to survey the riches of the jurisprudence of the "Romanoi" and on this basis to form a code which would bring law and order to his Empire. The work was accomplished in the amazingly short space of four years. The centerpiece was the Digest (or Pandects), a vast anthology of classical jurisprudence containing exerpts from thirty-nine authors drawn from the reading of some three million lines and arranged according to traditional categories and rubrics. The Institutes was a textbook, a sort of digest of the Digest following the plan of "our Gaius," while the Code was a collection of recent legislation. These works, published from A.D. 530 on, constitute the sacred canon of civil law, in a sense the funeral monument of Roman jurisprudence, the model of virtually all subsequent structures of Western law, and in many ways the prototype of systematic social thought.[5]

"A code is both a history and a system," remarked a modern jurist; and this was conspicuously true of the work carried out by Tribonian and his editorial colleagues.[6] To begin with, the Digest was the product of filial piety toward the fathers of Roman jurisprudence (*veteris iuris conditores*); and the emperor himself declared his "reverence for antiquity" and respect for the "monuments of ancient learning," in recognition of which Pomponius's history of law (*De origine iuris*) was included in the second title of the Digest following the introductory title on the philosophy, structure, and goals of law (*De iure et iustitia*).[7]

Yet at the same time Justinian had no intention of being bound by the past—"for how," he asked rhetorically, "can antiquity interfere with our authority?" So he commanded, vainly, that all contradictions be eliminated and, just as vainly, that all judicial or academic "interpretation" be forbidden.[8] Behind this heaven-storming ambition there were two motives: one that henceforth the emperor's will should be the only source of law (locus classicus of the idea of "absolute authority") and the other that social order should once and for all be guaranteed by a "perfect" system of law (locus classicus, perhaps, for the idea of enlightened despotism). So Justinian's "new law" became a model both for authoritarian government and for a kind of social engineering.

The rationale of Justinian's Corpus, then, was essentially a function of the ideology of empire as he conceived of it. The true basis of *imperium*, of course, had been military expansion; and the question arose as to the significance of Tribonian's scholarly undertaking for imperial glory. In the medieval gloss to Justinian's Institutes, nucleus of a modern Romanist mythology, this question is posed by a young student, who recalls the emperor's reference to himself and his followers as "soldiers": why, then, all the commotion about laws? "My son, this is how I answer you," Justinian is made to say by Accursius. "It befits every emperor to be ready for these two times, that is, for arms and for laws . . . The time of war he will govern by means of arms . . . and therewith he will become a conqueror and victor triumphant. The time of peace, however, he will govern by means of law . . . and thus he will punish the evil joys of the culprits; and by this he will become a man most religious."[9] *Cedunt arma togae* is the topos, "the sword gives way to the robe"; and yet this peaceful role required no less willfulness than conquest, as Justinian and Napoleon (and many law-makers in between) knew full well. If *imperium* originally designated military power, it came more extensively to signify the sovereign will of the prince over the private as well as public lives of his subjects.

Emulating God Himself, then, Justinian posed as lord of his own creation, claiming omnipotence through "the authority of the laws, which properly regulate all affairs, both divine and human." History was in effect commanded to stop—to stop not only through the suppression of all ancient sources of law except the imperial will, including the authority of the Senate and the juristic "right of responding" (*ius respondendi*), but also through the ban on interpretation and the denial that there were any contradictions (*antinomiae*) in the edited texts of the jurists. This dogmatic view was moreover to be maintained through a system of legal education designed to produce "new Justinians" (*novi Justiniani,* Justinian's freshmen, being the nickname bestowed on first-year law students in the three imperial schools of Constantinople, Beirut, and Rome). This system, which became a model for legal studies in the West in later centuries, was the training ground for that juridical priesthood which, initiated into the mysteries of law, would preserve order in the social cosmos envisioned by Justinian. Such was the social base of that "true philosophy" celebrated by Ulpian in the very first lines of the Digest—referring, it seems, to Platonic philosophy as contrasted with sophistry as characterized by Plato.

Yet Justinian was not so blind to human fragility that he expected history really to stop before his will; for in the final analysis, he admitted, "only divine things are perfect." "It is characteristic of human jurisprudence to be indefinitely extending," he continued, "and there is nothing in it which can endure forever, for nature is constantly hastening to bring forth new forms."[10] This admission furnished the loophole through which later jurists brought an endless stream of technically illegal "interpretations," thus contributing to the "vain discourse of posterity" feared and predicted by Justinian. The intimidating revival of a universalistic theory of law was more apparent in imperial and Stoic rhetoric than in the substance of Romano-Byzantine jurisprudence. In general, despite rationalistic pretensions and invocations of natural law, the substance of Roman tradition embodied human conventions, empirical case-law, and judgments (*res iudicatae*). In a word, it expressed a form of Nomos—a particularly complex form, since the Roman original was telescoped and transformed by Tribonian's alterations (later to be called *emblemata* or even *crimina Triboniani*), and it would undergo still more outlandish transmutations in a later European context.[11] Perhaps it would be better to say that the Corpus Iuris Justiniani marked out a battleground for a long series of confrontations between Nomos and Physis, confrontations which would be generative and decisive in the shaping of Western social thought.

True Philosophy

Justinian's publications, especially the Digest, constituted the Bible of the legal profession for more than a millennium after their appearance. They were literally an expression of "true philosophy" (*vera philosophia*), distinguished by Ulpian from the "simulated" rhetorical variety.[12] Yet at the same time these books represented "prudence" and a "practical art" aimed at human welfare, depending on concrete judgments of fact, and ending with applications of legal principles to particular problems. In this way, too, the canon of civil law represented a balance and an interplay between these two legal themes, the prudential and the scientific, the historical and the philosophical, enshrined in the Digest. The polarity is also apparent in the equally famous identification of jurisprudence with true wisdom (the *sapientia* of Augustine as well as Cicero), defined as "the knowledge of things divine and human."[13]

The intellectual framework of Romano-Byzantine jurisprudence is summarized in the first five titles of the Digest, a few pages which display not only the elements of legal science but also a vital segment of Western liberal education, at least from the twelfth century down to recent times. Law was a unique science in that it spanned the Aristotelian division between practical and theoretical knowledge, since it required both understanding the idea of justice and applying it to the human condition. It was unique, too, in that it presumed to bridge the gap between the individual and the universal, which is another way of saying between the private and the public spheres. But the individual remained the central focus, and the conceit of concentric rings seems appropriate for describing the succession of concepts presented in the first title, "On Law and Justice," which was based largely on the lost Institutes of Ulpian. The outermost circle is the field of natural law, defined (curiously and controversially) by Ulpian as "what nature teaches all animals."[14] Next comes the area devoted to the "law of nations" (*ius gentium*), limited to the human race in the sense of the collectivity of rational beings and illustrated by examples, reverence toward God and obedience to parents, taken from Pomponius. Later jurists identified this with what they called the "primary law of nature," which was that of pure reason, as distinguished from the "secondary law of nature." Still more restricted is the circle of particular national law (*ius proprium*), here to be understood as the civil law of Rome, though later the laws of other *gentes* might be substituted. As Gaius put it in the celebrated law *Omnes populi,* "All nations which are ruled by laws and customs make use partly of their own law, and partly of that common to all men" (*partim suo proprio, partim communi omnium hominum iure*).[15] The most general common denominator, however, remained always the idea of justice.

Moving from the first to the second title of the Digest is in a sense to move from synchrony to diachrony. The importance of studying the "origin of law" comes from the need to understand its *principium* (analogue of the Greek *arche*) in the sense both of cause and of source; but it also involves reconstructing the history of Roman jurisprudence, at least in part, as Justinian said in one of his prefaces, out of "reverence for antiquity" and for the founding fathers of the legal tradition, especially those honored with a place in Justinian's anthology. The historical survey presented in this title is an unusually garbled passage from Pomponius's monograph *De origine iuris,* which represents the *primum in genere* of legal historiography. In the course of the millennium since the Twelve Tables there had been several sources of law—*leges, plebiscita, senatusconsulta,* and the interpretive *ius honoratiorum*—though all were subsumed under imperial legislation after Justinian. The factor of time was also taken under consideration in the third title, especially in connection with the abrogation or supersession of laws, with the problems of custom and desuetude (*consuetudo* and *desuetudo*), and with the difficult question of "interpretation." Although unwritten, "long established custom" was declared by Hermogenianus to be as binding as written law, since it was based on the "tacit agreement of citizens." What is more, according to another jurist cited here, "custom is the best interpreter of law."[16]

The central problem of jurisprudence continued to be "interpretation," though Justinian's ban, designed to prevent judicial usurpation, was formally observed. But "the art of the good and the just" ultimately demanded attention to the whole range of hermeneutical questions from philology and literary style to philosophy—from the reading of texts to the judging of reality and the invocation of underlying principle. The philological and historical aspects were attached especially to the rubrics of the last title of the Digest, "On the Meaning of Words" and "On the Various Rules of Law" (*De verborum significatione* and *De diversis regulis iuris antiquis*), where problems both of linguistic propriety and of authorial, or legislative, "intention" were confronted.[17] Philosophically, jurists had to bring conventional rules into harmony with standards of natural law. Beyond this they had to apply law to social situations in a way appropriate to both and to the legal system as a whole, while at the same time being consistent with the particular demands of "equity." Eschewing the ancient rigidity of the law (*rigor iuris*), jurists were professionally bound to seek out the "reason of the law" as a balance between convention and nature.

It is essential to understand that, at least since the classical period, jurisprudence has been an independent field, conceptually as well as professionally. It has been subject ultimately to the standards neither of philology nor of philosophy. Although etymology might presume otherwise, law was derived from justice according to legal science (*ius a iustitia*), and the authority of particular rules was based on the law, never the reverse. The theory of legal interpretation always operated within these limitations, and so did specific questions about the meaning of words and judgments. In two respects of fundamental significance for social thought, legal hermeneutics differed from the philological, philosophical, and theological varieties. In the first place, jurists had to acknowledge changes in meaning according to context and consequently to accept that which most closely pertained to the case in question. Second, legal interpretation, being unable to avoid involvement in the world of "reality" and "action," was not text-bound to the extent that more familiar hermeneutical traditions have been.

In general Justinian remained faithful to Roman legal tradition and especially to the views of "our Gaius," who furnished the model for Justinian's own Institutes. In particular Justinian preserved, and passed on to posterity, the tripartite structure of Gaianism. The factor of human will remained central. Individual *voluntas* received legal definition in terms of "liberty" and that of the ruler in terms of "authority," while social stability depended on a balance between these private and public forces. A similar balance had to be maintained also between popular "custom," which represented the "will of the people," and legislation, which Justinian tried to identify exclusively with law: two opposed forms of Nomos which fixed the poles of social change, from unwritten *fas* and *consuetudo* to formulated *ius,* including deliberate legal reform.[18]

Perhaps the most famous expression of this polarity appears in the formula *Quod principi placuit,* standing at the head of title IV: "Whatever the Emperor has decreed has the force of law, since by a royal ordinance which was passed concerning his sovereignty [*maiestas*] the people conferred upon him all their own authority and power."[19] In this much used and abused paradox we can see archetypal expressions both of political absolutism and, in the second clause invoking the mythical *lex regia,* popular government. This dual theme, too, has run through the whole course of Western political thought, not only in conceptions of authoritarian and democratic government but also in the endless dialectic between legislative and judicial powers.

As for the extra-personal world of "reality"—"things"—the canon of civil law assembled a vast and eclectic heritage of experience and regulation. Human things—as distinguished from divine and common or public things—were either corporeal or incorporeal, either held by "emancipation" or not. In any case (as noted before) the concept of *res* was the object of that enormously complex social field which has been called the "classificatory genitive," another juridical trinity, this one involving the laws of property, possession, and prescription.[20]

Possession might seem to be the most elementary member of this triad, but it certainly had the broadest range, referring both to a condition of fact and a condition of law—capable, that is, of being at once "natural" and "civil." Civil (as distinguished from natural) possession required a form of consciousness and (good) will (*animus*) as well as physical occupancy. As usual its legal expression was produced by an "action of law," specifically a "possessory action," and once proven, it had the status of full property. The function of the law of possession was to maintain private justice and, beyond that, public order. It remained separate from the law of property, and indeed jurists insisted that between the two there was "nothing in common." Possession was closely associated with the notion of prescription, which required continuous possession in good faith over a specified length of time (ten, twenty, thirty years). Prescription, especially the *praescriptio longae temporis,* became socially important from the second century A.D., mainly as a remedy against negligent or absentee proprietors.[21]

Properly speaking, property (*dominium*) was the counterpart in private law of the empire; the first question to be asked was how it could be acquired, and second how it could be disposed of or passed on or restricted. As usual the basic condition was one of human "will"—legal intention (*animus*), donations, private agreements, testaments, and so on. Jurists hypothesized that property or dominion was established in the first place "naturally," by occupation and use (*usucapio*), and later by family succession or other legitimate transfer, whether natural (familial) or conventional (by artificial "will"). In the Roman tradition private property, as the material base of personal liberty, has in all periods remained the very foundation not only of social "reality" but also of political order and even, according to more recent apologists, of civilization itself. As such it has also been at the center of social and political controversy.[22]

In Romano-Byzantine law the third member of the Gaian trinity may be better represented by the concept of "obligation" than the more concrete category of "action," which technically was the only way to enforce interpersonal obligations. In a sense *obligatio* was the social cement which preserved order through the machinery of law, though depending too on individual good faith. Like possession, obligations could be natural as well as civil; but only the latter were juridically enforceable, especially when nature coincided, as in the obligation to keep compacts (*pacta servanda sunt*). Perhaps the best way to understand "obligation" is to see it as the controlling value of human negotiations, remedial as well as contractual. Essential to the judgment of questions of obligation were notions of objective "causation" and "fault," understood in terms of legal if not moral values (though jurists were not usually disposed to separate the two). Within this framework arose regulatory principles of sale, hire, and other economic devices, as well as partnerships and other kinds of association. Although this field of social and economic interaction might seem to have a logical and in this sense "natural" structure, in reality it depended upon social values, norms, and conventions, and so belonged to the realm of Nomos.

From the point of view adopted here, jurisprudence becomes a sort of surrogate social science. Roman jurists were certainly called on to judge matters of fact as well as of law, social "utility" as well as abstract justice, causation as well as responsibility; and the categories of the Gaian triad had sociological as well as juridical significance, encompassing in effect problems of social psychology, political economy, and "action theory." In its posthumous life in particular, Romano-Byzantine jurisprudence was received into all parts of the world formerly defined by Roman citizenship— into the extended world defined by the *ius gentium*.

Ius Gentium

Civil law was imperialistic, omnivorous, anthropocentric, anthropolatrous. To it, despite transcendent philosophical claims, nothing human has been alien. Because of the emphasis on personality and free action, it was in many ways—like Christian beliefs but independent of them—set apart from the naturalistic orientation of Greek philosophy, illustrating again the polarity between nature and convention. In Roman law each concept had its place: the first as a rational norm identified with natural law (*ius naturale*) and the second as the human substance of civil law and that extra-Roman accumulation assembled and rationalized as the "law of nations" (*ius gentium*).[23] But in contrast to the naturalistic or mathematical, especially Euclidean, strategy of reasoning from general principles, Gaianism gave prominence and priority to the human aspect, to "positive law," and then advanced empirically to higher levels of rationality and universality. In this process Roman obsession with "trichotomy" remained almost as ingrained as, though much less controversial than, the Christian Trinity; and indeed it formed, perhaps even more than Greek political philosophy, the basic structure for Western social thought. As Aristotelianism furnished the basis for the investigation of Physis, so analogously Gaianism served as a framework for the exploration of Nomos.

Civil law began with fundamental questions of existence, survival, and life in society. Liberty and property, protected and extended through legal action, were the cornerstones of Roman jurisprudence, the central themes of Rome's contributions to Western thought in a massive literature extending over many generations. The complexity of the Roman social fabric and legal mentality is reflected in the range of subjects considered by the jurists: in family law, status of women, slavery, the position of foreigners, guardianship, succession, dowries, legacies, and trusts; in proprietary and possessory law and prescription, the acquisition and transfer of ownership, restrictions on and crimes against it; in the law of obligation, contract, liability, partnership, and corporate organization; and in endless attendant questions of procedure, proof, and interpretation. Not for centuries would Western civilization produce comparable systems of legal and social science—and then in many ways derivatively.

Not only could civil law not be separated from the human condition; it could not even be confined to the Roman segment of that condition. "People belong to the law of nations" (*populi sunt de iure gentium*) was one rule of law—and another was that "actions belong to the law of nations" (*actiones sunt de iure gentium*).[24] The inference is that all the lesser breeds outside the law, their customs, business, and place in the world, had also to be taken into account—and that, indeed, every *gens* had its own legitimate "civil law." This was the extraordinary loophole in the Roman canon on which European jurists would later seize and elaborate.

In many ways the most impressive aspect, and most enduring consequence, of the expansion of Roman law was its incorporation of alien customs within the framework of this inter- and super-national law, which recorded some of the repercussions of Rome's imperial mission. Out of the rules governing exchange in the Mediterranean world (*ius commercii*) and warfare (*ius belli*) emerged a "common law" (*ius commune*) that transcended the particular law (*ius proprium*) of the Romans.[25] The result was that, as the gentile law was succeeded by the civil law, so civil law was overshadowed, at least potentially, by the law of nations, itself reflecting the Roman drive to world dominion—as well as by the growing tendency of Romans, again following Greek precedent and anticipating Christian attitudes, to identify their national tradition with humanity as a whole. In general the *ius gentium* was assembled on grounds of "reason," but a "natural reason" (*naturalis ratio* was Gaius's phrase)[26] which signified common sense rather than Greek rationality, although as Peter Stein has shown, it later "degenerated from an appeal that the law should be rooted in experience and reality into a lame excuse for not applying the law."[27] The "natural law" underlying the common law of nations was defined by Roman jurists not simply as abstract reason but, in the famous words of Ulpian, as "what nature teaches all animals," referring especially to the mating instinct and the "law of self-defense." The means of satisfying these drives differed widely, however, and international rules had to be determined through experience and formulated through positive jurisprudence considering such social problems as war, slavery, property, and institutions of economic intercourse.

The "law of nations" founded by Roman jurists as a by-product of world empire was an unfinished monument. Assembled from proto-anthropological observations made in the course of military and commercial contacts with "barbarians" around the Mediterranean, the *ius gentium* was an open and expanding system of international and comparative law whose career not only paralleled that of the empire but also outlasted it and, indeed, like civil law, would pass through several later incarnations, including modern international law (*ius inter gentes*). The "law of nations" of the medieval period and that recognized by Grotius and Vico obviously accommodated peoples and customs beyond any imagined by the Romans, but the basic principles and the recourse to natural law remained constant over the centuries. In a very real sense the ancient law of nations provided the broadest framework for the historical and comparative study of institutions and so a major conceptual base for positive anthropology. In short, the *ius gentium* was the very embodiment of "second nature."

Before the Roman Empire came to a formal, or at least symbolic, end in A.D. 476, Roman law had already overflowed its own national channels and had swept into its currents a growing number of alien traditions. To the racial and cultural provenance of many gentes, Rome was indeed, according to another legal formula, the "common fatherland" (*Roma communis patria*).[28] The classical phase of Roman jurisprudence was coming to an end in the third century, just as its ambivalent encounters with Christian views of law and society were beginning. In the bureaucratic period, from Diocletian to Justinian, the alliance between civil and ecclesiastical law was sealed; and the legitimization of Christianity by Constantine in 313 accelerated the fateful interpenetration of the two. In the Theodosian Code (438) the Gaian trinity was joined by its Christian counterpart, symbolizing the new ideological unity (if not uniformity) of Roman civilization. In the West this was also the period of the barbarian invasions and an interpenetration of another sort, namely, that between civil law and a wide range of Germanic customs. This triangular relationship between Roman, Christian, and Germanic cultures entailed a complex symbiosis of ancient law in the Western Empire. It was in this context that Roman law became truly the law of all nations, more stable and less inclined to schism than its religious counterpart.

What occurred in the West was the emergence, whether judged as evolution or degeneration, of Roman "vulgar law," based on tradition, precedents, and notarial practice and estranged in many ways from classical sources and legal science. It was a changing jurisprudence, as Ernest Levy put it, "governed by social and economic rather than legal considerations."[29] As the old Roman conception of personal liberty was qualified and hedged in by various political and economic pressures, for example, so the idea of property (*dominium, proprietas*) was shorn of its classical complexities and came to apply to provincial as well as Italian land, while possession came increasingly to designate permanent ownership and control, and prescription was established as an essential element of peaceable occupation.

In many ways this "vulgar law" departed from classical ideals of rationality and permanence, and through flexible and often unprofessional "interpretation" reverted in a sense to humbler notions of convention and utility. Touched by Christian values, empirical jurisprudence may have found a better way to "social justice" (as Edward Pickman has suggested), taking for instance a broader and more liberal, or at least more charitable, view of "persons" as well as of property.[30] In any case, despite efforts to marshal the forces of Physis in the efforts at codification culminating in the grand legislative vision of Justinian, Nomos again became king in the West—but in the context of another universalizing power which promised another sort of transcendence. In the Christian Logos, King Nomos had an even more formidable rival for the shaping of social thought.

The Romano-Byzantine Legacy

The Corpus Iuris Civilis is located at a pivotal point in the continuum of Western social thought. The problem of its meaning spans many centuries and must be established not only through "palingenetic" analysis of its sources and structures and determination of the innovations introduced by Tribonian into form and content, but also by tracing its later fortunes through a whole series of afterlives, reincarnations, and transmigrations. Despite Justinian's attempt to impose his imperial ideology, civil law has not represented a particular doctrine, political, social, or philosophical. It has been invoked in support of liberty as well as law and order, communal as well as private property, democratic and revolutionary as well as author-itarian and absolutist ideas; for the truth is that civil law has been a vehicle of many meanings and possible interpretations, depending on social context and convergence with other intellectual currents. In one way the Romano-Byzantine canon has remained consistent: it is the most comprehensive expression of the Western tradition of what from the twelfth century would be called "positive law"—the epitome, that is to say, of Nomos.

In its posthumous career Roman law has provided the vocabulary—the terminology, conceptualizations, formulas, premises, and as it were the "fore-structure"—for much of civilized life in Western terms.[31] In charac-teristically legalistic and practical ways it preserved philosophical ideas—of genus and species, for example, of modes and "forms," of reason and certainty, of cognition and "causation"; and did so on human levels dis-tinct from, and often more elementary than, the philosophical tradition, or curriculum. The "certain," for example—directly appropriated later by Vico for his own epistemological purposes—designates the object (*quid*) of a claim where the quality (*quale*) and quantity (*quantum*) are evident. Roman law also preserved categories of moral judgment—good faith and honesty, injury and culpability—and likewise in more practical and perhaps consequential terms, arising from the centrality of the notions of will, agency, and responsibility (*voluntas, intentio, animus, auctoritas, causa, iudicium,* and *obligatio*) in juridical thinking.

Most conspicuously, perhaps, Roman law established the terms and categories of social action and structure—ways of talking about, acting on, and judging questions of "contract," "interest" (*eo quod interest*), and above all property, along with the law of possession and prescription, the other two members of "the classificatory genitive," and with the varieties of theft (*furtum*). It defines levels of society (*condiciones, gradus*), from the lowest (*proletarius*) to the highest (*nobilitas,* or imperial *divinitas*), and kinds of social organization (*societas, universitas, ordo,* and so on); and it provides links with and justification for political action, especially through invocations of the public welfare (*salus populi* and *utilitas publica*). Not only family life and inheritance but acquisition and politics receive definition in civilian tradition. And of course it accommodates, discriminates, and passes judgment on change over time by characterizations of antiquity (*antiquitas, vetustas*) and novelty (*novum, novitas,* in a special sense), currency and obsoleteness, through such terms as "today," "now," and "formerly" (*hodie, nunc, olim*), and especially the sensitive question of priority and posteriority (for, proverbially, "posterior laws annul prior laws").

Above all, Roman law formed and in some ways institutionalized several fundamental polarities in Western culture which still, if only inadvertently through linguistic convention, inform Western social thought. Of central importance here is the distinction, inherited from Greek philosophy, between the "natural" and the "civil"—*naturaliter* in contrast to *civiliter,* for example, or "natural possession" in contrast to "civil possession." Analogously, civil law recognized a basic disjunction between matters of "fact" and of "law," though it is important to realize that the term "fact" itself was applied specifically to human behavior and again represented a legal and social rather than a natural and philosophical concept. The distinction between "public" and "private" was also essential to the structure of Roman jurisprudence even though the spheres were never precisely defined; and indeed concepts like "liberty" and "property" have become notoriously and increasingly political in the work of later jurists and publicists who drew, as most did, upon the legal tradition.

Less obvious but no less essential was the distinction between unwritten and written forms. Ritual and oral modes were preserved in the Romano-Byzantine texts, but by substance as well as definition civil law was *ius scriptum,* and so (in spite of being technically *ius non scriptum*) were the European codes which were formulated in Romanist terms. Even the notion of "act" (*actus*) signified a written expression or record of will, whether private or public; and lawyerly concerns with "instruments," "formulas," "rules," "testimony," "proof," and questions of falsification, "forgery," and "libel" (*libellus famosus,* a legal topic much commented on by modern polemicists) indicate that, even for "rustic" matters, civil law was reserved largely for literate culture, professional monopoly, and, by inference, political meddling and control.

In this connection the accomplishments and pronouncements of Justinian represented an "absolute" model in European social and political tradition down to Napoleon and beyond. The political implications of this have long been recognized, and indeed inflated—in the sense that the surviving and recurring "professional monopoly" of the lawyers has all too often been overshadowed by the more sensational political implications of codification and Justinianian legislative sovereignty. What has received much less attention is the transmission, interpretation, and adaptation of juristic language, perceptions, assumptions, categories, and styles of thought and writing in the larger tradition of social and cultural thought. One of the primary links between modern thought and ancient legal science was fashioned by the Christian Church in its worldly form; and this eclectic, mystery-laden, but no less imperialistic tradition is the subject of the next chapter in the story of Nomos.

FIVE

Christian Tradition

Sed Dominus noster Christus veritatem
se non consuetudinem cognominavit.

Cyprian, *Epistolae*, lxxiv

·

From Nomos to Logos

Christianity cast the old legal tradition in a new light. To the ancient
dialectic of Nomos and Physis the Gospel added a third term, a theological
synthesis which was the transcendent spirit, the Logos—but the Logos of
religious vision, not of rational analysis or persuasive discourse.[1] In the
Hellenizing interpretations of the early Christian Fathers, Christ stood
against sophistry and rose above Nature. He seemed to them a sort of
higher Platonist; indeed, Celsus even thought that he had read Plato (as
Origen thought that Plato had read Moses).[2] Christ, however, represented
the idea not of the Good but of God Himself, and the underlying dialectic
was not that between Nature and "second nature" but that between Nature
and Supernature. Once again, as in the age of myth, law was conceived as
an expression not of human will or even of universal reason but rather of
divine command; and the religious community founded itself not on old
customs but on a transcendent and metaphilosophical Nomos—which was
the Word, the Logos unknown even to Plato. Once again, in a manner of
speaking, *ius* became *fas*.

Like the Romans, the Jews had pursued their idea of law along intensely
and even imperviously national lines. The Mosaic law had a universal
complexion, which was implied also by the repeated insistence: "There
shall be one law for the citizen and for the stranger that dwells among
you" (for example, Lev. 19:34, 24:22; Num. 15:16). The Deuteronomic
code, however, and the judicial agents of post-Mosaic Israel, including the
legal experts, the Levitical priests, and later the Pharisees, spun out the
commands of Jehovah into incredibly complex and concrete particularity.
The resulting agglomeration of tribal customs, totems, and taboos was an
extraordinary manifestation of "Nomos" (as the Judaic conception of
law—*Torah*—was always rendered in the Greek of the Septuagint). A
fourth-century text, the *Collation of Roman and Mosaic Laws*, not only
emphasized the similarities between these two traditions of positive law

but also suggested that the latter was somehow derived from the former.[3] Hellenistic influence led biblical scholars to identify Judaic with natural law; but at least in part this resulted from the tendency of monotheism to identify the law-making with the creating Deity, and by inference what the Torah required with "the law written on the heart," which Christians came to understand as Conscience (*synteresis*).[4] For the most part—and despite the efforts of Hellenizing teachers like Philo, who argued for a universal law prior to the "enacted laws" (*nomoi*)—Judaism preserved its nomothetic character and, in the course of political afflictions under the Roman Empire, became even more legalistic.[5]

In an evangelical Christian perspective, then, Judaic law seemed to epitomize those merely (and pejoratively) "human traditions" which were contrasted with revealed (or for that matter, natural) law.[6] The polarity resembled the old opposition between convention and nature, except that Physis was subsumed in a divine Meta-Physis, which in effect restored the idea of law to its original religious context, as recognized by the Greeks and Romans as well as Jews and Christians. For Origen and Tertullian natural law was God's law, though not exclusively or exhaustively so; and this view would be taken over into canon law, whose professional needs would bridge the natural and supernatural worlds in the famous equation implying a sort of legal (if not theological) pantheism, that "Nature = God" (*Natura id est Deus*).[7]

Such a synthesis was admittedly far from the thoughts of the early Christians, for whom neither nature nor convention held any large attraction. Such was certainly the attitude of the man who did most to conceptualize the Christian offshoot of Judaism. Paul the Apostle, formerly Saul the Jew, and ever "all things to all men," insisted quite invidiously on the contrast between the old law and the new dispensation brought by Christ. "Christ hath redeemed us from the curse of the law," declared Paul in his epistle to the Galatians, attacking the "bondage" of Mosaic law in contrast to the spiritual "liberty" of Christianity."[8] A similar message had been issued by the first Christian martyr, St. Stephen, who indeed sent it at the cost of his life. "For we have heard him say," reported his Jewish auditors, "that this Jesus of Nazareth shall destroy this place, and shall change the custom which Moses delivered us." For this offense Judaic law prescribed stoning, and with the consequent conventional execution Paul was himself associated. The value of Stephen's teaching, and the injustice of his condemnation, dawned on Paul shortly afterwards and contributed to his own storied conversion. Yet the word he preached suggested not so much the iniquity of Judaic law as its irrelevance to the force of Christian conviction. Not human convention but ultimate truth, not legal bondage but spiritual freedom—these were the mottoes of the new Pauline faith that looked beyond the law.

For Paul the Gentiles were scarcely better off than the Jews, since "having not the law, they are a law unto themselves."[9] As Jews lived by circumcision, so the pagans lived by uncircumcision—that is, according to natural law, equivalent perhaps to the untutored conscience, "the law written on the heart." The Greeks, though they "spend their time in nothing else, but either to tell, or to hear some new thing," were the prey of unnumbered philosophic sects; and although they had indeed rejected Mythos, they had located the Logos within themselves and called it philosophy or science. Their invocation of "natural law" was as great an obstacle as Judaic legalism to Christian truth. Nomos and Physis were equally neglectful of, if not hostile to, Christ; for as Paul lamented, "the Jews require a sign, and the Greeks seek after wisdom."

What Paul preached in place of these conceptions was a transcendental and truly universal Logos. His epic, and epiphanic, journey to Damascus started a voyage that carried him beyond both law and nature. The first stage involved the discovery of a new sense of self, a conception of the soul (*psyche, animus*) that went beyond notions of human freedom and will to include "conscience" and preoccupation with sin—to include, that is, the whole of the human condition and not merely national self-images. Confronting the Athenians, Paul appealed to the latent cosmopolitanism concealed by their disputatious and xenophobic character by quoting one of their own poets (Aratus or Cleanthes): "For we are also His offspring."[10] And as Paul, "all things to all men," spoke as a Jew to the Jews and as a Roman to the Romans, so he displayed his Greek heritage before the Athenians. Paul's Logos was supernatural as well as superlegal—"Neither Greek nor Jew, slave nor free, male nor female" is the famous formula—and its universality was manifest on all levels, "One Lord, one faith, one baptism; One God and Father of all." Yet for all this evangelical idealism Paul realized the need of law, not of course "for a righteous man, but for the lawless and the disobedient, the ungodly and sinners, for unholy and profane, for murderers of fathers and murders of mothers, for manslayers."[11] And this, unfortunately, included a large portion of humanity.

Paul's ineluctable dualism, opposing spirit to law, natural as well as positive, was worked out more fully by early Christian apologists, most of them "gentiles" and inclined even more than Paul to a conceptual sort of anti-Semitism. To Origen, Tertullian, and other early Fathers, the pharisaical formalism of the Jews had been replaced by a "new law" and by a "new circumcision" which left only a spiritual mark.[12] For Christ was the new "law-giver," and his followers lived under this new "Christonomic" regimen. The Gnostic Ptolemy saw in this a sort of generational conflict, with Christ the Son acting as interpreter and critic of his Father's sometimes "tainted" commands, applying the Decalogue but rejecting as obsolete the demands for vengeance and merely formal or superstitious requirements

set down by Moses and the elders of Israel. The most extreme expression
of the paradoxical notion of "evangelical law" appeared in the work of
Marcion, who dispensed entirely with the "Old Testament" and thereby,
in effect, created the "New," though his claims of novelty and radicalization
of Pauline theology were too much for "conventional" authors to stom-
ach.[13]

The subversive implications of these attitudes were hard to conceal; and
scriptural fundamentalism, no less than appeals to pure reason, posed a
threat to all conventional "authority." As Paul had rejected Judaic law, so
Origen justified Christian resistance to the inequities and iniquities of
Roman law by invoking an ultimate law of nature, which was the Logos.
Marcionites even reversed the disclaimer of Christ (Matt. 5:17) to read,
"not come to fulfill the law but to abolish it"; and of course Christian
insistence on the value of martyrdom intensified their subversive image.[14]
No wonder that Jewish scholars had reacted with horror to Paul's kind of
fundamentalism; no wonder that Roman observers like Tacitus and Pliny
condemned Christianity as "deadly superstition" and even as atheism.

What the Logos represented was a new and untried conception of liberty
and justice (that is, righteousness) transcending the ideals of ancient law,
Judaic or Roman. What Christian conscience represented was a new and
unbound mentality transcending the rationalism and tribalism of ancient
civilization, including as it did a sense of evil and endless struggle (*psychomachia*) between flesh and spirit.[15] In a sense the central theme of
Christian experience was the operation of the Logos in warding off the
corrupting and binding effects of Nomos and the false license implied by
Physis. This depended, of course, on the "justice of God," which, represented originally as a "new law," necessarily became the starting point for
a new tradition—and so a new form of Nomos.

Christonomos

The "new law" of Christ was elaborated, interpreted, and in a sense codified
by the patristic tradition, which again exalted "fatherhood," following the
pattern of the Romans but now in a spiritual way, corresponding to the
community which Augustine called the "city of God," in contrast to the
civitas terrena of Rome. The Fathers of the church, apostolic, Greek, and
Latin, carried out the essential task of accommodating the Logos not only
to Jewish and Greek prefigurations but also to the imperial mission of
Rome; and for such purposes they had perforce to turn their attention to
"conventional" human problems.[16] The "apostolic Fathers," beginning
with Clement of Rome and Barnabas, found or fabricated traces of doctrinal continuity, especially through allegorical interpretation of the Old
Testament, in order to provide Christianity with historical legitimacy; and

post-apostolic apologists beginning with Justin Martyr launched into more direct defenses of Christian life-style and pleas for equitable treatment under imperial law. Running contrapuntally through these apologetic refrains were assaults on a pandemonium of doctrinal errors expressed in whole genres of literature against this or that human misconception or deviation (*adversus Judaeos, adversus paganos,* and, endlessly, *adversus haereticos*)— each of them "against the (new) law."

Out of this attempt to capture the Logos in written terms came the beginnings of a coherent Christian ideology, especially in the work of Irenaeus and members of the Alexandrian school (Clement, Hippolytus, and Origen). As a central target Irenaeus took Simon Magus, "from whom all heresies derive," and especially the neo-Judaic corruption of the spirit due to that legalistic and materialistic offense later condemned as the sin of "simony."[17] Clement of Alexandria, of Athenian parentage, recognized that Greek philosophy offered a preparation for true knowledge (*gnosis*) and justice; but he denied that the first cause or principle of righteousness (or justice) could be found in nature, since true culture (*paideia*) was taught only through Christ. Hippolytus (an "anti-pope" whose statue, inscribed with a list of his lost works, was discovered in 1551) criticized not only Judaic legalism but also the inverted materialism of ascetics, who took all-too-human pride in their rejection of meat, sex, and other commodities of the comfortable life.[18] These were some of the pioneers in the attempt to give human order and authority to Christian doctrine, including certain more legalistic forms of orthodoxy, such as binding creeds and canons.

The most powerful synthetic thinker among the Greek fathers was surely Origen, who sought to translate the Christian Logos into human rules and principles (*kanones, archai*). For Origen, writing in the third century, Christianity had established a social consensus and perhaps an extra-scriptural "institutional tradition" as well as a coherent doctrine; and he rejected the criticism of Celsus that this religion was either novel or revolutionary.[19] In various ways, faithful always to the Christological model, Origen tried to maintain a balance between spirit and flesh, maintaining that the incarnation allowed the transcendent Logos to establish ties with Nomos—and indeed with pagan antiquity—in a sort of socialized expression of Incarnation.

Origen's most characteristic way of expressing this metaphysical (and metanomical) verity was through the Book—central symbol of the Christian (as it was of the Jewish) faith—and in terms of the distinction between the letter and the spirit of a text. Origen's hermeneutics, derived most likely from the allegorical interpretation of Homer (which Origen knew through Alexandrian scholarship), was analogous to the distinction between word and meaning (*verba* and *voluntas*), and likewise "corporeal" and "incorporeal" things in civil law. Like legal "science," Christian "truth" was achieved by penetrating the literal surface of a text to the life-giving spiritual meaning. Conversely, this conceit made it possible to connect revelation with the accidents of history, including Jewish and classical culture. "All the things in the visible category can be related to the invisible," declared Origen, "the corporeal to the incorporeal, and the manifest to those that are hidden."[20]

And as spirit transcended letter, so the Logos transcended speech, "for although the languages of the world are dissimilar," remarked Irenaeus, "yet the import of tradition is one and the same."[21] The ultimate source of this dialectic was of course the twofold nature of Christ himself, and so of man made in his image. It was through this mystical, and mythical, synthesis that Christians related their transcendent faith and future hopes to their present predicament and past memories. In this way Christianity began to reconcile Athens with Jerusalem, Cicero with Christ, and so to find a balance between the Word and the laws—between revelation and human nature, which is to say "second" as well as primary nature.

How was the "new law" of Christ to be preserved in human terms? To begin with, through oral tradition, especially through the propagation of the "good news" by *kerygma,* carried above all by sermons; but of course the passage of time and the deficiencies of scribal culture complicated and often corrupted this process. Thus Christian rhetoric favored the idea of renewal, of a purified state which, if not preserved, must be periodically returned to. If the individual soul needed to the "born again," society as a whole, the earthly church, needed chronic "reformation"; and the myth of the "primitive church" runs through "reform" movements down to those of Hildebrand and Luther. Conversion itself was a way of being "reformed," and so in later times were admission to the regular clergy and various efforts of papal and conciliar legislation. Yet the idea of "reform" was not usually utopian, except perhaps in some monastic movements; it was intensely conservative and backward-looking. "If however the decrees of former councils have been neglected in the abuse of times," runs one sixth-century canon, "they must now receive the censure of a revival of order."[22]

The key in fact was "tradition" (*paradosis*), a conception which had associations with the Roman law of succession as well as divine transmission: "All things are delivered [*tradita sunt*] unto me of my father," Christ had declared. Change was unavoidable, but as Cyprian wrote (and this was quoted endlessly by canonists), "Let there be no innovation without tradition" (*Nihil innovetur nisi quod traditum est*).[23] In a spiritual sense tradition was implied by patristic efforts to fabricate doctrinal continuity with pagan and Judaic antiquity; in an institutional sense it was tied to "apostolic tradition," which Irenaeus assumed to be in the hands of the bishops. Early in the third century Irenaeus's pupil Hippolytus wrote a classic treatise on this subject (*Apostolike Paradosis*) and under this rubric considered the structure of church government as well as the social and ecclesiastical problems inherent in the cure of souls. Eusebius's concept of "preparation for the gospel" (*praeparatio evangelium*) was another, more speculative and mythical way of providing grounds for tradition, as was the gradualist view of Vincent of Lerins in the fifth century, patristic prototype of Cardinal Newman's evolutionist interpretation of theology.[24]

The mature conception of tradition was a product of scribal culture, which marked the end of the oral phase of Christian doctrine—or at least severely constricted it. Increasingly thereafter tradition was identified with parallel questions of apostolicity, orthodoxy, and catholicity; and by the time of Boethius it had been given a place next to Scripture itself (which time and the controversial problems of authenticity and canonicity) were also rendering "traditional").[25] In Western ecclesiastical terms, especially in the wake of the Protestant Reformation, "tradition" suggested in effect the modern form of Romanism.

Accompanying the establishment of Christian tradition was the emergence of a sense of a unique Christian society—a "congregation of the faithful," if not a "communion of saints"—which was defined in the first instance by exclusive access to the true principles of liberty, justice, and wisdom. "The Christians are distinguished from other men neither by country, nor language, nor the customs which they observe," wrote the author of the Epistle to Diognetus in the second century; rather they were defined by their cast of mind. "They are in the flesh, but they do not live after the flesh. They pass their days on earth, but they are citizens of heaven. They obey the prescribed laws, and at the same time surpass the laws by their lives." What the soul is to the body, this writer concluded, so the Christians are to the world.[26]

The Latin Fathers in particular tried to give human definition to Christian society. Taking his cue from Origen, Tertullian stressed the positive "rule of faith" (*regula fidei*), which provided extra-scriptural legitimacy for Christian tradition.[27] His own pupil Cyprian offered a more comprehensive defense of the "unity of the church" in terms that were at once allegorical (that is, Christological) and psychological ("unanimous," of one soul). In the work of later Fathers (Ambrose, Augustine, and Jerome) theological conceptions of the church were humanized—legalized and socialized— through ideas of popular consent (*consensus iuris,* according to Augustine) and the application of such terms as the Christian *patria, natio, gens, plebs,* and above all *Populus.* Such terminology implied juridical structure, independence, and legitimacy as well as sacramental foundation—*fas* again being fashioned into *ius* but this time in terms of a Christian pontificate.[28] Later this process would become even clearer, as the "mystical body of the church" (*corpus mysticum ecclesiae*) as conceived by theologians was transformed into a humanoid "corporation" as interpreted by lawyers.

In Christian thought there sounds once again the old theme of primary versus second nature, or custom—and both, of course, versus supernature. From Cyprian and Tertullian through the great canonists, Christians were reminded (after John 14:6) that Christ had proclaimed not "I am the custom" but "I am the truth."[29] Like Cicero and Seneca, Augustine and Jerome regarded "custom" (*consuetudo*), in the form of second nature, as a surrender to the corruption both of human nature and of human law and as further alienation from the spiritual heritage of Christ; and Clement of Alexandria spoke of "thrusting away custom as some deadly drug."[30] In early Christian thought, in short, "custom" normally suggested "bad custom"—a fall from reason or grace or both.

In theology the doctrine of the Logos triumphed by the fourth century, while Christological, trinitarian, and soteriological dogmas reflected the transcendent claims of Christian ideology. Yet many aspects of Christian life—ordination, penance, liturgy, monasticism, and the "lapsed," not to speak of property and crime—were hardly covered by scriptural rules, or at least not without extraordinary efforts of "interpretation."[31] Despite Paul's assertions of Christian "liberty" and equality, there were many arbitrary regulations and proprieties in the early church. Women were on a par with men, but of course they must not appear unveiled in church and must remain silent. Children must be obedient to parents, servants to masters, and above all, citizens to the powers that be—for the "things that are Caesar's" were manifestly (as well as biblically) a part of the realm of Nomos enjoying divine sanction. In general many Jewish and Roman legalisms were concealed in the works of the Fathers, and indeed it could hardly be otherwise because of their anxiety to avoid the spiritualist excesses of heretics or Gnostics like Marcion.

If Christ could retrospectively be identified with the Logos, Peter and his successors had to take a less immaculate pose. If the Word, Logos, was pure spirit, the "rock" (*petra*) of the church furnished the materially more secure basis of Nomos. With the burden of the "cure of souls" and the establishment of the church as a propertied corporation and eventually a political hierarchy, the accumulation of human conventions and "positive law" was inexorable, as was the transformation of "true gnosis," defined by Irenaeus as "the doctrine of the apostles and the ancient order of the church throughout the whole world"—as a structured *societas christiana*.[32]

This new society, a spiritual rival of nations based on blood relationships, was itself given blood-coherence by the early martyrs, whose sacrifices furnished the "seed of the church"; by later legal reinforcement, especially through the sacraments of baptism and communion, which defined membership in what came to be regarded as "God's family"; and by the later interpretation proposing that there was no salvation outside the society of the church—damnation being the equivalent of spiritual outlawry. In many ways Christianity lost its transcendent status and became increasingly (in the terms given currency by Guy Swanson) an "immanent" religion, which embraced, legitimized, and came to embody "human traditions."[33] Through a kind of process of social incarnation, Logos again made way for Nomos, and Fas for Ius.

Ecclesia sub Lege Romana

The church has been called the ghost of the old Roman Empire, but the metaphors of adoption and succession might be more appropriate, since in many ways the church took over the legal tradition as well as the governmental machinery of the Caesars and came, proverbially, to live "under Roman law" (*Ecclesia vivit sub lege romana*).[34] "Wherever there are Romans there is much vice," wrote Salvian in the fifth century.[35] But wherever there were Romans there was also law; and Christian thinkers inadvertently, and then more deliberately, took advantage of this legacy. On the highest level were the parallelisms between Christ and emperor. Both were "priest-kings" on the model of David. Both were "lord" and "savior" (*soter*) and shared a variety of hyperbolic epithets, including *theos* and *basileus;* both were ultimate sources of law (*basilikos nomos*). Beyond such cult terminology the organized church indulged in a wide range of imperialistic borrowings and ill-disguised imitations. In general the diocese was the successor of the *civitas,* as the episcopal court was of the prefect, while of course the Roman "Papa" took over the imperial title of Pontifex Maximus along with residency in the capital of the ancient Caesars.

As usual this process begins with the founder of Christian ideology. Paul denied that he had brought a "new legislation," but in fact his preaching implied a code of behavior and social norms as well as a new spirituality. How could it be otherwise? For Paul had been brought up in "the law," destined to be a rabbi, and he often protested that the purpose of Christ was not to annul but to fulfill Judaic law. Paul was also a Roman citizen, proud of his civil status, and ready to appeal to Roman imperial jurisdiction. "Is it lawful for you to scourge a man that is a Roman and uncondemned?" he had asked a Roman centurion in Jerusalem.[36]

In "rendering to Caesar," in placing Nomos above the Logos for the sake of expediency, Paul testified in more ways than one to the influence of Roman law. Even his commitment to the Christian faith Paul expressed in terms of Roman adoption into a family, with the implication not only that he had found a new Father and brothers but also that he would receive a share of the promised (spiritual) heritage. He and his converts became "heirs of God and joint-heirs with Christ," and the whole relationship was that of a contract, or a covenant. In a sense God (the Father) had the ultimate paternal power (*patria potestas*) and like his Roman counterpart could choose freedom or slavery, life or death, for his children. Other analogies, including that of *stipulatio,* which referred to a person's obligation to the church, and the marriage vow, which suggested the form of the Nicene Creed, lend support to the thesis that the framework of Pauline theology, anthropocentric and focused on the values of "liberty" and "justice," represented a sort of sublimated version of Roman law.

Christian tradition, even more profoundly than that of ancient Rome, was based on the principle of Fatherhood—embodied in the authority not only of God but also of patristic doctrine and above all the apostolic succession settled on the Roman Papa, as he was called from the time of Constantine. As the pastoral functions of ministers of the gospels, especially the "cure" and "regimen" of souls, implied a social dimension to the spiritual office, so papal claims to supremacy—*Papatus* would be the lawyers' term—implied a political dimension, which episcopal jurisdiction over "sin" would vastly enlarge.[37] Retrospectively, the justification for this secular initiative was based on interpretation of the so-called "power of the keys" to bind and loose "whatever," on earth as in heaven. The translation of this remark of Christ to Peter (Matt. 16:18–19) into legal terms—the petrifaction of the Petrine commission, to compound the original pun—represents the central theme of the story of canon law; and in this connection Roman law was again employed, though in a biblically and theologically transmuted form. In one way the Romanist tradition represented the enemy of the Word of God, since Justinian's Caesaropapist pretensions might be seen as a reincarnation of the "law" in Paul's Judaic and pejorative sense. In practical terms, however, the formulation of Christian Nomos was achieved largely on the basis of Roman legal science.

The symbiosis between faith and law was further reinforced by the international character of primitive Christianity and its imperial mission: "Go ye therefore and teach all nations" (Matt. 28:19). Beginning as an otherworldly offshoot of Judaism, Christianity became an expansive doctrinal empire, claiming total and exclusive dominion over the truth. Paul himself, marveled Clement of Rome, "taught righteousness [justice] to the whole world." His missionary ambitions extended as far west as Spain and included "barbarians" as well as humans properly (classically) speaking. Assimilating Christ not only to the Jewish messiah and to the Greek Logos but also to the conquering Caesars gave historical shape to the Gospel, creating an ideology and a genealogy worthy of a universal church. From this arose the two imperialisms celebrated by Eusebius: "Two great powers sprang up fully as out of one stream and they gave peace to all and brought all together into a state of friendship: the Roman Empire, which from that time appeared as one kingdom, and the power of the Savior of all, whose aid was at once extended to and established with everyone."[38] A perfect union not only of Caesar and Christ, he thought, but also of human tradition and universal truth. So the unified, Romanoid Empire of Constantine, for which Eusebius wrote his apology, was joined and enhanced by the divine unity celebrated contemporaneously at the Council of Nicaea, attended by Eusebius. Obeying the almighty emperor was ideologically reinforced by believing in the "One Lord, one faith, one baptism" preached by Paul and codified in the Nicene Creed.

In other ways the Logos was inscribed in the earthly community in terms of Nomos. Romanizing influences can be seen in the writings of the Western Fathers, and perhaps most conspicuously in the work of Tertullian, the first and most effective advocate for the Christian cause. Tertullian was a severe critic of the shallowness and inequities of Roman laws. He lamented their notorious proliferation, instability, unfairness (as in the charge of lese majesty leveled against Christians), and especially irreverence (which made the gods as well as principles of justice seem to be merely human creations).[39] Yet Tertullian had the mind of a lawyer (and indeed is usually identified with the jurist of the same name in the Digest); and he did not scruple to make use of the tools of Roman law, above all in his defense of Christians, invoking Judaic and philosophical as well as juridical precedents. For him Christianity was a legitimate tradition with ample human authority; and he was careful to avoid illicit interpretations, especially those of Marcion, whose abstract Hellenizing had led to heretical misappropriation of the doctrinal property of true Christians and provoked Tertullian to legalistic efforts of "prescription." Other religious ideas, such as the "satisfaction" owed by men for their sins, were presumably also derived from civil law. In his various social concerns Tertullian followed the lead of Roman law and indeed seems to have been working systematically toward some sort of Christian "code of life."

The ideals of Roman law persisted directly, if in somewhat diluted and distorted ways, in medieval thought. One summary, which later passed into canonist tradition, was the little textbook *On the Laws,* which formed book five of the encyclopedia compiled by Isidore of Seville in the seventh century. In these *Etymologies* Isidore sought, in a rather clumsy and speculative imitation of classical methods, to find the meaning behind the letter of key terms through speculative derivation. "Law" came from "justice" (*ius a iustitia,* though Isidore no doubt knew that linguistically the derivation was the reverse), and particular law from the act of reading (*lex a legere*), because of the requirement of written form (*lex scripta*).[40] Laws had been formulated by particular authors—Moses, Solon, Numa, and others—though the Romans had apparently replaced their original *fas* with Solon's laws, "translated" and set down in the Twelve Tables. Attempts to systematize civil law had not been successful after the "new laws" established by Constantine and codified by Theodosius. Isidore concluded with a conventional summary of the chief divisions of law (civil, natural, law of nations, public, and private) and a statement that law "ought to be" not only for the public good but also ought to fulfill the practical requirements of being "honorable, just, possible, according to nature, according to the custom of the country and adapted to the place and time." The result was that Roman law was shorn of much of its specificity and reduced to a general norm and set of categories which could be imported into Christian tradition without danger of pagan infection.

In many ways, then, the Roman papacy drew explicitly as well as implicitly upon the juridical wealth of the imperial tradition in the process of bringing about what Walter Ullmann has called the "Romanization of Europe." Taking up residence in Rome, the pope and the ecclesiastical hierarchy took over much of the machinery of urban government and administrative offices (such as that of "pontifex maximus") as well as abandoned temples; and after the legal demise of the *imperium* he began to establish his own claims to "princely" status (*principatus*) and legislative authority.[41] While displaying the prideful humility of the spiritual title "servant of the servants of God," the pope nevertheless also ascended to the office of earthly "lord" (*dominus*) and eventually, in imitation of Justinian as well as David, of priest-king (*rex-sacerdos*). The essential step was taken in the eighth century, when the popes declared their independence of the Eastern Empire and formed their epoch-making alliance with the Carolingian Franks. The result was a "revival of empire" in a secular sense, but the major beneficiary of the short-lived "Carolingian renaissance" was the Roman church, which was well on the way to becoming a world monarchy and surviving agent of the "Roman" (in the sense of "Christian") legal tradition.

Two Natures, Two Laws

The "two great powers" celebrated by Eusebius had an uneasy relationship from the fourth century on, when an incipient European civilization found a new ideological foundation but in a sense paid for it with a permanently divided soul.[42] Again, like Constantine's famous coin, displaying a cross on one side and the image of Sol Invictus on the other, church and empire were joined but obversely related. There continued to be mutual reinforcement, especially in the area of law. On the one hand the church pursued its social involvements, "hierocratic" organization, and imperial mission by drawing upon civil law; on the other hand Roman law was recast in a Christian mold, with the principle of the Trinity taking precedence in the great collections of jurisprudence made by Theodosius and Justinian. From Constantine there began a long, if uneven, tradition of legislation favoring the church and the priesthood in material as well as ideological terms and taking over the patristic campaign against paganism and heresy. The Emperor Julian made an idealistic effort to "restore the customs of antiquity" after repealing Christian laws, but this was a brief episode that left little trace in the legal tradition so honored by Julian in his anachronistic fashion. Before the sack of Rome by Alaric in 410 the old and the new law were indissolubly joined—like the two natures of Christ and of humanity, or so Christian ideologists hoped and argued.

Yet the tensions between the two traditions, or natures, one grounded in sin and the other in grace, persisted. This is evident in the work of Lactantius, that "Christian Cicero" of the early fourth century, who deplored the ingrained "cupidity" of the Romans, discrediting their professed ideals. The Romans "passed laws for themselves, under the name of justice, those most unfair and unjust measures by which they protected their thefts and avarice against the strength of the multitude."[43] By contrast he praised to the skies the form taken by Roman tradition under Constantine and the establishment of true justice, though it encompassed much of the substance of the old pagan law, as would be apparent from the collections of Theodosius and Justinian.

At the end of the century Bishop Ambrose of Milan, himself son of a pretorian prefect, sought to fuse the new morality of Christianity with ancient Roman virtue, centering on prudence and justice; but his discussion of the "duties of ministers" (*De officiis ministrorum*), modeled on Cicero's discussion of duty, subordinated Ciceronian moral philosophy to newer ideals of conscience. Ambrose had great respect for the imperial office and lauded Theodosius both in letters and in a funeral oration. Yet he did not hesitate (in the famous affair of the massacre of Thessalonica) to instruct the emperor that, while he might be above civil law (*legibus solutus*), he was subject to the rule of Christian conscience and perhaps to the penance which the church might choose to impose. In such ways Christ came to rival Caesar, or rather (as in Jerome's storied dream) Cicero; and the civil ideals of justice were given spiritual, which is to say ecclesiastical, form.

By this time the final confrontation of the two traditions had taken place, the spirit at last winning out over the flesh, or so the victors boasted. The conflict was strikingly symbolized in the famous affair of the altar of Victory in 382. On this altar, which dated from the time of Augustus, Roman senators had sworn to uphold the emperor's laws. Christian pressure led to its removal and then, after restoration by Julian, to a second removal and another protest by the senators. Their spokesman, Symmachus, entered a plea on behalf of tradition: "The love of custom is great," he remarked, and then asked, "Where shall we swear to obey your laws and commands?" The glory of Rome was bound up with its ancient traditions, and Symmachus asked that Romans be allowed "to leave to posterity what we received as boys." The response was given by Bishop (formerly governor) Ambrose, who spoke on behalf of "a progress which is better," as contrasted with the sins of the bloody Roman past. Prudentius, author of Christianity's best answer to the imperial verses of Vergil, seconded Ambrose by lamenting the fact that Rome, "who has appointed law and justice to the conquered nations," should have been tied to superstitions as profound as those of ignorant barbarians.[44] The party of "progress," in any case, won out over that of ancient tradition, and a decade later paganism was proscribed by the legislation of Theodosius. The Roman foundations of Nomos were shaken, though not replaced.

So the fundamental duality of Christian thought was raised to a political level, and the Pauline struggle between flesh and spirit, celebrated in elaborate allegory in Prudentius's poem *Psychomachia,* found a social counterpart in the rivalry of legal traditions. Or should we say, in terms more appropriate to the "juristic theology" being developed by the papacy, that the Logos assumed another human (now institutional) form?

The polarity received classic expression in the work of Augustine provoked by the sack of Rome in 410, popularly blamed on Christian influence. In the *City of God* Augustine presented a survey of the two Roman traditions in cosmic perspective (and on Pauline premises). The glory of the earthly city (*civitas terrena*) was based not on religion but on superstition and, like Israel, on fratricide (Romulus being the Roman Cain); and its so-called "victories" were the result not of virtue but of "lust for rule." Roman laws were not divinely bestowed but appropriated from other nations and founded in sin and violence, not true justice. Nor had they brought peace and concord. It would be more appropriate, Augustine thought, to erect a temple to Discord.[45] Worlds apart from this city "divided against itself" was the *Civitas Dei,* which was the true embodiment of "peace and justice," the motto of "political Augustinianism" over the centuries. So the Roman church, according to its own imperialistic style, plundered and tried to discredit, yet at the same time claimed succession to, the heritage of ancient culture. The most valuable part of this culture was obviously the legal tradition—source of liberty, justice, and the ideal, according to the Christian transvaluation, of "true philosophy."

The legal and political claims of the church were expressed most famously in the interpretation given to the biblical conceit of the "two swords." Compared with the royal power, wrote Pope Gelasius I in the late fifth century, "the sacred authority of the priests . . . is so much the greater, in that they must also render an account before the judgment of God for the king of man."[46] Papal authority, recognized by Justinian as well as Theodosius, was given the final seal of approval by Charlemagne. According to one of the most pervasive of all the cultural myths of the West—the "translation" or "renovation" of empire (*translatio, renovatio imperii*)—the legal heritage of *Romanitas* was identified with the religious heritage of *Christianitas.*[47]

Starting out as "Rex Francorum," Charlemagne died (according to the inscription on his tomb) "orthodoxus Imperator," who among other things had brought about a restoration of "written law." His "capitularies," assembled by "legislators," published as the "king's word," and enforced by a reorganized judicial and administrative system, were in effect the first legislation in the West since the fifth century; and after the imperial coronation in 800 they moved into areas of private law, such as matrimony, and into the social life of the clergy, regular as well as secular. After the *divisio imperii* of the ninth century the papacy was left for the most part to take over the remnants of the *imperium christianum*.

Despite invocations of Logos, then, papacy and empire alike became the captives of Nomos. The second "renovation of empire," that of the Ottonian emperors of the tenth century, revived the debate over the "two swords" but gave it a new twist because of the problem of the so-called "proprietary churches" (*Eigenkirchen*), Germanic antecedents of the national churches of the later Middle Ages, and the related issue of lay investiture. This issue, erupting in the eleventh century in the form of the "Investiture controversy," may also be seen in part as a conflict of legal traditions, and specifically (as Gerd Tellenbach put it) "as a conflict of the old (Roman) canon law with the 'Germanic' proprietary church law of the early middle ages."[48] The Investiture controversy recapitulated, in the political terms of feudal society, the old Pauline dialectic of liberty and bondage; but for the papacy it brought also the high tide of Romanism in its ecclesiastical form, signaled by the battle-cry of Gregorian reform—"Liberty of the church." *Libertas Ecclesiae*, or *Libertas Romana*, meant more than simply independence from secular power; it entailed also legal "authority" in a positive sense, that is, the power to legislate.

The encroachments of Nomos on Logos underlay both what Walter Ullmann called "juristic theology" and what Ernst Kantorowicz called "political theology"; and the keys of Peter (*claves iuris*, as they were sometimes referred to) were used to unlock the riches of legal tradition.[49] In pretending to hegemony over the entire church (*regimen totius ecclesiae*), Gregory was claiming an inheritance accumulated over some seven centuries of debate and profoundly indebted to Roman law conceptually as well as terminologically. The central aim of papal government was increasingly not merely the cure of souls and preservation of doctrine; it had become political liberty and justice. Moreover, deriving strength from the Christian Populus, the Pope, as *princeps* of the church, issued his own quasi-imperial decrees and constitutions for purposes of "public utility" as well as sound doctrine. The papal hierarchy was elaborated through metropolitan and super-metropolitan offices (vicars, legates), legal activities were organized and regularized through the chancery, and the elaborate political conventions of "hierocracy" were in process of formation.

Papalist ideology was countered by a revival of lay opposition, which centered on the Ottonian empire and likewise displayed a marked interest in the revival of Roman law. A tenth-century forgery, the so-called *Privilegium Majus*, appealed to the famous *lex regia* (itself spurious) as a justification of imperial authority; and in general the imperial propaganda enshrined in the *Libelli de lite* was filled with Romanist citations and allusions.[50] Illustrations of this appear in the writings of the jurist Peter Crassus of Ravenna, of the eleventh-century "humanist" Benzo of Alba, and of the anonymous author of the York tractates, which all appeal to the authority of the Roman Populus as well as to the divine endorsement claimed by Constantine and Justinian. To the massive revival of Roman law in the twelfth century this ideological war—"Papal Revolution," as it has been called, and if so, then "Imperial Counter-Revolution"—was an even more direct spur than the demands of a revitalized civic life. The proof of this is the lead taken by clerical intellectuals in shaping the legal tradition and in assembling the body of canon law, the second major system of social thought based on Roman legal science and an institutional expression of the foundational duality of Christian belief.

At issue in the various conflicts between "church and state" was not only control over Christian tradition but also the obedience of Christian souls under law. Like the Roman imperial establishment, the Roman ecclesiastical establishment was in various ways person- and value-centered—law-centered—the first basing its claims on the welfare of the people and criminal offenses thereto, and the other on the cure of souls and "sin." As the popular base of imperial government was suggested by the ancient and legendary *lex regia,* so that of ecclesiastical government was suggested by the reverse pomposity of the papal title, "Servant of the servants of God." The goal of the rivalry was, ultimately, jurisdiction over the "world of nations" defined not only by civil and canon law but by the larger "world of nations" encompassed by the emergent extra-Roman and extra-Christian *ius gentium*—the modern equivalent of the realm of Nomos.

Ius Canonicum

As the Word became flesh, as the Church became imperial, so spiritual tradition took institutional form; and the final product, the true embodiment of Christian Nomos, was the canon law.[51] The cornerstone of the canonist structure had already been laid when Christianity became a legitimate cult through Constantine's legislation of 313. The point of departure was the proto-canonist effort to provide social organization to early Christian communities. Beginning with the assembly of apostles and elders in Jerusalem in the middle of the first century, the theory and practice of the council (*synodos,* or *concilium*) acted to give form to the mystical body of

Christ; and in the second and third centuries several assemblies were called
to discuss problems of discipline, jurisdiction, and Christian life-style as
well as doctrine. Baptism, marriage, family relations, burial, clerical celi-
bacy, moral offenses, and, interminably, heresy were some of the matters
ruled on by pre-Nicene councils before conciliarism was taken over by the
Christian emperors. Meanwhile, there was a steady flow of pastoral letters,
which by the fourth century had been transformed, again through Roman
influence, into papal commands, interpretations, and the makings of a legal
tradition. From these two sources, as well as unspecified and sometimes
legendary "ancient customs," flowed the mainstream of canon law, which
was the principal agent in the transformation of the spiritual body of the
church, the society of trinitarian communicants, into a juridical community
and eventually into a world monarchy.

In 434 Vincent of Lerins wrote a famous defense of the idea of the
"progress of religion in the church of Christ," arguing philosophically that
everything changes and that, consequently, the church too "must grow and
make great and enormous progress by the advance of ages and centuries,"
though of course without changing the essential meaning of the Christian
message.[52] This growth could be seen not only in missionary victories and
the establishment of law but also in the organization of ecclesiastical leadership through a complex, again Romanoid, hierarchy. Prefigured in the
Old Testament, as Christian exegetes argued, this ecclesiological development was evident even before the second century, when the designations
of elder (*presbyter*) and bishop (*episcopos*) had been canonized, and perhaps also Roman primacy, as suggested by the letter attributed to Clement
I, third "papa" after Peter. Although Tertullian and Hippolytus recognized
all of the apostolic churches as "wombs and original sources of the faith,"
the special place of the Petrine commission, as of Rome, was accepted by
Origen and especially Cyprian, whose doctrine of the "unity of the church"
rested on a Romanist premise. By the time of Eusebius this premise had
become the motto of a new Christian imperialism.

The structure of international Christian society was fixed, or at least
foreshadowed, at the first ecumenical Council of Nicaea in 325, presided
over by Constantine but dominated by the bishops, who were seated
according to rank and whom the Emperor addressed as virtual "gods." In
the canons of this council the hierarchy was thus recognized, including the
primacy of the Roman bishop as well as the subordination of lay to
sacerdotal (*laikoi, hieroi*), and so was the juridical and legislative character
of the church. For the West a set of twenty canons treated current problems,
such as the "lapsed," heretics, excommunication, penance, and clerical
discipline. Ancient customs of particular regions were normally protected.
Perhaps the most foreboding implication was the principle of doctrinal
uniformity, though it was not given full legal expression until the time of

Theodosius in the late fifth century, when paganism was finally and permanently outlawed. It took the form of a written creed, which at the same
time had the status of human, that is, imperial, law.

Established in the Christian Empire of the fourth century, the canonist
tradition survived the political turmoil following the sacks of Rome (410
and 455) and the formal demise of the empire (476), emerged relatively
unscathed from the theological battles raging in the East, and actually
benefited from contacts with invading barbarians, whose customs contrasted favorably with the bankrupt values of old Rome. Although still
caput mundi, Rome was regarded by Augustine, Jerome, and other church
Fathers as the antithesis of the ideal of justice. A generation later Salvian
charged that she was worse than the barbarians who were destroying her,
and in the sixth century Pope Gregory the Great pronounced a famous
obituary: "Rome, once mistress of the world, what has become of her? . . .
Where is the Senate, where the People? . . . The city has been shorn of its
eagle wings on which it was once accustomed to fly in search of prey."[53]
One exception was the contemporary institution of monasticism, which
effected a return to purer values, drawing on the virtue both of ancient
Rome and of the "primitive church."

This was particularly apparent in the "rule" (*regula*, a term equivalent
to "canon," and recalling the *regulae iuris* of Roman law) of St. Benedict,
who took the family as the model for the monastic community, and paterfamilial power for that of the abbot.[54] The utopian ideals of the "regular"
clergy might often seem remote, but they occasionally had an impact on
ecclesiastical organization and reform, for instance in the "Pastoral Rule"
(*Regula Pastoralis*) of Pope (and former Benedictine monk) Gregory the
Great. For many generations, moreover, monasticism—with its simple "customs" contrasting with the written commands of the papal curia—stood
as a rebuke to ecclesiastical materialism and a reminder of the purity and
poverty of the early church.

As the church progressed from a primitive network of congregations to
a property-owning corporation to a juridical community and finally to a
world state, so Christian Nomos grew from informal customs to written
law maintained in ecclesiastical courts under the appellate jurisdiction of
the pope, supported by a growing force of notaries, attorneys (*defensores*),
archivists (*scrinarii*), and other bureaucratic offices. By at least 443, canonist collections were being generally "promulgated," and from the eighth
century they began to multiply.[55] From that time, too, the substance of
papal tradition began to be gathered in registers, although earlier, undated
letters had been collected for the legal precedents and principles which they
contained. This was the basis of the "chancery" (so-called, in imitation of
the empire, from the eleventh century), which became the great arsenal of
papal ideology. From at least the time of Leo the Great (A.D. 461) papal

legislation (*statuta, canones, decretales, constituta*) extended over most of the territories of the old empire. By the time of Gregory the Great (A.D. 604) the missionary expansion of Christianity had in effect established a new empire based on trinitarian dogma and what Gregory called "the society of the Christian Republic," and by the time of Charlemagne *Christianitas* was fully identified with *Romanitas* and the "revived" or "translated" *imperium*. In this way canon law, nourished also by the work of the councils and theologians, was in the process of becoming a new "law of nations."

The "Carolingian renaissance" gave a significant impulse to the formation of canon law. Charlemagne's "General Admonition" of 789 drew upon early canonist collections, especially the Dionysio-Hadriana (ca. 500, 774) and the Hispana (633), and in various ways reflected the canonist vision of an ordered society. His alliance with the papacy also illustrates how tradition might be furthered and even transformed by myth. In order to justify various Frankish "donations" the papacy needed a larger legitimacy, and this was provided contemporaneously by one of the most famous of all legal fabrications, published as the *Constitutio Constantini*. Building on the "legend of St. Sylvester" dating from the "Gelasian renaissance," this Donation of Constantine not only pretended that the pope had received his Roman territories from Constantine but also implied that the emperor owed his crown to the Roman pontiff.[56]

This document, debated and sensationalized in the later middle ages, exemplified and symbolized the process of fabricating a tradition, especially the semi-mythical link between papal government and Roman political tradition—taking back from Caesar, in a sense, "the things that are Caesar's." Such legal mythopoeia was itself traditional in an age which, though largely destitute of legal records, had revived an enthusiasm for "written law." If there could be "no change without tradition," then tradition itself, when unrecorded, had to be created, if possible re-created; and according to a process very much like the making of myth, privileges and laws had frequently to be invented, or at least reconstructed imaginatively, in order to provide the necessary legitimation.

The eighth and especially the ninth century constituted a great age of forgery—of Pseudo-Nomos—Charlemagne himself becoming an extraordinary focus for legends and the source of falsified as well as real rights and privileges. Canon law became the great vehicle for ecclesiastical fabrications, including the Donation of Constantine, which were woven into the very fabric of written tradition. Most famous were the forgeries of "pseudo-Isidore," a ninth-century collection, or confection, modeled on the Hispana and including older forgeries and a large number of allegedly pre-Constantinian decretals. The aim of these "false decretals," as of their rival "false capitularies," was not to announce new principles but rather to exaggerate the antiquity, or to enhance the authority, of conventional ideas; but above all it was usually to promote papal "plenitude of power" and the ecclesiastical hierarchy (as, contemporaneously, Benedictus Levita and others were doing on the imperial side). These so-called "forgers" were not trying to innovate, then, but rather hoping to fill out, to illustrate, and as it were to enhance tradition through a kind of speculative or divinatory interpretation. In any case this technique, and the texts to which it was applied, had become an integral part of the canonist tradition before the twelfth-century revival of learning.

According to Baronius, the great chronicler of ecclesiastical tradition, the tenth century was "an iron and dark age"; and certainly this time of "pornocratic" government in the church, marked by the rule of custom and by forgeries (whether designed to render these customs in written form or to invent new ones) as well as by growing lay influence, was a low point in the spiritual mission of Christianity. In the wake of the Carolingian collapse, rival national traditions, especially the Capetian monarchy in France and the Saxon empire in Germany, arose to complicate the policies and aspirations of the papacy. On a lower level the life and concerns of the church were affected by the secular customs and institutions of Europe, including the proprietary church and system of benefices, which entangled the ecclesiastical hierarchy in the webs of feudal society.

In some ways the papacy was able to take advantage of feudal law, to the extent indeed of claiming feudal hegemony over England, Sicily, and other European states, aided by the ambiguities in Christian and feudal conceptions of "faith" (*fides, fidelitas*) in social relationships. In other ways the church fell victim to feudal encroachments. From Roman times, ecclesiastical interests had been overseen in courts by lay "advocates" (chosen by bishops according to Carolingian law); but increasingly these patrons came from the noble classes and assumed, in fact and sometimes in law, the position of secular "lord," with the consequence that "canonical elections" became increasingly inoperative. On the whole the problems associated with property and proprietary rights (*ius regalium, spolii, fundi*) and with jurisdiction increased the laicization—and what might be called the "simonization"—of the church, its sacraments (especially penance), and its system of "justice." In such ways the church was moving from a "transcendent" to an "immanent" condition—from Logos back to Nomos.

Officially, the papacy continued to stand above the vicissitudes of positive law as experienced by Jews, Saracens, and pagans. "For these obey their own laws, though they are now of no avail for the salvation of souls and are not, like our own law, set forth and sanctioned by repeated declarations of the Eternal King."[57] So wrote Gregory VII, who (as Hildebrand) had never ceased invoking the Logos, recalling at one point the old formula that Christ's claim was to be not "the custom" but "the truth." Yet ecclesiastical law, too, was limited by human tradition; and what Charles Duggan has referred to as "a theory of the relativity and mutability of laws" was reinforced by canonist methods, in which there was a still more striking gap than in civil law between ideals and reality. The social and cultural casuistry which assumed that laws had to be interpreted in terms of place, time, and person (*locus, tempus, persona*) was in agreement with the demands of utility and especially of equity, which was an extraordinary "extension" of canon law from civil science. These attitudes were also essential for a discipline which presumed, in cooperation or rivalry with civil law, to constitute the fundamental science of human society.

Although proclaiming ecclesiastical "liberty," the Gregorian reform in fact promoted the idea of the church as a juridical community with its own concept of *iustitia* and so its own form of *ius*. The Petrine "keys," too, had acquired a juridical as well as a sacramental character, to the extent, indeed, that (according to the *Dictatus Papae,* which no doubt represented Gregory VII's views, whether or not he was the author) the pope was above judgment and was the exclusive source of law. The same theme sounds in another canonist collection ("in seventy-four titles") of the Gregorian period, which took its point of departure from a classic commentary on Judaic law, advising people, in matters too difficult for lay judgment, to go to the experts—the "priests of the Levites"—for the final say. Though speaking of "freedom," this text took as its major premise Roman primacy, and its message was the overriding need for law and order.[58] Naturally, the distinction between lay and ecclesiastic was absolute, the legal implication being that only those in the latter sphere, "ordained of God," could pass judgment. Support for these claims was drawn not only from legitimate tradition, including imperial decrees, but also from forged decretals, for example, a spurious letter of Gregory IV asserting the function of the pope "to keep a vigilant watch over everyone's status."[59] In general this implicitly polemical text illustrates the transmutation of ancient ideals, such as Cyprian's notion of ecclesiastical "unity," into claims of secular jurisdiction and social control—and the "body of Christ" transmuted into a body ecclesiastic.

Here indeed is the resurgence of Nomos, this time in the form of Germanic customs and feudal practices, assaulting the Logos; and the canonist tradition—a "Christian Torah"—responded by trying to assert and to fortify its own ancient customs as well as those more recently devised. Efforts to codify ecclesiastical law, most notably those of Cardinal Deusdedit, Anselm of Lucca, and Ivo of Chartres, went beyond particular ideological motives; for they were also informed by the desire to give order and legitimacy to the inchoate tradition that was becoming virtually a "common law" (*ius commune*) of Europe. These authors were also aware of the necessity of sorting out truth and falsity in canonist tradition; and Ivo of

Chartres in particular, in a fundamental treatise, discussed questions of forgery, degrees of authority, and the distinction between variable custom and generally valid, indeed "natural," law. From the late eleventh century these canonists tried not only to gather authoritative texts but, along the lines of ancient legal science, to reconcile and to "harmonize" them in a rational way. The culmination of this movement came with the monumental work of Gratian, completed about 1140, modeled in some ways on Justinian's collection and originally called "Concordance of Discordant Canons." The Decretum, as it came to be known, constituted the nucleus of the Corpus Iuris Canonici and the classic, if not entirely official, expression of what I have called Christian Nomos.[60]

From about this time (the period also of the revival of Roman law and Greek political thought) the lawyers—"canonists," "decretists," and later "decretalists," as well as their civilian or "legist" counterparts—began to take the lead in the systematic (if sometimes discordant) formulation of Western jurisprudence. In this opening phase of the posthumous European career of Nomos we can also see, in retrospect, not only a link between pagan and Christian ideas of law but also the remote beginnings of "modern" social thought.

SIX

Germanic Intrusions

Dit recht hebbe ek selve nicht irdacht,
it hebbet van aldere an unsick gebracht
Unse guden vorevaren.

Eike von Repgow

Sola Anglia usa est in suis finibus iure non scripto et consuetudine.

Bracton, *De Legibus*

•

Consuetudo

"The human race is ruled in two ways," wrote Isidore of Seville in the seventh century, "by nature and by custom."[1] In this formula, which opens Gratian's Decretum, we can see another reflection of the old duality of first and "second" nature, of Physis and Nomos—and what are humanly and historically the most fundamental sources of law. "Law originates in fact" (*lex ex facto oritur*) was a common medieval maxim, reflected in the Anglo-Saxon commonplace that "possession is nine points of the law."[2] Law was born of custom; and custom, as Baldus would later remark, was based not on theory but on "the experience of things." Ultimately, social rules were expressions of the unreflective (and in this sense "natural") behavior of people, and in a long perspective law can be seen as a retrospective idealization, or rationalization, of socially approved norms. These were the grounds of the Greek ideal of *arete* and the Roman *virtus* or *bonae mores* underlying the larger hypostasis of "justice"; they were the source, too, of the retrospective vision of the moral purity of the "primitive church," preserved in the austere customs of monastic communities, if not in the legalism of the Roman Ecclesia, which purported to reveal the institutional face of the Chistian Logos.[3] The growth of legal traditions and modern jurisprudence tended to obscure but never wholly to efface the primitive and popular roots of Nomos.

In the concept of "custom" we have at once the most concrete expression of Nomos and a theoretical access to the problem of the ultimate origin of law. Gaius, Pomponius, and other Roman jurists did not acknowledge custom as a legitimate source of law, and yet they recognized its practical force. The point was perhaps made best by Modestinus, last of the classical jurists: "All law has either been made by consent, or established by neces-

sity, or confirmed by custom." All three parts of this proposition, it may
be noticed, arise on a level beneath that of universal reason, which was the
basis of that "nature" recognized in classical legal science. Necessity, of
course, was its own law, or rather, according to Roman jurists, "had no
law," while the other two forces, custom and consent, were virtually identical. "Custom," in Ulpian's formula, "is the tacit consent of the people
confirmed by long-established practice"; it was the residue, or recollection,
of the ways of the fathers (mos maiorum). Habit, sanctioned by family
patterns, communal pressures, and cultural inertia, fixed social usages and
created a sort of proto-legitimacy finally expressed in "customary law"—
so that, in Roman "vulgar" law, "long-standing custom, approved by usage,
has not less authority than written law."[4]

From this it should be evident that custom, though it was the product
of historical contingency, found its major conceptual framework in Roman
(canon but especially civil) law. Consuetudo was the technical term from
classical times—balanced by its opposite, desuetude (desuetudo)—and it
normally referred to the legitimized form of what, according to the topos
established by the Sophists, was nominally "unwritten law" (nomos agraphos, ius non scriptum).[5] One of the major tasks of medieval jurists was
to reconcile the original concept of custom with unofficially written and
officially "redacted" forms of law.

Of course, "custom" continued to suggest the notion of "habit" in terms
of individual psychology (Aristotelian ethos and hexis), and this idea has
its own peculiar (though not unrelated) history. As usual, too, there were
connotations from rhetoric, which likewise took linguistic "custom," sustained by general approval, "for law." Both Cicero and Quintilian used the
term in the sense of a norm of the speech community, and Cicero contrasted
everyday life (vitae consuetudo) with the idealizations of Plato's Republic.
"Custom is the ruler of life" was a classical commonplace invoked by Pliny
as well as Quintilian and Cicero in an individual as well as a collective
sense. Other terms—such as mos, usus, and sometimes stilus or ritus—were
applied to social behavior in a descriptive sense; but "long," "longest," or
"inveterate" custom (longa, longissima, inveterata consuetudo) based on
tacit consent remained central to legal thought for centuries, as did its
sibling rival desuetudo, which implied obsolescence and loss of social legitimacy.[6]

Custom was "conventional" (in the sense of nomos) and often localized,
as in various restrictive phrases—consuetudo religionis, loci, civitatis—as
well as in the famous proverb attributed to St. Ambrose or St. Augustine
and commonly cited by later jurists, "When in Rome, do as the Romans
do" (Cum Romae fueris, Romano vivito more).[7] Yet custom was not
arbitrary and indeed was presumably grounded in common sense or, in

Gaius's famous phrase, "natural reason." Canonists, too, though they continued to contrast it pejoratively with "truth," took custom "for law" (*pro lege*) and regarded it, along with *lex,* as a species of *ius;* and indeed much of ecclesiastical tradition, sanctified though it was by conciliar and papal legislation, was derived from Christian *consuetudines,* especially the more general and rational ones.[8] So it was with the Roman tradition in both the eastern and western parts of the empire. What is most important to understand is that custom represented not merely a relic of bygone times but a continuing force; "for custom," according to one of the most frequently cited fragments in the Digest, "is the best interpreter of laws" (*optima legum interpres*).[9]

One characteristic expression of Christian Nomos appeared in monastic customs, which originated in spiritual maxims and lists of usages or bylaws. The Benedictine rule, however, began a long tradition, spawning commentaries, interpretations, and many local varieties of "old and reasonable customs," such as the influential usages of Cluny; and such customs underwent what David Knowles called a "gradual crystallization" before reaching a stage of written law—codes and "constitutions"—in the eleventh century. In this context the idea and term *consuetudo* received further elaboration and appeared in a variety of combinations—"good," "pristine," "holy," "daily," or "earlier" custom, as well as customs of particular places. Urban guilds also produced their own "customs," which (according to Baldus and other jurists) were distinctive in not needing the approval of the people and indeed, on occasion, in even being contrary to municipal statute.[10]

The idea of custom, along with the "positive law" which it helped to form, was always vulnerable to criticism from the standpoint of universal systems, whether religious or "scientific." Civil law, having originated in Roman mores, disappeared, in the West at least, in a wilderness of resurgent customs hardly accessible to us except through poorly recollected and vaguely construed "common law." In a long perspective, the pattern may be seen as a shift from "personal" to "territorial" law and in effect a blurring of the anthropocentric focus of civil law. But Western "vulgar law" was particularized in terms of time as well as place; and so, for example, old institutions such as private property tended to be replaced by more practical arrangements, including the possessory rights arising from "prescription" (especially the *praescriptio longae temporis* established in the second century A.D.). What Eugen Ehrlich idealized as an "inner order of society, localized and perhaps tribalized," replaced legislative and governmental regulation.[11]

This "de-universalizing" (the reverse of Ehrlich's "universalizing") process, too, represented a form of "interpretation" and had its own significance for social thought. Yet it was a process soon reversed by lawyers, as the concept of custom became Romanized—or perhaps re-Romanized—through legal interpretation, and so, despite local variations, given a general and even uniform rationale. In civil law beginning with Azo and in canon law beginning with Hostiensis, *consuetudo* was given rational form and contemporary relevance, and so again became a major category of social, historical, and cultural thought.[12]

By the sixteenth century, discussions of custom had become as systematic as other aspects of modern civil science. Peter of Ravenna pointed out the limits and qualifications of *consuetudo*, including the relation of custom to fact, conflicts between custom and law, the proof of custom, "bad custom," and desuetude, and then went on to offer a fourfold classification of the concept of *consuetudo*. Among contemporary customs he recognized ones which were "most general," which bound "all Catholics"; those which were "general," covering provinces; "special," which were limited to a single city; and "most special," which referred to the head of a household (*paterfamilias*).[13] Of course other varieties, such as ecclesiastical and secular, might be recognized—each of which had its own sources, conditions, and qualifications.

The interplay between custom and nature in the context of the new European social formations rising among the ruins and memories of Roman institutions suggests another phase in the story of Nomos and Physis. In one sense *consuetudo* stood at the opposite pole from the *natura* recognized by the old jurists—"No law, no senatusconsultum is sufficient for the variety of nature," wrote Andrea de Isernia.[14] In another sense—as in Ulpian's "what nature teaches all animals," or as the product of Aristotelian "nature" and natural "causes"—custom implied common citizenship in the world of nature. On this question, as usual, the "doctors disagreed." But in either case custom was bound to the human condition; it was changeable, associated with sin and corruption, and was ever time-, place- and race-oriented. "Local knowledge," in other words, was the very essence of Nomos.

And of course custom continued to be regarded by European jurists as "second nature" (*altera natura*), whether this was praiseworthy or not. "Ruling custom is more powerful than nature herself" (*consuetudo potens natura fortior ipsa est*) is one of a number of medieval proverbs recalling the ancient topos.[15] What Aristotle had said about custom (*ethos*)—that it depended on repetition (that it belonged to the idea of 'often' as nature belonged to 'always')—applied also to the medieval conception of *consuetudo*, which likewise was defined not by universality but rather by repeated and accepted usage. According to the commonly cited medieval adage (a radical simplification of Aristotle's conception of memory), "Twice makes a custom."[16] In this sense, too, "Law originates in fact."

Barbarian Law

The customs of European society, like those of Greece and Rome, can hardly be extricated from the myths that accompanied them; but the customs of early medieval Europe, unlike those of classical antiquity, first appeared in the context of an earlier civilization, or the ruins thereof, and never escaped the spell of antiquity.[17] The terminology and to some extent the form and substance of Roman law, that is, "vulgar" Roman law, assisted in the formulation not only of the various *leges romanae* devised for Germanic nations—most notably the "Breviary" of the Visigothic king Alaric II (506), the "Edict" of the Ostrogothic king Theodoric (508), and the laws of the Burgundians (before 516)—but also of the still more various *leges barbarorum* from the fifth century onwards. The Visigoths and Burgundians, too, had their "Germanic" laws; but most important in retrospect were the laws of the Franks, Salian as well as Ripuarian (published in the sixth century), and those of the Lombards (643–755). These two disparate, though politically related, traditions furnish one of the clearest illustrations of the rival cultural streams which joined to form the basis of European society and social thought.

The Romanist group preserved, for the West, most of what remained of legal science. The *leges barbarorum* displayed a fairly sophisticated legal philosophy, considering, for instance, the qualities of the legislator (*artifex legum*) and of the judge—eloquence as well as virtue and expertise. Law covered all orders of society, including women, illiterates, and incompetents; it had to agree with "nature, the customs of the city, and the condition of places and times" as well as fulfill the demand for justice, equality, necessity, and utility. Divine in origin, law was, like history itself, the "mistress of life" (*magistra vitae*) and aimed at "public utility"—sentiments which recurred centuries later in the Fuero Juzgo (*utilidad publica* is the phrase) and in the famous *Siete Partidas* established after the Gaian model by King Alfonso the Wise of Castile. By contrast the Breviary of Alaric, perhaps the most authoritative of the Western collections, showed a marked intellectual and social "shrinkage" (as Vinogradoff called it), eliminating, for example, antiquarian discussions of the source of laws and the varieties of personal liberty, and adding an elementary "interpretation" for the benefit of untutored practitioners.[18]

The indigenous "laws of the barbarians" were by no means immune from Romanist influence, if only because their redaction into "written law" carried with it a large weight of conceptual and terminological convention. Like Justinian, but a generation earlier, the Burgundian king Gundobad declared "in the name of God" that his collection of "laws past nd present" were to be kept "for the order and utility of the people" (*pro quiete et utilitate populi*) and "to be preserved for all future time."[19] The chauvinistic

Lex Salica, too, invoked piety and justice as the aims of social order, while King Rothair, in the earliest of the Lombard laws, echoed Justinian directly in "amending all earlier laws by adding that which is lacking and eliminating that which is superfluous." Building on this collection, his successor King Luitprand, spoke in similar accents. All of these collections were in fact summations of popular custom (similar in some ways to the Twelve Tables), but they were all issued under kingly patronage. They followed more or less explicitly the Roman model of legislation and as such represent perhaps the most fundamental reflection of social thought in the limited scribal culture existing before the eleventh century.

The so-called *leges barbarorum*—Germanic custom—contrasted unmistakably with Roman universalism, at least as preserved in its ghostly ecclesiastical form. The Germanic "invasions" were on the whole peaceful demographic movements occupying many generations, but the consequent racial and cultural conflict established an enduring dialectic in Western society. In legal terms this opposition was between the popular usages of communities still organized along tribal lines and a tradition based on authoritarian legislation which at least affected a rational style—or, more technically, between a legal system based on "personality," or tribal inheritance, and one based on "territoriality," which is to say, local jurisdiction carried over from imperial times. Between the time of Caesar and that of Tacitus the Germanic tribes on the European periphery of the empire had settled into an agricultural existence, but the successive waves of immigration continued, each leaving its imprint on social institutions and thought. Although the earliest of the barbarian laws date from the fifth century, the customs gathered in these "codes," like those of the Twelve Tables, were much older, in some cases from a period before tribal conversion to Christianity. Both the Burgundian and the Visigothic laws, for example, speak of "ancient" customs preceding the effort of redaction, which was assumed to be the act of "wise men" representing the popular assembly.

Between the finished work of Roman legal science and these unstructured assemblages of usages retrospectively sanctioned by political authority, there were profound and lasting differences. Germanic "codes" (though they were not "barbaric" to any but the Romans, as Roman codes had been to Greeks) were essentially expressions of tribal, or racial, privilege or "liberty," consisting specifically of elaborate tariffs of punishments to set members apart from aliens, especially Romans. These customs dealt above all with social disorder—crimes of violence ("scandalous" was the Lombard term), but more generally threats to family coherence, future as well as present. The severest of them, the Salic Law, was most offended by grave robbery and alienation of family property, whence the famous prohibition of inheritance by or through females. Its exclusive character is illustrated by a provision for families to expel foreigners by concerted action and by the sanctity of the paternal *terra salica,* comparable in significance to the Roman notion of property.[20] The "wergeld" of a Frank was twice that of a Roman, while others had no worth at all—were literally "outlaws," equivalent to the Roman and Greek conception of barbarism and the Christian state of excommunication.

Associated with the "barbarian" legal tradition is a view of Germanic national character which, especially since the Renaissance, has acquired the status of a grand cultural myth.[21] According to this Germanist myth, the northern migratory tribes were racially unmixed (since they forbade intermarriage) and, though led by hereditary kings, were democratically governed through the tribal assembly, or *Thing.* Although they were inclined to violence, feuding, and perhaps drunkenness, they displayed the rural virtues of uncorrupted morals—no usury among the Germans, Tacitus noted—and, above all, the love of liberty and law. The racialist myth of Germanism has never been more confidently expressed (not even by Tacitus, who had his own polemical point to make—the corrupt and virtueless condition of the Romans) than in the prelude to the Salic Law, which praised the strength, uncontaminated virtue, and good fortune of the *gens Francorum,* whose very name meant "free."[22] On this basis later jurists claimed that Frankish custom was closer than Roman law to natural law, according to which, "all men are free." As for the concept of law (called *e* in old German), it was a matter of debate whether it was related to the Latin word for eternity (*aevum*) or that for equity (*aequum*).[23] In all of these respects it has been conventional, ever since Tacitus, to contrast Germanic simplicity of manners with the supposedly "civilized" character of imperial Rome—and later, even more pointedly, with that of papal Rome.

With Charlemagne the amalgam of German and Roman, of customary and imperial, traditions began to affect institutions on every level. Just as this *rex-imperator* continued to endorse particular and local liberties through charters, so he aspired to larger social, political, and ecclesiastical control through his capitularies, which emulated ancient Roman legislation.[24] On the one hand, these capitularies reinforced Germanic customs, such as the *wergeld* and the *frida,* and acted to prevent innovations, such as new tolls, "except where they have existed of old." On the other hand, Charlemagne's administrative agents (*missi dominici*) served an imperial policy of recentralization, further sanctified by theocratic pretensions and papal support. To enforce his law he established a system of law-finders (*scabini, échevins*), which also promoted the amalgam of Germanic and Roman traditions. In his capitulary of Aix, less than two years after his coronation in 800, Charlemagne represented his legislation as being "in accordance with Salic, Roman, and Burgundian law" (that is, custom); and elsewhere he made similar appeals to the legitimacy of Lombard and canon law. Such eclecticism provided the practical basis for the revived Roman-law (but now the Christian and Western European) empire and accommodated a variety of traditions, each of which had its "own law" (*ius proprium*), comparable to the civil law of Rome.

Charlemagne's Sacrum Imperium did not last long, judged at least by its Roman prototype, nor did its legislative efforts. Yet its legal continuity was preserved by retrospective and mythopoeic interpretation; and it was richly productive in legal, political, and ecclesiastical precedents tied to "the legend and the memory of Charlemagne," establishing an ideological archetype for several European traditions, including those of Germany and France, and a model of "common law" apart from Romanism. At the same time the Carolingian collapse left secular Romanism and legal science at an even lower level than before—and left territories to be, in effect, a law unto themselves.

The ninth and tenth centuries were in fact the seed-time of European social institutions—the seminal period of *consuetudo*, when "personality" was wholly replaced by "territoriality," and when tribal custom was becoming adjusted to its environment and accommodated to the needs of an agrarian and military (and perhaps, in this sense, still "barbarian") society. It was a time of myth and oral tradition, of that unreflective social creativity which is the ultimate source of Nomos. Reconstruction of this creative process is in large part speculative, and with Marc Bloch we can only infer that "every collectivity was fashioning its own law." According to a ninth century formula, "justice" was nothing more than the "law of the land" (*lex terrenae*). A new society was being born; according to François Olivier-Martin, "The secret of this birth is undoubtedly enveloped in a mystery which always shrouds the intimate manifestations of social life."[25] It was the birth of law, a mystery deepened before the twelfth century by the scarcity of documents and the proliferation of a variety of legends and forms of religious consciousness. And the law in question was that disparate network of relationships given retrospective definition and form under the name of "feudal law" and eventually "feudalism."

Feudal Law

Gaining access to this part of the European legal tradition is notoriously difficult. Language throws some light on the mystery, to the extent that we can see new patterns emerging in the transformation and creation of terms. What is significant above all (or perhaps I should say beneath all) was the position of landed property. The Latin word *terra* acquired this proprietary signification from at least the Carolingian age; and so, more conspicuously, did the classical term *honor*, which was increasingly applied to the landed "benefice," as a conditional grant of territory was conventionally called.

Similarly, the words suggesting lordship—*dominus, senior*—were extended from political or tribal contexts to territorial proprietorship, to landlordship. Most crucial of all was the term, or rather family of terms, locating the central institution of European society in the post-Carolingian age: *feus, feuu, feusum, feuz, faeuum, foeum, feuum, fefum, feodum, feudum, feodum, feodium, fefodum, feuodium, feuodum, fedum, foedum.*[26] Etymologists are still debating the origin of this family of terms, agreeing at least that it is Germanic (*fehn, fehod,* referring to cattle, or possessions more generally), but acknowledging associations, even if accrued only later, with the Latin *foedus* (pact) and *fiscus* (domain).

In a word, out of all these terms, coinages, and miscoinages, the central mystery is what jurists later rationalized, and mythologized, as "feudal law" (*ius feudale, ius feudisticum*) and what modern historians and sociologists have further abstracted as "feudalism" (*feodalité, feudalismo, Lehnwesen*). Evolving from conditions of barbarian society, "feudalism" in its European form illustrates neatly the aphorism that "law originates in fact." In general the process, mostly complete by the tenth century, was the extension of the old Merovingian following (*Gefolgschaft,* called *comitatus* by Tacitus) into a larger and more complex social grouping known as "vassalage," which was formed, for the most part unconsciously (according to Bloch), by a curious amalgam of usages and institutions, which received legal definition in a variety of languages besides Latin, and which, by the thirteenth century, was extended over much of Europe and beyond.

The patterns of feudal society and the problems generated by these new arrangements led also to new ways of expressing and thinking about social relationships. The "feud" (*faida*) in a conventional sense, and blood ties in general, continued to be institutionally central, especially after the Carolingian collapse; but what was being rationalized as "feudal law," first in particular cases and then in more general extensions, suggested new conceptions of social solidarity. Conceptually, feudalism implied a universal human condition in the sense that the entire earth was in theory enfeoffed— of God, if not of man. Land remained the key and was literally inseparable from lordship (*dominium* in a private as well as a public sense), as expressed in the maxim, "Nul terre sans seigneur." That this lordship came in effect to be shared by the vassal was suggested by the distinction made later by lawyers between "direct" lordship and lordship of "use" (*dominium directum, dominium utile,* pertaining to lord and vassal respectively). Both involved "honor" in a social as well as economic and material sense; and of course with this honor came responsibilities toward the church and peasantry, centering especially on manorial jurisdiction, and a host of other problems, including "subinfeudation," primary allegiance (*ligesse*), and above all feudal possession, succession, and hereditability.[27]

Vassalage may be regarded as the cultural dimension of feudal society.

Beyond the feudal base, the landed "honor," there arose a variety of social, moral, legal, and ceremonial obligations attached to the contractual arrangement implied by "fealty," which became a fundamental secular as well as religious category, and attached also to the evil consequences of breaking faith—the original crime of "felony." Vassalage thus represented the most fundamental social tie, expressed in elementary possessory terms. "Lord, I become your man" was the formula established by St. Louis (*Devenio homo vester; Je deviens vostre hom*), and the promise could be extended far beyond the initial feudal relationship. So it was, for example, in the *Siete Partidas,* in which vassalage was defended as the "most natural" relationship and as the highest ideal of humanity. Such—as seen by the "feudists," anyway—were the implications of the institutional hybrid which has come to be called feudalism.

Many historians disapprove of the term "feudalism," much in the way that classical-minded scholars used to condemn the "Gothic disease" of Germanic customs. Historically, indeed, the term may imply a false uniformity, and certainly the conventions covered by the feudal terminology vary strikingly from Lombardy to the Germanic north, from Spain to the kingdom of Jerusalem. From historical evidence we can conclude at most that feudalism emerged in the form of local "customs and usages" which only later acquired social approval, precise legal definition, and the "universalizing" inclination noted by Ehrlich.[28] Older tribal traditions persisted, for instance, in the success of the principle of hereditability of the fief; and of course other institutional patterns—rural groupings and village communities falling outside the feudal relationship, as well as the ecclesiastical institutions intruding themselves into it—further obscured the contractual model which seemed, especially to lawyers, to give structure to society.

Yet "feudalism" does have a rationale from the point of view of social thought. No matter how viewed, this kaleidoscope of "feudal law" assembled or reconstructed by lawyers represented an original pattern. As customary relationships were set down in writing (*consuetudo scripta*—a contradiction in civil law), in particular formulas, and then in more considered statements, they coalesced—were forced to coalesce—into patterns which achieved legal and eventually philosophic status, thanks largely to the apparatus of ancient legal science, which was beginning to reappear in the late eleventh century. If only through the rationalizations of lawyers, the *ius feudale* was elevated to the quasi-philosophical status of *ius feudisticum.*

From the beginning it was possible to see, beneath the maze of disparate and divergent local customs reflected sporadically in formulas and charters, a basic functional as well as institutional duality, corresponding both to the ingrained Roman categories of persons and things and to the Christian polarity of body and soul: first, the social substance, the landed benefice "enfeoffed by possessors" and "subinfeudated" to others according to written contractual agreement; and then the personal relationship thereby formed, "vassalage" based on loyalty or faith (*fides,* or *bona fides*). This "faith," the prerequisite for a binding contract according to civil law, was a concept enhanced and reinforced by associations with Christian doctrine (especially Pauline "faith"), courtly love, and filial obedience. This curious marriage of social custom and religious ideal is the very prototype, one might say, of Marxian social theory: a material base, composed of the essential productive wealth of society, and a superstructure, reflecting the essential values and goals of the system, or at least of its ruling class. The fact and the law, we might conclude; and there is reason to suspect that Marx's own formulation was much influenced by the legal version of this duality.

Historians are no doubt right to distrust the rationalizations and fabrications of lawyers, but such suspicions are misplaced in a study of the process and tradition of social thought, which must attend to the abstracting and myth-making tendencies of jurisprudence. The first written basis for a theory of "feudalism" was not only a product of the revival of legal science but was, so lawyers alleged, a direct continuation of Roman legal tradition. This twelfth-century collection, known as the *Book of Fiefs* (*Consuetudines Feudorum,* later *Libri Feudorum*), was an assemblage of northern Italian custom, statutory law, and jurisprudence brought together by two jurists, Girardus Niger and Obertus de Orto, and interpreted continuously by commentators down to the eighteenth century. In this work the fief was defined simply as "property held in return for service," and a distinction was made between property and hereditary usufruct (equivalent to *dominium utile*). The process of rationalizing and homogenizing feudal rules is well indicated by the rubrics which served as topics for debate for many generations of feudists: who can bestow a fief, and who not; how a fief is acquired; who succeeds to a fief; and various problems arising between the lord and his "faithful."[29] By the sixteenth century "feudal law" was subjected not only to intensive historical investigation but also to analytical "method," which gave it status as a part of "moral philosophy." Here (and not in the discussion of Montesquieu, who drew upon the *Book of Fiefs* and the commentary it generated) was the true "invention of feudalism."[30]

Customary Law

How in fact was custom promoted from a social to a legal and even a political level? How did it come not only to "represent" a people (as Baldus said) but also to rule its behavior? How did it pass from unrecorded, collective memory to authoritative written form? How, more technically, was *consuetudo* transformed into *ius consuetudinarium*? And how, more specifically, did French *coutumes* become *droit civil,* German *Gewohnheit* become *Recht,* and English customs become *le ley commun*—"common law"?[31]

In theory the answer depended on simple social inquiry and judgment. Perhaps the most rudimentary explanation was given by the English civilian John Cowell in the early seventeenth century. "It is enough for the profe of a custom by witness in the common lawe (as I have credibly heard)," wrote Cowell, "if two or more can agree, that they have heard their fathers say, that it was a custome all their time and that their fathers heard their fathers also say, that it was likewise a custome in their time."[32] Custom, in short, was authenticated transcriptions of popular memory. At this point it is clear that we must confront, again, not only the prehistorical character of custom but the problem of the passage from oral to scribal and literate culture.

The notion of law originating in fact is well illustrated by the earliest accessible stage of European "custom," which was represented by individual transactions recorded in charters. In Normandy, for example, Romano-canonical influence was slight before the assembling of the earliest of French custumals, the *Très ancien coutumier de Normandie* (ca. 1200); and property transfers (to mention the most characteristic subject of surviving charters) were carried out by increasingly uniform "legal habits" (in the words of a recent historian). Already in the eleventh century such business was accomplished according to the "ancestral *mos*" or the "*mos* of the ancients" and with deference to general ideas of custom (*mos Normanniae, mos patriae, mos terrae*). By the end of the reign of William the Conqueror, to judge from this evidence, there was already a distinct provincial *coutume*— the "très très ancien coutume de Normandie"—perhaps the earliest in France.[33]

In the written formulation of such generalized customs the essential problem was that of "proof," or "approval," and it could be resolved in two ways. In primitive or preliterate societies no proof was called for; or rather, the members of that society were themselves "living proof" of their customs. In complex cultures a significant level of expertise was required. In medieval Europe this first meant law-finders or lay "sayers of the law" (*sapientes, diseurs de droit, Gesetzsprecher*), who consulted their own memories or consciences, and later, under new commercial and political pressures, more formally trained jurists, who claimed special expertise, or rather received it from higher authority.

In theory and in early practice not only the creation but also the recognition and declaration of custom belonged to the "people"; and in France at least this was accomplished through the institution of the *turbe,* which had Carolingian and even Roman precedents. According to the fourteenth-century *Grand Coustumier de France* by Jacques d'Ableiges, custom was "proved by a meeting of ten men worthy of faith" (*prouvés en turbe par dix hommes dignes de foi*); and a little later Jean Bouteiller, in his *Somme rurale,* declared that the proof of a custom was to be accomplished "by twelve of the wisest and oldest men of the place"(*douze hommes les plus sages et anciens du lieu*).[34] As Gilles Fortin wrote of the Parisian *coutume* three centuries later, "This customary law was for a long time observed without being written or engraved anywhere except on the hearts of the citizens who kept it; and if in doubt the proof was not in books but in assemblies [*turbes*] of those who knew the practice and ordinary usage."[35] An approved custom, then, was a form of social contract (*quasi ex contractu,* in the words of a sixteenth-century feudist).

The crucial point came in the reduction—or "redaction"—of local usages into written form. At first the production of *coutumiers* was merely a matter of private observation and judicial recording, exemplified by the *Libri Feudorum,* the anonymous *Etablissements de Saint Louis,* the *coutumes* of Beauvaisis by Philippe de Beaumanoir, the *Sachsenspiegel* of Eike von Repgow, and perhaps the treatises of Glanvil and Bracton, which all gained authority only in retrospect. These collections represented both a shift "from memory to written record" (in M. T. Clanchy's phrase) and a geographical extension of local customs through judicial decisions and formulations. This generalizing process was intensified, of course, by the impact of more formal "Romano-canonical" procedures and by the teaching of civil and canon law in the universities—and more especially by the imperial drives of feudal monarchy.[36] Indeed, the redaction of customs is a classic example of the convergence between, and mutual reinforcement of, writing, literacy, the expansion of the legal profession, and political power—a process in which custom as an expression of popular will was in large part overwhelmed.

The chronology and geography of European customary law as it emerged into the light of history is extremely complex, but there are common as well as national patterns, at least in the context of a reviving "written law." In France customary law was formulated in collections of provincial jurisprudence from the late twelfth century; but most important eventually was that of the municipal jurisdiction of Paris (*le Prévôté et Vicomté de Paris*), which achieved unofficial recognition as the general custom of France (*usus et consuetudines Franciae,* meaning northern France).[37] In England, according to Bracton, only "unwritten law and custom" applied; and so it was for many parts of the German Empire, which, however, did acquire a number of so-called territorial "mirrors," especially the *Sachsenspiegel,* part of which was specifically "feudal" (the *Lehnrecht* as distinguished from the *Landrecht*). In Spain, where the Visigothic tradition continued to be strong, the *Fuero Viejo* dates from the early twelfth century, as does the first recension of the *Book of Fiefs.* From the thirteenth century on, these collections of customary law multiplied; and it was largely through such vernacular *coustumes, utsages,* and the like that European *consuetudo* found expression and conceptualization, with important consequences for social thought in general.

France was the classic land of customary law, as of so many other institutional creations, but there were comparable developments in other parts of Europe. In Spain the pattern was more complex not only because of geographical particularism but also because of the intermixture of Roman and Moorish traditions underlying the later medieval diversity. After the Visigothic period local privileges were granted and usages recognized in *fueros,* the Spanish institution which in fact (*hecho*) literally became law (*derecho*), thus in a sense reversing the universalizing process perceived by Ehrlich.[38] One of the legacies of the Visigothic kingdom was the *Fuero Juzgo,* the "fountain of true Spanish law," as Grotius called it, but even this constitutional document failed to prevent the drift toward particularism. It was specifically rejected by Castile in favor of the so-called *albedrio* system, according to which judges settled cases and thereby set binding precedents (*razana*) for future use. Aragon, too, inclined toward judge-made, which is to say, local and customary, law, at least until the great thirteenth-century collection, *Las Siete Partidas,* modeled after the Institutes.

In Germany legal tradition was also confined largely to judicial sources, especially to the surviving Carolingian law-finders (*scabini,* or *Schöffen*), who rendered private justice; and the political chaos of the Holy Roman Empire from the thirteenth century onwards insured that this pattern would continue long after England, France, and Spain had established firm legislative foundations. Customary elements such as trial by battle and the ordeal were preserved longer, and Roman influence was officially held off until the "Reception" of the later fifteenth century.[39] The great figure in German vernacular jurisprudence is Eike von Repgow, who assembled the "Saxon Mirror" in the thirteenth century. For Eike law was a form of divinity—*Gott ist selve recht*—and he associated it with Old Testament wisdom as well as mythical origins, especially in the legends of Alexander. At the same time, law was for him also a reflection of society, a bequest of the "good forebears" (*gute Vorfahren*), and it signified above all freedom and peace (*Freiheit und Friede*). To this extent the "universalizing" process suggested by Ehrlich did produce, through Eike, a partial code in the influential *Sachsenspiegel,* which became the basis for later re-formations of Saxon law.[40]

English common law followed a more varied and circuitous channel and built up its own characteristic and in some ways independent mythology. To later lawyers English law seemed to be an expression of "immemorial custom," which had acquired legitimacy through humanly imputed, or invented, continuity and rationality, especially as contained in judgments originating in the royal (the "common-law") courts. In contrast to Continental traditions the common law developed to a large extent in terms of legal procedure; and indeed the earliest books of authority, beginning with Glanvil in the twelfth century, were little more than commentaries on the various kinds of writs, which is to say, "forms of action," analogous to the old Roman *legis actiones*. Despite the influence of civil and canon law (which has almost always been minimized) it kept for the most part a vernacular dress—that unique trilingual jargon called "law-French"—and remained professionally innocent of academic jurisprudence, at least until the sixteenth century. It was the boast of common lawyers from Bracton to Blackstone that English law alone escaped the rigidity of the *ius scriptum* and derived entirely from popular custom as expressed by the judiciary.[41] The matter is not quite so simple, however, and needs to be examined as a special case of the formation of Nomos in late medieval thought.

In France the development of custom from unwritten usages to memorable doctrine, from fact to law and learned jurisprudence, can be followed more precisely. The story begins in the thirteenth century when the central government began to show serious concern with local customs, bound up as they were with the rival interests of feudal, seigneurial, and urban courts. By an ordinance of 1270 Louis IX instituted the device of the collective inquest (*inquisitio per turbam; enquête par turbe*), or rather, adapted the old Carolingian inquest, which had been used in criminal cases, to the authentication of local customs.[42] This was the procedure referred to by Jacques d'Ableiges and Jean Bouteiller, according to which royal commissioners (*enquêteurs*) convoked a certain number of "wise men" and proposed a series of customs for their consideration. These *turbiers* not only affirmed the existence—technically, the "notoriety"—of each custom, but they also testified to the times, places, circumstances, and persons with which it had been associated: "If they ever saw judgment by the said custom," a report from the city of Rheims described the procedure in 1253, "and how many times, and by which judges, and between which persons, and at what time . . . and if all or the best part of the people, expressly or tacitly, agreed to introduce this custom."[43] Then, but only after unanimous agreement, the royal *enquêteurs* set the customs down in writing.

By the time *consuetudo* had become a form of *ius scriptum*, the revival of ancient legal science was, of course, in full swing, with the result that the procedures of Romano-canonical law were being substituted for oral, customary, and inquisitorial methods. The *coutumiers* of France displayed a most striking intercultural amalgam—a hybrid genre of vernacular text with technical and multiple Latin glosses, annotations, and interpretations, which was also a vehicle for the vital field of legal lexicography. It was in this context that the idea of custom was given rational and systematic formulation and that, as in the early ages of Greece and Rome, it again became a major shaping force in the history of law and social thought.

The Theory of Custom

In the paradoxical efforts to reduce custom (by definition "unwritten") to writing, there emerges once again the old contrast between first and second nature—Physis and Nomos. "Law is either natural or positive," we read in the oldest Norman *coutume*. Natural law comes from God, but the *ius positivum* "is established by men for the good of humanity and differs from province to province according to its difference sources."[44] This dichotomy persists throughout the entire history of Old Regime law and custom notwithstanding the developments of secularism and science.

Positive law—which refers to law that is "posited," without any relation, except through later confusions, to legal "positivism"—remained normally on the side of history. Its most fundamental form of expression was *consuetudo,* which was defined in the Norman *coutume* as "mores established by antiquity, approved by princes, and conserved by the people subject to them." Pierre de Fontaines, who was *bailli* in the reign of Louis IX, defined custom as something created by human action and "taken for law when the law is silent," a direct echo of Isidore of Seville. In the next century Bouteiller was more specific. "According to the ancients," he wrote, "a local custom is an establishment held and preserved in a country by the old wise men by agreement, and maintained according to the condition of the place where it was made as long as it is accepted and suffices."[45]

In this statement we can see four of the major attributes of customary law as it emerged throughout Europe in the Middle Ages. First, in contrast to civil and canon law, it was relative to place in ways that jurists came to formulate according to geo-historical and even ethnographical discriminations. Second, as custom was subject to conditions of geographical relativity, so it was tied to factors of time and temporal change, implying potential improvement and "reformation" as well as obsolescence and degeneration. Third, custom was the product of human "will" and "interest," which, though they may account for its changeability and corruptibility, also set it apart from the world of primary nature. Fourth, these conditions meant, implicitly, that custom was to be proved as well as "preserved" by the people of a country represented by the "wise men." It remains from the standpoint of social thought, to examine those conceptual aspects of European customary law as they existed in the later medieval period before the massive intrusions of legal science and political philosophy.

The geographical diversity of French customary law was proverbial: already in the thirteenth century Beaumanoir was complaining that "one cannot find in all of France two *châtellanies* using the same custom."[46] At the end of the Old Regime there were still perhaps three hundred local and sixty-five general *coutumes,* most with their own accumulated jurisprudence. Under pressure of jurisprudence the tendency was for the "special" or "particular" customs to be gathered into provincial aggregates, such as that of Beauvaisis, which Beaumanoir himself shaped through his judicial experience, and beyond that (from the fourteenth century) into still more general, virtually national, *coutumiers,* which were assembled in the major centers of jurisdiction, that is, the several Parlements. In France, notwithstanding private collections and movements of redaction, reform, unification, and, in effect, of codification, localism persisted in the face of all interpretation, comparative study, and systematization.

Juridically, this characteristic of French customs was expressed in the old maxim that "place determines act" (*locus regit actum,* or *formam actum*), referring not only to seigneurial justice (that of the "dominant fief") as one sixteenth-century jurist argued, but to the local *coutume* established by agreement of all three estates. These legal principles were reinforced by a variety of medico-astrological assumptions which linked customs with the "humors" of a people as well as the "climate" or "air" of a place, and which implied an analogy between the judge and the prescribing physician—another popular reflection, perhaps, of the idea of custom as "second nature."[47] This premise of fundamental ties between environment and social custom, so characteristic of a pre-scientific age, has informed French social and geo-historical thought about national tradition down to the days of Vidal de la Blache and Lucien Febvre.

The temporal dimension of French customary law is reflected in a variety of ways. One is what the redactors of the provincial customs recognized as folk memory, the "high antiquity" of the Breton *coutume,* for example, concealing barbarian usages antedating feudalism. Kinship patterns often survived feudal interests, but especially in the insistence on blood succession, expressed most commonly in the formula that private inheritances, like public ones, passed immediately and mystically from the dead to the living—"le mort saisit le vif" being almost as famous as its political counterpart, "le roi ne meurt jamais."[48] More conspicuously, the historical dimension of custom appears in the recognition of the instability of human traditions, whether through the identification of obsolescence (*desuetudo* being the obverse of *consuetudo*) or through the correction of "bad customs." Jurists did not hesitate to apply to antiquated laws the rule that "today the custom is changed" (*mutata est hodie consuetudo,* in the words of Odofredus), and as Vacarius wrote in his *Book for Poor Scholars,* "Things are dissolved by the same process by which they are created."[49] Even more than most human creations, custom had to be understood, at least metaphorically, in terms of generation and corruption.

Yet if they were a "second nature," customs were not "natural" in any deterministic sense, and philosophically their most important feature was that they were quite directly a creation of human will (with all of the further irregularities this implied). The paradoxical side of the notion that will was the "cause of a custom" (*causa consuetudinis*) was the fact that will, like custom, could be malicious, and that the largely feudal substance of French provincial customs represented the interests of the new aristocracy; for not by accident did "custom" become identified with rent or toll, and "bad customs" with unjust exactions. But to most jurists this was an aberration. Their underlying complacency arose from the belief that, as Roman jurists had also held, custom represented the "tacit consent" of the people, a legal fiction which became entangled with the mythical and mystical conception of a three-tiered society. And when it came to publication in writing, customs indeed had to be approved by each of the Three Estates.

But what was a "people"? The short answer was given by the medieval aphorism that "ten makes a people" (*decem faciunt populum,* perhaps memorializing the Roman *decemviri*), which applied to the *turbe* as well (defined in Roman law as ten or fifteen men, but not as few as three). There were, however, considerations of quality as well as quantity. The term and concept of *populus,* which had been transferred from ancient Rome to the Christian faith (*populus christianus* being commonly used by Augustine and Jerome), might be applied to communities ranging from a village to a nation or empire; but it was invariably defined by adherence to a "custom," whether local and particular or "general."[50]

With the advent of written forms, however, even with the proviso of popular "approval" and "tacit consent," custom lost its primary ties with its social base and came under the control of legal and political authorities. The classical formula designating *consuetudo* as the "best interpreter of law" was intended by jurists to enhance their own power, as suggested by the gloss of Azo, who defined custom as the founder and abrogator as well as the interpreter of law (*quod consuetudo sit conditrix legis, abrogatrix et interpretatrix*).[51] Another, less authoritative maxim (*cuius interpretatio, eius legislatio,* and its variations) suggests the true significance of the transition from "custom" to "customary law," which is that once again the legal experts have begun to take over. This indeed is the import of the twelfth-century revival of "legal science," in which custom joins civil and canon law in the arsenal of the "language of power" which jurists come in large part to monopolize. Despite mutability, irregularity, and national divergences, custom joined canon and civil law as a major vehicle of the European legal tradition—and the most characteristic expression of Nomos in the Western European context. Customary law preserved its integrity well into the modern period, especially in the context of "positive jurisprudence," including the judicial memory and lawyerly maneuvering preserved in various kinds of law reporting, in the "popular literature" of uneducated and half-educated men, and in traditional polemics against professional lawyers.

Myth also played a role in the preservation, or creation, of local and national "customs." The Italian and German "nations" naturally maintained a self-conscious connection with a posthumous but still allegedly authentic Roman tradition (though ambivalently in the case of the Germans), but other nationalities had to look to their own putative "fathers" for the most part.[52] In Spain there was awareness of—or wishful thinking about—a national custom (*costumbre* or *uso de Espana*), which later medieval authors idealized or contrasted with local (for example, Catalonian) customs; and of course the *Siete Partidas* figured prominently in this national myth, protected by "Blessed Lady Spain" and by various submyths, such as the notorious Aragonese oath ("Si no, no"). Even more conspicuous was the English conviction that its legal order had always been an expression of insular customs, despite the imposition of the "Norman yoke"; and by the sixteenth century the myth of "immemorial custom" had become a cornerstone of the legal profession. In general common lawyers rejoiced in the mysterious character of their vocation, emphasizing that it was based on a sort of "artificial reason" which could hardly be appreciated by the uninitiated, much less by foreigners. This was the "mysterious science of law" exported to the Anglophone parts of the new world.[53]

French jurists too, though the *raison civile* of their customary law was not nearly so convoluted as the "artificial reason" of the English, developed a mystique of national tradition to rival that of England and even Rome. *Consuetudo,* at first referring only to a particular privilege (or obligations of peasants to their seigneur), came to signify the way of life of a people, though this of course might include "bad customs" (*malae consuetudines*) as well as good, and "servitudes" as well as "liberties." But the larger social and political signification of *consuetudo* came to predominate, especially as applied to the "French people."[54] From the twelfth century on, the *coutume* of Paris became identified with the customs of France (*consuetudines Franciae*), even before it was identified with any political unit. From the sixteenth century, however, the idea of a "general custom" for the whole French nation became not only an instrument of national political consolidation but also a concept essential to the development of the modern sciences of society.

Such was the basis for the judicial and historical quest, begun in the context of medico-astrological theory, for the "spirit" of French law, as jurists (adapting the old formula of the *mens legum*) called the "second nature" of their own society. This spirit was located above all in local and provincial customs, especially that of Paris, which were progressively promoted from the level of particular "fact" to that of more general "law." In the words of Montesquieu, "These customs were preserved in the memories of old men, but insensibly laws or written customs were formed." Montesquieu was also aware of the political implications, for as he summed up the process, "Thus our customs were committed to writing, they were made more general, and they received the stamp of royal authority."[55] However imperfectly, custom was joined to royal jurisdiction as social base to superstructure, and in this sense it became civilized and politicized.

Custom never entirely lost its connection with "fact," and indeed what complicates the idea of custom in a social context is the problem that it often cannot be fixed by legal formulation. In part this is because of the process of *desuetudo,* the practical and theoretical counterpart of *consuetudo*; in part it is because many customs, as Marc Bloch has shown, have "no force apart from the wills of the inhabitants" and are preserved only in oral culture, where "human memory is sole arbiter."[56] One good example is the perennial, and annual, problem of boundaries (*bornage*), which could always, from the time of Beaumanoir down to the Civil Code, be settled by agreement (*amiablement; sans justice*) as well as legally (*judiciairement; par auctorité de justice*).[57] And in any case, as Eusèbe Laurière observed in the seventeenth century, only "where the crops are showing" could customary law protect possession or use. In practice, cultivated land was "subject to the law of nations and the common property of all" and subject to unspoken agreements. "How true it is," Bloch remarked, "that all rural customs take their origin from an attitude of mind."[58]

What made possible the development of customary law in a theoretical way was of course the revival of legal science in the Middle Ages. By the sixteenth century it is hardly possible to extricate native customs and oral tradition from the written tradition of professional jurisprudence, although by at least the sixteenth century legal and antiquarian scholars were attempting to do just this. The principal categories of social thought continued, however, to be the monopoly of civilians and canonists. Thus we must turn back to the ancient legal tradition, or rather, to its posthumous life in the context of European society and the new "world of nations" emerging in the eleventh and twelfth centuries.

SEVEN

Medieval Reconstruction

Consuetudo altera natura.

Azo, *In ius civile*

Hodie consuetudo mutata est.

Odofredus, *Lectura super Codice*

·

Twelfth-Century Revival

The modern legal tradition was born, or reborn, in the general cultural revival of the twelfth century; and it was the product of three converging intellectual currents. One was the body of ecclesiastical law, which was both a vehicle and a rival of Roman jurisprudence. Another was the practical, "vulgar" remnant of Roman law surviving in various areas of the West, especially in the cities of northern Italy and in the "provinces of written law" in southern France. The third was the related continuation of Roman education, especially the teaching of rhetoric—"expertness in discourse in civil questions," as Cassiodorus defined it in the sixth century—which provided a haven for the study of law on an elementary level, not only pedagogical and notarial but also epistolary (in the *ars dictaminis*, which arose in the Italian cities). In the "renaissance of the twelfth century" both Greek natural philosophy and Roman jurisprudence began to be rediscovered, with the result that once again Physis (in the scholastic form of Aristotelianism) and Nomos (mainly in the form of civil law) came into confrontation—the Greeks versus the Romans in posthumous alliance or combat.[1]

The arena for this confrontation was the "Studium," that modern version of the ancient "encyclopedia" which was the intellectual base of the new universities beginning to be established in that age. The *studium generale*, which was the original term for university (the *corpus intellectuale* as distinguished from the *universitas*, the civilian term for a licensed corporation) consisted essentially of the old circle of "seven liberal arts," with the addition of the higher "sciences" of philosophy, theology, medicine, and law. This body of elementary and professional learning, together with the institutions of church and empire, reflected also a growing awareness

of, or at least wishful thinking about, the cultural unity of "Europe."
Underlying this idea was a powerful cultural myth promoted by medieval
clerks concerning the "translation of empire" (*translatio imperii*) and a
parallel "translation of studies" or even of "wisdom" (*translatio studii,* or
translatio sapientiae), by which the best of ancient civilization was to be
passed on to modern nations. Out of the East, then to the Greeks, and
later to the Romans, came wisdom, the knowledge of things divine and
human—"le premier los et de clergie," in the phrase of Chrétien de Troyes,
who concluded with the hope that

> . . . at last to France, we pray,
> These arts have come to stay.[2]

And as the French, "as the most acute, received the Studium of the sciences
and liberal arts," concluded Alexander of Roes, "so the Italians had the
Church and the Germans the Empire. By these three, namely *Sacerdotium,
Imperium, Studium,* as by the virtues, namely the vital, the natural and the
animal, the Holy Catholic Church is spiritually vivified, enlarged and
ruled."[3]

The most concrete expressions of this cultural unity, or rather trinity,
were the Latin language and Roman law; and medieval scholars were
inclined to hypostasize and to mythologize these ancient legacies as well.
"Whoever speaks the Latin language . . ." declared one thirteenth-century
canonist, "is bound by Roman law."[4] From at least the eleventh century
on, the vocabulary, and hence to some extent the mentality, of civil law
informed the commercial life of southern France—in various contractual
arrangements, for example, and in the capacity once again to distinguish
between private property and mere possession—well before the academic
revival.

For more learned inquirers, Roman law, combining the resources of near-
classical Latin and the memory of civic and imperial institutions and ideals
of antiquity, was the most vivid reflection of ancient wisdom (*sapientia*)—
which indeed was just the way in which jurists had defined their discipline
("the knowledge of things divine and human"). Medieval "doctors of law"
were intensely conscious, and proud, of being the lineal descendants of
Justinian's law professors—called "antecessors," Odofredus thought,
"because they should precede others and exceed them in knowledge and
virtue" (*excedunt alios in scientia et moribus*).[5] Of course pretensions to
an ancient pedigree, to colleagueship with Papinian, Ulpian, and Gaius,
were paralleled and reinforced by the claims of medieval emperors to be,
via the Carolingian "translation of empire," the legislative successors of
Caesar and Justinian; and it was a central aim of restored civil law to
emphasize and to elaborate on this intellectual and institutional genealogy.
It was above all this emphasis on the specific historical pedigree, rather

than universal philosophical validity, that aligned the Roman (or Romanist) tradition with the conventional forces of Nomos.

Like the ancient Roman archetype, this modern Romanist legal science (*civilis scientia,* as it came to be called) had its own myths of origin. One was that the great law school of Bologna had been founded by the Emperor Theodosius II in 433. Another "fairy story," as C. H. Haskins called it, was the legend of the miraculous recovery of the oldest manuscript of the Digest (now in the Laurentian Library in Florence) after the capture of Amalfi by the Pisans in 1135. And still another was the tale that Irnerius single-handedly revived the teaching of Roman law at the University of Pisa about the same time by lecturing on this manuscript. The first two of these are pure fiction, the third something of an exaggeration, although the debate about Irnerius's significance goes on. In any case Irnerius was only one of a number of "masters of liberal arts" who included legal materials in their *lectiones;* and Bologna was not the first, but only the most important, center of civilian studies.[6] Blurred memories of classical law were preserved also at Ravenna (through Justinian's old exarchate), at Rome (through the papacy), and at Pavia (through the teaching of Lombard law). In the eleventh century there were various references to "doctors of law," for instance, in the compilation known as *Exceptiones Petri,* which drew upon Justinian's collection and celebrated the study of "the reason of natural and civil law."

It was nevertheless through Irnerius's teaching of the Digest (at least the first part, the "old Digest") that the lowly notarial art of the *dictamen,* medieval residue of ancient rhetoric, was elevated to the level of legal science and that the fundamental enterprise of obtaining "access to the authors" was inaugurated. The work was continued by Irnerius's pupils, especially the famous "four doctors," who were memorialized in a famous medieval verse:

> Bulgarus has the golden mouth,
> Martin in lore ranks high,
> Hugo the very spirit of laws [mens legum],
> And lastly Jacob, who am I.[7]

The intellectual elite represented by these *doctores legum* was involved with the life active as well as contemplative. They all served, variously, the municipal courts, papacy, and empire, the last most notably at the Diet of Roncaglia, which was attended by all of the "four doctors" and which produced one of the founding charters of the University of Bologna as well as a classic defense of civil law against its canonist rival. Frederick Barbarossa's constitution *Habita* of 1559 first bestowed upon these "doctors" the right of interpretation, of finding the true "spirit of laws" (*mens legum*), thus transforming "interpretation" from a treasonable offense into one of the major rubrics of medieval jurisprudence.[8]

The headquarters and intellectual arsenal of the jurists remained the university, which (that of Bologna in particular) reflected an immense range of divisions, cultural as well as professional and doctrinal, that affected the development of legal and social thought. "Ultramontanes" versus "citramontanes," subdivided into particular "nations"; "artists" versus "scientists," that is, the rivalries between the faculties of the arts, of law, theology, and medicine; "ancients" versus "moderns" expressed in various sorts of generational conflict; and of course "legists" versus "canonists" (Gratian himself being a contemporary and to some extent a pupil of the Irnerian school)—these are only a few of the patterns that set the terms for debate and shaped the thinking of the juridical community. Through various "migrations" (from Bologna to Padua, Vicenza, and elsewhere) and international movements of graduates of the Irnerian school (Placentinus to Montpellier, for example, and Vacarius to Oxford), this community became part of an international monopoly, divided by doctrinal and professional interests but linked by common allegiance to legal science and to a classical ancestry. The work of these pioneers, including a mass of (mostly unpublished) pre-Irnerian glosses, prompted another poetic outburst describing how, in the parade of thirteenth century learning,

> Civil law rode richly
> And canon law proudly
> Ahead of all the other arts.[9]

Soon civil law would claim precedence not only over medicine but eventually over philosophy and even over the "queen of sciences" herself, theology.

There was an ideological as well as an intellectual basis for the reemergence of the legal profession. This was the demand for a literate and politically expert class of civil servants, both ecclesiastical and imperial. This demand was intensified by political conflict between the reformed papacy of Gregory VII and the renovated empire of the Hohenstaufen, not to speak of the political, social, and economic needs of the self-governing communes of Italy, needs which led Arnold of Brescia, attacking the Gregorian papacy, to call for a revival of "the good customs and ancient laws of Rome."[10] In general, medieval emperors needed advocates, advisors, and apologists as well as soldiers and taxpayers, especially in the face of the political competition of the imperial papacy soon to be consolidated by Innocent III. As the papacy had modeled itself on the ancient empire, so the medieval "Holy Empire" followed the example of the papal monarchy—the emperor Frederick II learning his political lessons from his guardian, Pope Innocent III—and in this expropriation of the political and legislative resources of Roman law the national monarchies and city-republics soon followed suit.

The result was the creation of a new secular intelligentsia, graduates of the universities sponsored by pope, emperor, and kings, including not only civilians, or "legists," but also "canonists," who represented a post-theological movement within the church, and eventually in its leadership. Although civil and canon lawyers were ideological rivals, in a longer perspective they seem part of what one eighteenth-century scholar, on the analogy of the *respublica litterarum,* called the "republic of jurisconsults."[11] The greatest of medieval jurists often took their degrees *utriusque* and served either client—or both. Together they formed a sort of scientific elite—a "community of interpretation," Karl O. Apel has called it—which, perhaps more than the political philosophers of the Aristotelian school, formulated and disseminated the main doctrines of modern (or, as Otto Gierke, mindful of intervening Christian interpretations, preferred to say, "antique-modern") social thought.[12]

Civil Science

"Civil science" (*civilis, legalis, legitima scientia*), or even "civil wisdom" (*civilis sapientia,* in the words of the Accursian Gloss), was the name bestowed by medieval jurists on their new, but also very old, discipline.[13] From our perspective civil science, which may be seen as the infancy of modern European social thought, is divided conventionally into three phases. The first was that of the glossators, from Irnerius (ca. 1100–30) down to the authoritative *Glossa Ordinaria* of Accursius (ca. 1265), which assembled much of the scattered apparatus (some ninety-six thousand glosses) of the previous century and a half. The second was the age of the commentators, or post-glossators, extending from the late thirteenth century not only to the end of the medieval period but even into the nineteenth century, when the "pandectist" tradition (*usus modernus Pandectarum*) was still active. The third was the humanist school of jurisprudence arising in the sixteenth century and still continuing today in the work of certain "juristic classicists" (as Fritz Schulz has called them)[14] who have tried to undo those editorial mutilations deplored by humanists as "Tribonian's crimes" and to restore the pure conceptions of Roman legal science.

In the broadest view, these stages are somewhat arbitrary not only because other divisions cut deeper but also because the glossators, who carried out the ground-breaking work of recovery, shared basic aims with the succeeding schools—with the humanists the purpose of establishing the literal and "historical" meaning of ancient texts, and with the commentators that of adapting this meaning to contemporary conditions and justifying it in rational terms. In any case, they all belonged to a continuing intellectual and professional tradition which has given new life to ancient jurisprudence as well as a major impetus to modern thinking about society and its problems. As the search for the true Aristotle has been in many

ways the starting point for the history of natural philosophy, so the search
for the "true philosophy" of Roman law has furnished an essential base
and motive for the elaboration of social thought—Nomos in modern dress.

The forms of doctrinal activity within the revived legal science of the
twelfth century may seem rigid and artificial because of their latter-day
academic descendants. This science was based on a textual fetishism,
although it did involve the discussion of difficulties and contradictions
whose existence had been denied by Justinian.[15] Extracted from the text,
too, were rules of law (*brocarda*) and various questions, which all went
into the making of the "gloss," and of glosses thereon—"Glosses on glosses
of glosses"—and of the more elaborate pedagogical apparatus underlying
the main genres of civil science. The medieval glossators lived indeed in a
"logocentric" world, mastered by the texts they read.

Yet even though the central and originating experience was the "lecture,"
the feeling of excitement at the vicarious contact with Roman experience
must have been extraordinary at the time—for some scholars, perhaps, as
provocative and mind-expanding as, if somewhat less subversive than,
reading Aristotle and the *Libri Naturales,* which came under ecclesiastical
censorship in the thirteenth century. Juristic scholasticism provided the
framework for the secular study of human behavior, society, and political
constructions. Since the final goal, professionally as well as pedagogically
speaking, was the successful "disputation," it is not surprising that this
framework also produced academic factions, those endless "isms" applied
by disciples to the doctrines of their masters—"Bartolism" being the most
durable analogue to "Scotism" or "Thomism" among the philosophers.

If their first efforts were directed to textual exegesis, the progeny of
Irnerius soon, in classical fashion, split into parties over problems of interpretation—"our doctors" (*nostri doctores*) following Bulgarus and uphold-
ing the *rigor iuris,* and the "Gosians," named after Martinus Gosia, inclining to more liberal interpretation and even to "canonist equity." In the
effort to extract modern "utility" from ancient texts these pioneers busied
themselves with various "disputed questions" (*quaestiones disputatae*)
involving not only legal science but also moral philosophy, of which law
was still regarded as a part. If justice was giving everyone always his due,
how, for example (according to the famous distributive theory of Cicero),
could there ever be a truly just man? And of course there were more
practical questions of procedure, ignorance of law, and particular "cases"
about dowries, contracts, "interest," and other current social issues.

The conceptual level of these scholars is suggested by a fascinating dialogue, "Questions concerning the subtleties of law" (*Quaestiones de iuris
subtilitatibus,* perhaps by Placentinus, though formerly attributed to Irnerius), in which the "interpreter" instructs the "auditor" before an allegorical
assembly of Justitia and her attendant virtues (Religio, Pietas, Gratia, Vin-

dicatio, Observatio, and Veritas), together with Aequitas and Ratio, to whom Justice appeals on a particularly difficult problem. Can contemporary German emperors make changes in the Roman canon? Ratio (Reason) answers no, on the grounds that these "transalpine" kings lack an understanding of Roman law.[16] Nevertheless, this doctrinal drama is a "Gosian" work and fully defends the liberal—the rational, equitable, and moral—approach to interpretation.

But behind these hermeneutical divergences, professional aims were fairly constant. What the study of the Digest, Code, and Institutes demanded was a reevaluation of the larger questions of jurisprudence, beginning with the classical notion of Dike. Placentinus was aware of Plato's treatment but preferred Justinian's definition of justice as a quality of will—not unstable human will, of course, but rather the "perpetual and constant" divine variety celebrated by Ulpian. Above Justice, for most glossators, stood Equity, which was sometimes identified with God Himself, or at least with the source of justice and order, and which the judge (who determined the *ius*) or the legislator (who determined *lex*) was bound to seek, though ultimately both had to be content with a human approximation thereof—such being the implication of the "prudence" in *jurisprudentia*. The idea that truth was to be found not in rational argument but in judgments or even "in the Gloss" (*res judicata pro veritate accipitur; veritas est in Glossis*) was a common presumption among doctors of law.[17] And yet it was forbidden for judges to "change their mind," which is to say, to change the meaning (*mens*) of the law. These commonplaces suggest what Justice Holmes would call an "inarticulate major premise" of civil science: that the truth of law was accessible only through academic or judicial interpretation controlled by the licensed experts according to inherited forms of procedure.

This also applied to the idea of custom, though about this anomalous category—fact as well as law—"the doctors disagreed." A famous summary of the central issue, that is, the relationship between custom (*consuetudo*) and law (*ius*), appears in an anonymous collection of the early thirteenth century entitled *Dissensiones dominorum,* in which the contradictions in the classical and post-classical texts are exposed and elaborated: "Some say that no custom, whether special or general, contrary to law abrogates or derogates from written law, arguing on the basis of Digest XLVII. 12. 3. 5, and they hold this mainly because today it is only for the prince to enact law and so it is only for him to interpret law. They say that the written law abrogates a contrary custom, and so where written law exists custom is annulled . . . But others say that a custom that can be confirmed by express consent should be observed, for custom is nothing else than a tacit agreement, according to Digest I. 3. 35. But others distinguish between a special custom and a general custom contrary to law, so that if a custom is general and observed by all the people of an empire without distinction, it abrogates written law . . . But if the custom is special, as pertaining to a municipality or city, they distinguish whether it is approved by common consent, as a custom confirmed by a contested judgment . . . Others say that if a law [*lex*] be approved by custom, then it cannot prevail over custom . . . Others say that a good but not a bad custom prevails over a law. Others say that if a people knowingly follows a usage against law, it annuls the law, and if unknowingly, it does not, because it is preferable to believe that they erred."[18] "Some say . . . others say" (*Quidam dicunt . . . alii dicunt*), and so on, and the question is never resolved; but there is no disagreement about who is doing the saying, and they are the "doctors."

In certain ways the revival of legal science in the twelfth century seems to recapitulate the pre-Ciceronian "scientific revolution," especially in the exploitation of the conceptual devices of dialectic and rhetoric. This was related to the central problem of the twelfth-century revival, namely, translation from the Greek—though Aristotelian categories, causes, and predicaments were known through Boethius, while civil law was itself permeated with Greek terms and ideas, some of them undecipherable for centuries. The early doctors of law sought out means of conceptualizing the vast materials they were mining from the corrupt manuscript tradition of Roman law, most especially through classification (genus and species), causation (the fourfold Aristotelian scheme), and the distinction between nature and accident.[19] And then there was what a recent historian has called the "eternal return" of the celebrated Gaian triad (persons, things, actions), which provided the framework for the elaborate theory and practice of interpretation worked out by Roman jurists, also with the help of Greek ideas.[20]

In the extension of this science the old contention between Physis and Nomos once again made its appearance. Gaius's old idea of "natural reason" was highly ambiguous. Did it imply instinct or pure rationality—primary or "second" nature? According to Azo, natural law could be understood in several ways: as what is common to all animals (Ulpian's formula), as the common law of mankind only (the *ius gentium*), as the law of Moses (*ius naturale decalogi*), as the epitome of equity (*aequissimum*), or even, in a sense, as civil law.[21] Many enthusiasts for the contemporary (and also the newly revived) philosophy of Aristotle, leaned toward Nature in their arguments and judgments; yet it was the inescapable condition of their science, drawn from centuries of Roman experience, that they were constrained normally to resort to convention, in however rationalized a form.

Thus, in any case, was resurrected the old division between a "first" and a "second" nature; and the poles of interpretation were fixed: what is made by God, natural law, was "the condition of created things" (*conditio rebus creatis*); and what is made by man, the "law of nations," was the product of human labor (*industria humana*). According to the thirteenth-century

Summa Parisiensis, "natural law had its origin in first nature [*ex prima natura*] in the first creation of man, and afterwards was given and restored in the Gospel," so that, in general, law was "divided into natural law and customs" (*ius divitur in jus naturale et mores*).[22] And this left a major dilemma, never resolved, at least by jurists, as to whether human law (especially the *ius gentium*) was "according to nature" or "against nature."

The new form of this old division was reflected clearly in interpretations of the first two members of the Gaian trinity (accepted with little questioning by medieval jurists), that is to say, "persons" and "things." About personal liberty there was little disagreement: it was "natural," as was "equality," and both slavery and class division were creations of (sinful) man, as indeed was inequality between the sexes. The difficulties came basically from the question of property, the consequence of the intrusion of human will into the world of "reality," first natural and then social; and in a sense this controversy has never ceased (the rise of "socialism" and revolutionary movements notwithstanding). Unlike most canonists, legists tended to regard property (*dominium*) as a part of natural law, or at least a part of nature; and the same could be said for many contractual obligations.[23] The distinction between nature and convention can be seen clearly in the Roman law of possession, which could be either "natural" or "civil." In the first case possession was the result of simple and physical "prehension" or "detention," in the second of legal justification (*justa causa*), and therefore equivalent—to ancient if not modern jurists—to full property. Thus *possessio* (and the law thereof) virtually marks the boundary line between the states of nature and society, alien as this might be to the conventions of feudalism (and the law of "seizin").

Much the same could be said for the category of "action," which generated no less controversy, touching as it did upon deviant and proscribed (criminal) action as well as social action. It touched, too, on what is perhaps the most "conventional" of all legal topics, the "varieties of actions," in the phrase of Placentinus (that is, legal procedure), which constitute the very roots of law in a concrete sense. Whether in a private or a public sense, actions, or "acts," were of course accommodated to literate culture and, in fact, came to designate primarily written and "enacted" statements or records of human initiative.

In general what civil science brought to European thought was a means of grasping and controlling the new realities of medieval society. It offered the classical language of social analysis, of economic interaction, and of political action—in short, the language of power. The expanding vocabulary and logic of social thought, derived from legal sources and paralleling and reinforcing those of ancient philosophy, reflected a world of experience and human predicaments across an expanding horizon of social and political action.

The terminology and conventions of civil law made possible the designation and discussion of structures and phenomena hardly expressible in a society ruled by local custom and enchanted by religious metaphor. The pre-Accursian glosses started the exegesis of the rich vocabulary of civil law, beginning with the Institutes and moving on to the labyrinth of the Digest, trying to make sense of ancient ideas of "liberty" and "property" and to apply the threefold "division of the law" to the world of "today" (*hodie*).[24] Words, and so manipulable concepts, were found for complex social roles (identified by such terms as *conditio, status,* and *dignitas*), for groupings (*civitas, universitas, corpus, societas, ordo, collegium*), for relations (*contractus, obligatio, conjuratio*), and especially for expressions of will and power (*jurisdictio, dominium, administratio, judicatio,* and *legislatio,* not to speak of political terms such as *potestas, imperium,* and *majestas*); and this terminlogy permeated the upsurge of legislation made possible and promoted by Romanist lines of argument.[25] Central to all these concepts, of course, was the theory of law, including the practice of "interpretation," which transformed law into "civil science"—and even, according to traditional juristic hyperbole, into "civil wisdom."

Canonic Science

The classic compendium of Christian law was the Decretum of Gratian; and as Justinian's publications established the canon of "civil science," so this twelfth-century collection was the sacred vehicle of "canonic science" (*scientia canonica*).[26] As the first discipline had emerged out of rhetoric from the eleventh century, so the second was created largely out of theological sources. A simple "magister" like his contemporary, Irnerius, the monk Gratian laid the foundations of the new science by applying to ecclesiastical materials the dialectical method developed by teachers such as Abelard. In this effort Gratian's aim was almost as authoritarian as that of the editors of the Digest: both it and the Decretum drew upon centuries of experience and thought; both invoked divine authority, a deeply revered ancestry, and a holy mission; both underlay a powerful professional monopoly; and both assumed an absolute sovereign, a *rex-sacerdos* who guaranteed and applied the assembled law, and of course added to it. Both traditions were also subject to similar methods of interpretation (the *Glossa Ordinaria* of Johannes Teutonicus was the counterpart of the great compilation of Accursius), passed through congruent stages of scholarship, and had to contend with a "new" as well as an "old" law and eventually with humanistic revisionists.

In assembling the "old law" the antiquarian labors of Gratian and his colleagues represented a process (to be sure, a very legalistic process) of myth-making—in the sense certainly that myth operates as an "interpretation of mystery."[27] The original, indeed originating, myth was that of the trinity, formulated authoritatively in the first ecumenical council of Nicaea in 325 under the auspices of an emperor recently, but imperfectly, converted from paganism. The creed based on this conception represented a kind of loyalty oath to the earthly church as well as human testimony to its central mystery. Unlike the old secular triad of Gaius, the Christian threesome linked human society not to nature but rather to supernature: humanity (the Son) being joined to divinity (the Father), with the link itself preserved in time (through the Holy Spirit). In this Trinity we can see the grounds for all of the incorrigible dualities running through the history of Christian doctrine—not only nature and supernature (and nature and grace), but also history and metahistory, the city of man and the city of God, the mystical body of Christ and the social body of believers, and especially the Gelasian principle of the "two swords." Christianity was one society, in short, but "two orders." In such terms Master Gratian presented a comprehensive theory of law and the church as a juridical community, thus giving scholarly endorsement to the human unfolding of the Ecclesia, of "Christian society" (*societas christiana*), which progressed from natural through civil to divine law out of the mystical commission bestowed by God through his Son.[28] Gratian endorsed, too, the human roots of ecclesiastical institutions, including not only the synagogue and Jewish law, which "prefigured" the church, but also the Roman offices of flamen and pontifex, which anticipated the priesthood.

The principal junctures between humanity and divinity were located, of course, in the system of sacraments, which furnished much of the religious substance of canon law. Several of the conventional sacraments had obvious precedents in oriental religions—purification by water, eating the god's flesh, and other ritualisms—but in Christian society they came to serve a quasi-legal as well as a spiritual function. The eucharist, baptism, confirmation, and last rites all signified membership in the Christian community; marriage brought the family into this society; ordination established the basic social distinction and foundation of the ecclesiastical hierarchy; and penance—an "amphibious" concept involving sin as well as remorse and repentance—provided the basis not only for the regulation of individual conscience but also for the profits of ecclesiastical government. Reflected in the sacramental system as well as in canonist tradition was an ordered society possessing a legislating head and participating members who owed allegiance, were required to maintain sacramental communication with one another, and were subject, as the penalty for nonconformity, to "excommunication."[29] Out of these mundane concerns grew also regulations of morality and communal behavior under such rubrics as magic, sorcery, blasphemy, theft, drunkenness, gluttony, perjury, murder, incest, and rape; and finally, through assumed jurisdiction over sin (*ratione peccati*), ecclesiastical government became involved in secular politics.[30] Such in general terms was the rationale for the transformation of a transcendent religion into an immanent ecclesiology, of Logos into Nomos. From this transformation arose the question whether the *sacerdotium* was an expression of social conscience or of worldly corruption—the two being perhaps inseparable in the human condition.

In contrast to this "old law," the "new law" of the church was the product mostly of papal legislation and a continuing wave of commentaries on the entire tradition. Corresponding to Justinian's "novels" and the feudist appendage to the civil law were the "extravagant" decretals added to the Decretum by certain thirteenth- and fourteenth-century popes, while the interpretive commentaries were designated "decretist" and "decretalist" respectively. Like secular Roman law, too, canon law had been given increasingly systematic form, from Gratian's pioneering attempt to achieve dialectical "concord," through the "first compilation" made by the Bolognese professor Bernard of Pavia at the end of the twelfth century, down finally to the completed version of the Corpus Iuris Canonici published in 1317.[31] This legal scholarship was given official reinforcement through various authoritarian declarations, including those of that "papal Justinian," Innocent III, and later Honorius III and Boniface VIII, who likewise modeled their legislative declarations on the famous prefatory edicts of Justinian. Drawing on Roman precedent and experience, canonic science itself provided a model for secular systems of jurisprudence.

In the canonist tradition the old dialectic of Physis and Nomos recurred: Physis was virtually assimilated to the Logos—and, for many legal purposes, natural law to divine law. "Nature is God" (*Natura id est Deus*) is one formula, though, to be sure, an essential distinction is preserved between the Creator (*natura naturans*) and his creation (*natura naturata*)— in effect between Logos and Physis.[32] In a sense, canon law represented a reversion to the old Roman *fas* (a term indeed employed by Gratian), except that it benefited from the entire range of Roman experience and jurisprudence and was enhanced by association with transcendent religious belief and theological mystery. Canon law also suggested a higher standard of reason than civil law, or at least a higher standard of morality—for example, in the radical presumption that neither property nor associated human inequalities, including those between the sexes, should be counted as part of natural law. As a sort of resacramentalized natural law, canon law continued to be contrasted to laws that were merely human and "positive" (often in a pejorative sense), as in the attack of Peter the Chanter on the "instability of positive law," joined, not surprisingly, to a parallel assault on lawyers.[33] Yet in their aspirations to transcend human law, the spokesmen for civil and for canonic science were in general agreement; for like Justinian the successors of St. Peter claimed the right, in effect, to raise

Nomos to the level of Physis—the human to the divine—through the transforming medium of a creating "will" based on divine right.

Like civil law, however, canon law in much of its substance could not be identified with universal reason, still less with divine perfection or biblical revelation. This, of course, is where human tradition—Nomos in its temporal aspect—came in. "The old and ancient canons ought to be observed," went one canonist formula; and according to another, "It is not permitted to stray from approved institutions." Custom also played an important role; in canonist as in civilian terms it could be taken "for law" (*pro lege*) and was accepted, in the famous civilian formula, as "the best interpreter of law."[34] Increasingly, too, canon law was guided by secular standards of "necessity" and "utility" and was shaped by the confusing and depressing realities of late medieval society—and by a variety of secular challenges.

The New Ius Gentium

The twelfth-century revival of legal science had a crucial impact on the divergent national traditions emerging from the prehistorical world of oral tradition and customary law. In legal terms this world defined the modern *ius gentium* and once again had to be accommodated by Roman jurisprudence—thereby once again fulfilling the ancient axiom making Rome the "common fatherland" (*Roma communis patria*).[35] Of course Rome was no longer coterminous with civilization. It became common for jurists, especially "ultramontane" jurists, to point out that no emperor, not even Justinian, had been truly "lord of the world" (*dominus mundi,* a formula from the Code), nor, consequently, had his law been truly universal; and in any case every nation, according to Gaius, had its own law (*ius proprium*). It was in this connection that European monarchs could each claim to be "emperor in his kingdom" (*rex imperator in regno suo*). In France this was standard royalist doctrine, in Spain it was written into the *Siete Partidas* (*Quanto en lo temporale, bien asi como el emperador en su imperio*), and in England it was acceptable enough to be invoked by Thomas Cromwell as England was divorcing itself from Rome in the wake of Henry VIII's "great matter."[36] One of the implications of this doctrine was that Roman law might be utilized (whether or not it had been formally "received") as *ius commune* in matters of private law.

Yet even for descendants of the "barbarians," Roman civil law had a special claim to rationality: it was not only *lex scripta* but also, according to the civilian formula, *ratio scripta*. All national traditions of customary law applied to Roman legal science for terminology, procedures, methods of proof, standards of comparison, and social ideals, and did so even as they attacked the modern, "holy" Roman Empire. They did this through ingenuity and by application of the principles of "analogy" and "extensive interpretation."[37] The borrowings are apparent not only in the vast accumulation of Latinate interpretations of vernacular legal texts but also in various efforts, beginning in the late medieval period, toward national uniformity and eventually codification.

For European civilians the underlying question from the time of Irnerius was that of "reception," first on an informal and judicial and later on a formal, legislative, and political level. Although the full-fledged (capital R) "Reception" occurred in the Holy Roman Empire only in 1495, there were more surreptitious, utilitarian, and piecemeal importations of Roman material—"by reception but not by subjection," in the words of one French jurist, wary of recognizing imperial priority. The most comprehensive survey of the *fortuna* of civil law in Europe was the book of the English civilian Arthur Duck, *The Authority and Use of Civil Law among the Dominions of the Christian Princes* (1656), which traced the posthumous career of the *ius civile* in Italy, Naples and Sicily, France, Portugal, England, Ireland, Scotland, Poland, Hungary, Denmark, Sweden, and Bohemia.[38] Although the rulers of these territories rejected imperial supremacy, they were happy, through their lawyers, to exploit the riches of the Romano-Byzantine legacy and to model their own legal position on that of the German Imperator.

Romanization took many forms, and in formal, if not substantial, terms it is evident even for that *locus classicus* of feudal law, the northern Italian *Book of Fiefs* (*Libri* or *Consuetudines Feudorum*). Because of imperial sanction this work was represented and published as the "tenth collection" (*decima collatio*) of "Roman law," succeeding the legislation of Justinian and of course subject to the same sort of controlled "interpretation." The authoritative edition was made by Azo's pupil Jacopo Ardizone and the major gloss by Jacopo Columbi, and it was commented on by jurists of all persuasions, not to speak of literary critics like Petrarch. The assumption— another conscious legal myth—of its authentically "Roman" character was reinforced by the further speculative argument, typical of medieval jurisprudence, that the fief was derived etymologically, hence logically and institutionally, from the loyalty or "faith" which was essential to the agreement (*feudum a fidelitate dicitur vel a fide* was the formula which, despite its linguistic flaw, came to possess the force of law). Various Roman legalisms reinforced this line of argument and effort of legitimation. According to the glossators, for example, the vassal had only "natural possession" of the fief; the lord alone had "civil possession." Irnerius and his followers also assimilated the feudal relationship to the Roman contract (*pactum*), for the *feudum* was indeed a juridical "thing" granted in return for services.[39] Later on, more antiquarian-minded jurists occasionally assigned the "origins" of the fief to the old Roman clientele, which reflected a relationship analogous to that of lord and vassal. There were always objections, by a minority of jurists as well as philologists and historians, to such vulgar or precious Romanizing; but legally the principle of Roman origins survived as long as "feudal law" itself—and historically has persisted down to the present.

Although such forced Romanist interpretations reflected another mythical element in the legal tradition, they were accompanied by serious attempts to give rational form to the *ius feudale*. William Durandus, for example, tried in his *Speculum* to establish a feudal typology, distinguishing six, or perhaps ten, "species" of fiefs, with reference to canonist as well as civilian sources; and he admitted further that the institution of homage had been introduced through custom rather than written (that is, civil) law. Other jurists tried to assimilate feudal law (as they did civil law) to the four Aristotelian causes: the efficient cause being the legislator; the material cause (*materia* being the technical legal term for sources) the *Book of Fiefs*; the formal cause the distribution of the work into topics; and the final cause the settlement of disputes and, ultimately, the achieving of justice. As a result of such juridical ratiocination feudal law was lauded by one commentator as a "part of philosophy," which was to say moral philosophy, and even a kind of wisdom (*legalis sapientia*).[40] Still later, feudal law, like its canonist and civilian cousins, would undergo a further process of scientific rationalization and "methodizing." This is another reason for suggesting, notwithstanding the objections of some medievalists, that long before the time of Montesquieu, European jurists, through rational and comparative interpretation, had formulated a kind of *féodalité avant la lettre*.

A still more ambitious and official product of Italian legal science in the Middle Ages was the so-called *Liber Augustalis,* or "Constitutions of Melfi," promulgated by Emperor Frederick II for the Kingdom of Sicily in 1231.[41] While the "material" of this collection reflected the chaotic condition of thirteenth century Sicilian society, the form was an expression of absolute imperial will which, in its heaven- and earth-storming goals, hearkened back self-consciously to Justinian and Augustus. As God made man in His own image (Frederick's proem quoted from the Psalms), so He set the emperor above all men—"elevated [him] beyond hope of man to the pinnacle of the Roman Empire"—through his godlike power to be "lord of the world." Peace and justice (*pax et justitia*) are the themes dominating this, the first great monument of medieval jurisprudence. It was based on a highly idealistic vision of a well-ordered society, controlled from the center and organized according to the ideas derived from ancient, and in some cases alien (Islamic), legal traditions. Besides the legal status of women, adultery, prostitution, medical malpractice, air pollution, gambling, and watering wine, the code treated in fine detail violent crime and the police force to control it. If not quite the "birth certificate of modern bureaucracy" that Jacob Burckhardt judged it to be, the *Liber Augustalis* was an unprecedented attempt to impose, upon a confusion of medieval customs, the authoritarian ideals and the *religio licita* of ancient Rome.[42]

The German part of Frederick's imperial inheritance fared much worse: as a result of imperial neglect German law proceeded for the most part in its old customary channels, much in the way that English common law did, except for the lack of a central government and court system. Imperial legal science continued to be centered in the Italian universities. The influence of Roman law was apparent in the German "mirrors"—the *Deutschenspiegel* and *Schwabenspiegel* in particular, and the glosses of the *Sachsenspiegel*—but the full force of the Roman tradition had to await the formal "Reception" of Roman law in 1495, and even then it was restricted mainly to imperial courts. The emergence of Roman tradition as a basis of a modern common law, referred to by German jurists as the *usus modernus Pandectarum*, was in general a considerably later development.[43]

The Spanish legal tradition seems to have maintained a more direct contact with Roman sources, at least in part because of the preservation of Visigothic laws via the *Fuero Juzgo* and *Fuero Real*, although these also borrowed materials from local *fueros* formed from particular customs. According to Duck, Roman law was "received by consent" (*receptum est consensu; ex earum justitia et ratione receptas*).[44] This was obvious in that greatest of Spanish legal monuments, the *Siete Partidas* of Alfonso el Sabio of Castile, assembled in the mid-thirteenth century. Gathered together here was material not only on the principal parts of private law (property and possession, obligations, marriage, and wills) and criminal law but also on religious questions and especially the theory of law, custom, and interpretation. The law was intended for the whole "people," including all three classes, "upper, middle and lower"; but in discussing the primary rubric of "personality," or the "condition of man" (*status hominum*), more distinctions were added to those of civil law in order to accommodate clergy, infidels, and the feudal nobility. Ideally, law itself was based on nature, society only on a vaguely similar quality called "natural feeling," for instance, in the "natural obligation" to love and to obey not only one's parents but also one's lord. In this way even the complex and artificial arrangements of feudal society could in a sense be naturalized—or, through violation of faith, denaturalized.

In France civil law, or the oral transmission thereof, had been continuously accepted as "common law" in certain provinces of the south (*pays du droit écrit*) corresponding roughly to the territory of former Roman occupation; and so the ground was well prepared for the massive, and generally welcome, invasion of Romanism in the late twelfth century. The revival of legal science was promoted most obviously through the universities, beginning in Montpellier, where the glossator Placentinus came to teach from 1160, and through the translations of Justinian's law available to legal practitioners beginning at least in the second quarter of the thirteenth century.[45] The first led to an increasingly philosophical treatment of Roman texts; the second led to vernacular borrowings and comparative studies, such as Pierre de Fontaines' *Advice to a Friend* (*Conseil à un ami*), and the *Book of Justice and Pleading* (*Livre de jostice et de plet*), apparently from the school of Orleans, which became a leading center of legal studies after the prohibition of 1219 on the teaching of Roman (though not canon) law in Paris. In French academic jurisprudence there were notable convergences between the study of the new legal science and the equally new natural philosophy of Aristotle; but, professionally, philosophy and jurisprudence (the latter reviving its claims to be "true philosophy") went their separate ways—forming institutional embodiments, in a sense, of Physis and Nomos.

From this time on, civil science in France followed a two-track course: on the one hand, local customs "universalized" in the form of *coutumiers* with the help of Roman concepts and methods, and on the other hand, civil law in the university faculties interpreted, reciprocally, in the context of and for the benefit of French social (as well as political) institutions and thought. A good example of the first is the pioneering commentary on the custom of Beauvaisis by Philippe de Beaumanoir, who contributed richly to the conceptualization of custom and its elevation to the level of written law.[46] An example of the second is Jacques de Révigny, who taught at the University of Toulouse in the last quarter of the thirteenth century, and who was reputedly the first to introduce the new dialectical method of scholasticism into legal interpretation, an approach soon to be taken over by Italian jurists. He also took the lead in adapting Roman law to the needs and standards of the French monarchy, shifting significantly the notion of "common fatherland" from Rome to the French crown (traced back to Charlemagne and further), and to this extent contributed to the division of civil science along national lines.[47]

English law participated marginally in the twelfth-century revival of jurisprudence, beginning with the teaching of Master Vacarius, who went to Oxford from the school of Bologna, and the work of Henry de Bracton, who relied extensively on Azo's exegesis of Justinian's Institutes. Early English jurists such as Bracton and "Glanvil" found in Roman and canon law a technical language, methods of argumentation, rules of procedure, and particular maxims with which to give shape to English customs. In his introductory *De legibus* Bracton offered definitions according to Romanist convention and a "summary" of *consilia* and *responsa*. For him law (*ius* or *lex*) was "the general agreement of the commonwealth" (*commune praeceptum virorum consultum prudentium*) and, in contrast to the divine nature of justice, a product of human will, while jurisprudence was identified with wisdom, according to the famous formula of Ulpian ("the knowledge of things divine and human"). Bracton also retained Gaius's equally famous formula that "all law pertains to persons, things, or actions" and cited him for conventional views of the *ius naturale* and *ius gentium*.[48] Yet all of this was intended only to serve the needs of English "civil law," which was essentially customary and unwritten in character, or provenance; and in fact Romanist influence never supplanted national traditions despite numerous convergences over the centuries. English "common law" for the most part cut its own channels and must be charted independently of, in some ways in contrast to, Continental civil science.

European civil science took a worldly, and world-spanning, view of its projects. Yet it also had to confront and to cope, to deal, and eventually to live with alien forms of social life, especially in the case of Saracens and Jews, as Alberico de Rosate and other jurists acknowledged. Even in its Christian incarnation, the Roman *ius gentium*, with its premise that every social group had the right to make its own laws, made possible such accommodations; and indeed canon lawyers contributed significantly to the notion that even infidels had some rights to liberty and property.[49] Yet the conventional interest in tracing and celebrating the humanitarian impulses of modern international law should not let us forget the narrow conceptions of "humanity" informing European jurisprudence. By civil law Jews could not hold office or be physicians or magistrates, and such anti-Semitic conventions were still common in the sixteenth century, as suggested by the work of such distinguished legal scholars as Giason del Maino and Ulrich Zasius. Such xenophobia has often been a companion of the "local knowledge" demanded, or invited, by conventional jurisprudence and by the political authorities it served—or resisted.

The legacy of ancient legal science was ambiguous, manifold, multiform; and it is certainly an oversimplification to identify it exclusively with notions of sovereignty and state-building. Implicit in both civil and canonic science were also ideas of reform, representation, resistance, and other qualifications of the exercise of imperial will. Yet it should be added that the Romano-Byzantine collections of the *ius civile* did offer an extraordinary paradigm—indeed the locus classicus—of legislative sovereignty, and that the decretist view of the *ius canonicum* reinforced this political model with analogous conceptions of papal monarchy (including claims of *principatus* and actions proceeding *de motu proprio*).[50] It is hardly surprising that monarchs and their ideological champions drew on legal science to enhance their authority and political initiative, in the private as well as public sphere, as Justinian so brazenly had done.

For political thought it has usually seemed sufficient to trace the fortunes of ideas of sovereignty, structure of government, problems of church and state, forms of resistance, and the like. For social thought it is essential to inquire as well into patterns of private life, questions of "local knowledge," and inarticulate assumptions of linguistic (and therefore social) relationships. In these terms the force of custom and its legal offspring, including social analysis, geographical and historical discrimination, and judicial interpretation in general, has to be considered. On this level of inquiry we can see emerging what is perhaps the essential dialectic of modern social thought, which is the alternation between submission to the forces of history and efforts to master and direct these forces—between law as a product and concomitant of social behavior and the "tacit consent" of the People, and law as a form of imperial will and social planning. These rival views, too, are part of the legacy of medieval "civil science" and of the modern kingdom of Nomos, which took shape in the wake of the "receptions," formal and informal, of civil law.

EIGHT

Jurisprudence Italian Style

Consuetudo repraesentat mentem populi.

Bartolus, *Ad Digestum*

Posterior consuetudo tollit legem priorem.

Baldus, *Ad Digestum*

·

Mos Italicus

In the late thirteenth century European "civil science" entered a new phase, a juristic variant of "scholasticism" formed by the introduction of philosophical concepts and apparatus.[1] Though identified later with Italian jurisprudence (*mos italicus iuris docendi*), this rationalizing and modernizing method was at first developed by French jurists, especially Jacques de Révigny and his pupil Pierre de Belleperche, in the later thirteenth century. As Italians like Placentinus and Guido de Guinis had brought Bolognese legal knowledge to France, so a later generation, beginning with Cino da Pistoia, carried scholastic methods back across the Alps for the benefit of the *Citramontani,* including most notably Cino's disciple Bartolus de Sassoferrato (d. 1357) and "grand-disciple" Baldus de Ubaldis (d. 1400). The "jurisprudence Italian style" established by these men and such colleagues as Alberico de Rosate (d. 1354) and Lucas de Penna (d. 1370) reached its highest point in the fourteenth century; but the major phase extended from the time of Dante's friend and contemporary Cino da Pistoia down to the time of Erasmus's friend and contemporary Andrea Alciato, who composed a verse on the grand succession of civil scientists down to his own mentor:

> In law first place to Bartolus goes;
> Baldus in court preeminence shows;
> Third, Paolo Castro, teacher of note;
> Then, Alexander's opinions we quote,
> Followed by Giason del Maino's light,
> And others we honor, for books if not right.[2]

In the long perspective this "Bartolist" school formed a major link, conceptually and professionally, between ancient legal science and modern social thought.

The international rivalry between the "citramontanes" and "ultramontanes" had its origin in the Bolognese university structure, with its subdivision into nations. Yet Italian law students and their "barbarian" colleagues had a common, international, and unshakable commitment to civil
science, which they took to be a realization of the ancient ideal of "true
philosophy," a full-fledged "encyclopedia" or *Studium,* and indeed a world
in its own right. Was even theology, "queen of the sciences," necessary for
the law? "I answer no," Accursius had replied, "because in the law everything is contained"—even, added a later jurist, "true theology."[3] Civil
scientists agreed, too, on the central role of "natural reason" in jurisprudence and the necessity of rationality or "rationability" in construing laws.
Where they differed, and differed fundamentally, was in their conception
of legal authority. The French jurists in particular, avant garde of the
moderni, denounced the triviality and obsequiousness of the Accursian
Gloss (*glossa diabolica, glossa pessima*) and the contradictions and "chat-
ter" (*truffae, burdae*) of the glossators. Cino, though he honored his teacher
Jacques de Révigny as "master of all philosophers," deplored this irreverence, while Baldus was outraged at these ultramontane jackasses (*isti asini
ultramontani*) "who are never happy except when criticizing the Gloss."[4]

So were sown the seeds of an ideological struggle which would break
out more violently in later generations, especially in the Franco-imperial
conflict of the sixteenth century. The legal issue was perhaps best defined
by commentaries on the famous title from the Code, *Omnes populi,* which
declared that "all peoples are ruled either by civil law or by the law of
nations," likewise formulated by Roman jurists. "But what of those who
are not so ruled?" Accursius had asked. His answer—"that they are not
civilized men"—was hardly satisfactory to ultramontanes, who objected
that nowadays (*hodie*) the empire had been "translated" to Germany.[5]
Furthermore, there were many jurists, Spanish and English as well as French
and Germans, eager to point out that (contrary to the glosses on another
famous title, *Cunctos populos,* from an edict of Theodosius) the emperor
had never been "lord of the world"—whence indeed the potent ultramontane, and canonist, formula recognizing each national monarch as at least
de facto "emperor in his kingdom" and so not bound by imperial laws.[6]
In this sense civil science was created "not by reason of empire," according
to a famous formula, "but by the empire of reason" (*non ratione imperii
sed rationis imperio*).

Even Italian jurists had their doubts about Gaius's assertion that "all
people" were ruled by Roman law. Was this true for the modern world?
"I respond that not all are," wrote Baldus, "for many cities are ruled by
their own statutes." If the emperor was still technically the only source of
law (and ruled in Italy, for example, through imperial vicars), the right of
people to make their own law (*ius proprium*) could still be justified, Baldus

continued. Did not the imperial rule against a people's making "illicit statutes" imply that they could make *licit* ones? In this way Baldus, elaborating on his master Bartolus's principle that the city was in effect sovereign (*civitas sibi princeps*), built up the case for the legitimacy of institutions independent of Roman forms.[7] His conclusion, altogether consistent with civilian tradition, was that particular peoples and their governments (*populus* and *regimen*) were in fact determined not by Roman law but by a modern law of nations (*novissimum ius gentium*), which, like the old one but still more diversely, was "used by all societies."[8]

So "jurisprudence Italian style" was Romanoid rather than Romanist and derived its authority not from antiquity as such but rather from its own special reconstruction of legal principles. Beginning with the founding father, Cino—*conditor iuris*, Bartolus called him, thus honoring him as a legislator—Italian jurists created their own tradition and thereby, as always, their own myths. At the center of this mythology stood, eventually, Bartolus of Sassoferrato, who overshadowed even Papinian and whose opinions came to possess statutory force. Bartolus combined legal theory with practical experience—combined, that is, study of the Romano-Byzantine canon with treatises and opinions (*consilia*) on a wide range of contemporary social and political problems. Civil science insisted on reason, but like its canonist sibling it was a "reason" tied always to authority; and no jurist was more authoritative, academically as well as judicially, than Bartolus. Many civil scientists were convinced that the only good jurist was a Bartolist (*nemo jurista nisi bartolista*); and even Alciato, who was suspicious of his style and crude attitude toward classical texts, admitted that "without Bartolus we should have no science."[9] Needless to say, there were many critics, beginning as early as Petrarch, who mocked and denounced "Bartolism" as an Italian defilement of the pristine sources of Roman law, but professionally and methodologically it represented a "scientific" orthodoxy that in some ways prevailed into the nineteenth century.

Like its eponymous hero, Bartolus, the profession of law has also accumulated its legends, beginning with the infallibility of its authorities, proclaimed by Justinian himself, who also denied the presence of contradictions in his "new law." According to Baldus, it was positively illegal to allege an error in the law (*doctor iuris non potest pretendere iuris errorem*), although there were ways of circumventing even this rule.[10] Civil science was an imperialistic field intellectually, claiming precedence first over the arts, then over medicine, and even over theology. Its devotees not only took pride in tracing their professional and scientific pedigree back to the Roman jurisconsults but also laid claim to "nobility" because of the elevated status of their discipline (*propter magnam scientiam* was the conventional phrase)— and not only nobility, added a sixteenth-century jurist, but even "immortality," if only in the earthly sense of posthumous fame. Jurists were still, in Ulpian's phrase, "priests of the law." Yet priesthoods are always suspect, especially when they are also a social and economic elite; and hardly less than usurers and soldiers, the lawyers were the targets of the bitterest satire and denunciation, the source of a powerful counter-mythology. Not only could lawyers be "mean and mercenary," as Cicero had lamented, but they were, by instinct as well as method and motives, duplicitous and out for hire to the devil himself. Long before Luther's famous complaint it was proverbial that "a lawyer's a bad Christian."[11]

In fact the legal profession reflected, morally and perhaps socially as well, the heights and depths of the human condition in late medieval Europe. It was an international force, in effect taking over the guidance of secular institutions as canonists had done for the church. From its trivial Italian beginnings the legal profession expanded demographically as well as academically; and its primary vehicle was always that intellectual embodiment of tradition (*corpus intellectuale*) which was the university. In 1300 there were perhaps twenty European universities with some significant instruction in the law; by 1500 the number was closer to eighty.[12] Despite ideological differences within communities of students and masters, their common language and methods gave them the coherence virtually of an international intelligentsia rivaling the clergy, but possessing a secular and in some circumstances even an anticlerical character. What guaranteed the success of the profession of law was the general "triumph of the professionals" noted by John P. Dawson, which took over the distribution of justice on every level from the popular to the political, and which established a vast complex of court systems forming their own relationships and rivalries.[13]

As in antiquity, then, and in many respects in imitation of ancient language and patterns, the legal profession had a practical as well as a theoretical branch; and the two were interdependent because university training (or its equivalent in the English Inns of Court) was prerequisite to a legal career. Thus to the corporate structure of academic jurisprudence was joined the guild structure of notaries and lawyers, established on a national as well as a civic level. Of course there were many national variations; but this general outline suggests the character of the linguistic, scientific, and professional community—the European "republic of jurisconsults"—which for at least five centuries preserved "jurisprudence Italian style."

The political role of the lawyers starting in the thirteenth century is well known, and so to some extent is their social position; but it is more difficult to perceive and to assess their contributions to social thought. Until at least the eighteenth century the study of civil law represented a major phase of liberal education, and more specifically of classical learning, and from that most fundamental level acted to shape the thinking of many Europeans introduced to the elementary texts of the Institutes if not of the Digest. The significance of the lawyers in "starting the Renaissance," as Roberto Weiss put it, has long been recognized; but of course they were even more directly productive in other intellectual enterprises, not only official and polemical but also (in the context of theoretical jurisprudence) economic, sociological, anthropological, and even philosophical.[14] Jurists who served as advocates and judges as well as teachers and authors accumulated vast stores of insight and experience in litigation and disputes over personal liberty, property, succession, and many other matters of private law and criminal offenses against it. Through such social experience gained in the laboratory of the courtroom and expressed and judged in terms of civil science, the revived legal tradition—a continuation, as Max Weber saw it, of the old *ius honoratorum*—extended further the realm of Nomos explored by the Greeks and then taken over and settled by the Romans.[15] The central question continued to be how to understand, to exploit, and to apply the precedents and examples inherited from the old legal tradition.

The Interpretation of Law

The key to civil science in the Italian mode was the construction of a theory of interpretation—though this was in violation of Justinian's official ban. "We forbid all persons now living as well as those who are to come," Justinian had declared, "to write any commentaries on these laws." In the Code he went further and prescribed capital punishment (*pena falsitatis*) for unauthorized interpretation. How medieval jurists came to ignore this injunction was explained by Johann Oldendorp in his commentary on Emperor Frederick Barbarossa's constitution *Habita* of 1159. This imperial act bestowed the "double privilege" of interpreting imperial law on authorized *doctores legum* on grounds of pedagogical utility and religious propriety, that is, making ancient law intelligible to students and bringing it into line with Christian truth.[16] So, as a sixteenth-century jurist concluded, "Interpretation is a necessary part of law."[17] The rubric *defensio interpretationis* came to shelter not only the central issue of modern jurisprudence but also a new genre, which was legal hermeneutics. The primary foci for this *ars hermeneutica,* as Leibniz later called it, were the two titles, in the last book of the Digest, "On the Meaning of Words" and "On the Rules of Ancient Law," which generated commentaries upon commentaries and made fundamental, if seldom appreciated, contributions to social thought.

One of the central themes of interpretation was the age-old polarity between letter and spirit, the locus classicus for lawyers being the formula of Celsus that "laws must be understood not according to the letter but their force and effect" (*vis et potestas*).[18] For medieval jurists like Baldus, of course, there was an additional assumption that Christian faith would lead beyond the deadening letter to the life-giving spirit, and like Paul he expressly warned students against reading the Law "Jewishly" (*judaice* or *more Judaeorum*). Such lack of imagination was in violation of the spirit as well as the letter of Justinian's prohibition, as many later critics pointed out; and indeed what began as a small loophole ended up as a large gateway to judicial discretion and what one historian has called the "creative function" of professional jurists. It was an important doorway, too, for the obiter dicta which have contributed to social thought in many ways besides the normative and the speculative.

Put another way, this hermeneutical question concealed a issue crucial to jurisprudence across the centuries, which was whether the construction of laws should be strict or liberal (*restrictiva* or *extensiva*). The consensus seems to be on the side of the "more benign" as against "rigorous" judgment. "Interpretation should be not literal [*ad literam*]," wrote Baldus, "but rather meaningful [*ad sensum*], for the sense of the words should prevail."[19] One should go beyond the literal *expositio vocabuli*, then, to the "explanation of the true meaning [*ad verum intellectum*], understood according to the reason rather than the shell and exterior of the words." The principle of judicial discretion also involved the complicated question of equity, which (according to an old rule) was the basis for interpreting laws and contracts (*fundamentum interpretandi leges et pacta*). Laws were subject to change and improvement through other juridical devices, including "corrective laws" (*leges correctoriae*) and the legislative principle that "posterior laws correct prior ones." Finally, law was shaped by what Odofredus, following the lead of Azo (and Paulus before him), called the "triple force" of "custom" as "founder, interpreter, and abrogator of law" (*triplex est potestas consuetudinis: est legum conditrix, est legum interpretatrix, est legum arrogatrix*).[20]

The first important step beyond the legal fundamentalism of the glossators was taken by the French leaders of the party of the "moderns" (*moderni*), who were deeply suspicious of the Accursian Gloss and who in any case could not accept the authority of the "emperor's law" over the French monarchy. Hence they became committed to the search not merely for legislative "intention" (*mens legum*) but also for the underlying, or perhaps overarching, "reason" and justice in a particular legal text. In a sense they were the first to criticize what recent literary scholars have identified as the "intentional fallacy." "Not the intention of the legislator but the rationale of the law" (*nec ex mente sed ex ratione*) was the formula of Jacques de Révigny, and Pierre de Belleperche went still further in the direction of judicial discretion (*nec ex mente sed ex interpretatione*), which is to say, usurpation of the author's role by the critic.[21] This fashion was followed in Italy (whose relation to the emperor was also an adversarial one), beginning especially with Cino da Pistoia, who had studied with the French commentators and who continued their efforts to give what they called "interpretive extension" (*extensio interpretiva*) to ancient law, and so to modernize as well as to rationalize it. This was extended further by the use of analogy (*interpretatio analogica, extensio de similibus a similia*), and other rhetorical and dialectical devices.[22]

Jurists were fully aware of the perils of interpretation. Their judgments had always to be made, in legal jargon, *civiliter* rather than merely *rationaliter* or *regulariter*—according to the *ius civile*, that is, and not by pure reason or an unadorned rule (*nuda regula*); and they had always to remember the first of these rules, that "all definition is dangerous" (*omnis definitio est periculosa*).[23] Yet the meaning of laws had to be established in practical terms and for justice's sake, and several modes of *interpretatio* came to be recognized. Lucas de Penna identified four of them, beginning with the "authentic," referring to legislative intention, the original "spirit of the law." The second, "judicial interpretation," meant the precedents established by the principal courts, though these were not binding and could never contradict the legislator. "Customary interpretation," on the other hand, was binding; and when necessary Lucas even recommended that the *interpretatio consuetudinaria* of neighboring provinces be invoked. Last came professional or academic interpretation (*interpretatio professoris*), which he regarded as only "probable," though often useful to judges and in any case the best approximation to practical wisdom.[24]

On the question of interpretation Bartolus was, as usual, the most comprehensive and authoritative commentator. Like his colleagues he preferred the simplest approach, the so-called *interpretatio declarativa*, which depended on "propriety" (*proprietas*) and "primary authority" (*ex primo authoritate*). At the same time he admitted interpretation by analogy, and he recognized degrees of latitude—*late, latius, latissima*—which he illustrated by commenting that contracts might be construed broadly, wills more broadly, and privileges most broadly. The major loophole of interpretation, however, was provided by the requirements of reason and equity; and Bartolus widened this loophole by identifying rationality (*ratio*) not only with intention (*mens*) but also with liberal interpretation (*extensio*).[25] Beyond that he was able to bypass strict construction (*interpretatio stricti iuris*) by resorting to the standards both of natural law and of the law of nations—recalling the maxim that both "actions" and "peoples" belonged to the law of nations (*actiones sunt de iure gentium; populi sunt de iure gentium*).[26]

Bartolus also recognized interpretation by etymology, or "allusion," but only if it did not conflict with the proper definition. The etymological imagination, active ever since the time of Plato, provides still another example of the interplay between Physis and Nomos, corresponding as it does to the problem of the basis of language: did it originate in nature or in convention? Most jurists, while recognizing the grammatical arguments for the latter opinion, adopted the former view for purposes of their own science. They were well aware, for example, that linguistically "law" could not be derived from "justice" (*ius a justitia*, according to the Gloss); but as Jacques de Révigny had argued, logic and legal propriety demanded this etymology. As a sixteenth-century Bartolist argued, grammarians would not fight so hard against jurists if they understood this properly, "for . . . justice was prior in time"—having been created by God, while law was merely the work of men. Just as "bad grammar does not invalidate a legal instrument" (as Bartolus once noted),[27] so linguistic or historical error does not detract from legal principle (as defenders of the Donation of Constantine were still insisting in the sixteenth century). So it was with etymology, whose purpose, Claude de Seyssel noted, was to get at the essence of something (*quidditas*), his own example being the relation between fief and faith (*feudum a fide seu fidelitate*).[28] Though long aware of the "barbarian" origin of feudalism, jurists insisted on its Roman nature on the grounds of imperial authority (testified to in the *Book of Fiefs*) as well as juridical interpretation.

One question of special urgency in legal hermeneutics was that of the interpretation of statutes, and here jurists had to tread carefully. The assumption was that the "meaning" of a law was identical with the intention of the law-maker, who alone, therefore, could determine this meaning (*statutorum interpretatio fieri debet per conditores,* according to one formula). This self-denying ordinance was an axiom of Italian jurisprudence. As Baldus put it, "a statute cannot receive extensive interpretation" (*non recipit interpretationem extensivam*); for this, according to Alberico de Rosate, was reserved for those who formulated the statutes (*illi qui condiderunt*). Yet it was the judge who had to apply the law and to resolve problems. Here the assumption (one might say the fiction) of the identity of the words and the spirit of law was most useful, since "propriety" applied in principle to the latter. If there could be no exceptions to the law, there might be to its words, and Bartolus even spoke of "irrational statutes." In any case, justice must be served. Bartolus's colleague Alberico de Rosate agreed with the basic premise that "the author of a law should be its interpreter" (*legis auctor debet esse interpres*), but he insisted on the necessity of extensive interpretation in many (for example, criminal) cases. "The statutes demand decapitation of murderers, but are madmen or infants decapitated?" he asked. "Certainly not, because of their age or, in the case of *furiosi,* because their condition is punishment enough."[29]

Renaissance humanism, likewise an italianate intellectual movement but highly critical of professional jurisprudence, had a significant impact on hermeneutics, conceptually as well as textually. For the humanists Roman law was a brand of literature, and scholars such as Maffeo Vegio, reversing the Petrarchan pattern, were converted from poetry to the study of ancient law.[30] Most fundamental in this connection was the continued search for the "historical sense" of legal texts, Greek as well as Latin. Lorenzo Valla in particular made significant efforts to establish the common language as well as the particular words of classical authors (the *langue* as distinguished from the *paroles,* in terms of Saussurean linguistics). Out of the rather desultory textual criticisms in Valla's *Elegancies of the Latin Language* (ca. 1444) came what was still in the nineteenth century called the "elegant"— and more or less paraprofessional—school of jurisprudence.

Valla's example was followed by a distinguished line of sixteenth century exegetes and especially legal lexicographers, who likewise, but more professionally, discussed the Digest title "On the Meaning of Words." Less positively, Valla ridiculed the style of Bartolus, the practice of speculative etymology, the creation of neologisms and abstractions, the neglect of the literary and historical specificity of Roman culture, and the contempt for the "authority of antiquity" (a phrase also used by Justinian) displayed by the commentators.[31] For "civil science," however, Valla's influence seemed to be marginal and even pernicious and conservatives like Bonifacius Amerbach and Alberico Gentili specifically contrasted the "grammatical" excesses of Valla with the sober science of the true "interpreters of law."

In the effort to make law a *studium liberale* the true pioneer was Andrea Alciato, who, though highly critical of Valla, was proud to be the first in a thousand years to teach civil law "in a Latin manner." Alciato's contributions to legal hermeneutics, set down in a monumental commentary on the same title, "On the Meaning of Words," combined the elegant insights of humanist philology with the practical accomplishments of Bartolist science. Alciato had an entirely conventionalist view of language, "for whence should words arise if not from the custom of men?" (*unde enim vocabula inventa nisi ex hominum usu?*). For legal texts he distinguished four modes of interpretation, beginning with the literal, which meant linguistic "propriety" tied ideally to the intention of the author, though in case of doubt one might resort to etymology—not, however, "frivolous etymology," as, perhaps, in the attempt to derive *ius* from *Justinian.* The second type of interpretation was "improper" (*improprietas*), though this did not necessarily involve error, since it might rest on convention, a "fiction," or perhaps a foreign term which did not produce misunderstanding. Third was interpretation according to common usage (*ex usu*), which was permissible, though given the vagaries of the vernacular there was always a tendency for "use" to degenerate into "abuse." The analogy with customary law was obvious, for as Alciato remarked, "What is common usage today cannot be presumed to have been so formerly or before the memory of living men." Like *consuetudo, communis usus* was valid for a limited time, say ten years, but legal interpretation often demanded the search for an older meaning (*antiqua significatio*).[32]

Fourth and last came *extensio,* which was the means both of limiting and of expanding the meaning of law (*ab huius modis ratione et lex restringetur et extendetur*). Here Alciato discussed a wide range of conditions and ways of pushing interpretation beyond propriety and custom, many of them drawn from the tradition "handed down" from Bartolus but enhanced by more recent learning. In the fourth book of his classic commentary "On the Meaning of Words," Alciato discussed a number of literary "extensions," including proverbs, figures, and tropes (not to speak of puns). He surveyed the whole range of Quintilian's *tropoi,* from metaphor to irony and "barbarism," mainly in legal terms; and he noted neologisms and anachronisms, pointing out, for example, that the word "tyrant" had once referred to a "good prince." Alciato not only drew upon but also supplemented the *Adages* of his elder friend Erasmus, providing an "index of proverbs peculiar to jurisconsults"—such as "having one foot in the grave" (*pedem in fovea habere,* from Pomponius).[33] For civil law, like theology, was a form of literature as well as a "science" and had also to be understood in those terms. Henceforth this, too, was to be a prime axiom of civil science, at least in its theory and self-image, as well as a way of "extending" interpretation.

In general, jurisprudence Italian style, following classical precedents, took a linguistic as well as a philosophical turn in its approach to the understanding and the judgment of human behavior, collective as well as individual. This linguistic sensitivity was applied not only to the texts of Roman law but also, in a comparative and practical way, to modern language and its divergence from tradition. The "Bartolo-Baldist" tradition showed a kind of hermeneutical awareness that social reality and social values were always expressed—at once revealed and concealed—in words, and that language necessarily formed at once the condition, the point of departure, and the juridical goal of their profession.

Ratio Iuris

In various ways jurisprudence Italian style, though an expression of Nomos, aspired to the level of Physis: though an authoritarian art, that is, it claimed to be a rational and universal science. The first purpose of this school was to adapt the resources of ancient law to the needs of late medieval society through ingenious identifications and analogies—modernization through rationalization, in general terms. So fourteenth century jurisprudence began to incline again to the devices of natural reason, and indeed to the complex ratiocinations of Greek philosophy. This was especially true of that most philosophical of jurists, Baldus (*philosophotatos* was one epithet), but it was true also of Cino da Pistoia and his French mentors of the thirteenth century.[34]

The dialectical framework was well described by Cino: "First I shall make divisions," he wrote of his classroom procedure, "second give an account of the case, third offer comparisons, fourth make objections, and fifth pose questions." At all times, however, the purpose of the civil scientist was to establish the "spirit" or "reason" of law (*mens, ratio, intellectus, sententia,* or *voluntas legis* or *legum*).[35] As Alciato himself had written, "reason is the soul and life of a particular law" (*ratio est anima, vigorque ipsius legis*); and the search for the "spirit of the laws" was a constant theme of social thought from Celsus to Bartolus and Baldus—and from those Italian masters to Vico and Montesquieu. How, responsibly and effectively, could civil scientists call up this spirit?

This aspect of the twelfth-century revival reflected, quite directly, a reversion to the ancient "scientific revolution" in law embodied in the writings of the classical jurisconsults, especially Ulpian and Gaius. Bartolism deployed the various devices of Hellenistic science, including the systematic use of distinctions, divisions, and the concepts of genus and species; but by far the most important was the endlessly complex idea of "cause." In a legal sense the term referred to the issue in dispute or to be argued out, and in this connection there emerged moral and political notions of "just cause," together with standards of public utility and emergency which could potentially override laws. "For cause," Giason del Maino suggested, "laws may be transgressed," referring to cases of "necessity" (which had its "own law"), if not utility.[36] It is obvious that this conception of "cause" could be extremely useful in judicial interpretation, as it could be in the invocation of laws "higher" than those on the books.

Because of the impact of Greek science, however, the central meaning of "cause" tended to be much more rigorous and rational, in one sense, indeed, being identified with reason (*causa, id est ratio,* in the words of Alberico de Rosate). Or according to another formula, "Cause is the reason without which there is no law." In this sense "cause" was linked not only to the "spirit of the law" (*mens sive causa legis,* in the words of the Gloss) but also to processes of logical explanation, by means, for example, of various "rational conjunctions" ("because"—*quia, quoniam,* and the like). The term had an objective as well as a subjective aspect, since it referred to the generating "impulse" on which a causal event depended and without which it disappeared (*cessante causa cessat effectus* was the lawyer's version), as well as to analytical judgments passed on the process.[37] Like their philosophical colleagues, moreover, jurists were capable of distinguishing between causes direct and indirect ("occasions"), "proximate" and "remote." Such was the basis of the naturalism and rationality (*rationabilitas*) of jurisprudence Italian style.

"Fortunate he who understands through causes," wrote Vergil (*Felix qui potuit rerum causas cognoscere*); and the lawyers had their own more prosaic version: "Science is knowledge through causes" (*scire est per causas cognoscere*).[38] What is more, "the legist and the canonist know through causes" (*legista et canonista cognoscunt per causas*). These formulas, rehearsed by a sixteenth-century French Bartolist, established the basis for the claim of jurisprudence Italian style to be a true, which is to say, a naturalistic, "science." Knowledge through cause and effect, celebrated by poets as well as philosophers and jurists, acquired a more precise meaning in the twelfth century, and this was the famous system of "four causes" devised by Aristotle. Feudists as well as legists applied this apparatus of cause and effect (which included notions also of substance, form, and purpose) to give rational structure to the law-making process.[39] The "efficient cause" was the will of the legislator, whether people, prince, or magistrate, corresponding to the prime mover; the "material cause" referred to the facts of a case, or texts of the law; the "formal cause" represented the rubrics, interpretations, or conclusions; and the "final cause" was the settlement of cases and achievement of "justice" in a general sense. Here is the first systematic effort to set up a naturalistic science of society, and implicitly the basis for a rudimentary sort of social engineering, predicated on rational jurisprudence as well as legislation. Since the time of these scholastic interpretations, of course, the legal concept of "causation" has been "extended" further, though often more narrowly, by modern jurists who have cared little for these early intellectual struggles.

The search for the "reason of law" was tied to an even larger conceptual framework—and larger expression of Physis—than the Aristotelian theory of causation; and this was the old concept, now in Christian guise, of natural law. Ideas of the *ius naturale* ranged from Ulpian's famous definition of it as instinct ("what nature teaches all animals"), whence came also the basis of the *ius gentium,* to the Stoic and Ciceronian view that it corresponded to universal reason, interpreted by Christians as equivalent to the Ten Commandments (*ius naturale decalogi*). A basic distinction was always preserved between a creating and a created nature—God being *natura naturans* and humanity *natura naturata*—and this in turn corresponded to the distinction between "primary" and "secondary" natural law, which is to say, between a primitive state of nature and one derived from it since the fall, reflected largely in the *ius gentium*. For Baldus, custom could itself be understood as a kind of "natural law" in the process of continuous (and "daily") creation.[40] In any case, natural law was regarded as "most equitable" (*ius aequissimum* was Baldus's term), and it served mightily in the hermeneutical process of "extension." The controlling idea was always that of equity (Aristotelian *epieikeia* in particular); and, as natural law could be equated with divine law, nature with God, so "equity" was raised to a transcendent level: *Natura, id est Deus; Aequitas nihil aliud est quam Deus.* This, needless to say, was an honor never bestowed upon "custom."[41]

Usus Modernus

Yet if italianate civil science aspired to the level of pure reason, in practice and even in theory it usually had to be satisfied with more conventional goals: Nomos was still, in a manner of speaking, king. Although invoking natural law, jurists could in fact formulate only "positive law"; for as Azo remarked, with reference to Justinian's hopes for legal perfection, "to forget nothing and never to err belongs rather to divinity than to humanity." Or as Placentinus (among many others) put it, "Man is the author of laws, God of justice." What made the artificiality of civil law most conspicuous was the fact that it had to rely so often on analogy (*argumentum a similia*, in the words of Jacques de Révigny) and on various hypotheses and "fictions."[42] However useful, it could be the height of irrationality as well as anachronism to resort to Roman contract law for modern European society, to adapt the Roman dowry to the royal domain or fisc, to identify the knight with the Roman *miles,* and especially to apply Roman property law to feudal arrangements. Distinguishing between direct and indirect ownership (*dominium directum* and *utile*) was a rational solution,[43] but it could only be maintained by introducing complications from medieval law, which was itself subjected to fictitious analogies, such as those of the Parlement of Paris with the Roman Senate and the fief with the Roman *emphyteusis.* It was in any case through such arbitrary constructions and what would later be called "artificial reason" that medieval jurists sought the *ratio legis.*

In this connection it should be noted that civil scientists were by no means lacking in a "sense of history." Occupationally they could not help being aware of linguistic change and especially anachronism, which in legal terms was the significance of "desuetude" (*desuetudo,* the opposite of *consuetudo*). Even the glossators had shown a kind of historical consciousness in their use of the formula *hodie* (employed also by Justinian's editors for their own purposes of *aggiornamento*). This conceit was the basis for defining contemporary law (*ius hodiernum*) and distinguishing it from what had formerly obtained. "Nowadays the law, or custom, is changed" is the way that Odofredus put it (*hodie ius mutatum est; hodie consuetudo mutata est*). In the beginning men were free, Placentinus quoted from the Institutes, but today not. Formerly, according to the *lex regia,* power had resided with the people but today no longer; formerly there had been a Roman senate, formerly the responses of jurists had been a source of law, formerly usury had been permitted, formerly the status of men (and especially of women) had been highly restricted—but "today," perhaps unfortunately, no longer.

Moreover, there was a certain built-in, even theoretical relativism and sense of process in civil (as well as canonic) science, expressed most clearly in the repeated injunction to take into account time, place, and personal condition; and indeed the concept of equity, though related to the ideal of universal justice, was tied to particular and perhaps "exceptional" circumstances.[44] As Bartolus and his disciple Baldus continually warned, human behavior was the product of individual will and accidents, and legal interpretation had always to take cognizance of these.

"Nature and the acts of men," as Baldus observed, "continually produce new forms." In this context "nature" implies not only regularity but also fundamental change; and civil scientists were acutely aware of the need to confront the forces of this change and the problem of mutability. In speaking of the "new forms" produced by nature, Baldus was no doubt thinking of Justinian's admission that "nature is constantly hastening to bring forth new forms," but he had not the same faith in legislative foresight. "New cases require new remedies," he continued; "so new material arises, and so it is necessary to apply to the jurist." "The science of law cannot exist without the acts of men," Baldus also declared, and elsewhere, "jurisprudence is the science of accidents." If "equity" could suggest a higher form of justice, it could also be defined by Lucas de Penna as an "exception to the law." If Physis depended on stability, Nomos accommodated itself to change (*nihil perpetuum sub sole,* quoted Baldus); and its devotees, the civil scientists, had to develop a method that was empirical and perhaps historical as well as rational.[45]

The great figures of Italian civil science went beyond this and made a virtue of necessity. Cino da Pistoia, for example, a man who read poets and historians as well as jurists and philosophers (and who had studied with the French *moderni*), was well aware of what he called the "novelties of modern scholars" (*novitates modernorum doctorum*), and indeed, at the outset of his famous lectures on the Code, he took as his motto the principle that "all novelty is pleasing" (*omnia nova placent*).[46] He was exaggerating, of course, for much modern scholarship was nonsense, including the amateurish opinions of the canonists (*idiotae,* as he called them, hardly less disrespectfully than did his friend Dante). What Cino meant was that ancient doctrine could not be fully recovered without modern interpretation and adaptation and that, furthermore, the human condition as jurists had to confront it was continually producing novelty. Cino was joined in this conviction by Bartolus and Baldus, who went so far as to welcome these antinomies (*contraria*), whose very existence had been denied by Justinian, on the grounds that they opened up new possibilities of interpretation and resolution of questions.

One of the inspirations for jurists' appreciation of the process of change was the Digest itself, reflecting as it did the whole life-cycle of a civilization.

"It is called old," observed Azo, "because it contained the confused legislation of almost fourteen hundred years from the founding of Rome at the
time of Romulus down to the time of Justinian." Of the five recognized
"species" of law, four (the *plebiscita,* the *senatusconsulta,* the *responsa
prudentum,* and the *lex pretoria*) were obsolete. At the other extreme was
the feudal law, which was also scrutinized by civil scientists. "My first
question," remarked Baldus in his "golden" commentary *Super Feudis,* "is
whether the *Book of Fiefs* should be considered authentic . . . For it is not
part of pretorian law, nor does it follow the normal order of the Corpus
[Juris], and . . . it contains many irregularities and inadequacies which are
not of the nature of true law, the 'art of the good and the just.'" As a good
imperialist, Baldus himself could not share the doubts of the "ultramontanes," and he concluded that "the book is proved by custom to be authentic and useful" because it had been accepted and commented on by canonists and civilians alike, and so it should be accepted "not only in legal
practice but also in legal science." Other jurists objected to this Romanist
thesis on etymological as well as historical grounds. "Both 'fief' and 'vassal'
are new names [*nova nomina*] and are not contained in Roman law," as
Andrea de Isernia pointed out. This argument, which was quite in accord
with Baldus's own position that feudal law had emerged from custom,
represented a kind of juridical "nominalism" and, in a sense, another small
victory for Nomos.[47]

Underlying these local and ad hoc notions of legal change was an attitude
that could only subvert the uniform and universalist tendencies of Physis:
a sort of historical and geographical relativism which required human
institutions to be interpreted in terms of particular conditions and environments as well as precepts and ideals. "Human laws," as Lucas de Penna
put it, "vary according to the disposition of the land and differences in
time [*secundum dispositionum terrarum et varietates temporum*] . . . and
so from the diversity of times flows the diversity of things." This attitude
was reinforced by the anthropocentric and voluntarist implications of the
old Gaian trinity (persons, things, actions), accepted almost without question by glossators and commentators; for the inference was that the "status
of persons," a legal rubric philosophically equivalent to the "human condition," entailed variety and variability and was certainly inadequate for
what Alberico de Rosate called "the modern condition of men" (*modernus
status hominum*). "In modern times there are various states of men which
are not treated in this title," he pointed out. "And because the state of man
is in constant motion and never at rest," he proposed to bring the discussion
up to date by considering questions concerning Jews, Saracens, heretics,
and different sorts of Christians, lay and ecclesiastical. This open-minded-
ness, obviously necessary for transforming the *ius antiquum* into a *usus
modernus,* was essential as well for a modern science of society.[48]

It may be going too far to suggest, as does Harold Berman, that juris-prudence represents a model of "modern science," if only because of the ambivalent attitudes toward naturalism; but there are at least four general intellectual linkages. One is the connection through naive empiricism, prec-edents being in a sense the conceptual "data" of jurists. Another is the fact that long before Galileo civil scientists appreciated and even celebrated the positive aspects of change and its "causes"; and to that extent, as humanist critics well understood and lamented, they lent their support to the party of the "moderns" in its endless "quarrel" with the "ancients." Third is the analogy between jurisprudence and mathematics, based at least on notions of "harmonic" (proportionate rather than equal or arithmetical) justice. Last and perhaps most significant is the fact that long before the burst of interest in the "logic of probability" in the mid-seventeenth century, jurists had displayed doubts about the possibility, in their own practice, of achiev-ing certainty; and they had opened up an important line of questioning about probable logic. The significance of juridical investigations in this area, and the development of legal procedure, is illustrated in the work of Leibniz, especially the young Leibniz, in whom legal learning and a math-ematical interest in a "logic for contingent events" converged.[49]

In general, jurisprudence Italian style aspired to be a perfect union of theory and practice—of physis and nomos—and the connecting link was nothing else than the concept of positive law. Civil science pretended to be rational and universal, but it was also bound to human values and the human condition. If it could claim theoretical stability through its goals of justice and order, it nevertheless "cannot exist without the acts of men, "as Baldus insisted. "Our science concerns accidents and human deeds, which are as diverse as the minds and hearts of men." Once again the emphasis was on human will (*voluntas*). "Nature is ruled by the heavens . . ." Baldus remarked of the *ius naturale,* "but the will is free."[50] The special function of law was to supplement nature, or perhaps to surpass it, by placing limitations on free will not by necessary but for the sake of social stability. Yet beyond the small horizons of particular judgments, the more general goals and methods of civil science continued to be defined by natural law. Reconciling nature (in this larger, originally Stoic sense) with the human condition was the basis, ultimately, of the claim of civil law to be, in the endlessly repeated phrase of Ulpian, "true philosophy."

Nevertheless, questions of practical judgment had priority in the thought and writing of jurists like Bartolus and Baldus. In general the practioners and theoreticians of civil science had to be experts not only in the law but also in the social, cultural, and to some extent historical analysis of the particular manners and traditions of a people. They traded in "local knowl-edge" and in the "second" as well as primary nature of society—that is, its historical character as well as its environment. The jurisprudence which

they constructed out of ancient texts and modern experience treated also
the condition of persons and social relations, and claimed to do so in terms
of "cause" and effect; but at bottom their science was indeed a "prudence"—not so much an *episteme* (in currently fashionable terms) as a
phronesis.

Civil Humanism

"Wherever the Latin tongue holds sway," wrote Lorenzo Valla, "there is
the Roman Empire."[51] Except for the shift of emphasis to language, this
boast was practically a paraphrase of views long held by civilians and
canonists about the coterminality of Latinity and civil law. "Whoever uses
the Latin language are called Romans," according to the *Summa Lipsiensis,*
"whence all Latin peoples are bound by that law." It is all too often
forgotten that Roman law was an essential ingredient not only of the
twelfth-century revival but also of the Italian Renaissance. No one was
clearer about this than Francesco Petrarch, who, though despising professional lawyers, had the deepest reverence for the "fathers of jurisprudence,"
as he called them, enshrined in the Digest, while Valla granted them an
honorable place in his *Elegancies of the Latin Language,* a lexicographical
epic which celebrated, through civil law as well as language, the posthumous conquest of Europe by the Roman Empire—thereby fulfilling the
ancient maxim representing Rome as the common fatherland: *Roma communis patria.*

The main task for the intellectual progeny of Petrarch, not only rheto-
ricians like Valla but also philologists like Angelo Poliziano and Pietro
Crinito, was to do for contemporary jurists what Petrarch had started to
do for Cicero, which was to uncover and clean up the textual monuments,
and then to interpret them in their proper historical context. As Rabelais
remarked of the Accursian Gloss, "The books of law seem like a beautiful
robe of gold, triumphant and marvellously precious, and embroidered with
shit."[52] The work of the commentators made restoration still more difficult,
and Valla in particular defended the Latin language against the "treason"
(*Latinitatis maiestatis laesae*) of Bartolus and his school. The major com-
plication, however, was the fact that the extant texts of civil law were not
only fragmentary but also corrupted by the Byzantine editors—the so-called
"Tribonianisms"—and in need of expertness in Greek. In this sense, too,
Hellenismus was the key to *Romanitas.*

The identification of Romanism and humanism—*Romanitas* and *humanitas*—had been an article of faith with the ancient jurisconsults, but it was
a thesis that needed demonstration anew for modern enthusiasts like Dante
and Petrarch, whether or not they had had legal training. One of the first
of Petrarch's disciples, Coluccio Salutati, wrote an invidious treatise "On

the Nobility of Law and Medicine" in order to celebrate the human virtues of law and to deplore the mechanism and determinism of medicine.[53] The rivalry between these two disciplines was a common topic of debate among the commentators, too, but usually over the respective claims to "scientific" status. Salutati was concerned instead to carry on the message of Petrarch, who had similarly criticized the naturalism of the so-called Averroists of Padua, infesting the medical faculty in particular. In the broad tradition of legal humanism this attitude was elaborated not only by devotees of the liberal arts like Salutati but also by liberal- and literary-minded jurists like Alciato, for whom civil law was indeed a liberal art (*studium liberale*) as well as a science.

Much, perhaps too much, has been written about "legal humanism," especially in contrast to civil science. No more than late medieval theology, can the "scholastic" jurisprudence of the fifteenth and sixteenth centuries be represented as a degeneration from the practice of Bartolus or the *conditor iuris,* Cino; on the contrary (and by analogy with the argument of Heiko Obermann regarding late scholasticism), civil science enjoyed a "harvest time" just before, and during, the Reformation period. One of the main reasons for this was the fact that, though pretending to be in effect a "hard" science, jurisprudence was also deeply concerned with human questions, moral as well as political. "Civil science is the true philosophy and to be preferred to all other fields because of its purpose," wrote Giason del Maino's disciple Claude de Seyssel; and this purpose, he added, "consists not in speculation but in action" (*non in speculatione sed in actione consistit*).[54] Thus it was, as Baldus had said, a practical as well as a theoretical science, pertaining not only to the "contemplative" but also to the "active" life.

"Civic humanism," even more than "legal humanism," has been the subject of much debate and, likewise, some exaggeration—and most likely for the same reason: that humanist rhetoric has been allowed to drown out, as well as to discredit, the more pedestrian work of the older-fashioned professionals, who lived indeed in a different world of thought and discourse.[55] As, in the case of legal humanism, the conceptual efforts of civil science were overshadowed by literary issues, so in the case of "civic humanism" they were overshadowed by political posturing and propaganda. In fact, attitudes developed within jurisprudence Italian style which were largely independent both of the political "crises" associated with "civic humanism" and the "Machiavellian moment." As historians used to notice, civilians like Bartolus and Baldus expressed not only technical legal expertise but also the values and aspirations of a new *civilita,* a commitment to the ideals of citizenship and the *vita activa,* and a favorable attude toward republican "liberty" and even resistance to "tyranny"; and what is more, they had a much broader concern for social, as distinguished from political and constitutional, questions. They also displayed a certain "craving after worldly fame" (*perpetua nominis desiderium*), from which Ernst Kantorowicz inferred, in reference to the Accursian gloss, "the dead live through glory," that "perhaps this path, too, was first trodden by the jurists."[56] These are a few of the reasons for regarding "civil humanism" as a cast of mind no less distinctive than those of "civic" or of "legal" humanism.

As guardians of the ancient legal canon, civil scientists were also masters of social and political thought in ways not accessible to political and social philosophers committed to Aristotelian naturalism; and it is fascinating to see the jurists giving shape and meaning to their world through linguistic and hermeneutical virtuosity. On several levels their mission was to socialize—or more precisely to "civilize"—their contemporaries. They thought and judged "civilly" (*civiliter* meaning according to the *ius civile*, as *regulariter* meant according to the *regulae iuris*, and *communaliter* meant according to consensus). They were agents of "civility"—*civilitas* being equivalent to *Romanitas*, sociability, and even, anachronistically, "civilization."[57] Like humanists but earlier and more professionally, they sought to bring the urbanity of the *civitas* and the responsibility of the *civis* to late medieval and early modern society. For Italian jurists, invoking an ancient topos, the civic status became a "second nature," which required its own definition and rules.[58] Civism was given definition, too, by its negation, which was the condition of being exiled or under ban, a political sort of excommunication that corresponded to civic death.

In various ways Italian jurists acted to socialize the political and to politicize the social. Drawing (again like the humanists) upon Greek political philosophy as well as Roman legal science, they were led in many ways to "think big"—to extend their horizons and to distinguish larger social patterns, assessing the nature and behavior of collectivities as well as individuals. They developed—that is, they inherited and "extended"—a massive vocabulary and conceptual apparatus designed to comprehend, that is, to establish intellectual "cognizance" (analogous to *cognitio* in the legal sense) and scientific jurisdiction over the wide range of social groupings and forces that agitated the cities and countryside of Europe.

Obviously, the "reason of law" was quite distinct from—indeed, frequently the opposite of—"reason of state." This latter concept, also italianate but developed in a very different tradition of political thinking, came to override considerations of ordinary law, custom, and morality, according to an exaggerated separation between the private and public spheres. One of the principal differences between "civic humanism," and "civil humanism," between Baldus and the likes of Bruni and Machiavelli, is that the former remained tied to the legal tradition, with all of its conventions, apparatus, and inhibitions. Yet there remained also a certain overlap, especially in the belief in the central role of human motives and responsibility and in the need for experience as well as theory in making human judgments.

The factor of will, being the central premise both of private law and of the law-making process, contributed also to the convergence between the revived legal tradition and the *vita activa,* which was celebrated as the life-principle of the city-republics of the early Renaissance. It was the jurist who first, or at least most professionally and responsibly, encountered, assessed, and reacted to social reality on almost every level, trying to accommodate the active life—domestic matters, economic activity, status of persons, crime, and so on—to the rule of law, with the help of the axiom that, in the words of Bartolus and Baldus, "Custom represents the will [or reflects the mentality] of the people" (*consuetudo repraesentat mentem populi*).[59] This is reflected in monographic literature more than commentaries, but above all in particular legal briefs and case books, those great collections of *consilia* which remain largely unexploited by historians. In many ways jurists such as Bartolus and Baldus—judges of both fact and principle, concerned with private interest and social utility as well as scientific truth and public policy—were the best observers of the civic life of Renaissance Italy, and to some extent critics of such political excesses as "tyranny" and unjust war.

None of this is to deny that late medieval and Renaissance civil science often served evil or corrupt political masters, and often defended what we would regard as evil interests and causes; but this is the potential condition of any discipline, even one that professes devotion to the highest principles of truth and justice. It is only to suggest that, in view of its empirical base and professional legacy, its technical and ideological apparatus, its terminology, and its broadly human concerns, jurisprudence Italian style may well appear in retrospect as the first (and most pervasively, if surreptitiously, influential) modern form of systematic social thought, and that in linguistic and formal ways, whether or not we care to recognize them, its ghost still haunts us.

NINE

Tradition and Reform

Consuetudo optima est legum interpres.

Innocent III

Niemand sol der Wahrheit die Gewohnheit furzihen.

Martin Luther

·

Theological Jurisprudence

With civil science, canonic science was a sibling rival for the Roman patrimony and in a sense had even stronger claims to authority through the "Petrine Commission," which gave ecclesiastical lawyers a direct line to divine law. The "two laws" continued to reinforce each other and to cross paths—or swords—intertwining and interacting in various ways while preserving much the same language and methods. Their correlations were strengthened by the fact that so many jurists took their degrees *utriusque iuris,* a manifestation of the lay-ecclesiastical dualism likened by Innocent III to the opposition, yet mutual relation, between the sun and moon, the two principal luminaries of Christendom.[1]

This invidiously ingenious metaphor was appropriate in more ways than one, for not only did the church claim solar preeminence in political terms, but it also pretended to a larger and more vital function in life. Despite transcendent pretensions, canon law corresponded humanly to a "juridical community" definable apart from the realities of feudal society. For canonists this community was distinguished above all by access to the sacraments, especially the "necesssary sacraments" of baptism and the eucharist. Canon law covered all aspects of private life, from cradle to grave—and beyond. Nothing human (or divine) was alien to it; it was, as Gabriel Lebras said, a *droit social,* redefining in ecclesiastical terms many social and even blood relationships (such as "spiritual consanguinity").[2] Conscious of the limitations imposed by sin, canonists developed their own conception of equity (*aequitas canonica*), going beyond the rational and utilitarian conventions of civil law; and they promoted "faith" (*fides*) from a religious and social virtue to a legal and, by extension, "scientific" principle. In certain ways, because of its range and pretensions as well as its international character, canon law had perhaps an even greater impact on social (if not political) thought than its secular sibling.

Even more than the Germanic beneficiaries of Justinian, the Roman beneficiaries of St. Peter were inheritors of imperial ideology; for beyond pretending to construct a perfect system of human laws, they claimed "the power to interpret divine law" (*potestas interpretandi legem divinam*). From this came the rising tide of decretals and "decretalist" commentaries thereon—and from this, given the heaven-storming as well as earth-shaking aspirations of the successors of St. Peter, came also the significance of canon law beyond the closed ranks of the ecclesiastical hierarchy. Claiming at once a divine origin (through the "Petrine commission"), a social mission (the pope as "servant of the servants of God"), divine endorsement (as "vicar of Christ"), and royal status (as "priest-king," Old Testament style), the papal office created by canonist science was deeply involved (*ratione peccati,* "by reason of sin") in worldly matters; and while maintaining, down to the present, the language of imperial Rome, it contributed seminally to the shaping not only of European institutions but also of modern social thought.[3]

Canonists were even more successful than their civilian rivals in raising themselves to high administrative office, up to and including the papacy. Decretist science, analogous to the work of the civilian glossators, was represented not only by scholars like Huguccio, teacher of that most imperialist pope, Innocent III, and Johannes Teutonicus, author of the Glossa Ordinaria, but also by several later popes who gave legislative impetus and codified form to ecclesiastical law, which was at last officially published in 1317. The decretalist commentators on papal legislation—the so-called "new law"—were a more mixed and international group, being divided, like the civilians, into "citra-" and "ultra-montane" parties and inclined either toward the new monarchism of Innocent III and Boniface VIII or toward a more conventional Gelasian dualism. Beginning with Hostiensis and Innocent IV, the decretalist tradition built a mighty edifice on the foundation of the Decretum and decretal letters, extending hierocratic doctrines into many areas of private law. It also sparked a wide range of social and political controversies leading up to the Great Schism, to the emergence of the various national churches, and finally to the ideological explosions of the Reformation and Counter-Reformation.

Canon law has represented, among other things, a bridge between the universal church, hence divine grace, and local and national communities. The centralizing force of canon law was reflected especially in the ecclesiastical court system, whose apex was the Roman Rota; and it was reinforced by natural tendencies to seize legal advantage by appealing to this papal supreme court and to the Curia. Counterbalancing these were centrifugal forces—imperial, national, and civic—encouraging political separatism, defined most famously according to the "ancient" and modern "liberties" of the Gallican church of France. Not surprisingly, canonist thought was more successful than secular legal science (tied as it was to the anachronistic universalism of world empire) in promoting ideas of national and royalist ideology. The most famous formulation, repudiating Roman claims of world lordship, represented the national monarch as "emperor in his kingdom" (a treasured and much discussed phrase grounded in Innocent III's bull *Per venerabilem*); but there were many other conceptions enhancing kingship, with its theocratic and imperial attributes, which themselves found classic expression in canon law. These political by-products of canonist polemic contributed to the worldly transformations of canon law in a society increasingly pervaded by national interests and lay prejudices. They contributed, in other words, to that process of "secularization" which was itself a key concept of the canonist tradition, in terms first of property and then of attitudes toward the human condition in general.[4]

In certain ways natural law was more important to canonists than to civilians, to the extent at least that it could be associated with divine law. Johannes Teutonicus distinguished four senses in which the term "nature" could be used: first, the biological meaning, "the power inherent in things by which like procreates like"; second, the conception of Ulpian defining nature as "the stimulus or instinct . . . arising from sensuality"; third, the more humanly limited subdivision of this instinct which was based on reason, similar to Gaius's "natural reason"; and finally, the grounds for such precepts as "Thou shalt not steal," which provided the connection with divine law.[5] Another famous hyperbolic formula identified nature with God Himself (*natura naturans* as distinguished from *natura naturata*), so that the concept might potentially be applied to the entire ladder of creation—the whole "great chain of being," including human links and even social forms. Thus inflated, the concept of the natural might seem to lose all precision, but its effect was to render many areas of study susceptible to philosophical analysis and Aristotelian dialectic, and of course it provided a marvelously effective instrument and weapon for a legal tradition that claimed as its Client, as well as Patron, the divine Author of Nature Himself.

Yet nominally Physis remained subordinate to the Logos—nature bowed to supernature—in canonist tradition, and this left an indelible imprint on legal style and doctrine. This is evident in the "political theology" discussed by Ernst Kantorowicz and the correlative "juristic theology" discussed by Walter Ullmann, which mark the long transition from mystical to legal conceptualization—from Christology to jurisprudence, which is to say, from the church as the body of Christ (*corpus Christi*) to the church as a licensed corporation (*corpus juridicum*). The idea of spiritual unity, of a "congregation of the faithful" or "community of the saints," in the Augustinian formulation of Christian society, was preserved; but for practical (that is, for proprietary and political) reasons, more human and perhaps more "natural" ways of expressing this unity were sought, and eventually found, with the assistance of pagan law and philosophy. In particular, mystical bodies found theoretical incarnation in Roman ideas of corporation and in the organistic analogies of Aristotelian natural philosophy. With such conceptual help canon lawyers devised the ideas of consent, counsel, and representation to provide human legitimacy for ecclesiastical institutions and policies. The convergence of theology and jurisprudence, especially in the form of ecclesiastical corporation theory, produced some of the first sociological abstractions in post-classical Western thought, as Gierke showed over a century ago and as recent historians have been illustrating more fully.

In this tradition of corporation theory the theme of unity was constant, from its purely spiritual expression in Cyprian—the Nicene Creed ("I believe in one God, the Father . . . ")—through the quasi-juridical paraphrase in Boniface VIII's *Unam Sanctam* ("one head" for the mystical body of the church, "not two, like a monster"), down to modern naturalistic arguments for monarchy. The conceit of the *corpus mysticum* was applied, with quite unmystical connotations of legal integrity, not only to the church but also to the crown, to the estates of the realm, and to the Parlement of Paris. Among the ingenious variations on this theme were those of John of Salisbury and of Nicolas of Cusa, for whom the creation and interpretation of law were absolutely central to the life processes of social bodies. Going beyond "head and members," Cusanus (who had canonist training) suggested analogies between the making of laws and the processes of digestion, with legislators playing the efficient role of the teeth and the judiciary corresponding to the liver—though fortunately he did not follow the digestive allegory through to its final cause and natural culmination. Jurists like Lucas de Penna resorted to such analogies for more practical purposes, such as the inference of fiscal and political "inalienability," which arose from the social integrity and perpetuity imputed to the republic and corresponding to the spiritual unity of Christendom.[6]

Yet at the same time there persisted, in a variety of forms, that Christological—and derivatively anthropological—dualism of Christian political thinking, from the Gelasian motif of the "two swords" to the king's "two bodies," which also reflected the connection between nature and grace, or body and spirit. The king's second body, which "never dies," brings immortality, hence dynastic and legal continuity; and so it was with other corporate bodies, including society itself—the *populus, congregatio fidelium,*

or *communitas sanctorum.* Naturalistic metaphors and analogies continued
to be applied to social collectivities—especially those of "head and members" and of generation and corruption—but questions of structure and
value were worked out by the lawyers, canon as well as civil. It was under
the jurisdiction of Nomos that the conceptualization and terminology of a
significant part of the vocabulary of social analysis—*populus, universitas,
concilium, societas, electio, collegium,* and many other such terms—was
developed.[7] Beyond the political variety there was also a sort of "social
theology" which jurists developed and, of course, loaded with a large freight
of legal conventions.

   In general the effect of the ancient legal heritage on canonist tradition
was toward rationalization, secularization, and (in this Weberian sense)
modernization, especially through notions of office and legal representation,
which made a bishop (as well as a king) an administrator (*tutor* and other
civilian terms) rather than a simple proprietor or feudal lord. Yet in other
ways the curious blend of Romanist ideas and Christian institutions produced more far-fetched analogies, such as the notion of marriage as applied
to the relationship between bishop and church, or king and domain, with
the inference that the physical property in question, the fisc, had the legal
status of a dowry and so was "inalienable."[8] The idea of corporation was
itself a sort of myth, being conceptually the equivalent of the Aristotelian
concept of species or, according to theological analogy, angels (as *primum,*
or rather, *solum in genere*); and therefore it was subject to logical criticism
by "terminists" such as William of Ockham, for whom only individuals
had natural or human existence. Yet, while (as canonists pointed out)
collectivities might consist only of individuals in reality, they had their own
separate "personality" before the law and a kind of sacred and social
"unanimity" (*unanimitas*).[9] Such legal fictions—the fallacious legal "realism" of "incorporation"—were prominent among the targets of Ockham's
"razor," which threatened not only the worldly constructions of the lawyers
but also the church itself as a corporate, hence property-owning and power-
wielding, institution (though such arguments were basically "unrealistic"
in more than one sense).

   In any case, the church represented the earthly "form" of the "congregation of the faithful" and as such was subject to generation and corruption—as well as, endlessly, "reformation." As the church was a political
and legal model for European governments in the later Middle Ages, so it
was a prototypical target for social reform and a prototypical vehicle of
modern thinking about questions of social structure and process and attendant human problems—"topics which, under modern conditions," as
Walter Ullmann argued many years ago, "would be dealt with, not by the
lawyer, but by the sociologist."[10]

Canon Law in the World

The Christian church was an "amphibious" body—a *societas* as well as a *corpus mysticum*—and this dualism lay at the roots not only of ecclesiastical "reform" but also of social involvements and conceptualizations of major benefit to European society. The concept of sin, rather than greed or ambition, marked the entry of the church into the world. "Because of sin" (*ratione peccati*) and attendant on the primary task of the cure of souls, the church claimed a certain jurisdiction over the private as well as the public sphere; and this of course reinforced its "amphibious" condition and the dualisms it produced, which were summed up most clearly, perhaps, by the formula "power and love" (*potestas et caritas*). On the one hand and in the first instance, the church was a "transcendent" foundation, a divine gift from the "sky-god," and a sacramental system set above human experience; on the other hand and subsequently, it was an earthly creation subject to the weaknesses, needs, and desires which inform the human condition, and a system of "positive law."[11] Yet these paradoxes also made possible many of the insights and constructs which canon law has given to Western social thought.

From the eleventh century on, the *ius canonicum* constituted an international common law which had cognizance over moral as well as political affairs, over the "internal forum" of conscience as well as the "external forum" of legality. Like Roman law, but with larger justifications, canon law placed its focus on and drew its values from the individual "person" as discovered by Greek philosophers, defined by the civil lawyers, and exalted, in a variety of ways, by medieval theologians and Renaissance humanists alike. Like the civilians but on higher authority, the canonists emphasized the liberty—the "free will"—of the individual soul, and thereby his (and increasingly her) responsibility before the law. "But," in the words of Rufinus, "because persons are higher than matters [*personae digniores sunt negotiis*], therefore Master Gratian had dealt with persons first, on whose account matters occur."[12] This emphasis had immense significance for many areas of social behavior which are self-evidently to be understood in terms of private "wills"—especially marriage and contract, perhaps inheritance, and certainly crime. In the long run these attitudes tended to favor persons normally excluded from the advantages of civil law, such as women, prisoners of war, and even infidels and slaves. By extension such moralistic and voluntaristic assumptions were also extended into the public sphere, where the pope again claimed jurisdiction "because of sin." In this way the anthropocentric, and to a degree anthropomorphic, premises of "Gaianism" were reinforced, in a sense spiritualized, and made even more systematic.[13]

It was one of the implicit tendencies of the canonist tradition to exalt customs, the popular norms of a particular group, above written law imposed by authority, especially secular authority. Decretalists like Hostiensis and Odofredus were outspoken in preferring *consuetudo,* or immemorial usage, to *ius positivum,* with or without specific papal endorsement.[14] According to canonist opinion, indeed, "custom" was the only source of law besides nature and reason; and according to one canonist definition, justice itself proceeded from nature through custom. *Consuetudo* was thus the most "natural" expression of justice—and, as decretalists like Gregory IX quoted from the Digest, the "best interpreter of law"—while *desuetudo* represented its decay or obsolescence. More than civilians, who tended to exaggerate the rationality of Roman law and underestimate the sinful nature of man, canonists were inclined to acknowledge and even insist on the mutability of human laws, which had always to be interpreted "according to the cause, the place, the time, and the person" (*ex causa, ex loco, ex tempore, ex persona,* in Gratian's words). As one eleventh-century churchman had put it, "One must take into consideration geography, the nature of the times [*qualitas temporum*], the weakness of man, and other unavoidable realities which normally change rules; for by power many things are changed for the common good of the churches . . . Sometimes contradictory canons are issued in one council and prohibited in another. Yet this should not frustrate those who, in terms of our temporal life, want virtue to overcome vice, and truth falsehood."[15]

The broadmindedness and sensitivity displayed by canonists toward the human condition was not wholly disinterested, it may be noted; on the contrary, it was a flexibility that permitted the extension not only of their science but also of questions of power (*non solum scientia sed etiam potestas,* as Gratian had said) and of ecclesiastical "interest" and "utility." In some ways canonists had a freer hand than the civilians in emphasizing judicial over legislative authority, and on these grounds they transformed the ancient notion of equity into wide powers of judicial discretion. "Equity is the true mean between rigidity and license," declared Hostiensis (*Aequitas vero media est inter rigor et dispensationem*), and therefore "equity is justice." "Extension" or "extensive interpretation," as it came to be called, played no part in the Decretum; but the decretals and their commentaries developed, even more liberally than civil science, a theory of interpretation which (reinforced by the papal power of "dispensation" and, later, by casuistic doctrines) became an essential part of canonist science. Like the civilians, too, canonists sought not merely the letter of the law, which was nothing more than its body or substance, but rather its reason (*ratio iuris*), which was its soul and indeed its "final cause."[16]

The discretionary drift and populist overtones of some canonist arguments might furnish support for resistance, revolution, and even tyrannicide; but more directly they meant reducing the domain of natural reason and natural law. The major juridical consequence of Adam's fall was to undermine the human capacity of natural reason, hence to resort to convention justified through authority and faith. Laurentius Hispanus was perhaps the first canonist to distinguish between reason and legislative will, hence to open up possibilities for judicial criticism of enacted law.[17] In this way the Logos acted to increase the significance of Nomos; for many of the institutions regarded by the civilians as "natural"—preeminently private property, but perhaps also slavery (as a division of property)—were relegated by canonists to the realm of convention. Much the same might be said for the famous *aequitas canonica,* which became a shelter for interpretations in no way defensible as "natural" or even "civil." One may suppose that this is one of the roots of the development of a casuistry sometimes necessary because of the practical as well as theoretical problem of reconciling the divinely ideal with the humanly real.

Another implication of the canonist tradition was the invasion of the innermost recesses of conscience, consciousness, and so of private law, arising from the difficulties incurred by the cure of souls. The principle of the Trinity has merited a special title in the collections of civil law since Theodosius, but the sacramental system and moral theology were by no means so prominent as in canon law. The central mystery, and the point of contact between humanity and divinity, remained the eucharist; but more crucial legally was the sacrament of ordination, since it established the basis of social ordering, the clerical monopoly over the other sacraments (hence mediation between man and God), and, juridically most important, the point of entry for the clergy into the private life and consciousness of the laity. In the social as in the political field the problem posed by "sin" justified massive intrusion into the "internal forum" of human behavior. The social condition itself was bound most directly to that "sacrament of entrance," baptism, just as extreme unction opened the door to eternal life, and the sacrament of marriage and attendant interpretations brought the family under canonist jurisdiction. As sin introduced criminal and immoral behavior into the purview of canon law, so requirements of orthodoxy made doctrinal deviance—heresy, apostasy, and infidelity—an object of legislation and jurisprudence. Powers of inquisition and excommunication were directed at control of thought and will even more, apparently, than of behavior. In general, the rise of ecclesiastical law represented a challenge not only to secular authority but also to the basic civilian distinction between the public and private spheres.

The major sacramental overlap between the individual and the social was penance, which was transformed from a certain spiritual requirement or test into a legalistic device which commanded obedience as well as repentance, a standard of moral as well as doctrinal behavior, and material as well as moral support to the Christian community. Penance surely required a particular state of consciousness—indeed, a "change of mind," following the Pauline model of conversion. Yet according to many authorities a particular act of confession was as important as an attitude of contrition. Not only doctrine, according to another conventional distinction, but also discipline defined penance in an institutional sense; and the further convergence with the ecclesiastical innovation of plenary indulgence, adapted (from the thirteenth century on) to the fiscal needs of the papal government, added to the legal consequences of this sacrament. Indulgences, as interpreted and applied from the time of Boniface VIII, represented only one of the forms of bureaucratization and "corruption" by which human laws and simoniac customs seemed to detract from the spiritual mission of the church.[18] Other curial practices and dispensations acted to turn the church further away from the Logos, as it were, and toward a form of Nomos—"human tradition," sometimes in a pejorative sense—which appeared to critics as a resurgence of Judaic law. Such were the major conditions of and impetus to recurrent movements of ecclesiastical, legal, and social "reform."

The effort to join public interest and private morality—*potestas and caritas* in the most literal sense—was most obvious, perhaps, in the arena defined by political economy. As canonists had attempted to set down rules for military conflict, so they tried to regulate commercial competition and contractual agreements, which invited not only indulgence of private wills but also injustice. As they devised ideas of the "just war," so they formulated a doctrine of the "just price" and other curbs on excessive profit, mercantile deceit, and unfair exchange, and above all that juridical device, pregnant with social as well as economic significance, known as "interest." Canonists also dealt with the difficult problems of private property (*dominium*) and, perhaps more actively than civilians, developed and extended possessory remedies for the recovery or "restitution" of goods unjustly taken. Indeed, the development of a modern law of possession, though largely neglected by historians, who have been overly and anachronistically impressed with "private property," was in some ways no less significant than questions of titled ownership, especially because it served as a basis for the moral critique of "private property" and its social costs.[19]

Adjacent in a sense to the canonist tradition and the "secular clergy" was the separate world of the "regular clergy," which offered a unique perspective from which to see, judge, and criticize (if not to "reform") the secular sphere—especially in its radical critique of "property."[20] Beginning with its own process of "conversion," monasticism developed its own distinctive customs, laws, "rules," work habits, and life styles; founded on a vision of the Logos, it created its own forms of Nomos and ways of thinking about the social world. Essentially, however, the first premise of monasticism was a rejection of this world and of its primary institutions—family, property, economic exchange, and social and political engagement. In this way the monastic tradition at once rejected the old "law" in favor of spiritual freedom and, ironically, created its own mundane rules, which made it, remotely, an inspiration and then, more immediately, a target for new forms of "reformation" and "protest" in the sixteenth century.

Following the ancient Roman model, canonists also made repeated efforts to organize the materials of their Decretist and Decretalist tradition from the bull *Rex pacificus* of 1234 down to the *Quum pro munere* of 1580, which finally defined the whole body of canon law, the Corpus Iuris Canonici. In these attempts to give shape and authority to their "canonical" texts, church scholars and canonists contributed importantly to the modern idea of codification, with the aim of joining political authority and the organization of a particular society and its values in a single legal system of law.

If the focus of canon law was in some ways narrowly personal, in other ways it ranged over large international, intercultural, and even universal boundaries. Canonic science took as its field of competence the entire "modern law of nations" extending beyond the boundaries of Christendom, and it expanded in at least two of the same directions as the ancient *ius gentium,* namely, the laws of war and peace and those of commercial relations, especially in regard to Jews, infidels, and other modern equivalents of the "barbarians." For canonists, warfare, as an institutionalized form of violence, was virtually an analogue of jurisdiction; and it was considered according to the same combination of ethical and legal criteria. Within the law of nations, and, in effect, of nature, violence was justified if directed to self-protection (the old civilian principle of *vim vi repellere licet*), the recovery of property, or the defense of country. Whether self-defense against legitimate authority was permitted was a difficult question, but it found a place among the seven species of war recognized by Hostiensis. By confrontating problems generated by feudal warfare, by the crusades, and by later colonial conquests, canonic science helped in many ways to establish the foundations of the modern field of "international law," which represented the kingdom of Nomos in its most extended form.[21]

Conciliarism and Reform

The culmination both of ecclesiastical law and (as critics saw it) of lawlessness came in the fourteenth century with, first, the Babylonian Captivity, when the papacy resided for the most part in Avignon and was in effect a satellite of the French monarchy, and then, especially, with the Great Schism opened by the double election of 1378. This dilemma, which threatened the spirit as well as the body of western Christendom, sent scholars back to the texts of canon law and other parts of the legal tradition for remedies and precedents, including secular ones. Short of a miracle, the best solution seemed to be the conciliarist thesis (*via concilii*), proposed first by a pair of German scholars at the University of Paris, the canonist Conrad of Gelnhausen and his theological colleague Henry of Langenstein, though it would not be officially implemented for another generation.[22]

Conrad resorted to the Augustinian (and Pauline) principle which might be called the church's two bodies, arguing that the spiritual aspect was primary and was to be identified not with its human and Roman head but with the whole "congregation of the faithful." The further argument that the ecumenical council was the most adequate representative of this *congregatio fidelium* was difficult to maintain in canonist terms, despite the availability of decrees from the ancient councils and the qualifications placed on papal supremacy in cases of heresy, madness, or other incapacity. So these early conciliarists turned to broader legal principles, especially Aristotelian equity (*epieikeia*) and the proto- (or crypto-) constitutionalist rule "What touches all must be approved by all" (*quod omnes tangit ab omnibus approbetur*).[23]

Conciliarism triumphed at the Council of Constance (1415–17) and received legal expression in two famous decrees, *Sacrosancta* and *Frequens,* which set the council above the pope and made it into a regular governing and judging body; and it persisted in that "revolutionary synod," as a recent historian has called it, which was the rump Council of Basel (1431–49). Whereas the initial program of conciliarism declared a council superior to a pope in cases of heresy, schism, and the need for reform, the radical Basel interpretation was absolute superiority, making the church into a legal and theoretically self-governing community. "Baslean Conciliarism" in effect applied republican principles to the mystical body of Christ, sometimes with reference to the discussions by Bartolus and other civilians about the independence of Italian city-states—an ecclesiological sort of humanism similar to the civic variety. In general, however, two forces stood opposed to this ideal of a world ecclesiastical republic: resurgent papalism beginning with Martin V, which made the papacy into a major Italian power; and the resurgent national churches, which found support in the legislation of the Council of Basel, though their foundations had been laid during the ecclesiastical chaos of the schism. Papal policy led finally to the condemnation of conciliarism as an "execrable" doctrine, while nationalism destroyed its universalist base.[24]

Yet conciliarist ideas were preserved under cover of the national ecclesiologies, which had been recognized implicitly in the voting procedures ("by nation") at the Council of Constance and by the Basel decrees. The most notable result was that charter of "Gallican liberties," the Pragmatic

Sanction of Bourges of 1438, which, like the Decretum and the decretals, attracted massive commentary and became an essential ingredient in a legal tradition as well as in an attendant ideology of royalism. The core of this tradition (actually half a mythology) of "ancient liberties" was not only the mass of legislation of the Valois and Capetian dynasties but also, by a fictitious legal continuum created by the king's lawyers, the Carolingian legislation concerning the Frankish church, especially the *Libri Carolini*. Feeding into the channel of Gallicanism, too, were the precedents set by the Parlement of Paris when its jurisdiction was much expanded, and the polemics generated by the controversy between Philip IV and Boniface VIII. Much of this material was gathered in the monumental *Somnium Viridarii* (*Songe du Vergier* in the modified French version) compiled during the schism and reinforced by imperial propaganda, which derived especially from Marsilius of Padua and William of Ockham. But essential at all times was the ideological treasury of canon law, which in a famous formula taught that kings "had no superior in temporal matters" and generally contributed to the political theology underlying divine-right kingship.[25]

Conciliarism was condemned by the papal bull *Execrabilis* in 1460, but it enjoyed a number of posthumous careers—in the context of the national churches, especially of the "Gallican liberties" codified in the Concordat of Bologna of 1516; in the form of constitutional theory, especially in sixteenth- and seventeenth-century England; and in the early hopes of Lutheran reform. Within the church, moreover, conciliarism was appropriated by the papacy and, in its Tridentine form, became an adjunct of papal authority.

Beginning with the canons and decrees of the Council of Trent, canon law entered a third phase—its *ius novissimum*—which brought it into the modern world in various ways. For one thing, canon law was subjected to the historical scrutiny of humanist scholarship, leading not only to Protestant and Gallican critiques of Catholic tradition and apochryphal texts but also to the work of the Roman *correctores* in the 1580s. Canonists were also led to make reevaluations of concepts of "law," "custom," and "tradition" in general, and so of social as well as ecclesiastical theory.

An important extension of the canonist tradition in this period was the so-called "second scholasticism" begun by such Spanish theologians and jurists as Francisco de Vitoria, Domingo de Soto, and Francisco Suarez. Their work, which highlighted the sixteenth-century Thomist revival, took as its point of departure the discussion of human law in St. Thomas's *Summa theologiae;* and it focused on problems of moral theology and philosophy, especially in the realm of economic exchange, and the moral and legal questions provoked by encounters with new forms of society in the Indies. Suarez, trained in canon law as well as theology at the University of Salamanca, centered his conception of law on the idea of free will, and his view of the *ius gentium* on the assumption that all peoples created their own customs and "positive laws."[26] This was a common assumption among Spanish jurists—as a commentator on the *Siete Partidas* put it (quoting from the *Libri feudorum*), "The authority of Roman law is not of small moment, but it does not extend so far as to override the usage and the general customs of the people"—and the principle was applied without difficulty to the peoples of the New World.[27] "La Seconda Scolastica" was largely a creation of Thomist and Jesuit scholarship, and its tendency was to subsume law under theology and moral philosophy. Nonetheless, it had a substantial impact on the "antique-modern" school of natural law; and indeed the Protestant Grotius, for example, cited these Dominican and Jesuit scholars more frequently than he did Bartolus and Baldus.[28]

In the post-Tridentine world, canon law came to terms with modern society and "secularization" (which itself was an old canonist term suggesting in a technical way the intersection of churchly and worldly interests), in part by devising casuist and "probabilist" doctrine accommodating formerly suspect economic behavior, and in part by promoting the specifically Christian notion of the *ius naturale*. This fusion of universalist legal theory and parochial legal practice seems to carry canon law outside the mainstream of modern (at least secular) social thought and to render it for the most part a matter of official tradition, legislation, and in-house commentaries. In the age of print even "custom" was regarded in effect as statutory law or the opinions of canonists. In post-Tridentine doctrine, "tradition," with its lowly companion, custom, was transformed into a legalistic, and in effect politicized, notion of papal authority (*magisterium*). It is true that canon law has remained in substance a *droit social* (in the words of Le Bras), and its illustrious past, if not its more parochial recent career, remains a significant heritage for the history of social thought. Yet from a modern and secular perspective, it has served not only as a model but also as a target of criticism, and this negative contribution needs attention in connection with modern conceptions of "law."

The Bondage of Law

If canonist doctrine served to intensify authoritarianism on a national as well as an ecclesiastical level (on the Pauline grounds of "rendering to Caesar"), it could also lend support to the most extreme radicalisms (on similarly Pauline grounds of the primacy of divine over human law). In general the exaltation of "law" justified not only the constitutionalist foundations of conciliar theory and what Walter Ullmann has called "populism" but also ideas of resistance to political authority, in that sense revolution, and even, from at least the time of John of Salisbury, political assassination.[29] The notion that God's law was prior to man's, and Scripture to human rules, suggested the most fundamental threat to secular as well as ecclesiastical authority.

The history of the church has been marked by a series of movements of spiritual reform, in effect Pauline revolts against the regimen of human law—the attempt, as it were, to restore the Logos to its rightful place above Nomos in Christian thought. From Dante's assaults on the *decretalistae*, through the programs of Wycliffe, Hus, and various minor evangelicals, and the humanist criticisms of Erasmus, Romanist conceptions of the "law" were subjected to fundamentalist criticisms. In this connection law was represented variously as the commandments of God, the dictates of reason, the will of prince or people, and that law of conscience which Paul found inscribed on the human heart—as nature, supernature, and as "second nature." Like Paul himself, law was "all things to all men."

Luther drew upon this legacy, finding his point of view and his language in his lectures on Paul, especially the epistles to the Romans. Through the efforts of Luther, the Pauline rejection of human law and the exaltation of "Christian liberty" caught the attention of a large segment of European society and inflamed the consciences of many members of a new generation, not only in religious but also, increasingly, in political terms. The target and focal point of the Lutheran "Reformation" was the human structure of canon law from the very outset—which is to say, from the first of the ninety-five theses of 1517, which (following the philological arguments of Erasmus and Valla before him) reinterpreted Matthew 3:2 ("Repent ye . . .") to signify a command to feel repentance rather than to do penance. In so arguing Luther was doing more than attack a conventional definition of a sacrament; he was also challenging the legal "power of the keys" both technically, by questioning the authority of the Vulgate translation, and juridically, though this did not become explicit for another three years.[30] That his aim was to deny the so-called power of loosing and binding, and beyond that the whole canonist tradition, was demonstrated publicly in December 1520, when, in the company of students and faculty of the University of Wittenberg, he ceremoniously burned the volumes of the Corpus Iuris Canonici, adding to these several other bookish symbols of curial authority, including the papal bull which had condemned him.[31]

"As they did to me, so I have done to them," Luther remarked; but in fact his grounds were more than personal justification. He was asserting the law of Christ against the false "human traditions" expressed in the decretals of Gregory IX and other usurping Romanists, and the various falsifications to be found even in the Decretum, including the Donation of Constantine, about which Luther had recently read in Ulrich von Hutten's edition of Valla's famous exposé.[32] Even worse than this "great unchristian lie" was the pope's claim that he was above all human judgment (*a nemine judicatur; nullo potest judicari*), from which, Luther charged, "all misfortune has come into the world." And so Luther concluded his denunciation of the power of the keys and papal subversion of secular authority with the declaration, "Therefore, the canon law is rightly to be destroyed and rejected as a poisonous thing."[33] The next year he went on to his famous campaign—in his vernacular *Address to the German Nation*—against the "three walls of the Romanists": the papal claims to a monopoly of scriptural interpretation, to exclusive right to call a council, and to exemption from secular jurisdiction, each of which was a violation of both human and divine law.

Yet despite these gestures of defiance the Lutheran movement was based on a deep respect for law in the sense of the rules of human order and the basis for worldly peace; and it is no wonder that Luther himself sent out "mixed signals" on the question of obedience to law. A good example of this ambivalence was the position of Philip Melanchthon, who followed Luther's critique of Judaic and canon law but who was at the same time a champion of civil law—the "emperor's law"—and its teaching in Lutheran universities. In his academic orations Melanchthon praised the forefathers of the legal tradition, including Irnerius and Bartolus, and more generally celebrated "that erudite doctrine of law" (*hanc eruditam doctrinam iuris*), which protected against war, barbarism, and civil confusion— words quoted three centuries later by Savigny in his efforts to revive jurisprudence in Germany.[34]

Luther's anti-canonist campaign was taken up by other evangelical critics, most notably by John Calvin, who also contrasted the "law" unfavorably with Christian liberty but who (like Melanchthon) looked favorably on (and indeed drew upon) the tradition of human law, whose purpose was "to protect the community from unjust men." In the 1543 edition of his *Institutes of the Christian Religion* (which owes more than a little, perhaps even its title, to Roman law) Calvin included a survey of the degeneration of the church from its pristine apostolic ideal and the supersession of faith and the Christian *mos maiorum* by canon law and papal legislation.[35] Calvin was followed in his assaults by his young protégé François Hotman, whose *State of the Primitive Church* (1555) continued the attack on Roman tyranny as a negative model of Christian society—and foreshadowed his notorious *Francogallia* of 1573, which amounted to a sort of "state of the primitive French constitution," likewise directed against pernicious Roman influence.[36]

Hotman's little essay was written in support of a much more significant critique of Romanism, which was the unprecedented and politically inflammatory commentary made by his elder colleague, Charles Dumoulin, on the whole corpus of canon law. A Gallican jurist still at that time in the evangelical camp, Dumoulin combined philological criticism in the style of Erasmus and Valla with heavy-handed Protestant vituperation against the

Roman "Antichrist." Like Luther he deplored the falsifications with which the Decretum was ridden, such as the so-called "apostolic canons" and the misattributed sermons of Augustine; but even more he objected to the scandalous lies by glossators, most notably (following Luther) the "false and heretical gloss" declaring that the pope "is judged by nobody." Invoking the example of the *ecclesia primitiva* and the motto *sola scriptura*, Dumoulin assailed the "stupid practice of the canonists" (*stulta praxis canonistarum*), their claim to be exempt from royal jurisdiction, their credulous acceptance of apochryphal texts, and especially their terrible "Trojan horse," the Petrine commission. In Dumoulin the radicalism of "Baslean Conciliarism" and Lutheran fundamentalism was joined to the weapons of "ultramontane" civil science in the war against Romanist legalism.[37]

In this period of evangelical fervor Dumoulin followed reformist fashions in attacking not only the "false and Judaic" conventions of canon law, such as the tithe, but, more fundamentally, human laws in general—"positive laws which prove nothing" (*jura positiva quae nihil probant*), as he complained, at least in an ecclesiastical context. Yet Dumoulin reveled in his Gallican heritage, regarding himself as a successor to Pierre de Cugnières in particular; and although he continued to scorn the "Sorbonist sophists and theologasters," he soon returned to his national commitments and Gallican convictions. Indeed the general drift of his legal thought was toward establishing the independence of French traditions of "positive law," including royalist ideology, customary laws, and the "ancient liberties" of the Gallican church. What civilians, canonists, and feudists had done for their own professional canon, Dumoulin proposed to do for all of the branches of French law; and his authority (and "legend") as a legist, a canon-breaker, and a canon-former would be unrivaled down to the Revolution—and beyond.[38]

More generally, Dumoulin's professional achievement represented another victory for Nomos as well as for the French monarchy, marking the intersection of canon and feudal law with Protestant criticism of papal "law," and of old-fashioned civil science with a modern, but very unclassical, sense of history and of national individuality.[39] More controversially but no less fundamentally than the legal humanists, Dumoulin celebrated his own "new method," which combined the *mores italicus* and *gallicus* and which treated law as an expression of a particular society, a vital dimension of national culture, and a conceptual field where a comparative approach was the key to general understanding and practical application: ideas which would become essential to legal and social thought in the modern "world of nations" down to the French Revolution—and beyond.

Protestant and reformed divergences from the old church were founded upon the most fundamental critiques—even the nominal rejection—of "law." Yet the human condition, involving not only "sin" but a wide and expanding range of social issues, forced the new confessions to establish their own orthodoxies and legal traditions, which (when they did not maintain canon law on grounds of utility) tended to recapitulate in social and institutional terms the experience of the early church and to form their own "laws of ecclesiastical polity" (in the words of Richard Hooker). In this connection Hooker likewise had recourse to the old distinction between "primary" and "secondary" laws.[40] In general, the habits of questioning, doubting, and criticizing produced by the Reformation and its aftermath had repercussions in legal, social, and political, as well as in religious and philosophical thought. Not only Christian belief and the study of nature but also ideas of law and society called for review and reevaluation in both national and international terms; and the debates over canon law provoked discussion not only of confessional issues but also fundamental questions of the function of law, custom, and tradition.

It was in the post-Reformation context of religious, social, political, and intra- and inter-national divisions—and hopes of restoring Christian unity—that the modern sciences of society and culture began to take shape. "Social science," like its antecedent and surrogate, the science of law, has always claimed to be universal; but in reality the human sciences have developed along specific and even local lines, and this parochialism must be respected as we follow the fortunes of Nomos in its various national channels.

TEN

English Developments: The Common Law

Usus altera fit natura.

Fortescue, *De laudibus legum Anglie*

For use almost can change the stamp of nature.

Shakespeare, *Hamlet*, III, iv

•

La Commune Ley

"For its ends England employs only non-written law and custom," Bracton declared in the twelfth century.[1] English common law (*ius commune; la ley commune*) was in process of formulation from the twelfth century on, but as "general immemorial custom" it pretended to deeper roots and thereby created its own mythology and way of looking at the English past. This custom—West Saxon, Mercian, and the Danelaw in particular—had been preserved, at least in distorted form, in various collections of *leges* assembled after the Norman Conquest, such as those of Henry I, which one historian has called "the first book of comparative law."[2] Combining Frankish with Norman and Anglo-Saxon law (and, perhaps consciously, rejecting Roman personalism), the Leges Henrici declared that "all causes are to be decided by judges with true understanding of judgment [*vera concilii ratione*] and are to be decided with equality without respect of persons."[3] These collections of laws all began by deploring the diversity of customs in different counties and shires and "the evil and hateful practice of lawyers," and placed all their reliance on a properly controlled royal system which operated "according to the law of the land."

The Norman influx brought in a new ruling class and the influence of Continental law, Roman and ecclesiastical as well as feudal. Yet native English institutions persisted in many ways, especially through the popular (hundred, shire, and township) courts and various marginal jurisdictions. The institution of the jury, too, had Anglo-Saxon as well as Frankish precedents and helped to maintain ties between English society and Norman government. Through its two major forms, the jury of presentment (accusation) and the jury of trial, this popular institution dealt with questions both of fact and of law, especially by declaring (not unlike the French *turbes*) what did or did not constitute a valid custom.[4] It was through the royal courts stemming from the Curia Regis, however, that mainstream common law developed—the King's Bench and the Court of Common Pleas—which were superimposed on the pre-Conquest court system. From the outset English law seemed to be the joint creation of the "reasonable men" of the sworn neighborhood assembly and the professional judges, who were eventually organized in the order of the coif and trained in an apprentice system institutionalized in the Inns of Court.

One major characteristic of the English legal tradition was the way in which it preserved oral modes of proof over the "dead hand" of writing, not only in pleading and teaching (the "moot" trials) but also in judgments. In the seventeenth century Matthew Hale still celebrated "Oral tradition" as a basic component of English law. Collective memory was flexible (even when constituted by judges), whereas written documentation and procedures were fixed and easily subject to political control, "strict interpretation," and the subversion of customary arrangements, as in the unpopular displacement of "folkland" by "bookland" and in the *Que warranto* proceedings beginning in the thirteenth (and appearing again in the sixteenth) century.[5] Another significant by-product of oral tradition was the judicial habit of invoking "immemorial custom"—in the phrase made famous by Sir Edward Coke, who used it to reinforce his own authority, if not (as Plucknett suggested) to establish his own judicial brand of "fundamental law."[6]

On the whole and (as legend would have it) despite recourse to Roman conventions and terminology, English law followed its own "nature" and never lost touch with its roots in custom. From that source it developed almost entirely in terms of procedural law, that is, through demands for redress formulated in various kinds of writs (*brevia*), more or less equivalent to the ancient Roman legal actions (*legis actiones*). These writs were concerned above all with problems of property (*dominium*) and possession (*seizin*), and without them no appeals for "justice" could be initiated. The earliest treatises on "English law"—"Glanvil" in the twelfth and Bracton in the thirteenth century—were hardly more than commentaries on the principal royal writs. Both opened with the old Roman theme paralleling arms and laws, might and right; both insisted on the point that England was ruled by "unwritten" custom which, through royal endorsement, had attained the status of true law; and both argued that the foundation of English justice was the legal profession. The members and masters of this profession gained their credentials through training in the method of pleading through the system of writs and initiation into the "mysteries" of judicial procedure, which became, increasingly dependent on precedent and "local knowledge"; and they were, like the ancient Roman *prudentes*, the undisputed experts of social thought.[7]

In his "Summa" of English law, following, at least formally, Azo's work on the Institutes, Bracton adopted a nominally Romanizing interpretation, beginning with the inevitable Gaian triad. The natural (as well as divine) attribute of the first member of this trio, personality, was liberty; but in the civil state, that is, under the *ius civile* (or *ius proprium* of any people), things were not so simple. Social arrangements included class distinctions, starting with dukes, earls, and barons (*duces, comites, barones*); women were in an inferior condition; some persons were in bondage or in the power of another (*alieni juris*, notably the villeins or *servi*); and of course churchmen were a class apart in more ways than one. Much more important for Bracton than the status of persons (over twenty times more important, to judge by the space devoted to it), was the second Gaian rubric, which covered "things"—not because of problems of classification (things common, private, sacred, and so on) but because the overriding issue in civil society, and especially, it would seem, in English civil society, was the acquisition of things (*de adquirendo rerum dominio*), and of course their retention, use, and inheritance. In a word, and reminiscent again of early Rome, private property, in a complex feudal context, was the central question of English society and social thought. It was the central question, too, of Gaius's third rubric, legal action, a topic which led Bracton to consider the specifically English devices of the writ and the "pleas of the crown."[8]

Though "Romanesque in form," as Maitland summed up Bracton's unfinished work, it was "English in substance," being based on a vast amount of judicial experience, including some five hundred decisions. Yet Bracton did emphasize the popular—or as Walter Ullmann would say, "populist"—character of English institutions by assimilating native customs to Roman private law and the idea of *consuetudo* and by insisting not on public authority but rather on the force of social consent, expressed most famously in the Roman-canonical maxim introduced by him: "What touches all must be approved by all" (*Quod omnes tangit ab omnibus approbetur*).[9] According to English legal convention, too, justice could be sought even against the king. A comparison that immediately suggests itself is the contemporaneous French insistence on "approval" in all matters of custom—and the efforts of the French monarchy likewise to gather all customary, or "civil," matters under its own jurisdiction.

According to learned opinion as well as tradition, or at least professional rhetoric, then, English law was "found," not "made": oral, not written, in provenance; judicial, not legislative, in character. This emphasis was preserved even with the development of statutory law, since such law was

established only through the Parliament, itself a "high court" and at first
hardly distinguished from the King's Bench.[10] What is more, statutes and
especially customs were subjected to extensive interpretation by judges,
with a flexibility going quite beyond Continental jurisprudence; nor was
the king himself allowed to make changes in the law.

To this should be added the growing power of the legal profession and
the multiplicity of jurisdictions, including the paraprofessional justices of
the peace, and especially the emergence of the Court of Chancery with its
roots in a peculiarly English form of "equity." Although justified in terms
of Roman *aequitas* (and Greek *epieikeia*), English "equity" actually evolved
as a body of precedents in the court of the Chancellor and represented
extraordinary (and, Maitland noted, non-statutory) jurisdiction, and a
power of "interpretation" which common lawyers found offensive and
even threatening. The judge in Chancery was supposed to make these
interpretations "as a skillful artisan . . . even out of the grounds or fountaines of the same law," but in fact he often invoked divine, canon, or civil
law; and it is small wonder that his jurisdiction became known as a a
"court of conscience" (the conscience, that is, of the Chancellor).[11] In
general, while English law pretended to be in accord with—and common
law actually identical with—nature, in fact the complex of Anglo-Norman
legal traditions represented a massive creation of human legal convention
and myth, a new province in the kingdom of Nomos.

The myths of the common-law and parliamentary traditions were confirmed and reinforced in the seventeenth century, when modern scholarship
lent its authority to definitions of "feudal" and "fundamental" law and to
questions of "legal memory." One common denominator was "custom,"
and royalists and Puritans—Tories and Whigs—alike appealed to it.
According to David Jenkins, English law had three grounds—custom, judicial records, and acts of Parliament—but of these only the first was "original," the other two being merely written confirmations of custom, which
was alone truly "fundamental."[12] Over the centuries this has been a major
and largely unquestioned premise of English social thought.

Second Nature

"Custom becomes a second nature" (*usus altera fit natura*), quoted Sir John
Fortescue in the course of "praising" the laws of England from the vantage
point of the King's Bench in the later fifteenth century.[13] This was his way
of arguing that English law was "natural" in the sense not of universal
perfection but of the sub-lunar process of generation and decay and the
organic character of English society, analogous to the famous formula of
Ulpian identifying nature with instinct, or that of Gaius identifying it with

common sense. English law was natural, "like the nerves of the body physical" (*lex* derived from *ligando,* binding) because it was "caused" by the spontaneous generation of popular usages in the course of time, and because it was established by "common consent" and confirmed by "common interest." "Natural," too, is the life of such people, which, under lawful and kingly governance, takes the form of a "body mystical" analogous to the "body natural" described by Aristotle. The analogy suggests, of course, that what is involved is a "second nature," which is to say, the collective habits and social patterns expressed by English customs, especially as these are subsequently reduced by writing "into a constitution or something of the nature of statutes."

The evolution of the English legal profession and the emergence of the Inns of Court, as well as the policies of the crown, ensured that the career of English law (its *ius proprium*) would follow its own course. This is perhaps best illustrated by the pattern of linguistic development, which is unparalleled on the Continent. Some English terms were retained in the language of the law, and Latin terms were resorted to; but from the thirteenth century on the prevailing idiom was that curious professional hybrid called "law-French." English jurists still spoke of "sac and soc" (the jurisdiction and profits derived from the land), and royal courts and learned authors like Bracton preserved the technical terminology of the civilians; but through the weight of professional tradition, especially in the training given at the Inns of Court and in the standard collections of cases, the Yearbooks, law-French was the major vehicle of legal development down at least to the seventeenth century. English lawyers argued, wrote, taught, and presumably thought in terms much closer to the French *coutumiers* than to the Digest, utilizing not the Roman law of *possessio,* for example, but rather the customary provisions for *seizin* and *disseizin.*[14] English law not only emerged from custom, as Bracton said, but also, at least through judicial convention or legal fiction, continued in that condition.

In many ways English common law preserved its ties with custom and developed its own means of justification and legitimation. What it lacked was a full-fledged jurisprudence, a philosophy of law comparable to that formulated by Ulpian and his classical colleagues. There are suggestions in Bracton and Glanvil, but in general it was left to modern jurists, beginning with Fortescue and, a generation later, Christopher St. German, to supply a conceptual framework for what Fortescue called "the mysteries of English law." Both he and St. German undertook to show the inevitable rationality of Common Law. Both resorted extensively (if often surreptitiously) to civil law; and Fortescue in particular emphasized the sanctity of law, even human law, referring not only to biblical texts but also to Ulpian's famous designation of jurisconsults as "priests of the laws."[15] In part Fortescue's book was a "mirror of the prince," and its message was that the center of royal education should be not arms, as Machiavelli was soon to argue, but the art of law, especially the English law to which the king was bound.

Fortescue, while drawing on scholastic views of natural law, consistently focused on the human or "positive" side. For him all law which was not "of nature" was either custom or statute. English custom was "most ancient," older than that of Venice or even Rome (so French jurists also argued); and statute merely gave it later, more authoritative expression. For Fortescue as for St. German, the main business of common law was property, or rather, that feudal version which took as its unit the "fee," the English equivalent of the fief. What distinguished English from French society (at least before the French Revolution) was above all the respect for property, expressed, for instance, in the prohibition of the billeting of troops and of arbitrary taxation without consent—and of course in the notorious severity of English criminal law and the law of debt.[16] Property, indeed, was the subject of the greatest legal treatise of that age—"Littleton on Tenures"—which William Camden compared with Justinian's Digest and which Coke (defiantly answering Continental criticisms, especially François Hotman's accusation that the work was unintelligible) proclaimed to be as close to perfection as a book could be.[17]

The drift of St. German's argument, too, was toward celebrating the unique and indigenous character of English tradition, but he aspired to a higher enhancement by fixing English law within the framework of an "eternal law" equivalent to God's own reason. This *lex eterna* was manifested in three ways, St. German argued—through that "natural reason" referred to by Gaius, through divine revelation, and through human law, including legislation. To the main question, "to know wherupon the lawe of Englande is grounded," St. German posited six bases, all of them, in effect, human law. The first two categories he designated as reason and divine law, but in fact the substance of the first included criminal law (murder, perjury, breaking the peace, and other "primary" aspects of the *lex rationis*) and property law (the "second aspect"), and that of the second included matters for canon law courts or ecclesiastical cases consigned to royal courts. The remaining categories were "general custom" (referring to the "courts of record"), useful maxims (which "a large volume would not suffice to declare"), various particular customs, and finally the statutes. Above all, St. German wanted to reconcile the mass of English law, including antinomies and paradoxes, with general reason and its theological equivalents, "conscience" (*sinderesis*) and "equity" (*epieikeia*), which were associated with the court of Chancery.[18] At that time the Chancellor's court was guided by the ineluctable "conscience" of none other than Thomas More, who had more than a passing interest in both "natural" and "divine" law, the first in his *Utopia* and the second in his assaults on Protestant notions of "conscience."[19]

The arbitrary and, some would say, irrational character of common law is undeniable; "for how, " asked St. German, "may it be proved by reason that the eldest sone shall onlye enheryte his father & the yonger to haue no parte . . . ?" Another example, cited by Fortescue, that a man could not succeed to a brother by a different mother even if the property escheated, seemed again to be a rule without reason. "But," he added, "the difficulty of such a case does not in the least perturb one learned in the law." St. German admitted that "to discern the lawe of god and the law of reason from the lawe posytyve is very harde," but he too was undisturbed. He acknowledged, for example, that the law of property in general seemed to violate the law of nature, which is to say, reason, certainly according to canonists like Gratian and civilians like Irnerius. Goods ought to be held in common, he wrote, and property law was a relatively late convention. Yet such admissions did not prevent him from justifying English property law on grounds of nature as well as custom (*secundum naturam et secundum consuetudinem patrie*).[20] Whatever the grounds—the law of reason (*lex rationis*) or the reason of the law (*ratio legis*)—such arguments amounted to a kind of judicial discretion. "The rule of construction goes under various names," as St. German's modern editor summed up the matter. "Aristotle calls it *epieikeia,* the legists call it interpretation, the canonists call it dispensation, and the *politici* call it good faith." Common lawyers, we might add, just called it "nature."[21]

In any case, it was above all on the basis of the law of private property, which was a material yet sanctified extension of personal liberty, that the professional monopoly and national mythology of common law were established—assisted by the extraordinary growth of litigation (especially over debt) and of the proportion of attorneys in the population beginning in the later sixteenth century. For Blackstone anyone who violated the sanctity of property and possession was "guilty of a transgression against the law of society, which is a kind of secondary law of nature."[22] Eventually, divested of feudal trappings and expressed in the still more naturalistic terms of Lockean political theory, what might be called the property fetish of common law helped to prepare the way for modern liberal ideology.

At the end of the sixteenth century Richard Hooker developed the nativist arguments of Fortescue and St. German much more elaborately and extended them to the ecclesiastical aspect of English tradition. Defending Anglican tradition from Protestant subversions of "law," Hooker set about systematically, or at least comprehensively, to justify English institutional arrangements as both "reasonable" and "natural"—at least within the limits imposed by original sin, which reduced an original and "sincere,"

"primarie" condition to a "depraved," "secundarie" condition. His conclusion, like that of Fortescue, was that "Civill society" and "civill law"
in an English context were regulated according to a justified and even
admirable "second nature."[23] The notion of laws indigenous and "fundamental" to English society was reinforced, too, by political convergences
between common law, Puritanism, and parliamentary opposition to the
crown in the generation before the civil war.

If all of this helps to explain "how God became an Englishman," it
explains, too, the more philosophical point which Edmund Burke, in the
interest of conservative politics, made about man's "moral nature." Physical
nature man shares with the beasts, but his moral nature makes him a
creature of prejudice, opinions, habits, and sentiments, all of which "form
our second nature, as inhabitants of the country and members of the society
in which Providence has placed us."[24]

What has been called (by Maitland, among others) the "common-law
mind" seems to be summed up, if not caricatured, in the pronouncements
of Sir Edward Coke—made, to be sure, in the heat of controversy, but
nonetheless suggesting the nature and style of English legal and social
thought. Coke certainly illustrated the guild-mentality and chauvinism of
his profession. Rome had made imperial claims and liberal gestures, but in
this little island a better way had been found. Of all laws, Coke declared
in his daringly "extensive" and polemical commentaries on the law reports,
those of England "are the most equal and most certain, of greatest antiquity
and least Delay, and most beneficial and easy to be observed."[25] It was
appropriate that Coke's authoritative commentaries, like Justinian's Institutes and the Napoleonic Code, should be turned into verse for the amuse-
ment and easier recollection of beginning students.

Coke took an extremely proprietary attitude toward the common-law
tradition and its literary canon, which for him included not (as in France)
the work of historians ("I pray thee beware of Chronicle Law reported in
our Annals, for that will undoubtedly lead thee to error") but only books
of those such as Bracton, Glanvil, Littleton, St. German, and Lambarde,
and "the reading of the several Reports and Records of these laws," which
alone "contain the faithful and true histories of all successive Times, as
well concerning the Punishment of Evil . . . as concerning the Reward and
Advancement of Men of great Merit and Virtue." Yet the common law
represented an ancient mystery as well as a modern science, and ultimately
Coke's professional conclusion was that "the grounds of our Common Law
were beyond the Memory or Register of any Beginning." What English law
was before the statutes—that is, the prehistorical customs and "second
nature" of the English people—only the experts, the initiates into the
mysteries of common law, could declare. Only they could "speak the law"

(*judex est lex loquens* is one of Coke's many maxims); only they could bring about an advancement of legal learning.[26]

Ideologically, what is most significant about common law for the history of social thought is its instinctive, though eventually doctrinaire, insistence on the popular character of institutions. Politically, this was embodied in the Parliament, and especially in parliamentary rhetoric. Parliament, too, was "natural," drawing as it did on the myth of the three estates, and (as Lambarde observed) was "*Natural* in that it hath an imitation of the natural 'bodie' of man, truly called a *little world*." Socially, the popular character of English law took a variety of forms and was perhaps best symbolized by the old customs, set down in the *Book of Fiefs* long before Magna Carta, of judgment by peers, trial by jury, and in effect "due process." Trial by jury, related to the French *enquête par turbe* and the German *Weistum*, which determined the validity of a custom by inquiry of a certain number of "good men," was an illustration of the old belief that law was an expression of society, as was the emphasis placed by common lawyers on case law and precedent.[27]

Less apparent and never theoretically formulated, but no less fundamental, were the methodological premises of common law. Philosophical allusions aside, the true basis for interpretations made by Fortescue, St. German, and their later colleagues was (aside from the statutes) the series of Yearbooks and later law reports, which, out of particular cases, summed up England's legal experience and *leyes natifs ou positifs,* as Henry Finch referred to the legal base of any "civil societie." Finch acknowledged the reception of "Rules prises del autres Learnings" but only because they had in effect been naturalized by English experience.[28] Books such as Thomas Phaer's *Newe boke of Presidentes* (1543) illustrated and reinforced the empirical cast of mind encouraged in the Inns and in legal practice. As Fortescue wrote of the rules of common law, "These principles are not known by force of argument nor by logical demonstration, but . . . by logical induction through the senses and the memory." "For generalities," as Coke remarked in defense of his own commonsense methods, "never bring anything to a conclusion."[29]

In its reliance on such piecemeal and ad hoc procedure and in its antagonism to Roman theorizing, English jurisprudence seems neatly congruent not only with that juridical cast of mind known as legal positivism but perhaps also, as in the case of Francis Bacon, with that philosophical cast of mind known as British empiricism—which in general has continued to inform Anglo-American thinking about society and culture (at least its own). "The life of law has not been logic," as Justice Holmes put it: "it has been experience."[30] In this way, too, the "common-law mind" has managed to preserve its own "nature"—or rather, its "second nature." Yet no culture, not even a professional culture, is an island, and English social thought had continually to contend with intellectual threats and enticements from abroad.

The Law of Laws

Civil law had a continuous, if sometimes tenuous, existence in the English legal tradition. At one time, as Arthur Duck noted, the study of written law led to "the high road to rewards"; and in the sixteenth century it was still indispensable in various diplomatic, maritime, and ecclesiastical matters, as well as in the prerogative courts and other jurisdictions outside the common law.[31] These included the Council and the courts of Admiralty, Star Chamber, Arches, the Marshal, the Constable, and above all Chancery, where (as one of Coke's colleagues put it) "lextremitie et rigor al common ley est qualifie."[32] Until the end of the century most masters of the rolls, and many ambassadors, were civilians. As for canon law, which had never been clearly distinguished from civil law, it continued in force in some civil matters even after Henry VIII's break with Rome (except where explicitly forbidden by statute). Concerning Roman law in general, Richard Hooker remarked philosophically upon "the great use we have thereof, both in decisions in certain causes arising daily among ourselves, and especially for commerce with nations abroad, whereunto that knowledge is most requisite."[33]

In Tudor England, even after Henry VIII's break with Rome, civil law maintained an intellectual and scholarly presence for at least two institutional reasons. One was the formation in 1511 of "Doctors' Commons," a kind of civilian bar association, which had more than two hundred members over the next century, including distinguished scholars such as Erasmus's friend Cuthbert Tunstall, Thomas Smith, Julius Caesar, and Walter Haddon. The other was the establishment in 1540 of regius professorships in civil law both at Cambridge and at Oxford, whose charge was, among other things, to offer comparisons of civil and common law. The first tenant of the Cambridge chair was Smith himself, and in his inaugural lecture he praised the Continental masters of humanist jurisprudence and declared that civil law was a "divine science," a "truly common law to all grades of men."[34] Fortune seemed to smile on the study of civil law when, in 1560, Elizabeth went to Oxford to attend a disputation, and especially when, in 1587, the regius chair was given to Alberico Gentili. Although he was in flight from popery, Gentili (in contrast to Smith) clung to the methods of "jurisprudence Italian style."[35]

To civilians of all persuasions, of course, and indeed to most men of letters, Roman law was philosophically and socially, if not necessarily politically, far superior to the barbarian accumulations of medieval Europe, including common law. "The study of English law is as far as can be from true learning," remarked Erasmus; and his friend Thomas More, seeking a basis for the social criticism of his *Utopia,* had perforce to turn to the resources of natural law as preserved in part by Roman jurisprudence.[36] In other ways the classical wisdom reflected in Roman law had been absorbed in the humanist program of education, which had invaded even the practical curriculum of the Inns of Court by the sixteenth century. The great virtue of civil law, however, was that it formed "one body and system," as Robert Wiseman wrote during the enthusiasm for law reform in the wake of the Puritan Revolution; and on this basis alone it deserved to be regarded as the "law of laws."[37]

Yet the "common-law mind" took a very different view of all this. To William Lambarde English law was "like a wall built of stone and oak to defend a city."[38] The enemies at the gates continued to be those twin menaces, civil and canon law—which, coiled like two snakes about Mercury's wand, as John Selden put it, inspired a sort of fascinated horror in most Englishmen. Obviously, this attitude had deep roots in the English legal tradition. Continental civilians had regularly interpreted and "extended" European customs, but in England this was in violation of a professional monopoly. Coke called it "a desperate and dangerous matter for Civilians and Canonists . . . to write either of the Common Laws of England, which they profess not, or against them which they know not."[39]

By Coke's time the anti-Romanist prejudice was virtually "second nature" with common lawyers. "Comparisons are rightly to be judged odious," observed Fortescue; and so they were, especially as he employed them. To enhance his "praise of the laws of England," written in the wake of the Hundred Years' War, Fortescue indulged in a whole series of odious and invidious comparisons between common and civil law, that is, the civil law practiced in French courts as Fortescue understood it. With small regard for historical accuracy, what Fortescue did was to juxtapose an idealization of the law of the English courts of record with a caricature of those of France, and his purpose was transparently polemical. Civil law he represented in terms of its arbitrariness (establishing the truth by testimony of only a couple of witnesses instead of a sworn jury), its cavalier attitude toward family property (allowing bastards to succeed), its brutality (the recourse to torture), and above all its tyranny, suggested especially by the famous (and famously misconstrued) civilian formula (*lex regia*), "What pleases the prince has the force of law"; and of course he found the French monarchy guilty by association. By contrast, the "political *and* regal" (*regnum politicum et regale*—in effect and in retrospect, the parliamentary and monarchical) government of England belonged to a wholly different and more humane species.[40]

The Reformation aversion to popery further stirred up this anti-Romanism. In 1535 Henry VIII ended the teaching of canon law, and common lawyers urged further restrictions. In 1547 a group of students from the Inns of Court presented a petition to the Protector Somerset to arrest the decay of common law by curbing the crypto-Romanist jurisdiction of Chancery; and they complained bitterly about those who, "being civilian and not learned in the Common Laws, determyne the waighty causes of this realm according either to the saide Lawe Civile or to their own conscience."[41] And in his *De Republica Anglorum,* written in 1565, Thomas Smith—though he preserved a respect for the comparative approach to institutions—showed no sign of the enthusiasm for civil law that he had displayed twenty years before. Citing the old adage that "law originated in fact" (*ex facto ius oritur*), he gave up his Romanoid idealism and reverted to the insular view of Fortescue, who insisted and reveled in the fact that English law was "different from the fashions used either in Fraunce, or in Italy, or in any other place where the Emperors lawes and constitutions (called the civill lawes) be put in use."[42]

This sort of "juridical nationalism" took a social as well as a political form. During his exile in Strasbourg John Aylmer, for example, protested both the "burden" of civil law and the "cannon shot" of ecclesiastical law as well as such alien practices as testamentary succession—"for nothing soner destroieth great houses, than the division of thenheritance, as it appeareth in Germany." Aylmer also extended his arguments into the linguistic realm. "We have a few hunting termes and peddlars Frenche in the lousye lawe brought in by the Normans," admitted Aylmer, ". . . but the language and the customes bee Englyshe and Saxonyshe." There might be some French "blood," he added, but there were not French "hartes."[43] English "nature" went deeper than words.

The rivalry between the universalist arrogance of Roman law and the insular pride of common law was suggested by the legal and social language of the Tudor period. Civil lawyers interpreted their materials *civiliter* with implicitly "political" values associated with the "republic," but for Englishmen "civil" and "civil science" (*scientia civilis* in Thomas Cooper's Latin-English dictionary) had private and moral connotations. Social reformers, such as the so-called commonwealth party under Edward VI, as well as common lawyers, tended to couch their public discourse in "common" and "communal" terms for the presumed benefit of the "commonwealth." As Thomas More's son-in-law, John Rastel, wrote, "A good resonable commyn lawe makith a gode commyn pease and a comyn wealth among a grete commynalte of people."[44] In style, at least, English legal discourse, reinforcing the contemporary vernacularist fashions that resisted foreign imports (even trying to substitute "witcraft," for example, for "logic"), seemed informed less by "political" than by social, economic, and perhaps moral considerations.

A few English jurists looked across the channel for assistance and inspiration and even shared Continental notions of "perfect jurisprudence." In *The English Lawyer* (1631) John Doderidge, for example, summarized a "method for the managing the Lawes of this land." For those who (in Doderidge's words) "covet to contemplate with their inward eye the *expresse and perfect image of an English Lawyer,*" Doderidge recommended not only the works of Alciato, Budé, and the great legal humanists but also those of the sixteenth-century methodizers of jurisprudence who turned to dialectic, whether in the form of Aristotelianism or of the innovations of Ramus.[45] In his *Epieikeia,* written at the end of the sixteenth century, Edward Hake identified "equity" with that same "spirit of the law" celebrated by the ancient jurists and, more recently, by Melanchthon, in contrast to the "quercks and quiddityes strained from the trew sense of the law" by medieval commentators." Hake expected that this "spirit" would be taken "owt of the ground and fountaines" of common law.[46]

Under the Tudors civilians and common lawyers differed in legal style and tradition, but professional divergences became incendiary political issues under the Stuarts, when the stock of civil law was rising sharply. "And I think that if it bee taken away," wrote the first Stuart king in 1609, "it would make an entrie of Barbarisme into this Kingdome."[47] For James I, however, the civilizing force of Roman law (which he had enjoyed as ruler of Scotland) consisted not so much in its classicial elegance or rational order as in the support it lent to royal authority. Inevitably, this attitude turned common lawyers even more alarmedly against the old Romanist threat, which was expressed in civilian works such as John Cowell's *Interpreter* (1607) and Alberico Gentili's *Regales disputationes* (1605), whose message appeared to be (according to a later critic) simply the absolutist claim that "the people have given their power to their prince to be a tyrant and to tread them under foot at liberty."[48]

Civil law was thus guilty by association with royalism and became a symbol of tyranny, much as Machiavelli had been a generation earlier. Concerning this same formula (the *lex regia* and its corollary principle, the *princeps legibus solutus*), namely, that "a Prince is not tyed to the laws," Wiseman explained, in much the same terms as Etienne Pasquier had used earlier in the century in his own comparative study of Justinian's Institutes, that it did not have to be taken literally or "cruelly," and that it only referred to the prince's customary prerogatives.[49] Like custom and common law itself, such conceptions had to be in accord with reason and justice, not to mention common (and juris-) prudence.

English civilians taught, but common lawyers would not learn—especially in times of constitutional conflict and civil war—that Roman law also had its human, its social, and even its popular and "common" faces, and that it had a rational organization which might serve to improve and

to "reform" the disorder and inequities of English law. Various efforts were
made, in England as elsewhere, to harmonize civil law and native custom.
Roman and common law should not be opposed "like the two faces of
Janus," wrote William Fulbeke (alluding perhaps to the "disdainful comparisons" of Fortescue), "but rather be joined like the three graces"; and
Fulbeke practiced what he preached by writing a pioneering and comprehensive "parallel" of the common, civil, and canon laws.[50] His colleague
John Cowell made a still more substantial contribution to this enterprise
through his *Institutes of the Lawes of England,* which (like the similar
works by Pasquier and Guy Coquille in France) followed the method and
order of Justinian's textbook. There were other attempts to restore credit
to civil and canon law, such as Thomas Ridley's apologetic *View of the
Civile and Ecclesiastical Law* (1607) and Arthur Duck's *Treatise on the
Use and Authority of the Civil Law in England* (1648), which both envisaged a common—but a common European—heritage of social institutions
and thought.[51]

The cosmopolitan and comparative vision encouraged by the study of
civil law can be seen in the work not only of civilians but also of scholars
such as Selden, Spelman, and Roger Owen, who viewed English law in a
European perspective and who were pioneers in ideas of legal "evolution."
Commenting on Fortescue's "praise" of English laws, Selden argued that
English and European customs, despite later divergences, had a common
grounding and similar growth. To ask the question with which Plato opened
his laws—"When and how began your common laws?"—was a "trivial
demand" (words repeated a generation later by John Bridall), because it
implied speculations about an imaginary and unrecorded state of nature.
English laws were the product of centuries of being "increased, altered,
interpreted, and brought to what they now are," and so had to be understood in historical and comparative terms. There was no monolithic "immemorial custom," wrote Selden, "but questionless the *Saxons* made a mixture
of the *British* customs with their own, the *Danes* with old *British,* that
Saxon and their own; and the *Normans* the like."[52]

Spelman continued Selden's line of inquiry and interpretation. Trained
as a lawyer but devoted to antiquarian studies, Spelman linked the study
of English land law to that old and battle-scarred question of civil science,
"the origin of feuds." Maitland went so far as to suggest that it was
Spelman, not the Normans, who had introduced Continental feudalism
into England—although in this connection Spelman referred to the modern
work of Cujas and Pasquier as well as to medieval sources. In general,
Spelman concluded, "I think the Foundation of our Law to be laid by our
German ancestors, but built upon and polished by Materials taken from
the Canon Law and Civil Law."[53]

In legal as well as antiquarian terms the influence of civil law continued to be felt, and in the later seventeenth century George Mackenzie was still proclaiming its "Excellence and usefullnesse."[54] It was commonly invoked in various hopes and schemes of legal reform, most famously in Bacon's project for a "union of law," which would offer an equitable balance between the "public" and "private" poles of society—that is, government and property—and would help to demystify and deprofessionalize English law, yet give it an order that would enhance both its rationality and its utility.

Most important, perhaps, civil law continued to furnish a standard of comparison (even if "odious"), a fund of legal analogies, and a source (often unacknowledged) of general historical wisdom, especially as expressed in formulas and maxims—"foundations of the law" Bacon called them—many of which had been absorbed not only into common law but also into the general culture. Once again, of course, these maxims were accepted not as expressions of historical experience but rather, in the words of William Phillips, as "Conclusions of Reason," which it was "not lawful for any one to deny." The modern field of international law, in which Gentili and Selden were pioneers, was another by-product of Roman law— though again it was formulated increasingly in "natural" terms.[55] This is another story, but it is worth noting here that the debate over the modern law of nations played a large role in the expansion of social thought from the time of Selden and Grotius, who applied the *ius gentium* to the problems of a divided and expanding Europe and the confrontations of alien cultures throughout the "world of nations."

Yet these generous views of law as a part of literature and philosophy were hardly representative of the assumption or even the horizons of the common lawyers. For most of them it was enough to have a practical grasp of the texts and the trade secrets of their professional guild; and William Noy's *Compleat Lawyer,* for example, was little more than a catechism of the laws of tenures and estates—which, he opined, represented the very beginning of civilization. In the wake of the civil war, with Roman law generally discredited, English common law lapsed severely into its insular habits and alienation from Continental scholarship; and though it was abolished along with the monarchy law-French was restored from 1660 to 1773. All along, the Inns of Court had enjoyed, at best, only peripheral connections with Continental learning, especially of the humanist variety; but from the Stuart period to the mid-nineteenth century, as Holdsworth concluded, they were in a state of almost complete collapse; and the legal literature of the later seventeenth and eighteenth centuries reflected this condition.[56]

Professionally, then, the common law was increasingly impervious to Continental fashions, certainly as far as legal reform was concerned. The centuries-long professional feud with civil law reinforced the inclination of

English lawyers to ground their jurisprudence and their social thinking on
their own insular experience, even though they often equated this experience with "nature" and with "reason" in a sense foreign to Continental
legal philosophy. As William Lambarde instructed one of his juries, "The
law or policy of this realm of England . . . is a peculiar government, not
borrowed from the imperial or Roman law (as be the laws of the most part
of other nations) but standing upon the highest reason selected even for
itself." Or in the famous words of William Dugdale, "Common law is none
other than pure and tried Reason."[57]

Pure and Tried Reason

"Pure and tried reason" is a nice phrase, but in the context of law it is
ambivalent and perhaps paradoxical—smacking of Baconian or Newtonian
efforts to join experience and reason in a universally valid method applied
to the study of Nature. "Tried" the common law certainly was, but "trial
and error" may seem a better characterization of its development; and as
for "pure," the English legal tradition had none of the abstract rationality
of Stoicism, of modern civil science, or even of such fashionable modern
theories as Ramism, with its bifurcations. Much more appropriate for
common law was the idea of "artificial reason," gained only through the
study of the canon of common law, the training offered in the Inns of
Court, and the "practice" of law in the common law courts.[58]

In the opposition between "artificial reason" and "natural reason" we
have another episode in the long-standing rivalry between Physis and
Nomos, and there is no better illustration of the problem than in Thomas
Hobbes's conception of the primacy of natural law over any of the professional and practical varieties. In his *Elements of Law,* written in 1649,
Hobbes tied his idea of law wholly to an abstract theory of psychology—
of the behavior of the body natural paralleling that, expressed in the
Leviathan, of the body politic. In the former work Hobbes also made a
basic distinction between two sorts of learned men—the "mathematicians"
(*mathematici*) and the "dogmatists" (*dogmatici*).[59] The first group were
humble and dedicated themselves to natural reason and first principles,
while the second claimed privileged authority and were satisfied with sur-
rendering to custom and what was accepted through common consent—a
locus classicus, in short, of the contest between primary and "second"
nature, a contest for which Hobbes offered a simple and brutal resolution
in his *Leviathan.*

The opposition became clearer in Hobbes's later work, *A Dialogue
between a Philosopher and a Student of the Common Laws of England,*
published in 1681 and directed presumably at the views of Coke. In this
dialogue the main question is why mathematics should be more rational

and certain than the law, so that mathematicians err less often than jurists. The Philosopher and the Lawyer agree that "reason" is the "soul of law" (*ratio anima legis*, in the well-known formula). "As for this reasoning of yours, I think it well enough," remarks the Lawyer. "But there ought to be also a reverend respect to customs not unreasonable," such as those celebrated by Coke—who (he adds) ought to be praised for "drawing to the Men of his Profession as much Authority as lawfully he might," since this adds to the authority of the king. In any case, the sort of "reson" represented by Coke is "an artificial perfection of Reason gotten by long Study, Observation and Experience, and not every Mans natural Reason." And not only the authority of the common law but also prudence recommends this reliance on "positive law," for a judge would be delinquent and a barrister "but an ill Pleader" who has only pure reason for an ally in deciding about jurisdiction, for example, or complex problems of *meum et tuum*). In response to these arguments the Philosopher protests that this line of argument appeals to "mere *Rhetorick* to reduce the Jury, and sometimes the Judge also," rather than a search for justice. Understood rightly, continues the Philosopher, written law cannot be against reason; and he invokes the ancient legal distinction between the letter and the spirit of the law, which "is not only the Law . . . signified by *Grammatical* construction of the Letter, but that which the legislator should be in force; which Intention, I confess, is a very hard matter indeed many times to pick out of the words of the Statute."[60]

The terms of this debate are clear and need not be pursued. What is important to note is the way the Philosopher equates the "intention" of the legislator with reason—the *mens legis* with the *ratio legis*. This was a common asssumption of Roman jurists—and indeed the Philosopher observes in passing that common law is historically in only part of Roman law—and it suited Hobbes's own political program, but it does not seem quite in accord with the identification of law with "natural reason." In other words, juxtaposing the will of the prince and the rationality of the law would seem to revive the distinction between reason based on nature and reason based on human artifice, analogous again, perhaps, to a natural body and the "artificial body" of the Leviathan.

Sir Matthew Hale, historian as well as common lawyer, rejected the position of Hobbes (that is, the "Philosopher") on standard professional grounds. Hale admitted the presence of a "subject Reason" common to humanity but argued that this reason was developed along specialized lines, some men, for example, being more inclined, or applying themselves more energetically, to mathematical reason and others to medicine or—most complex of all—to the law. The "Difficultie of makeing, interpreting and applying Laws" arose from several conditions, including the disparity between individual and common convenience and the incommensurability of moral actions. Moreover, it seems imprudent to risk social discord for some "new Theory" instead of preserving an ancient law. "And this adds to ye difficultie of a present fathomeing of the reason of the Lawes, because they are the Production of long and iterated Experience wch tho' itt be commonly called the mistriss of Fooles, yett certainly itt is the wisest Expedient among mankind, and discovers those defects and Supplys wch no witt of Man coud either at once foresee or aptly remedye."[61]

Like Fortescue and St. German, Hale acknowledged that some English customs were beyond the power of reason to grasp, and this occurred especially in matters of property and succession. "Now if any the most refined Braine under heaven would goe about to Enquire by Speculation, or by reading of Plato or Aristotle, or by Considering the Lawes of the Jewes, or other Nations, to find out how Landes descend in England . . . he wou'd lose his Labour, and Spend his Notions in vaine, till he acquainted himselfe with the Lawes of England, and the reason is because they are Institutions introduced by the will and Consent of others implicitely by Custom and usage, or Explicitely by written Laws of Acts of Parlemt." Political modifications, too, he added, might be made "by longe custome and usage wch carries in it Selfe a facile Consent of the Governrs and Governed, or is at least an Evidence or Interpretation of the Original Institution of the nature of the Governmt."

In this way Hale celebrated the "second nature" which he and the "community of interpretation" to which he belonged had created by means of their "artificial reason." In his *History of the Common Law* Hale described more fully the canon of this tradition, its origin in unwritten law and oral tradition—"incompetent" as these are without written "monuments"—and its divergence from Roman law. Not only was common law excellent in itself, Hale argued, "but it is singularly accommodated to the frame of the English Government, and to the Disposition of the English Nation, and such as by a long Experience and Use is as it were incorporated into the very Temperament, and, in a Manner, become the Complection and Constitution of the English Commonwealth."[62] In terms of civil science Common Law was not only the *ius proprium* of England; it had in effect seceded from the *ius commune* of the European community.

Hobbes of course had many other critics, most of them fired by religious outrage but at least one of them opposed on legal grounds. In his *Leviathan Found Out* and *Behemoth Arraigned* John Whitehall supplemented Clarendon's arguments, objecting in particular to Hobbes's efforts to alter custom, which (he charged) were "principally aimed at supplanting our Common law." Whitehall also defended the principle of prescription, especially in matters of property, and the legitimacy which time had bestowed on English law. "For 'tis by the Common law that most men enjoy their estates, either real or personal. Now if length of time should not justify that property . . . down goes the Common law and law and property with it. Then let the strongest take all, Witty Mr. Hobbes!"[63]

In contrast to Continental social thought, English controversy of the Restoration period continued to turn on questions of the "immemorial" (in effect, the prehistorical and essentially popular) character of English institutions. In 1680 William Petyt's *Antient Right of the Commons Asserted,* attempting to prove "by records and the best historians, that the Commons were ever an essential part of Parliament," stirred up protest by royalists, who were convinced that English "legal memory" began only in 1198 (Richard I's coronation). William Atwood and Robert Brady were among those who opposed Petyt's subversive antiquarianism and arguments *ab antiquo* with—likewise historical—demonstrations that the constitution of Parliament was a creation not of the Anglo-Saxons but of the crown itself.[64] In a dialogue published in 1694 John Tyrrell, "Mr. Freeman," tried to persuade the civilian "Mr. Meanwell," again on historical grounds, that the true innovation, and an illegal one at that, was not the House of Commons, whose existence was ancient and "fundamental," but rather the principle of divine right.[65]

The culmination of this conservative and conservationist attitude came in William Blackstone's *Commentaries on the Laws of England,* a latter-day *Summa* to set beside the work of Bracton five centuries earlier. In the wake of Newtonian science, Blackstone had become even more adept at the sort of naturalistic rhetoric displayed by Coke, Fortescue, and other members of the common-law canon, and also at balancing the "scientific" and "mysterious" aspects of their tradition. For Blackstone, too, "reason" and "nature" referred not to abstract and universal rationality but to the "spirit" and "genius" of English common law, and especially to arrangements for the protection of liberty and property worked out over the centuries.[66] This was what he meant when he characterized English law as "a kind of secondary law of nature"—perfect in its own way, no doubt, but, for all that, a form of "local knowledge."

Beyond the Common Law

From the standpoint of social thought, offshoots of the common-law tradition were in many ways more significant than the mainstream English profession; and this applies especially to Scottish jurisprudence in the seventeenth and eighteenth centuries. By 1800 the lawyers, coming to outnumber and intellectually to outweigh the clergy, became a shaping force in the early stages of the Scottish Enlightenment, most especially in the area of social thought.[67] Efforts to understand and to evaluate the mixed heritage of Scottish law—Roman, English, and native custom—through historical investigation and ideas of natural law were seminally important in the development of "Scotch knowledge."

Aside from Thomas Craig's work on "feudal law," mostly a commentary on Scottish land law, there was not much in the way of legal literature in Scotland before Lord Stair's *Institutions* of 1681, a pioneering work which, with comparable display of general learning, accomplished for Scottish law what Grotius did for the Netherlands, Pasquier for France, and Cowell for England. Stair followed both Gaius's organization and his famous formula, that "the laws of men are either common to many nations, or proper to one nation, or"—adding a third alternative, perhaps to fit the Scottish situation—"peculiar to some places or incorporations, as were the municipal laws in the Roman republic." In general, Stair derived Scottish law "from the common law that rules the world and compared it with the laws civil and canon, and with the customs of the neighboring nations," although these, and especially the "popish law" of Rome, "are only received according to their equity and expedience." Like English law, Stair acknowledged, "our law is most part consuetudinary," though possessing closer ties with Continental feudalism; unlike it, however, Scottish "consuetude" was regarded as superior to statute law, which was peculiarly "liable to desuetude."[68]

Later Scottish scholars extended Stair's historical approach and gave it theoretical reinforcement with the help of more up-to-date Continental ideas. Gershom Carmichael, called "the real founder of the Scottish school of philosophy" by William Hamilton, introduced the work of Pufendorf to the University of Glasgow; and, tempered by Scottish respect for religion, "natural law Continental style" became a permanent feature of Scottish social thought in the work both of jurists and of moral philosophers, including Carmichael's successor at Glasgow, Francis Hutcheson.[69]

Among jurists the leading figure was Lord Kames, who began with the assumption that the study of law was only rational when it was followed historically. More specifically, Kames nourished the hope of tracing the "progress of manners, of laws, of arts from their birth" through the "dark ages," perhaps with the help of "hints from poets and historians" as well as the principles of natural law.[70] The culmination of this line of argument came with the famous "four-stage" theory of economic and social progress, which achieved its mature formulation in the work of three of Kames's protégés active in legal studies during the third quarter of the century— James Dalrymple, who was admitted as advocate in 1748; John Millar, who was professor of civil law at the University of Glasgow in the 1760s; and especially Adam Smith, who delivered his lectures on jurisprudence in those years.[71] The "four-stage" concept was also discussed at this time or even earlier by Turgot and by A. Y. Goguet, whose book on the origin of laws was translated into English and published in Edinburgh in 1761.[72]

According to this theory, implied if not formulated in civilian tradition, mankind progressed from barbarism to civilization through periods dominated successively by hunters, shepherds, farmers, and merchants—with congruent patterns of legal, and of course mental, development. This cornerstone of Enlightenment thinking, wishful though it may seem to some, represents not only a materialist version of the progress of "ideas" but also a sort of historicization of the categories of jurisprudence—from beginnings in "natural law" to custom and then (with settlement, cultivation, and trade) to more "civilized" notions of human society and written legal devices. It also depends on the vital principle of the overriding importance of property in particular and the new discipline of political economy in general. The marriage of economics and metaphysics which underlay the work of moral philosophers such as Carmichael and Smith and which produced "Scotch knowledge" has been essential to the history of modern social thought, but it carries the story beyond the confines of the professional tradition of civil science.

The British legal tradition left its mark, too, on colonial America, which carried out a "revolution" against a government but in no sense against the legal system—and which indeed might claim to be even more faithful to the principles of common law than the Parliament of George III. One of the transmitters was a product of this same Scottish school, James Wilson, who gave the first course of lectures on law in the new American republic (1790–92). "In free countries," he told his students in Philadelphia, "in free countries especially that boast the blessings of common law, sprung warm and spontaneous from the manners of the people"—and here he cited Fortescue, Hooker, and Pufendorf, as well as Spelman, Gibbon, and Blackstone—"Law must be taught as a historical science."[73]

What Wilson did was essentially to endorse the original claim made by Bracton, which was that English law was a prototype—and by the eighteenth century an archaic survival—of custom. Wilson established this commonplace in his second lecture (having celebrated, in the first one, in Washington's presence, the deliverance of the new nation, which had just "passed the Red Sea in safety"). "Let me mention in one word everything that can enforce my sentiments," he declared: "the common law of England is a customary law." So it remained, though in the custody of the jurists; and so he hoped the law of the new nation would be, though likewise under the leadership of professionals, including the students addressed by Wilson.

The founding fathers were, most of them, lawyers and, many of them, respectful of the European legal tradition, civil law included. As a young man John Adams had been a great admirer of Roman law and had once borrowed a copy of Justinian's Institutes from the Harvard Library with the intention of translating it. "A lawyer in this country must study common law, and civil law, and natural law, and admiralty law," he wrote.[74] His old friend Thomas Jefferson was in absolute agreement and, at the end of his life, recalled writing, as a young man himself, "The lawyer finds in the Latin tongue the system of civil law most conformable with the principles of justice of any which have been established among men, and from which much has been incorporated into our own." For a federal law suit of 1810 in Louisiana, Jefferson reviewed his knowledge of this subject and in the course of his brief even praised civil law in the old civilian formula, "written reason."[75]

Yet for the most part American law followed the "natural" course set by English common law and, politically, by the school of natural law and natural rights. As a consequence American thought, even more than its English counterpart, has been torn between a technical system of jurisprudence and a highly abstract system of political thought, and has in various ways been cut off from the sort of integral social thought created by the older tradition of European civil science and the "world of nations" which it inhabited. This may help to account for the generally foreshortened and narrow-ranged view which American scholarship, following good Anglo-Saxon precedent, has tended to take of the history of the sciences of society and of culture.

ELEVEN

Jurisprudence in the French Manner

Mos praecedat consuetudinem . . . Res iudicata consuetudinem confirmat.

Connan, *Commentarii iuris civilis* (1557)

·

Mos Gallicus

The "French method of teaching law" (*mos gallicus iuris docendi*) is another reflection of the nationalization of social thought. It was named after Alciato's disciples at the University of Bourges, who turned against Bartolism and self-consciously tried to formulate a "method" based on a combination of humanist learning and old fashioned legal science as developed by "ultramontane" jurists. Among the leaders of jurisprudence in the French manner were four famous scholars who happened to have the same first name (and were "French"), and who were memorialized in a contemporary punning verse:

> Among the François of law, the leading lights are four:
> Of interpreters François Duaren is first in legal lore;
> And then François Connan, counsellor we esteem;
> And third François Baudouin, Hellenist supreme;
> And François Hotman, in words the leader of all, some say;
> Followed by Baron, Doneau, Dumoulin, Gribaldi, Budé.[1]

This list is not complete, and indeed it slights the eldest and perhaps most original of Alciato's disciples, Eguinaire Baron, and ignores altogether the most famous and influential of all sixteenth-century legal scholars, Jacques Cujas; but it does suggest the making of a modern professional cult, and an attendant mythology, which rivaled (while it built upon) "jurisprudence Italian style" and which in important ways broadened and deepened traditional civil science.

For two generations and more, starting in the late 1520s when Alciato arrived and continuing through the bitter years of civil war, the law faculty of the University of Bourges was a cockpit of methodological and ideological (that is, confessional) strife—and, what is more to the point here, was the avant-garde of legal scholarship and thought. The new "method" championed by the first generation of *Alciatei* (as Gentili called them), beginning with Baron and Le Douaren, had three basic ingredients: first, mastery of the new philology, which had been imported to France by Guillaume Budé and which examined the Digest with the intention of restoring Greek passages, interpreting literary allusions, and elucidating philosophical concepts; second, a sense of original context and of historical change, essential for a discriminating evaluation of the legal tradition; and third, legal "reform" of the ancient legal canon, perhaps its reorganization, and thereby fulfillment of its moral, social, and cultural ideals.[2] These qualities were not entirely absent from "jurisprudence Italian style"; but they did not receive the priority given them by the advocates of "jurisprudence in the French manner," who neglected the accumulation of scholastic *opiniones* in order to devote themselves to this threefold program of critical reconstruction of the words of law, historical interpretation of its development, and realization of its formal aspirations to be "true philosophy" (*vera philosophia*). This realization, however, must be understood in terms not merely of the methodological rhetoric but more specifically of the conceptual practice of the French school.

The program of humanist jurisprudence was formulated not only in the essays of Baron, Le Douaren, and their progeny, but by a formal statute, issued by the law faculty of the University of Bourges in 1548, concerning "the order, way, and rationale of interpreting laws" (*de ordine, via, et ratione interpretandi iuris*).[3] This new "reformed jurisprudence" was suspect in some circles, partly because of its associations with the new "reformed religion," which had taken foothold in Bourges (and would soon split the faculty), but mainly because of its impracticality; and indeed the city fathers of Bourges complained that their professors (Baron and Le Douaren) had indulged their innovative "method" to the neglect of conventional legal education sanctioned by the Parlement of Paris. Yet the international renown of the University of Bourges rested on just these academic indulgences and the publications of their squabbling and sometimes unprofessional professors.

Much has been written about the scholarship of "legal humanism," and indeed it is a movement which is still active in the search for "interpolations" and for the various historical contexts—ancient Roman, Byzantine, and medieval—in which civil science developed. Critiques of "Bartolism," of "Accursianism," and of "Tribonianism"—such were the successive layers of editorial and interpretive exegesis which had to be uncovered before the letter, and so the true "spirit," of Roman law could be recaptured. This massive work of legal palengenesis was well underway among the second generation of the school of Bourges, roughly those whose careers spanned the years of civil war, beginning in the early 1560s with the third and fourth "François"—those deadly rivals Baudouin and Hotman (followers of Baron and Le Douaren respectively)—and their more cautious colleagues,

Cujas and Doneau; and their work made abundant use of this scholarship. A third generation, many of them students of Cujas, carried the message and methods of their mentors over into the study of vernacular laws, institutions, and culture.[4]

Certain qualifications ought to be registered about the desire of the French school to establish the "historical sense" of canonical texts. Although Cujas, like Erasmus, affected to be proud of the epithet "grammarian," in fact his life's work was concerned with discovering the *legal* meaning of Roman texts, and with doing so mainly through internal analysis. As in the case of more strictly "literary" texts, there was a strong element of identification and *mimesis* in the effort to reconstruct the discourse and mentality of the ancient jurists, including their values and ideals.[5] This effort sometimes involved anachronism, although Renaissance jurists were well aware of the difficulties of translating ideas created in a pagan and republican society into a Christian, feudal, and monarchical modernity.

How to make this translation was a matter of serious methodological disagreement; and in general there were, corresponding to the letter and the spirit of legal texts, two approaches to textual exegesis: one tied to a concern for manuscript tradition and "authority," which eschewed speculation; the other based on a willingness to make conjectural emendations and, in the search for true "meaning," to reach beyond particular words to the standards of language in a more general sense.[6] This had been the approach of Lorenzo Valla in his *Elegantiae Latinae linguae,* which was based on the "authority" not of Cicero, Quintilian, or any other single author, but rather of "antiquity" as a whole (*auctoritas antiquitatis*). This was the approach, too, of sixteenth-century jurists reaping the great harvest of juridical lexicography, which was another by-product of humanist scholarship.[7] This method, reaching beyond the letter for larger historical meaning, preserved the deepest traditions of civil law and eventually formed links between it and modern social science.

Related to philological criticism was the emergence of a historical perspective on civil law, which was significant for legal interpretation as well as for purely antiquarian study, following the lead of Pomponius's commentary on the Digest title, *De origine juris,* as lexicographers followed the *De verborum significatione.* Even for French jurists Roman law remained the model, and Roman legal history established the common pattern of change. So they devoted themselves not only to the chronicling of Roman legislation but also to monographic examinations of particular phases of Roman law, including the Twelve Tables, early republican and classical jurisprudence, the laws of the Christian Empire, and finally vulgar, feudal, and customary law. One of the central figures in the field was Baron's protégé, François Baudouin, who published a brief survey of

Roman legal history, a study of the ecclesiastical legislation of Constantine, and another of the "new law" of Justinian, as well as a treatise on the "method" of universal history in its relation to law—a method which was a sort of threefold "conjunction" of history, grammar, and jurisprudence, and which proposed in effect to establish Christian jurisprudence as a modern science of society.[8]

But the most important "conjunction," though seldom appreciated sufficiently, was that between civil science and philosophy, and this had to do above all with the systematic aspect of law. All the members of the school of Bourges touched on this problem in one way or another, beginning with Baron and Le Douaren, bitter rivals on most subjects but not on the need of civil law for "reform." The primary vehicle of this enterprise was the professional commentary on the standard canon of civil law; but French jurists had to attend to a wide range of problems beyond the Romanist tradition, including the "feudal" law of French provinces, the "liberties" of the Gallican church, the legal and political privileges of the king ("emperor in his kingdom," in the old canonist formula favored by the royal legists), and in general the special provenance and independent "spirit" of the French cultural heritage.[9]

This national slant, with the attendant royalist ideology, was perhaps the defining condition of the French school of jurisprudence. Since French jurists did not accept the authority of the "Roman" emperor, their conceptual framework, as well as their "intelligible field of study," was the law of nations—not the *ius civile* but rather the *ius gentium* (or, in Baldus's terms, the *ius novissimum gentium*). As usual this modern *ius gentium* was understood to exist in two modes—*primarium* and *secondarium*. "The primary [law of nations] means what is in accord with natural reason," as Baron put it; the secondary meant what in fact was reflected in the collective behavior of peoples—the actual customs and positive law of European *gentes,* including the legal tradition of the French monarchy. Or as Baron's former pupil, Hugues Doneau, put it, the primary form was based on "right reason" and was equivalent to natural law itself, while the secondary law of nations arose from necessity and utility, so that together they illustrated the ancient dialectic of nature and culture as well as the *termini* of the historical process.[10] It was this modern version of the old concept of "second nature" that furnished the point of departure for the French contribution to jurisprudence and to social thought.

The World of Nations

In the hands of French jurists civil science was elaborated within a series of concentric circles of legal tradition and experience—from the civil law to the law of nations and finally to natural law; from Roman experience to international history to universal reason. In keeping with the teaching of Gaius that all peoples were ruled partly by their own law (*ius proprium*) and partly by that common to all nations (*ius gentium*), French jurists regarded the *ius civile* as merely the *ius proprium* of the Romans with no more authority in France than either canon law or the feudal law of the *Book of Fiefs*.[11] On these grounds they turned to the "law of nations," both "primary" and "secondary," as their proper field of study and practice; and like their earlier Italian colleagues, but more systematically and methodically, they carried on their inquiries in a comparative fashion.

Since the mid-1520s Baron, first professor of law at the University of Bourges, had been involved in the study of comparative law within a philosophical framework. His researches into what he termed "that divine legal wisdom of Roman and Gallic law" (*divina illa iuris sapientia ius Romanum et Gallicum*) were no doubt reinforced by the contemporary political rivalry between the emperor and the French king; but conceptually his concern was with a fundamental issue both of philology and of legal science, namely, the old question of legal interpretation—in this case, literally one of translation. This question had been addressed by Leonardo Bruni in his early fifteenth-century essay *De recta interpretatione* and, a century later, with specific reference to civil law, by Guillaume Budé in his *Annotations on the Pandects*.[12]

Baron's starting point was a set of "bipartite commentaries" on the Institutes and Digest of Justinian. His general procedure was to analyze successively the rubrics of civil law and to suggest French counterparts or parallels according to the comparatist formula; *accommodata huius tituli ad mores Galliarum et leges Regias*. For the Roman concept of equity, for example (which had been extensively discussed by Budé in classical terms), Baron recalled the French usage, "what is profitable and reasonable" (*profitable et raisonable, ou utile et iuste*). Other comparisons were made between the *interpretatio prudentium* and the "application of the laws" (*practiquer les loix*), the *Senatus consulta* and the *ordonnances de la cour de Parlement*, the *plebs* and the *tiers estat*, and so on down into the lower levels of society, including parallels with feudal usages of other nations.[13] In these comments Baron found occasion not only to assert the superiority of French customs and institutions but also to illustrate both the similarities and the varieties of modern European legal and social patterns.

For Baron and his colleagues Roman law provided not an authoritative system but rather a conceptual model (as it did for Machiavelli, in his more exclusively political and behavioralist fashion), with attendant philosophical, political, legal, and social categories and standards of judgment. More severely than Alciato and more philosophically than Budé, Baron denounced the shallowness of the glossators. "This law," Accursius had declared of the Digest title on magistrates (I, 1, 5), "is not to be considered"

(*non legitur*). "And why not, Accursius?" asked Baron. "Because it has
been revoked by a new law? Or because what you need cannot be supplied
by the magistrates of that age? For the same reason I do not identify the
great offices of the Roman Empire with those of the Kingdom of France,
for example, the *senechaux* and *baillis* with the proconsuls; yet the mode
of jurisdiction is virtually the same."[14] In this way Baron suggested the
parallels, structural and historical, if not legal, between Roman and French
customs and institutions.

The central category of the study of comparative law was, as noted
before, the idea of custom (*consuetudo*). "Custom" arose not from words,
Baron continued, but from facts and actions—that is, from the manners of
the ancestors (*mos maiorum*) which had gained common acceptance, and
later the interpretations of wise men (*interpretatio prudentum*) and judicial
decisions (*res iudicatae*). Baron also remarked on the difficulty of "proving"
customs but added that in his own day, with the redaction of provincial
coutumiers, customs had no force unless written down in an edict.[15] In
sixteenth-century France as in the Roman Republic the law-making power
had passed from the people exclusively into the hands of the prince—the
royal edicts (*leges Regias*) being equivalent to the imperial constitutions,
although the administration of justice (*haute, moyenne,* and *basse*) was
more differentiated in the French monarchy.

In private law the differences between modern France and ancient Rome
were even more striking; for as political absolutism was moderated by the
Parlement and Estates General, so the old Roman "tyranny" of paternal
power (*patria potestas*) was excluded from French society. In the matter
of personal status, too (the rubric *status hominum*), French law was more
complex and more liberal than civil law, which distinguished only slave
and free. Baron pointed out in particular the position of "naturalized"
foreigners and that of women, which was inferior but not wholly subordinate. In French customs as well as civil law, of course, man was declared
"by nature free"; but the vagaries of the "secondary law of nations," which
brought war and slavery, had eroded this primal freedom. "Second nature"
brought a variety of social constraints and inconveniences.

In this "bipartite" approach to jurisprudence Baron was in some ways
following the procedures of the medieval commentators, except that he
was concerned to discriminate between rather than to accommodate or to
assimilate ancient and modern law. Baron's path to civil science, that is,
was not that of pure reason but rather that of empirical, historical, and
comparative studies—opening up further that "world of nations," in Vico's
famous phrase—and in this he was followed by a distinguished sixteenth-
century progeny, including François Baudouin and Jean Bodin, who, though
in some ways epigones, overshadowed their master.

Another French pioneer of the comparative study of law was the second

"François" of the verses quoted earlier—François Connan, former school friend of Calvin (at Bourges in Alciato's time) and a practicing jurist (*maître des requêtes de l'hôtel*), whose commentaries on civil law appeared in 1553, two years after his death. In his attempt to portray the nature of human law and society Connan began with a conventional survey of Roman legal history, following the Digest title "On the Origin of Law," from customary origins to civilized code—from the Twelve Tables, which "interpreted" Roman usages (*mos Civitatis*), down to Justinian's legislation. Law in general was the "form of a people" (*forma populi*) and received concrete expression in particular decisions to resolve human conflicts. With the advent of written law, custom was supplemented and confirmed by judicial authority (the *ius honorarium*) and decisions (*responsa prudentum* and *res iudicatae*), but being "approved by usage and time" (*usu et tempore comprobatum*), it always retained the power to "interpret" law according to the famous formula of the Digest (*consuetudo optima legum interpres*). As "civil reason" replaced the natural variety, the Roman genius for creating social institutions for the public good (*facilitas in legibus novandi,* in Connan's words) produced the tradition still underlying, if not governing, modern civil science.[16]

Yet French feudists necessarily had to expand their horizons to include not only civil law but also the modern "law of nations." It was from this more cosmopolitan perspective that François Connan offered his interpretation of legal and social history. Of the "world of nations" Nature remained the lowest common denominator. For Connan nature was not only the basis of the liberty of the "solitary" person, it was also the "fount" or "foundation" (*fons, fundamentum*) of social forms such as marriage and child-bearing. Beyond the familial *societas,* the beginning of civilization depended on the application of "natural reason," possessed (as Gaius had said) by all *gentes,* to human relations; and it first took the form of *mos.* The word *mos* was from *modus,* Connan etymologized, and "signified the form, state, and condition of a thing," which through repetition was accepted as custom. Like Baron, Connan celebrated the superiority of French custom to that of Rome, as in the more liberal treatment of women. Like Vico two centuries later, he believed in the indigenous character of customs, so that (for example) he inferred the institutions of feudalism to have originated not in Roman law but rather in Gallic customs passing into European society by way of the Franks.

Consuetudo, unwritten law (*ius non scriptum*), was at once an outgrowth of nature and a residue of mores. Though distinguished from prescription, custom was also "approved by usage and time" (*usu et tempore comprobatum,* in Connan's words) and "through age acquired the force of nature" (*consuetudo . . . sua vetustate naturae vim obtineat*), invoking here the famous phrase of Pindar about "king custom." It was limited by the laws of nature, that is, generation and corruption, and was always accompanied by its opposite, "desuetude." Custom could be created by any corporate group, especially by a *populus;* and precisely because of its proximity to nature and human behavior, it was, as Connan declared, "most certain law" (*certissima lex*) and the key to "equity" (*aequitas*).[17]

Yet if society, with its customs, arose out of nature, it was also in a sense alienated or "deflected" from it (*deflexit de via naturae*); for under pressure of collective needs, humanity rose above its instincts—or, in Christian terms, fell from its rational state—with "utility" replacing "reason" in its behavior. This was what Connan meant by his invocation of the old formula of custom as "second nature"—and his recollection of the similar, and likewise "barbaric," origins of Greek law (*nomos, thesmos*) as well as the civil law of Rome. For him *altera natura* referred to the emergence of a "secondary" natural law out of the "primary" phase, the supersession of "natural law" properly speaking by the "law of nations"—of a "state of nature" (in the parlance of the next century) by a state of society. In the wake of this alienation from divinity and descent from—or ascent to— humanity came all the rewards and punishments of the *ius gentium,* including kingdoms, servitude, war, private "possession," and other "barbaric" creations of early laws (*priscae leges*), which introduced an "iron age" (*aetas ferrea*) characterized by avarice, ambition, slavery, the "use of money," and the right of self-defense (*vis vim repellere licet*). It also produced conventions and institutions related to property and commercial activity, such as testaments and contracts.

Finally, as social usage "preceded custom" (*mos praecedet consuetudinem*), so the *ius gentium* preceded the *ius civile* of any nation; and out of the popular collectivity (*populus*) came organized society, especially in the form of the "city" (*Civitas*), and with this the institutions of written law and "civil society." In this condition civil liberty replaced the lost "natural" variety, property (*dominium*) replaced mere "possession," and humanity approached a state of, if not utopia, at least "equity" (*aequitas*), which Connan took to be the final cause of civil science and the end product of evolution of law.

Yet, having in effect "historicized" the relationship between nature and custom, and so the perception of civilization, Connan rejected the notion that justice itself was in any sense the product of mere convention. He posed the question in Platonic terms (*Ius natura ne sit an opinione*), recalling the cynical position of Thrasymachus in the *Republic,* which identified justice with mere utility. Without minimizing the role played by *utilitas* in the formation of law, Connan rejected it as an adequate representation of the civil (or certainly the natural) ideal, which sought a foundation or basis in "right reason." Nor did history suggest that there had ever been a nation so "barbarous" as to lack either the impulse to punish evil and reward good or, indeed, some form of religion. Justice did not arise, then, from the particularity of laws (though Connan agreed with the "grammarians" that the conventional derivation of *ius a justitia* was nominally wrong) but was rather antecedent to it—residing indeed in the spirit, mind, will, or soul of men (*ius in hominum mente ortum habere*), as according to legal convention it resided in the "spirit of the laws" (*mens legum*).[18] In this way Connan anticipated the issue of the inherent "sociability" of humanity, which later raged especially around the work of Thomas Hobbes and of his critics.

One of the assumptions of Baron and Connan's view of "civil law" (the civil law not merely of Rome but of any of the *gentes*) was its indigenous and historical character. Here again we return to one of the defining features of customary law, which was its proximity to the geographical, cultural, and historical variables of human behavior as expressed in the medico-astrological terms of Renaissance social thought. According to Pierre Ayrault, another alumnus of the law school of Bourges as well as a royal magistrate, the result of this "variety and mutation of law" was that laws from different places seemed incompatible and even contradictory—"in one place apparently rational, in another beyond all common sense." This also reflected the "necessary revolution," as Ayrault called it, which sent all societies through cycles of generation and corruption. So it had been with Rome; so it would be with other inhabitants of the world of nations. But the civil scientist had always to be conscious of this changeability and this consonance between laws and the underlying social "humors" and climate, as reflected in local custom. Legislators had to approach their work as "good, industrious painters," Ayrault wrote, and judges as scrupulous doctors prescribing for different patients. To suggest the complex relationship between law and society Ayrault often had recourse to metaphors. Law was like the sun, like fire, like a river—constant despite the changing scene, yet always adapting itself to that scene.[19]

On this level, law was obviously less of a "science" than an "art" or a "prudence," and in another work Ayrault showed in vast detail how law was actually the product not of philosophical reflection or scientific deduction but rather of many individual judgments or cases—*res judicatae*, in the old civilian rubric—which Ayrault collected in the form of a Digest. In this Summa of legal positivism Ayrault declared that "*res judicatae* are the first, only, or leading part of law" as well as the main locus of equity. Justice, he added, was based on the sort of "tacit consent" expressed most concretely in such cases, and law was little more than an accumulation of judgments (*Constitutio quid aliud est quam quod ex multis iudiciis et opinionibus?*). What was needed above all was legal experience and a knowledge of custom, which was the final arbiter (*Usus ille docendi magister* was the maxim he cited.) His conclusion, inevitably, was that law and its parent, justice, could in human terms be nothing more than the expert judgment of professional magistrates like himself, who knew the lay of the land as well as the requirements of their profession.

This line of thought was continued more notably by Jean Bodin, whose "method of history" and theory of politics were both framed within the law—and the world—of nations being explored by the school of Bourges. Bodin's maxim that "the major part of universal law resides in history" applied to the work of jurists like Baron and Connan as well as to his own *Methodus*.[20] From civil law, too, Bodin took his taxonomy of history—human, natural, and divine—and his emphasis on geographical and climatic factors. Like law, history aimed at being a form of wisdom ("the knowledge of things divine and human"). This alliance between law and history, formulated by Baudouin and endorsed by Bodin, was proclaimed in an even more doctrinaire fashion by Bodin's disciple, Pierre Droit de Gailliard, who declared: "All the law of Rome and of other nations is nothing more than that part of history which describes the customs . . . of each nation." Such was one terminal of the train of thought set in motion by the *mos gallicus iuris docendi* and drawn upon "extensively" by later investigators of the "world of nations," including Grotius, Vico, and Montesquieu.

Systematic Jurisprudence

Jurisprudence in the French manner was inspired by philology and informed by a "sense of history," but its essential aim was philosophical.[21] The disciples of Alciato continued to be concerned with the distortions of the legal canon due to Bartolism, Accursianism, and Tribonianism (according to the terminology used by Hotman, Cujas, and others); but they were disturbed even more by the fragmentation, disorder, "antinomies," and inequities displayed by Justinian's collections, especially of the Digest; and indeed the efforts of the school of Bourges were directed increasingly to correcting these defects. Connan, Le Douaren, Doneau, and Jean Coras were among the leaders in this attempt to "reform" civil law, although almost all jurists at least talked about introducing systematic "method" into law or "reducing it to an art"; for if civil law was "true philosophy," it needed a formal structure and social goals to match.

In fact the basis for such a structure was already contained in the old legal tradition: this was the arrangement of Gaius, which distributed law into the categories of persons, things, and actions. In this sense, too, civil science was arranged in a series of concentric circles, beginning with the free, needful, willful, and responsible individual, and going on to include the world of natural things which could be acquired and used for sustenance (and passed on, perhaps, to a later generation). This marked the arena of private law, and to that we might add the larger circle of public law and that "public utility" to which private actions were theoretically subject[22]—though jurists did not need Machiavelli to teach them the potential contradictions between the sphere of ethics (or economics?) and politics. This was in fact just another—a socialized—version of the old problem of the individual and the universal, and hardly reconcilable except through an act of faith or utopian arguments of some sort. In any case, the conflict between private and public "interest" was a basic problem of legal as well as moral and political thought, and it could be resolved equitably only by the expert in civil science.

In one essential respect French jurists accepted and tried to further the enterprise of jurisprudence Italian style, and this was, in a very special sense, the rationalization of law. The basic impulse was similar to that of Jacques de Révigny and Pierre de Belleperche in the thirteenth century, who had wanted not only to distinguish the "letter" from the "spirit" of the law but also, within the "spirit," to separate the "reason of the law" from the intention of the law-giver; since they necessarily preferred royal authority to that of the emperor.[23] But besides this political motive, there was also the higher ideal inherent in civil law since classical times, which was its fulfillment as "true philosophy."

In the sixteenth century this ideal was pursued by French jurists, especially alumni of the school of Bourges, along several lines. As usual, of course, they had recourse to the theoretical standard of "natural law," "primary" as well as "secondary"; and unlike civil law, which was "mutable," as Doneau reminded his readers, natural law was "immutable" (*ius civile mutabile est; iura naturalia immutabilia sunt*).[24] They also invoked the analogy of mathematics and geometry, especially in connection with "harmonic justice," and they preserved and even extended the connections between law and logic. Although applications of "dialectical method" to the law, such as the little textbook published by François Hotman in 1573, were offered largely for pedagogical purposes, they did contribute to efforts of legal "reform."[25] The drift of these analogies was to establish the "scientific" nature of jurisprudence in general, an issue which has dominated social thought down to the present day.

"Whether or not law is a science" was a question central to the theoretical work of Jean Coras (better known nowadays as the judge in the case of Martin Guerre); and his affirmative answer was quite in keeping with the Italian and the French schools of jurisprudence, which both wanted to defend the status of their discipline against theologians, philosophers, and especially doctors of medicine. To be sure it was an "art," but it was also a "science" because it dealt with its materials in terms of causes (*per causas*)—referring to the Aristotelian system of "four causes," despite the fact that the legal idea of "cause" had very different connotations from the idea of physical causation. For purposes of systematizing law and connecting it to the political context, however, the Aristotelian concept served very well, as Bartolists had long realized. Whether the "prince" or the "people" acted as the efficient cause of law, its "formal cause" was the collective (not merely individual) nature as *forma populi;* its material cause included the particular rubrics of civil law within the Gaian distribution; and the final cause was the common good of the community—*salus populi suprema lex esto,* as Coras summed it up in the ancient proverb from the Twelve Tables.[26]

It was under these conditions that civil law could express its inherent "reason" (*ratio legis*) and become "true philosophy." Both Connan and Doneau carried on their reappraisals of civilian tradition under the old flag of *vera philosophia,* signifying that civil science, placed in correct historical perspective and philosophical context, was the consummate form of wisdom, the foundation of social justice, and, as Connan put it, the most concrete expression of all philosophy (*hac nostra scientia explicitam omnem philosophiam esse*).[27] In his efforts to interpret and to reorder civil science Connan recalled in particular the old designs of Cicero and Caesar to "reduce law to an art" (*ius in artem redigendo*), Aristotle's view of "civil science" as architectonic, and especially Plato's conception of justice.

These aspirations served also to support the necessary condition of their philosophical enterprise, which was the theory and practice of legal interpretation. In opposition to Justinian's prohibition, Doneau defended the *interpretatio iuris* as essential in view of the fragmentary and especially the disordered state of the Digest. For Doneau the purpose of interpretation was suggested perfectly by the old view of Celsus that the understanding of laws referred to their spirit and force, not merely their letter, and by the conventional distinction drawn between "restrictive" and "extensive" construction. In a modern sense, Doneau sought the "reason of law," and perhaps more than any of his colleagues, at least in terms of his impact outside of France (which, especially in Germany, continued into the nineteenth century), was admired for his efforts to transcend civil law and in effect to adapt it to the modern "world of nations."[28]

Yet invocations of natural law, mathematical form, and scientific certainty, while figuring prominently in rhetorical celebrations of jurisprudence, did not greatly alter the substance of civil science. The topics of legal dialectic were drawn in large part from the titles of the Digest; and attempts to "re-form" civil law usually resorted to the arrangements of classical law, above all the Institutes of Justinian, which was itself modeled on the seminal textbook of Gaius. A monumental, if not classic, illustration of this is the work of Gregory of Toulouse, especially his *Republic,* written in part to counter Bodin's book of the same title and the ideas of that "most pernicious man," Machiavelli, by positioning the law, rather than the prince, at the center of the social world. Gregory's other systematic work, the *Syntagma iuris*, likewise based on an anthropocentric cosmos, followed the old Gaian trinity—persons, things, actions—in its efforts to recreate juridically God's Creation. For Gregory, "method" was an "imitation of nature," a pale and pedantic one at that, sublime in conception, perhaps, but grotesque in form; and what he produced was not a derivation of natural law but a Summa of civil law—an expression not of Physis but, very eclectically, of Nomos.[29]

Such Romanist, or Romanoid, structures were common enough in the seventeenth century; but by then the more abstract fashions of natural law, reinforced by Spanish scholasticism and Protestant Aristotelianism, had changed the style of legal argumentation.[30] Yet these elements were themselves part of the older legal tradition; and in a sense the "philosophical school of law" was an extension of, rather than a departure from, modern civil science.

Coutume and Coutumier

With qualifications, much the same can be said of the vernacular tradition of customary law, not only because of the extensive overlay of Latin commentaries but also because of its structure and various comparative efforts, beginning most notably with those of Baron and Connan. Yet French *droit coutumier* tended increasingly to distance itself from Roman conventions and Latin terminology.[31] The study of French customs, encouraged by forces of "juridical nationalism," was reinforced by the so-called vernacular humanism of scholars like Louis Le Caron and Etienne Pasquier, who pursued careers in the republics both of letters and of jurisprudence. Their achievement was to carry the methods of the school of Bourges over into the study of native French customs and institutions; and drawing not only on the "quarrel of Ancients and Moderns" but also on the Gallican-Romanist and Habsburg-Valois rivalry, they were still more incisive and invidious in their judgments about the superiority of their own legal and cultural heritage.

Perhaps the most striking spokesman for "juridical nationalism" in France was Louis Le Caron ("Charondas"), a historian of Roman law as well as a devoted investigator of medieval French law. It was Le Caron's distinction to reinforce the social and conceptual aspirations of jurisprudence with the philosophy of Platonism. "The divine Plato has elegantly declared that true philosophy [*vera philosophia*] concerns itself with the life and customs of man," he wrote while still a student of Baudouin at the University of Bourges; and a year later, writing in the vernacular, he invoked the old civilian topos: "I say that true philosophy is contained in the books of the laws and not in the useless and inarticulate libraries of philosophers, who in effect are men of great learning . . . but incapable in public matters.

Wherefore jurisprudence may indeed be called the true philosophy" (*la
vraye philosophie*).[32]
This is a perfect expression of the attitude I have called "civil humanism,"
which insists on the public and social character of "the office of the philosopher" (in Le Caron's phrase). The "true philosophy" of jurisprudence—
la science politique, as Le Caron also called it—demanded a return to the
cave of human conflict: not merely to "know thyself" and to seek the
"sovereign contentment" of the individual, as Le Caron's disillusioned
contemporary and colleague, Montaigne, seemed to be teaching (and to
which Le Caron explicitly took exception), but more important, to aim at
"public utility" and the "sovereign good" of the whole community.[33]
Le Caron's way of seeking this "sovereign good" was to turn away from
the pleasures of literature and to devote himself to the restoration and
reformation of the French legal tradition, including a pioneering edition of
Bouteiller's *Grand Coutumier de France.* Like Le Douaren and his contemporaries at Bourges, Le Caron became fascinated with the notion of a
system of law drawn from indigenous materials. In fact he declared to
Charles IX, "You are not subject to the laws of the Greeks and Romans,
nor are your magistrates bound by them, except to the extent that they are
in accord with reason."[34] Characteristically, Le Caron celebrated the
national heritage of law in philosophical as well as national terms. "French
law," he wrote in his *Pandects of French Law,* "is composed of all the
parts of universal law, the science of which is called jurisprudence, civil
science, or wisdom, and called 'royal' by some. It constitutes the major
part of moral as well as political philosophy and is most useful to human
society."[35]
In this enterprise, antiquarian and ideological by motive but philosophical in purpose, Le Caron was joined by other legal scholars devoted to the
vernacular tradition, into which comparative law in the style of Baron was
introduced. Le Caron's friend Etienne Pasquier, Antoine Loisel, and Guy
Coquille were the most prominent of those who, following Gaian convention, composed "Institutes" of French law on the model of Justinian's
textbook, itself modeled on the book of Gaius (which was not rediscovered
until the nineteenth century). Pasquier, better known for his lifelong
"researches" into French cultural tradition (including the history of French
law and of civil law in France), began a translation of Justinian's Institutes
in his later years; but as it progressed, the work (written in the early
seventeenth century, though not published until the nineteenth) was transformed into a comparative study of French laws and institutions. Coquille's
Institutes of French Law (1607) was composed along much the same lines,
trying to subsume French laws and institutions under conventional civilian
rubrics.[36] By far the most original, however, was Loisel's *Customary Institutes* (also 1607), which sought the spirit of French law in conventional

wisdom—literary sources, proverbs, and folklore—as well as in legal maxims and customary law, and which suggested a new field of investigation, the anthropology of law.

Loisel's book formed a link between the ancient "rules of law" and modern maxims, many of them enshrined in the French Civil Code. The legal *sententiae* he assembled were arranged according to the Gaian plan beginning with the "person"—first the king and his will, and then the "subject" (*noblesse* as well as *roturier*) and his liberty, and then proceeding to things—but most of the substance was feudal and even anti-Roman (for example, "paternal power has no place in France"). Naturally, Loisel's materials displayed a reverence for custom, both because of its age (*ancienneté a autorité*) and because of its popular source (*voix du peuple, voix de Dieu*).[37] Many of the proverbs expressed a distrust of lawyers ("Mad is he who goes to trial") and of written law in general (*le titre non fait pas le maistre*, and *possession immemoriale vault le titre*). "One leads a cow by the horns but men by words," Loisel quoted, "and a simple [oral] promise is worth all the 'stipulations' of Roman law." And against the "rule of rules," which Loisel took as the motto of his book, was the popular insight: "There is no rule without fault."

The pioneering works of Loisel and his colleagues, though historically well grounded, were systematically invidious in their comparisons of the hybrid French tradition and Romanism. The common professional aim of finding a national as well as a rational foundation for French law was even more evident in another work published at this time (1603, though written in 1567). Hotman's *Antitribonian* offered comparisons with civil law hardly less "odious" than those of Fortescue a century earlier.[38] Hotman attacked Roman law not only as irrelevant to French society but also as a kind of italianate disease infecting France with the evils both of Roman tyranny (absolutism and paternal power, for example) and of popery. Hotman's work was more radical than the conventional Gallicanism of Loisel and his colleagues, especially in his view of the pathogenesis of modern (italianate) French society, but it rested on the same sort of social analysis and vision of legal "reform."

Another major theme was evident in the work of these sometime practitioners of the *mos gallicus,* and this was the fundamental role of judicial interpretation in matters of the formulation and improvement as well as the application of laws. At the end of their long careers Loisel and Pasquier corresponded about this ancient issue, still sensitive in their own day. Pasquier's main question had to do with the decline of the *responsa prudentum* in Roman law and the desirability of preserving its modern analogue, judicial authority.[39] This was a problem of historical scholarship, but it also touched on the doctrinal premises, independence, and destiny of the French legal profession. Loisel's position on the issue is made clear

in a work he completed in 1600, which he named in honor of his friend—
Pasquier, ou dialogue des avocats du parlement de Paris—and in which
Pasquier (as well as François Pithou and others) figured as an interlocutor.[40]
Loisel's dialogue was a hagiography of the French legal profession and a
history and a celebration of the professional tradition, to which these
scholars all belonged, going back to its organization in the thirteenth
century. In effect the book defined the central "community of interpretation" as the school of "jurisprudence in the French manner," which itself
was a province in the larger tradition of social thought that I have been
calling the kingdom of Nomos.

The Spirit of French Law

French customs came under the cognizance of civil science with the introduction of writing, "a witness very hard to corrupt," remarked Montesquieu in his discussion of "the origin and revolutions of the civil laws
among the French," describing their passage from an oral to a civilized—
a social to a political—condition.[41] From Montesquieu's analysis it was
clear that, despite the invocation of "nature," historical understanding was
an essential part of legal interpretation. "If we go back to the origin of
laws," wrote a seventeenth-century commentator on the Norman custom,
"we will have to admit that customs preceded, and sometimes formed the
first part of, positive law, although they are placed last."[42] Thus "custom"
marked the point of intersection between fact and law, between might and
right, and in a sense between the state of nature and the state of society;
it was, so to speak, the pineal gland of the body social, where collective
and contingent behavior was transmuted into general principles and social
norms.

French scholars, from Beaumanoir to Marc Bloch, have been well aware
of the variety, irregularity, and sometimes iniquitous character of custom
in its oral stages, since, in the words of one commentator, "formerly they
were not recorded by public authority but only taught by common usage
passed from father to son."[43] Indeed, this was one of the basic conditions
of the "prudential" (as distinguished from the "scientific") aspect of their
profession. They understood the geographical and temporal relativity of
the provincial *coutumes,* which varied "according to the disposition of
manners and of the times." They also appreciated the continuing force of
desuetudo, that persistent shadow of *consuetudo;* and indeed one sixteenth-
century jurist, Philippe Bugnyon, devoted a whole treatise to law which
"today" (*hodie*) had fallen "out of usage" (*ab usu longe recessit; hors
d'usage*) because of the contradictions, multiplicity, mutations, and (in a
modern sense) "abuse" of laws.[44]

By the end of the fifteenth century, oral "proof" and judgments about

popular "notoriety" had been almost entirely supplanted by written procedures; and customs had become an integral part of literate culture and
political authority. The "redaction" of customs, by which *consuetudo*
became *ius consuetudinarium,* was a process undertaken by the government, following petition by the three estates of a particular town or province; and the purpose, as Pierre Angleberme wrote in the early sixteenth
century, was "not to declare new law but to preserve the memory of the
old" (*causa memoriae*).[45] The next step was both more threatening and
more theoretical. In the famous ordinance of Montils-les-Tours of 1453,
Charles VII declared his intention "not only to publish the ancient customs
but also to reform, to abrogate, to add new articles and new customs, and
to interpret them." A century later this became the charge of the first
president of the Parlement of Paris, Christofle de Thou, as reformation
succeeded redaction in the royal policy of political unification.[46]

In general the reform of customs can be seen as a kind of ceremonial
reenactment of the original social compact. The text was established
through elaborate negotiations between the king's officers and the representatives of the three estates. These discussions not infrequently turned
into bitter disputations about the exclusion of ancient liberties or the
introduction of "new customs," and more than once De Thou was charged
with exceeding his authority. The "soul" of the redaction—and the "spirit"
underlying the text of the *coutumier*—was the record (the *procès-verbal*)
of these discussions.[47] The myth of "consent" continued, and "tacit" acceptance of a custom by these estates was preserved; but of course, once settled
and authorized by ordinance, the written *coutumier* became binding on all
inhabitants of a province—literally and legally a "contract," as one eighteenth-century commentator put it, "and a public convention [which] one
is obliged by conscience to execute and to observe."[48]

These *coutumiers,* reformed and unreformed, accumulated a vast quantity of interpretation—a whole genre of works deploying learned introduc-
tions, parallels with Roman law, and the most refined legal, literary, and
philosophical criticism, as well as defining a community of jurists, stretching
from Beaumanoir to Montesquieu and beyond, who were concerned with
fundamental questions of liberty and property, feudal and "bourgeois"
status, social structure and change, cultural differentiation, and local and
national traditions. From at least the time of Jacques de Révigny, the major
premise of the arguments of French feudists had been the rejection of the
authority of Roman law in France. "Justinian never set foot in France,"
wrote Bernard Automne in his comparison of Roman and French law
published in 1610, "and on the contrary was defeated by the French" (that
is, the Franks).[49] In the words of another seventeenth-century feudist, "Baldus and many other doctors have said that, although the Gauls submitted
to the domination of the Roman Empire and its constitutions, they never

followed them, and that this people, jealous of their liberty and taking Roman laws as servitude, created [*se fit a la fantaisie*] particular customs in each province."[50] There were contrary opinions; but as Hotman, Pasquier, Loisel, Le Caron, and many other champions of what has been called "the school of customary law" argued, these were only misrepresentations made later by ill-informed or hostile products of the Italian school.

Yet the more orthodox Romanist position remained strong. Guy Coquille illustrated the conflict of these two schools by the famous confrontation between "two great personages of our time, who were successively presidents of the Parlement of Paris"[51] "Pierre Lizet held the Roman civil law as our common law [*nostre droit commun*] and accommodated to it as best he could our French law, which he regarded as a law to be restricted when contrary to Roman law. Contradicting this view, Christofle de Thou regarded the customs and French law as "our common law" and called Roman law "written reason." This partisanship was seen in the world of scholarship, too, where Jacques Cujas was reputed to be the leader of the Romanist and Charles Dumoulin the leader of the feudist party; certainly this was part of the legend which grew up around each of these ornaments of the golden age of civil science and which persisted into the nineteenth century.

Dumoulin's campaign to bring "union and concord" to French law was carried forward on several fronts, including royal and ecclesiastical as well as customary law; but his fundamental message was always the indigenous character of French legal tradition and its freedom from the taint of Romanism, ancient or modern. In particular he argued that the "common law of France" was to be found in the customs, and especially the custom of Paris—"the head of all the customs of this kingdom and even of Belgian Gaul" (*caput omnium huius regni et totius etiam Galliae Belgicae consuetudinem*)—"the law peculiar and common to the Franks and the Gauls" (*illae consuetudines erant ius peculiare et commune Francorum et Gallorum*).[52] Feudal customs could be traced back to Charlemagne but had no connection with Roman institutions (*feudorum origo non a iure Romano, sed a consuetudine*), and so legal unity had to be established within the same native canon and in the same national terms.

This was the second aspect of the "grandeur" of the monarchy of France that had been celebrated by Claude de Seyssel in his famous trinity of "bridles" on (and enhancements of) royal authority—"religion, justice, and police." "Truly," Seyssel wrote, " . . . this rein and bridle [*frein*] is greater and more praiseworthy in France than in any other land, and has been maintained for so long that it scarcely can be broken, though it may be bent, and although there are imperfections in this justice as in all other human affairs."[53] Seyssel's work, which summed up his career as a teacher of civil science and as a counselor of the French monarchy, offered a useful formulation of the grounds and terms of Renaissance social theory and criticism.

The customary foundation of legal unity was the premise of most feudists, especially commentators on the Parisian *coutume* down to the French Revolution, and indeed afterwards. Thus Dumoulin's successor and biographer, Julien Brodeau, writing a century later, declared French customs to be "not merely statutes or local usages but civil and common law," especially that of Paris, since this city was "the center of the State" (*le centre de l'Estat, le sejour ordinaires des Rois et de leur Cour*).[54] About the same time, another commentator on the *coutume* of Paris, Claude de Ferrière, extended civilian conceptions by arguing that this custom "unites our law, interprets it, and sometimes corrects it" (*elle unite la loi, elle l'interprete, et quelquefois elle la corrige*).[55]

In the wake of Dumoulin's seminal work a new sort of "proof" of custom began to be recognized—namely, proof on the basis of history. Another seventeenth-century jurist and commentator on Loisel's *Customary Institutes,* François de Launay, drawing extensively on the work of Dumoulin, Loisel, and others, celebrated the extreme antiquity of French customary law, "for Charlemagne himself did not distinguish between laws and customs" in his capitularies. Not scrupling to cite the Accursian principle that custom overcame law (*consuetudo superveniens vincit legem*), Launay came to the same conclusion as Dumoulin had done, that "Roman law is not our common law" (*Le droit Romain n'est pas notre Droit commun*).[56] Perhaps the most ambitious effort to realize Dumoulin's enterprise of bringing order to French customary law was the great collection assembled by Claude Berroyer and Eusèbe de Laurière, the *Bibliotheque des coutumes* published in 1699, adorned with historical studies of each provincial custom and an essay on interpretation.[57]

Declaring independence from the Romanist tradition, French feudists began to establish their own "methods" and rules of interpretation. These methods were modeled generally on those of civil science; but as Coquille warned, "In order not to be slaves, imitators, or worshipers of foreigners, let us not embroil the interpretation of our customs with the puzzling rules of statutes." According to the customary "method" of Paul Challine, following the lead of Dumoulin, French *coutumes* had to be understood in their own terms (*se doivent expliquer par elles-mesmes*), should be abolished by non-usage, and, especially, should be related to the "common law" and to social context.[58] When particular customs were defective, application should be made not only to the royal ordinances and to the reason (the rational part) of Roman law but also to unwritten usages, neighboring customs, and the "general spirit of French custom" (*l'esprit general de toutes les coutumes de France*). Needless to say, this defense of native custom served as well to enhance the interpretive authority and judicial discretion of the jurist.

In 1679 Louis XIV established professorships of French law in eleven universities, charging them, among other things, with teaching law in a comparative fashion; and from that point on the battle between the Romanists and the Germanists had an institutional locus. The issue, as usual, involved not only the provenance of French culture but also the means of further reform and, in Dumoulin's words, the "union and concord" of French law. As Claude de Ferrière wrote, "The unity of law or custom in the kingdom is the desire of all good men, but political reasons [raison d'etat] and the interest of peoples prevent it."[59]

One of the best defenses of the Romanist path to reform was assembled by Jean Bouhier, who was president of the Parlement of Burgundy, a commentator on and historian of the Burgundian custom, and a critic of the presumptions of the champions of the Parisian custom and of judicial discretion. To Bouhier the superiority of Roman law was demonstrated by its systematic form, its creation by professional "interpreters" instead of "ignorant men," and its grand intellectual tradition—"simply Reason par excellence," he declared, repeating the old anecdote about De Thou and Lizet, head of "the party of Roman law" (partie du Droit coutumier).[60] From the very beginning (de toute ancienneté) Roman law had been "common law," and indeed had been "received" in France no less than in Germany, and therefore the notion of a "spirit of customary law" was a "true chimera."

Testifying for "the partisans of customary law" was a long line of feudists following the trail blazed by Dumoulin—commentators on the coutume of Paris and various provinces, authors of monographic and polemical works, and historians of medieval law. One of the best of these legal vulgarians was Pierre Grosely, an admirer and product of Renaissance scholarship, who had offended Bouhier with his anti-Romanist opinions. In his study of the vast literature on the coutumes Grosely claimed to have grasped the true spirit of French law (l'esprit particulier de notre Droit coutumier actuel)—which, like the mythopoeic constructions of Coke and other English common lawyers, was in effect immemorial and possessed a continuity and "unanimity" going back at least to the inhabitants of septentrional (Frankish) Gaul. This "spirit" of French law, Grosely added, was something quite different from the more abstract speculations of his learned friend Montesquieu—though Montesquieu, too, favored the thesis of Germanic origins of French law.[61]

In the French school of jurisprudence, the Romanist as well as the Germanist branches, the idea of custom presided at the birth, and remained close to the heart, of discussions of the nature and history of society and culture. By 1789 the provincial coutumes in France numbered more than two hundred, and they had accumulated an extraordinary amount of textual commentary and contextual investigation. They constituted a sort of feudist canon, in which Dumoulin's work, republished in the eighteenth century, was seminal and continuously authoritative. They were entangled in age-old issues which united as well as divided the orders of French society. In one sense they represented the target of a vast national enterprise resembling that never-completed human process that Hans Blumenberg has called "work on myth."[62] At the same time they addressed important practical and "scientific" questions and helped to define some of the fundamental terms of social analysis and theory, including personal liberty, private (as well as feudal) property, class structure, judicial order, and the problems of social change which parties and schools of thought, both enlightened and benighted, found it increasingly hard to ignore.

In general, "custom" required jurists to give serious consideration to factors of geography, history, and local, or national, character—the "second" as well as the primary nature of people, and their "civil" as well as their "natural reason." "People are naturally inclined to follow what is most in conformity with their condition and their manners and what concerns their common interest," wrote Ferrière; and these "common inclinations of peoples, arising from the diversity of government and climate, we call 'civil reason,' which is the foundation of customs and laws."[63] Thus jurists came to appreciate the significance of "local knowledge," a kind of rudimentary sociology or anthropology of knowledge, and the "prudential" as well as "scientific" aspect of the law—at once jurisprudence and civil science.

They understood, too, the tradition of Nomos of which the discussion of custom was part. "This law the Greeks called [*nomon*] *agraphon,* that is, unwritten," wrote Angleberme, "which (says Plato) they call the laws of the fathers [*patrias leges*] . . . and long-standing usages, approved by conscience and observed as laws"—that is, as written laws, "which the Greeks call [*dikaion*] *nomikon* and which passed on to modern Europe by way of the Athenians and the Roman law of the Twelve Tables."[64] This is another way of paying homage to King Nomos.

More than two and a half centuries later, less than a decade before the Revolution, another jurist was still celebrating the French customs as "fundamental" and "social laws" (*lois fondamentales, lois sociales*). In general, P. G. Michaux argued, European customs were in no sense the result either of the Roman imperial domination or of the governments of particular states; on the contrary, they were "the creation of these nations as a whole" (*le propre ouvrage des ces nations en corps*). What the natural lawyers had to say about the origins of institutions, private as well as public (and especially that of property) was nonsense, he added. "We emerged into a social and political order . . . not as imagined by Pufendorf and other [social-contract theorists] but rather as revealed in our customs" (*non tel que Pufendorff et d'autres authors le suppose, mais tel que nos Coutumes le font concevoir*).[65]

In the work of this community of jurists we can see the first stage of the

French contributions to the modern sciences of society and culture—all too often overshadowed by the derivative and sometimes superficial discussions of political philosophers and especially by the champions of Physis, of "first" nature. By the seventeenth century, obviously, the investigators of "second nature" were very much out of the intellectual fashion dominated by the champions of a new form of naturalism, which Otto Gierke called "antique-modern" natural law; and it is essential to inquire into the rival tradition of rational jurisprudence, which came to prevail in an age first of enlightened despotism, then of liberal monarchy, and then finally of social revolution.

TWELVE

The Philosophical School

Les loix naturelles reglent et tout l'avenir et tout le passé.

Domat, *Les Loix civiles* (1689)

Le droit de nature n'existe point.

Dubuat, *Maximes du Gouvernement* (1778)

•

The Search for Method

The classical idea that jurisprudence was "true philosophy" was taken quite literally by European jurists, ultramontanes and citramontanes, scholastics and humanists, theoreticians and practicians alike, who associated it with the claim that their discipline was also a true "science." In the sixteenth century this notion was further enhanced by attempts to reform the study of law by joining it to dialectical and systematic "methods" of various sorts, beginning with Aristotelian categories but coming to be informed also by the "encyclopedic" and liberalizing impulse of Italian humanism, which admitted law to the charmed circle of the liberal arts, and by the "new logic" of Rudolph Agricola, Philip Melanchthon, and especially Peter Ramus, based on an alliance between rhetoric and logic.[1] The purpose of such reordering and "methodizing" was in the first place pedagogical and mnemonic, but it also came to promote the "scientific" and practical character of jurisprudence and its ancient claims to represent a form, perhaps the highest form, of wisdom.

The intersection in particular between topical logic and legal interpretation in the sixteenth century produced a new genre devoted to the theory and practice of judgment and criticism of legal texts and situations. In a stream of monographs extending at least from Constantinus Rogerius's *De iuris interpretatione* (1463) to Leibniz's *Nova methodus iurisprudentiae* (1667) and beyond, jurists sought a proper approach to legal understanding. In treatises by Christopher Hegendorf, Matteo Gribaldi, Claudius Cantiuncula, Johannes Apel, Nicolas Everardus, Johann Oldendorp, Pietro Andrea Gammaro, Bartolommeo Cepolla, Stephanus Federicus, Conrad Lagus, Johann Freigius, François Hotman, and others, legal hermeneutics came into its own and added a more or less formal methodological dimen-

sion to civil science and social thought more generally—or rather, it formalized and modernized the methodology created by "jurisprudence Italian
style" and its European offspring.[2]

"Method" was an extraordinarily popular piece of academic jargon in
the sixteenth century that, for champions of the old as well as the new
learning, signified, according to one standard view, correct order (*iustus
ordo*), "without which nothing can be taught or properly judged."[3] In legal
terms it was often associated with Cicero's famous proposal to "reduce
law to an art" or, less radically, with the conventional arrangement of
Justinian's (and Gaius's) "institutes" (a word which in fact might be translated as "method").[4] Correct "method," however, also required the understanding of legal texts and, in practical judgments, social actions as well;
and so it incorporated a whole system of what Leibniz and others would
call the hermeneutical art (*ars hermeneutica*).[5] But "method" had a political
as well as a rational face, for its ultimate goal remained the common good.
As Oldendorp warned, legal error not only undermined justice; it also
threatened the republic with social and political corruption (*error corrumpit
politicas ordines et introducit confusionem poenitendam*).[6]

Whether inclining toward conventional Aristotelian dialectic, categories,
and "causes" (like Gribaldi and Gammaro) or toward the newer, rival logic
associated with Ramists like Freigius and Althusius, sixteenth-century
jurists were agreed on the primacy of language. "Things not words" (*res
non verba*) was ever a motto of scholars, but it was also a classical topos
and in no way contradicted the premise that conventional language was
the medium of civil science. Indeed, in the wake of the humanist movement,
there was a veritable "linguistic turn" away from the abstractions and
conceptual excesses of scholasticism and toward the concrete experience
and wisdom of the classical legal canon. This intensified concern for language, reinforced by the advent of printing, was manifested in the production of critical editions of texts, which was perhaps the chief contribution
of "legal humanism."

The linguistic turn in Renaissance scholarship can be seen even more
conspicuously in the emergence of another new genre. This was the tradition of juridical lexicography, which was itself basically an extension of
the Digest title on the meaning of words (*De verborum significatione*),
though in modern times it had to consider problems of vernacular law,
which is to say, the translation and comparison of terms in the manner of
Baron and Pasquier. As Barnabé Brisson wrote in his great dictionary of
the same title, "Since the meaning of texts is obscure, we must have recourse
to the proper usage [*proprietas*] of a word and what and whom it designates, and we must explain and extract the sense of what they say."[7] In
various ways legal method had to concern itself with larger contexts and,
taking inspiration from parallel works of Valla and Erasmus, to go beyond

the gloss (which treated "single words") to larger, and inferentially social and historical, meanings, as Alciato and others were doing in their teaching. In more fashionable terms, legal critics had to understand not just isolated words but also the common, yet changing and ambiguous, language of the law—not merely the *paroles* of judicial discourse, according to the Saussurean distinction, but also the *langue* and the social meanings and political implications which it embodied.

Yet if jurists, following the likes of Erasmus as well as Alciato, were convinced of the priority of language and of literal signification, they also believed that their final aim was finding the larger meaning of the law— the "interior" rather than the "exterior" sense, in the words of Oldendorp. "The letter kills, the spirit brings life," as Federicus quoted from St. Paul (*litera occidit, spiritus vivificat*); and indeed, from the time of the Bartolists, the "spirit of the law" was the vital and legitimizing principle of the legal profession.[8] As for the early Commentators, there remained the problem whether this "spirit" was to be identified with the intention (*mens*) of the law-giver, with the rationality of the law itself (*ratio*), or with extensions designed to achieve higher moral or political goals; but in any case it required not only professional judgment beyond mere literal construction but also formation of a sophisticated hermeneutics.

"Extensive interpretation" (*interpretatio extensiva*) was the art of finding this spirit; and according to Cepolla, this was an operation which "was introduced by secondary natural law," that is, human judgment and specifically human "causes" as distinguished from the general rules associated with primary nature.[9] Hegendorf suggested that it was equivalent to Ciceronian "ratiocination," and he elaborated this with reference to Aristotelian causes, to the "new logic" of Agricola and Melanchthon (with pre-Ramist bifurcations) and to the new "jurisprudence" of Alciato. Following Alciato, Hegendorf went on to list several "canons" of interpretation, including literal interpretation (determination of simple verbal "propriety"), "probable" judgments of authorities such as Bartolus and Baldus, unaided reason, custom (the "best interpreter"), and criticism of legal opinions.[10]

Johann Oldendorp contributed in many ways to the search for legal "method"—through lexicography, the history of Roman law (beginning with the Twelve Tables), comparative law (canon and civil as well as natural and positive), and the history and theory of modern interpretation. Like Hegendorf, he tried to establish standards of legal construction (*regulae de significatione verborum et rerum*) and "forms of interpretation," which amounted in a sense to rudimentary "rules of sociological method" that likewise treated questions of judgment and inference, the proof of facts, and the application of law, which presumably connected spheres of language and action. [11]

In the style of Melanchthon's *Loci theologici,* Conrad Lagus's "method" of law attempted to give "commonplace" form to jurisprudence with respect to history as well as to philosophy. "The first part of legal doctrine is philosophical, that is, seeking the truth and the rationale of all laws to the extent that human intellect can attain this," Lagus wrote. "The second part, which prescribes the forms of law applied to carrying on business and punishing offenses for the benefit and conservation of human society, is historical."[12] For Lagus, law was an accumulation of experience requiring rational form to reach its practical goal, which was both the common good (salus publica) and the interest of state (necessitas publica); and indeed, building on the efforts of Eike von Repgow, he applied his method to forming an ordered and even "philosophical" "compendium" of Saxon law. Custom was indeed the "best interpreter," but it needed to be joined to rational and systematic form to reach perfection.

What is essential to understand about this sort of legal methodizing is that it was carried on mainly within the bounds of legal science; and discussions of "commonplaces," "topics," "seats of argument," "partitions," and other dialectical constructs were "legal" in form and substance as well as name. Matteo Gribaldi, while drawing upon Aristotelian inspiration, made a careful distinction between categories that were "natural" (transcendentals, predicables, and predicaments) and those that were "legal"—those in effect belonging to the sphere of Physis and those associated with Nomos. "Legal transcendentals" were concepts such as ius and bonum (in a specifically social sense); among the predicables were concepts such as thought, deed, and expression (mens, dictum, factum); and the predicaments included social variables and factors of "cause," "person," "place," and "time" which practical legal judgment had to accommodate.[13]

Fundamental to sixteenth-century notions of method, and indeed implicit in the legal tradition, was the assumption that social matters were of a different order from natural ones. "Philosophy is twofold," in Hotman's words: "natural, which turns to the observation of nature, and moral, which turns (as Cicero says) to life and manners."[14] Indeed, this was the issue underlying the tired old debate of whether law was a "science" or an "art," theoretical or practical. The proper answer, of course, was both— both a science that treated causes and reasons, and an art, a "prudence," that treated matters of human will, error, experience, and individuality. "The interpretation of laws treats contingents," Gammaro wrote, "for laws vary"; and so, if not law itself, then at least "the interpretation of law is not a science."[15]

That jurisprudence was at bottom, and by provenance, to be regarded as phronesis rather than episteme, was also evident in the fact that its judgments and especially "extensions" were often, and perhaps usually, "probable" rather than certain. This was especially true of conventional arguments from "prejudice" (praeiudicium), which was essential to the study of law.[16] Implicit in conventional method was the idea of "corrective law," which was the assumption that later glosses tended to correct earlier ones; but, for all that, judgments remained matters of "opinion" and consensus (*opinio communis*). And the consensus, in the search for a proper legal method, was that the practice, if not the theory, of law could never escape these human conditions. Modern social thought drew upon these empirical, historical, and prudential habits of thought which were elaborated by the old legal tradition, and in this way preserved its ties with the tradition of Nomos.

Perfect Jurisprudence

Civil science in the Renaissance aspired to be even more than a profession and an encyclopedic discipline at once theoretical and practical. For in addition law was a "science," seeing that it was universal, treated things in terms of causes and reasons, and claimed superiority not only to medicine but also to philosophy and even theology. Yet law was also an art, depending on human judgment and aimed at the common good; and because it "consisted not in speculation but in action," as Seyssel had repeated, it was in this respect, too, "superior to all other sciences."[17] Louis Le Caron and others extended this commonplace view into an extraordinary professional chauvinism by attaching legal rhetoric to the ideals of Platonic philosophy. "Not content with the glory of being identified with the highest philosophy," Leibniz wrote in 1667, "jurisprudence is driven to occupy alone the throne of wisdom."[18]

The key to this drive was the old, and the new (in Otto Gierke's words, the "antique-modern"), natural law, which had been formulated variously, and over many centuries, in Greek philosophy, Roman jurisprudence, Thomist theology, and humanist scholarship, and which was reinforced and transformed by the "new science," the mathematical philosophy of the seventeenth century. The foundations of modern natural law were laid by the so-called "second scholasticism" of Spanish theologians such as Vitoria and Suarez and by philosophical jurists such as Oldendorp, Coras, and Gentili, not to speak of Bodin and Althusius; and the structure itself was established largely on the grounds of Ramism and Protestant neo-Aristotelianism.[19] The major advocates of natural law in the seventeenth century—representing the methodological *communis opinio*—include Hugo Grotius, Samuel Pufendorf, John Selden, Thomas Hobbes, Leibniz, and Jean Domat, although such minor figures as Samuel Rachel, J. W. Textor (who was an ancestor of Goethe), J. F. Finetti, and J. G. Heineccius are in many ways more pertinent to this discussion of social thought.

Seventeenth-century "jusnaturalists," as they came to be called, formed an international family of squabbling scholars devoted to rationalizing and systematizing law and moral philosophy; and in general, despite religious and ideological differences, their intellectual style prevailed for two centuries, more or less, down certainly to the early nineteenth century. Their common goal was rational jurisprudence (*jurisprudentia rationalis*) and universal justice (*justitia universalis*); and in this enterprise they came increasingly to rely on abstraction and devices of pure reason, especially logic and mathematics. Leibniz's "new method of jurisprudence," for example, though it drew on the *mores italicus* and *gallicus*, was designed to proceed according to a *mos geometricus*, following not Gaius's *Institutes* or Aristotelian or Ramist logic but Euclid's *Elements* or a metaphysical counterpart thereof. The "perfect jurist" proclaimed by Leibniz was not merely the man of encyclopedic learning—the *uomo universale*—he was the methodical Man of Science as conceived by Bacon or Descartes.

In his pursuit of "perfect jurisprudence" Leibniz looked to nature and to psychology as ways of simplifying and bringing order to the old legal tradition. For him jurisprudence remained person- and subject-centered, but he regarded nature as the "cause" of individual "liberty" and will. He proposed to reduce the Gaian triad to a simple duality, the category of "action" being superfluous. So he preserved only the concepts of person, defined as a moral agent, and thing, defined as the object of natural possession, which was itself fundamentally only an extension of liberty (self-possession). This revision reflects both the old dualism of nature and society and the new dualism underlying the "metaphysical foundations of modern science," expressed even more radically by Descartes as a distinction merely between two classes of "things," one conscious and one material—*res cogitans* and *res extensa*.[20]

The drive toward abstraction and universality can be illustrated by the modern *fortuna* of the ancient Roman "rules of law" (*regulae antiqui iuris*) gathered in the last book of the Digest, which had been glossed conventionally for centuries. Not that these rules had philosophical status; on the contrary, the very first *regula* proclaimed their conventional basis: "The law may not be derived from a rule, but a rule must arise from the law as it is."[21] On the whole the practitioners of civil science were wary of abstractions, whether in the form of definitions ("all definitions are dangerous" was another commonplace) or of excessive generality and rigor (*summum ius, summa iniuria* was the motto of many discussions of "equity" and flexible interpretation).

Characteristically, however, seventeenth-century jurists looked with new eyes on these maxims—"Liberty is a thing beyond price," for example, and "Slavery is death," not to speak of "Women cannot hold public office"—and promoted them from their original level of rather ordinary Roman common sense to that of universal propositions, natural principles, and quasi-geometrical "axioms."[22] From Le Douaren and Coras to Leibniz and

Domat, the analogy between law and geometry was another way of bringing jurisprudence into line with the values, or rather value-free claims, of natural science; but the successes of the "new science" of Galileo, and the attendant separation of historical erudition from true "philosophy" (of whatever doctrinal persuasion), gave these quantifying and calculating conceits new force and conviction and the appearance of certainty.

Nature remained the starting point and the goal for most members of the "philosophical school of law," as critics later more or less indiscriminately referred to the champions of jusnaturalism and universal law. Their project was in general to rationalize and to universalize jurisprudence by reducing its principles not "to an art" (in the famous Ciceronian phrase) but to "natural order." This was the goal of Jean Domat's systematic study, *Les Lois civiles dans leur ordre naturel* of 1689, which sought the "spirit of the laws" (*l'esprit des lois*) in their most general formulation and which was based (as Leibniz remarked) on "a certain small number of principles from which the rest follow and which act as rules to give neat solutions to disputes."[23] In similar fashion French feudists such as François Bourjon and Pierre Merville tried to reduce the customs of Paris, Normandy, and other provinces to "principles" and to establish a sort of "reasoned" law not only for the use of advocates but also for "philosophical" ends, including the control and reform of society.[24]

One of Domat's contemporaries, Louis Boullenois, under a similar debt to Descartes, went so far as to propose a Cartesian jurisprudence that would dispense with conventional learning and deliver itself over to "meditation" and calculation. In theory this meant beginning with the juridical "person," but "person" understood in abstract psychological terms positing primary "natural" motives, whether acquisitive and aggressive or positive and "social."[25] In practice this came increasingly to mean isolating and ordering the economic interests of man in a rational way that literally transformed the law into a mathematical science—a civil arithmetic which was the juridical equivalent of Physiocracy and was based on a similar sort of reductionist anthropology. By thus joining "the passions and the interests" and defining the economic nature of man, Louis Boullenois hoped to contribute as well to political reform—"to lead French customs to unanimity" and in this way "to reduce a great kingdom to the same law"—a hope which he shared, of course, with the Physiocrats of a later generation.

Yet the labors of natural lawyers were continually disturbed by debates not only over methodology but also over questions of value, human as well as theological. Leibniz himself, although he found the pioneering work of the "incomparable Grotius" insufficiently rigorous (that is, not properly deductive), nevertheless kept his conceptualizations on a providential base and in that sense supernatural, and he rejected the views of Pufendorf and especially Hobbes for their hyperrationalism and for their apparent desire to reduce all things human, and perhaps divine, to the common denominator of Nature.[26] Both Grotius and Hobbes attracted swarms of critics who made similar objections, and so, no less voluminously, did Pufendorf.

Here again we can see the ancient contest between Physis and Nomos being played out, in revived and perhaps exaggerated form. Again, too, we can see the reemergence of the old dualism of a "primary law of nature," which was based on necessity and universal reason, or at least instinct, and a "secondary law of nature," which involved human free will (with or without attendant theological considerations).[27] In this new confrontation, the old forces of Nomos were linked with a tradition of learning which the champions of the new science, empirical as well as mathematical, were anxious to discredit if not, with Descartes, to ignore altogether.

Grotius by no means shared the skeptical approach of Descartes and indeed drew extensively on Roman law and both the medieval and the modern legal tradition of scholarship. Yet he professed the same sort of universalist aims even as he invoked classical wisdom in their behalf. For his masterwork, *The Law of War and Peace* (1625), Grotius took as his standard "not those written laws, indeed, but the immutable laws of heaven" (referred to in Sophocles' *Antigone*) as well as the "natural reason" of Gaius and medieval jurists such as Baldus. Like Leibniz later, Grotius also lamented that "old and detestable illusion"—expressed most famously by Thrasymachus in Plato's *Republic*—"that justice and injustice are distinguished the one from the other not by their own nature, but in some fashion merely by the opinion and custom of mankind" (*hominum inani opinione et consuetudine*).[28] Many others, including Leibniz, referred to the cynical suggestions of Thrasymachus, which seemed to prefigure and to reinforce the scandalous and in effect "value-free" arguments of Hobbes and later Spinoza—and to recall the distasteful opinions of Machiavelli and other champions of "reason of state."

Yet even in the "age of philosophy," as Whitehead called the seventeenth century, the idea of custom was not wholly supplanted by abstract naturalism; and unfamiliar and unfashionable as the subject is, the resistance to universalizing "science" in the seventeenth and eighteenth centuries should not go unnoticed. Grotius, Domat, and even Leibniz, despite their rationalistic rhetoric, preserved much of the substance, terminology, and forms of Roman law, including the Gaian trinity and the Gaian recognition of the overarching framework of the law of nations accommodating particular as well as general law—*ius proprium* as well as *ius naturale*. Grotius himself wrote on the "human" laws and customs of Holland (*Menschlicke wet* and *de ongeschreven wetten*) in terms of Roman civil law (*Burgerwet*), concerning such practical questions of private law as, "What are the rights of persons to things and the means of defending and pursuing the same?"

"There are two kinds of law used in all nations of the world," wrote Jean Domat, following this same conventional distinction. "One is natural law, and the other is the laws proper to each nation, such as customs authorized by long usage." Thus Domat paraphrased, and in a sense naturalized, the famous observation of Gaius that "all peoples observe in part their own special law [*ius proprium*] and in part a law common [*ius commune*] to all men"; and he accommodated not only a law based on "natural reason" but also a localized custom based in effect on the accidents of history and on "arbitrary" human will (*voluntas, arbitrium*).[29] As God created nature—or indeed, to recall the medieval formula, was himself nature (*Deus, id est Natura*)—so man created a "second nature," which was custom.

Although the consensus inclined to celebrate the conceptual hegemony of natural law, some jurists managed to recall the practical and local character of their discipline. One aspect of this which again reflected the "scientific" pretensions of the law was the employment of empirical modes of proof and argument. Legal "induction" owed more to Aristotelian rhetoric than to Baconian method, for it involved not quantifiable data but rather historical experience and precedent, not pure reason but rather the "logic of probability," which (as Ian Hacking has argued) arose in the mid-seventeenth century during the heyday of natural law.[30] Long before this there had been a connection between judicial logic and probability, which indeed had formed one of the topoi of sixteenth-century legal method; but again new scientific fashions came into play. For Leibniz, "the whole of judicial procedure is a kind of logic applied to questions of law."

Theological differences aside, the central issue among natural lawyers was the origin of society and of attendant institutions, especially property; and the main division was between those who assumed the fundamental "sociability" of humanity and those who did not. Grotius, Leibniz, and most jusnaturalists, Catholic as well as Protestant, defended the idea of an essential communal impulse (*appetitus societatis*) underlying human society and requiring a "social law" (*ius sociale; droit social*), while Pufendorf and, most notoriously, Hobbes approached the question of social origins from the standpoint of speculative and individual psychology—by inference "individualist" and by suspicion atheistic.

According to Georges Gurvitch, it was the great achievement of Grotius to shift the discussion of the collective behavior of humanity from religious and supernatural to secular and natural terms—or, as Leibniz saw it, to "join the scholastic doctrine of the eternal law of God with the principle of the social" (*lex Dei eterna cum principio socialitatis conjunxit*).[31] Drawing on Spanish scholasticism as well as Protestant Aristotelianism, Grotius employed medieval terms such as *universitas* but construed them as human collectivities without suggesting the old "mystical body" (*corpus mysti-*

cum); and most important, he interpreted human motives as an expression not merely of free will or acquisitiveness but of collective life and natural "sociability." To this extent Grotius maintained a balance between conceptions of Physis and Nomos.

Some jurists were even more concerned to recall and to recognize the importance of contingency and local knowledge in matters of legal judgment. In disagreement with Grotius and most contemporary opinion, Samuel Rachel, for example, insisted that the law of nations arose not from the law of nature but rather from "arbitrary" agreements and customs (*ius arbitrarium*)—corresponding to the Greek distinction between nature and law (*dikaion physikon* and *nomikon*) and perhaps to the scholastic distinction between providential and human law, largely neglected by Roman lawyers.[32] The *ius gentium* was a product of human will, in short, and not of reason, though modern jurisprudence might well try to remedy this defect through naturalistic reductions.

Contemporaneously with Domat and Rachel, J. W. Textor argued, or recalled, that the "secondary law of nations" was the product not only of natural law but also of the reception of custom—not only of reason (which was "primary natural law"), in short, but also of arbitrary usage. Out of this—*ex facto*—arose institutions of mating, bringing up the young, self-defense, ownership, and eventually the economic, political, and military rivalries between states. The consequence drawn by Textor from these circumstances was precisely that of Grotius and of Jean Bodin before him: not only was history relevant to the philosophy of law, but it represented the field in which law emerged and had to be interpreted.[33] The *ius gentium* represented the locus of human social experience and had to be viewed in a comparative and historical fashion. According to this minority opinion, in short, jurisprudence was the study, in the first instance, not of primary but of "second" nature.

Professional jurisprudence could hardly survive in the rarified atmosphere of pure reason and radical naturalism, and the upshot was usually some sort of synthesis between the old art of law and the new science of nature. One illustration is the encyclopedic and eclectic work of J. G. Heineccius, which brought together the learning and the lessons of legal humanism with those of jusnaturalism. For Heineccius jurisprudence, largely in its Romanoid form, continued to be "true philosophy" (*vera philosophia*, which was the theme of one of his academic essays) and the archetype of wisdom (*sapientia*), human and divine.[34] For the nineteenth century, Heineccius's work, which encompassed the history of law, philosophy, and scholarship, was still one of the most authoritative and moderate expressions of the "philosophical school of law," as it was retrospectively (and sometimes pejoratively) called, since it took into account experience, learned tradition, prudence, and practical judgment as well as the aspirations of enlightened reason and universal Nature, and since it stressed the "sociability" of mankind.

Nevertheless, the message and the legend of the Philosophical School as established in the eighteenth century was the doctrine of naturalism. "Perfect jurisprudence," as a consequence, was equated with jusnaturalism and from the seventeenth century on had turned increasingly to the natural-science model of social thought, to the neglect of the old tradition of "civil science." The old legal canon continued to form, as it were, the subtext of social discourse—"The theory [of Rousseau] is still that of the Roman lawyers," as Henry Sumner Maine remarked[35]—but it was concealed behind the language of naturalism. Old notions of human will and freedom were preserved, but in highly generalized forms, and were linked to an equally generalized anthropology which proposed to move directly from a theory of psychology to a theory of society and to programs of reform. Under these conditions the story of Nomos and the considerations of "second nature" became indeed "secondary," a sort of minor subplot, at least outside professional circles and in terms of the large questions of public debate concerning political power—and of course, in the later eighteenth century, political revolution. The "spirit of French law" was sought in custom and in the history of law and culture; the "spirit of law" more generally, though drawing perhaps on accumulated legal learning and experience, could apparently be established only within the larger framework of "nature."

The Spirit of the Law

From ancient times the search for the meaning of laws, the spirit as distinguished from the letter, was a central theme of social thought—"not merely the words" of the law, in the famous words of Celsus, "but their force and potency."[36] For the Glossators and especially for the Commentators this essential meaning remained the target of legal interpretation, and neither the legal revisionism derived from humanist influence nor the vogue of jusnaturalism changed this fundamental goal of jurisprudence—the quest for an underlying, or overriding, Spirit.

It was under cover of natural law that Jean Domat (who had studied at the University of Bourges) sought the "spirit of the Laws" (*l'esprit des Loix*), going beyond the more conservative enterprise of feudists to establish the "spirit of customary law." He began with the characteristic Enlightenment rejection of that old lawyerly standby, "prejudice." "I have not drawn my principles from *prejudices*," he declared, "but from the nature of things." For Domat the essential step was distinguishing between "arbitrary laws," based on human will, and "immutable laws," based on natural reason, and interpreting and ordering laws on the basis of the latter. One example given by Domat was the Roman law which provided that a man, in case his son died before reaching majority, might deprive the mother and transfer inheritance even to a stranger. Papinian had defended this practice through a fiction—the "spirit of the principle" of paternal "liberty"—which had a basis neither in nature nor in French custom, and which did not reflect the "written reason" to be found in other parts of Roman jurisprudence. Thus the "spirit of the law" was to be established, much in the fashion of Connan and other alumni of the law school of Bourges a century earlier, by adjusting the intention of Roman law through natural law and reason and determining its "spirit" through principles of equity.[37]

For Domat "the spirit of the laws" was one of three factors contributing to social consolidation and harmony. The other two were "the spirit of religion" and "the spirit of police"—distinctions which recalled not only the medieval conceit of the two swords but also the social trinity that, according to Claude de Seyssel, informed the national "grandeur" of the "grand monarchy of France" (religion, justice, police). Domat invoked the spirit of religion in terms of a spirituality reminiscent of that of his friend Pascal—reflecting an "inner spirit" corresponding to the "external order of society" (*l'ordre exterieur de la societé*). "The spirit of police," Domat added, "is to maintain public tranquillity among men and to keep them in this order regardless of the dispositions of their interior life" (*independemment de leurs dispositions dans l'interieur*).[38] And the spirit of the laws brought the ideal of justice to the contradictions between public order and private interests.

The search for the spirit of the laws was carried on more famously, more systematically, and with a wider range of learning by Montesquieu, whose *De l'esprit des lois* was also advertised as a work without grounding in legal conventions and prejudices—"born without a mother" (*prolem sine matrem creatam*) was the book's epigraph. Yet in many ways, despite philosophical and historical reflections and amplifications, the discussion was carried on in the old tradition of legal commentary, to the extent indeed that a later admirer called Montesquieu's book an "eloquent interpretation" of Ulpian on the nature of law. Montesquieu began his book with general definitions corresponding to the Digest title "On law and justice," went on to a discussion of the three species of constitutions after the fashion of the second title, "On the origin of laws," and then proceeded to the law of things (commercial law), the status of persons (liberty and servitude), family, and succession.[39] In the course of this exposition he made abundant use not only of standard Roman authorities but also of later commentators and of such modern discoveries as the fragments of Ulpian published in the sixteenth century. The last sections of the book corresponded exactly to the collections of feudal law (the *Libri Feudorum*).

More fundamentally, Montesquieu's forays into the field of comparative law followed trails already blazed by jurists, who for centuries had wrestled with problems of the "conflict of laws"—written law and custom as well as secular and ecclesiastical law—and who had had to take into account principles of territoriality, social differentiation, and geographical and cultural relativism. Montesquieu has been portrayed by Raymond Aron as a pioneering sociologist; but if so, this is due in large part to the intellectual legacy of European jurisprudence.

Initially, Montesquieu tried to bring Nomos and Physis back together by defining law, in the style of vulgar Newtonianism, as the "necessary relations between things" social as well as natural. Yet like Domat he recognized a distinction between the natural law of physical existence and the "positive law" of the moral world, where human wills created variety and instability; and he rejected the abstract universalism of conventional natural law. In order to determine the "spirit of the laws" in general, Montesquieu introduced the consideration of geographical, economic, social, cultural, and historical factors; but in keeping with the commentators on Roman law since the time of Jacques de Révigny and Pierre de Belleperche, he construed these factors in causal terms. "Mankind are influenced by various causes," he wrote: "by the climate, by the religion, by the laws, by the maxims of government, by precedents, morals, and customs; whence is formed a general spirit of nations."

Central to Montesquieu's reflections was the old conception of custom, and indeed a significant part of the book is devoted to tracing the life cycle of French *coutumes* from barbarism to more enlightened times. For Montesquieu each of the barbarian laws had its own "spirit," corresponding to the natural factors outlined earlier; but legislation, in the form of the Carolingian capitularies and later the legislative reforms of St. Louis, created a larger order. The spirit of French law was expressed above all by those laws which "suddenly appeared all over Europe" and which, Montesquieu added, "have done infinite good and infinite mischief." The last books of *The Spirit of the Laws* treated "the theory of the feudal laws"; and again following the conventions of legal scholarship (as well as the modern researches of the Abbé du Bos), Montesquieu retold the story of the "origins" of the fief and of vassalage and their later transformations.[40]

Writing brought rationality, but it also brought secrecy. Referring to Le Caron's commentary on the *Somme rurale*, Montesquieu commented on the transition from oral to literate culture in this way: "The usage of writing fixes the ideas, and keeps the secret; but when the usage is laid aside, nothing but the notoriety of the proceeding is capable of fixing those ideas." And, added Montesquieu, this secret style of proceeding which attends the decline of feudal justice "is the present practice."[41] From the time of St. Louis and the ascendancy of written procedures, French law had become a confusion of local customs, feudal practices, and Roman law, until the "grand epoch" of Charles VII, when customs, with popular consent, were made more general. In historical terms the resulting Franco-Romano "common law," which Montesquieu also called "the great *corpus* of our French jurisprudence," came (in one of Montesquieu's favorite expressions) "little by little" (*peu à peu*) to form the basis of the "spirit of the laws" in France—and would undergo a further process of generalization through analyses such as Domat's and his own.

Montesquieu presented an encyclopedic mixture of historical insight and theoretical reflection concerning the European legal tradition and its embedded issues, and in this connection he gave a sensitive analysis of the idea of custom as a category of social thought. Montesquieu did not share the contemporary enthusiasm for legislative reform—in effect social engineering, which for him represented despotism. He did envision social improvement on the basis of reason, but for him "the spirit of the laws" determined the conditions and limits of such enlightened reform. "It is the business of the legislature to follow the spirit of the nation," he advised, adding that "we do nothing so well as when we act with freedom, and follow the bent of our natural genius." His lesson was, indeed, that manners and customs could not be changed by laws but rather had to undergo change themselves; and then, through experience and learning as well as pure reason, the laws and institutions of a nation might be accommodated to them. This was why laws had to be understood in their geographical and historical context. This was why, too, a philosophical understanding of society could not limit itself to the body of the laws but had ultimately to seek out its "spirit." This premise signaled a transition from traditional "civil science" to a true and self-conscious science of society.

The Problem of Codification

But civil science, as "true philosophy," had its practical as well as its theoretical side; and Enlightenment notions of "philosophy" insisted on this aspect of the legal tradition. These practical concerns found a focus in the codification movement, which reached a high point in the eighteenth century and which represented perhaps the most fundamental issue of modern social thought. Was it possible to formulate the customs and laws of a society, which reflected its underlying national "spirit," in a written code? Could Justinian's project be repeated in particular national contexts, given the social divisions and turmoil of modern European society? The most "enlightened" answer was of course in the affirmative, as was that of jusnaturalism. In general the result was to shift the emphasis, within the legal tradition, from jurisprudence to legislation—from the "will" of the people to that of the government.[42]

In various ways the idea of a "code" represented a ruling metaphor of Enlightenment thought. "We live under three codes," wrote Diderot: "the natural code, the civil code, the religious code." In 1756 Morelly's *Code de la nature* proposed a model of legislation "conforming to the intentions of nature," that is, to the "true spirit of laws."[43] Historically, a "code" had been an accumulation of positive law, but the invasion of jurisprudence by rationalism confirmed the tendency to identify codification with the ideals of natural law. This was also the case with Bentham, who called his universal standard "utility." As a French critic of the old legal tradition put it in 1788, "Our history is not our code"; and this iconoclastic assumption may be taken thenceforth as a central theme of revolutionary jurisprudence, as well as of the Philosophical School.[44]

Throughout Europe in the eighteenth century the notion of a national "code" was often on the minds of jurists, who of course had the models of Theodosius and especially Justinian to inspire them. Among the most successful imitations of the Romano-Byzantine Corpus Juris was Frederick II's *Liber Augustalis* and Alfonzo IX's *Siete Partidas,* but there were other Romanoid efforts within the tradition of canon as well as secular law; and from the fifteenth century on, ideas of establishing systems of law were commonly joined to efforts of "state-building." This was only in part an expression of national policy, for not only Charles VII and Louis XI of France but also René of Anjou and Emperor Charles V were among those who hoped to secure their social base through the reform and regularization of, thus the "cognizance" over, local laws and customs.

Nor was the codification movement limited to official policy, for complaints about the confusion and inequity of laws and petitions for their reformation arose also from representatives of the people, who recited much the same litany of abuses, delays, and irregularities of justice. For more than two centuries before the French revolution, *cahiers* of the three estates called for such remedies, as of course did legal reformers like Chancellors Michel de L'Hôpital and Henri-François d'Aguesseau, as well as practical and philosophical jurists of all political and confessional persuasions. In France the locus classicus was Charles Dumoulin's "Oration on the Union and Concord of the Customs of France," which was later taken not only as a manifesto of the reformation movement but also as prophetic of later efforts to form a French code. "Nothing can be more laudable and useful in any Republic," Dumoulin had written, "than the reduction of all the very diffuse and often absurdly differing customs of this kingdom into a single, brief, very clear, and most equitable harmony" (*in brevem unam, clarissimam et aequissimam consonantiam reductio*).[45] In many ways the efforts of Robert Pothier, "father of the Code," carried on, in a synthetic way, the work of Dumoulin as well as Domat.[46]

Prominent among the "intellectual origins of the Civil Code" were both private systems of jurisprudence and royal legislation, from the seminal statement at Montils-les-Tours in 1454 to the Estates General of Blois in 1576 and, a century after that, the reforming ordinances of Louis XIV. With the encouragement of the champions of natural law, codification became a standard part of the program of enlightened despotism throughout pre-revolutionary Europe—and then an equally standard aim of revolutionary and Bonapartist governments. More than most questions, that of codification, which touched on the "general will," transcended particular "interests" and ideological concerns.

On the basis of the social principle (*socialitas,* or *sociabilitas; sociabilité*) elaborated by Pufendorf and others, Samuel Cocceij provided philosophical justification for the Code he assembled for Frederick the Great of Prussia (1751), to the extent indeed that "this new corpus of law," as he concluded, "may with reason be called the Law of Nature itself" (*le Droit de la Nature meme; Ius naturae privatum*). Yet the Roman model was not forgotten, and Cocceij followed the efforts of Justinian to preserve the law in its original purity and intention. "For this reason Professors who teach our youth are forbidden to instruct them in violation of the terms of the law, even in search of its spirit and intention, amplifications, limitations, or exceptions." The same went, of course, for the judges; for only the King himself could speak for the Law—and (by inference) for Nature.[47]

This line of argument has led some historians to suggest that natural law was devoted not only to rationalism but, in a less disinterested way, to the "rationalization" of established authority and existing institutions. Thomas Hobbes was the most unqualified and provocative defender of this sort of authoritarian attitude, and it was perhaps his bluntness as much as his materialism that made him an embarrassment to so many moderate and moralistic natural lawyers.[48] In any case the terminology, rhetoric, metaphors, and analogies of "antique-modern" natural law became part of the ideological weaponry of absolute monarchy and its growing monopoly over the theory and practice of jurisprudence and its long professional heritage.

Yet the impulse toward codification spanned the entire political spectrum from absolute monarchy to legal reformers such as Gaetano Filangieri and "philosophical radicals" such as Jeremy Bentham, though always in the name of modernity. Bentham was an extreme example of an anti-jurist who wanted to discard the old legal tradition and found law on a theoretical psychology—a "science of human nature" and a conception of "spirit" taken not from the sociological reflections of Montesquieu but from the mechanism and "moral determinism" of Helvetius. Bentham scorned the fuzzy conservativism not only of Montesquieu but also of Blackstone and Burke; and he made fun of the "fallacies of authority," including what he dismissed as the "Chinese argument" ("the Wisdom of our Ancestors") and the "hobgoblin argument" ("no Innovation")—though he substituted some fantasies of his own ("Everyman his own lawyer," which was analogous, as Halevy pointed out, to Luther's "priesthood of all believers).[49]

Though based on empirical premises, Bentham's utilitarian jurisprudence followed a natural-science model of legislation and judgment and aspired to a wholly quantitative and value-free conception of society—or rather a society whose values were calculable and divorced from questions of practical reason and judgment. Bentham displayed the characteristic Enlightenment scorn for "prejudice" and "interest" as well as "natural rights"—categories of jurisprudence which had become factors of theoretical psychology and targets of "philosophy"—and he in effect proposed to establish a social science in terms that were not only empirical but also, in a radical sense, nominalist. Nor would he recognize rational grounds for opposition to his codification proposals, for such could only arise from "corruptionists" and "knaves," which was to say, the "lawyer class" and the "class of party men in general." Later Bentham advertised his services as a codifier "to All Nations Professing Liberal Opinions."[50] Bentham's contempt for conventional wisdom and his subordination of "customary law" to legislative authority were extended by John Austin into a theory which, identifying "positive law" with legislative will, was quite in keeping with Enlightenment assumptions, if not aspirations.[51]

On the whole, the inclination of legal and social thought during the Enlightenment was toward the making rather than the finding or even the reforming of law. The "spirit of the law" was commonly identified with "the spirit of legislation," and the strategies associated with Physiocrats and codifiers were increasingly joined to hopes of social control and direction.[52] This was quite in keeping with the imperial rhetoric of the Romano-Byzantine legislation of Justinian and what may (in Kuhnian terms) be called the "normal science" of law. The French Revolution, however, called for a wholly new paradigm, implied perhaps by the Philosophical School, and worked out theoretically by enlightened absolutism, but never enforced in broadly social (private as well as public) and deeply national terms. The aims and the efforts of revolutionary legislation were taken, by admirers and critics alike, as the practical culmination of the Philosophical School of Law.

The Death and Rebirth of Nomos

In France the codification impulse emerged in the months before the Revolution of 1789, as is apparent in a number of the *cahiers de doléance,* and it became a major part of the program of revolutionary reform. If the Revolution represented the "triumph of philosophy," it began with the destruction of the past, including the whole structure of customary law.

One of the first items on the revolutionary agenda after the famous night of August fourth, that "St. Bartholomew of property" (as Aulard called it) which "entirely abolished the feudal regime," was the devising of a new constitution and, in this connection, "a new judicial order."[53] This question was debated intensely for months by the advocates on the Committee on Feudalism (*Comité de féodalité*) in terms of the ideals and goals of natural law, which had come to permeate the language of the legal profession.

In these debates the old issue of legislative versus judicial power was rehearsed in terms that were at once extreme and intensely practical. From his seat on the left of the National Assembly, Adrien Duport took the most radical position, identified loosely with the theories of Rousseau. Duport also took the lead in undermining the institutional base of his own profession. "No more judges!" he exclaimed at one point. "No more courts!" Duport argued that the achievement of justice was a purely logical process—a syllogism in which the facts formed the minor premise, the pertinent law the major, and the judgment the conclusion. In a democratic regime laws were not mysteries controlled only by privileged experts; they were "social conventions" which could be applied by any "citizen." Duport's ideas went too far, of course, and even his colleague Robespierre put in a kind word for the lawyers at this point.[54] Yet they were in keeping with the most advanced opinions of the time (including those not only of Bentham but also of the young Napoleon Bonaparte, who had likewise envisioned a society without lawyers). They were in keeping, too, with the extraordinary acts of 1790, which included the suppression of the Order of Advocates and the transformation of its members—*avocats, juges, procureurs,* and other varieties of the *gens de robe*—into ordinary "men of law" (*hommes de loi*), who became the spokesmen for the "General Will." Bentham was one of the first to offer a "new plan for the organisation of the Judicial Establishment in France" (December 1789), a plan which was quite in line with those of the more radical members of the Assembly, who likewise wanted to abolish the "lawyer class" and deliver (in Bentham's phrase) "power to the People."[55]

In the extensive debates over the "new judicial order" the most fundamental of questions, beyond that of the constitution itself, was that of codification, that legal face of national unification which lawyers had discussed for centuries, though with small chance of success until the revolutionary abolishment of the society of orders. "There will be made a code of civil laws common to the whole kingdom," declared the Assembly in September 1791; and two years later J. J. R. de Cambacérès presented the first "project" for a code.[56] It was a time of Jacobin euphoria and awakening of National Will, expressed just two weeks earlier in the famous *levée en masse.* "The age so devoutly wished for has finally arrived to fix forever the empire of liberty and the destinies of France," proclaimed

Cambacérès. He dedicated two further projects (in 1794 and 1797) to the "grand edifice of civil legislation," and Jacqueminot a fourth, before an official commission formulated the plan which evolved into the Civil Code of 1804.

The Code Civil, *né* Code Napoléon but first entitled "Code of the French People," was represented in official rhetoric and in public opinion, or at least popular imagination, as a derivation of pure reason and of "natural law." For the People "the truth is one and indivisible," declared Cambacérès, and so should be their law. The purpose of this law was to "regenerate," to "perfect," and to "foresee" absolutely "everything." This was quite in keeping with the legislative ambitions of the First Consul (soon-to-be Emperor), who fancied and represented himself to be the new Justinian. Drawing upon the Rousseauist *Volunté générale*—counterpart of the Roman *lex regia*—Napoleon both claimed a popular mandate (and abolished the Consulate), and hoped that his work would be (in Justinian's words) "valid for all time."

In the "preparatory work" and preliminary discussion of the Code (which the First Consul himself often attended) the old question of "interpretation" arose, and the mere mention of the word, according to Regnier, created a shock among the Citizen Redactors. Napoleon dealt with the issue just as Justinian had done—and indeed just as Robespierre had reacted to the problem in discussions of "judicial power"—by reciting the old rule that interpretation of the law belonged exclusively to the power that made it. Otherwise all the abuses of the Old Regime would be restored and, warned Citizen-Redactor Maillia-Garat, "the empire of custom would be reborn."[57]

It was quite directly in connection with this great legislative enterprise and attendant controversies that the modern conception, and terminology, of "social science" took form. In 1799 Cambacérès himself had presented a *Discours sur la science sociale* to the Institute, in which he rehearsed in modern terms the old theme of law as *vera philosophia*, precisely with reference to the problem of codification. "Legislators, philosophes, jurisconsults!" he proclaimed. "Here is the moment of social science and, we may add, of true philosophy" (*le moment de la science sociale, et nous pouvons ajouter, de la véritable philosophie*). For Cambacérès the science of society included moral philosophy, political economy, and legislation, and its aim—in keeping with the ideas of Condorcet and the Idéologues— was "to perfect social relations" (*de perfectionner les relations sociales*). The task of *la morale* and *l'économie politique* was to accomplish this with reference to "the passions and the interests," respectively; that of *la législation* was to attend to human rights, which were the essence of the revolutionary impulse and ideal.[58]

Yet the victory of Physis over Nomos claimed in effect by Jacobins and Bonapartists, as so often before, was more apparent than real. As Esmein remarked, the Redactors still spoke the language of Dumoulin and D'Aguesseau.[59] Rhetoric and ideological pretensions aside, Napoleon's creation was in substance and form a most conventional and traditional edifice. The "doctrinal origins" of the Code can be traced back not only to Old Regime jurisprudence, most notably the work of Domat and Pothier (accounting for more than half of the 2281 articles), but also to Roman law, which furnished the primary model for Napoleon and his Committee of Redactors, headed by Cambacérès. This was the case in particular with the crucial doctrine of "absolute" private property and the paternalistic view of the family, which was to parallel the authoritarian character of the Empire itself. "The Revolution . . . made possible a new creation," wrote one of the earliest commentators on the Code, Riffé, in 1803; yet just a page later he added, "This Code is founded mainly on Roman law."[60] So, too, in certain ways, would be French legal philosophy and education, and in some ways the infant discipline of "social science," for the next generation—though not without noteworthy opposition. The legacy of Nomos could not in practice be cast off merely by the rhetoric of naturalism and rationalism and by the hubris of virtuoso legislators.

On the surface, however, and especially in terms of political and constitutional debate, the European legal tradition was transformed through the speculations and controversies of natural-law ideas, Enlightenment ideals, and revolutionary efforts; and it was in the early nineteenth century that the champions of rational jurisprudence were lumped together—again according to time-honored legal convention—into a "philosophical school." In the wake of revolution, jusnaturalism became a sort of stereotype and a legend, characterized by simplistic and abstract conceptions of human psychology and material relations, and by ignorance, or avoidance, of historical context and scholarship. Concepts of "liberty," "property," "contract," "utility," and the like were separated from questions of tradition and human value; and anthropocentric systems, traceable back to conventional Romanoid structures such as the Gaian trinity, were apparently replaced by natural-science models of social order and regulation. Nevertheless, Enlightenment aspirations, followed eventually by revolutionary disillusionments, prepared the way for another reaction, another struggle between the forces of Physis and Nomos—and the final stage in the transition between the old "civil science" and the new "social science."

THIRTEEN

The Historical School

Vormals richtete.
  Konige.
  Weise.
    wer richtet denn itzt?
Richtet das einige
Volk? das heilige Gemeinde?
  nein . . .

Holderlin, "Zu Sokrates' Zeiten"

·

Historical Jurisprudence

History played a role in the legal tradition almost from the start, especially from the time of Pomponius's work "on the origin of civil law," which was incorporated into the first book of the Digest.[1] In that connection its function was to suggest both the "sources" of law and its "causes"—the idea of "principle" (*principium* or *arche*) accommodating both of these legal notions. Throughout the scholastic career of civil and canon law the respect for history in this sense was preserved, and it was made into a virtual fetish by humanist scholars and pedagogues and Renaissance historians of the law. The history of Roman law was carried down to the modern period by Valentinus Forster, another product of the University of Bourges, and others. The most comprehensive survey was Arthur Duck's *Use and Authority of Civil Law in the States of Christian Princes* (1653), which treated feudal as well as civil and canon law down to his own day in areas where these institutions still had force. The practice carried over into vernacular traditions, too, as exemplified by Hermann Conring's *Origins of German Law* (1643), which offered a contrast to natural-law fashions; and similar studies were undertaken for other national and international legal traditions.[2]

In various ways "history" was also basic to the new "methods" of law formulated in the sixteenth century, establishing an alternative to, or an empirical basis for, philosophical approaches. Like Bacon's natural science, sixteenth-century jurisprudence depended on both experience and reason. Such was the twofold structure of law as described by Conrad Lagus in his treatise on legal interpretation—although in the law, too, "history" often suggested an empirical base, a collection of examples or precedents, rather than temporal form or chronological explanation. Jean Barbeyrac and Johann Eisenart (Conring's younger colleague) both invoked the old program of François Baudouin for a "conjunction" between jurisprudence and the study of history, as in effect Montesquieu was to do a generation later.[3]

Another Digest title that continued to encourage a historical approach to the law was the one "On the meaning of words" (*De verborum significatione*), which brought to the attention of scholars questions of interpretation, etymology, and linguistic change.[4] Such questions became more complex in the medieval period when "interpretation" implied also the translation of barbarian terms into Romano-Byzantine, or Romano-canonical, terminology. Translations of and commentaries on classical texts, treatises of comparative law, and lexicons became the essential auxiliaries of legal history and contributed to the sense of and research into legal change over the centuries.

This continued to be no less the case at the height of natural-law fashions, "anti-historical" as they seemed to be. Grotius insisted on the importance of a "knowledge of history," and Montesquieu declared, more famously, "We must elucidate history by laws and laws by history."[5] The new genre of legal history, ancient and modern, flourished in the more specialized work of such scholars as Conring, Giovanni Gravina, André Terrasson, and Johann Gottlieb Heineccius. Like Montesquieu, Terrasson insisted that philosophy and history were "absolutely necessary" for a knowledge both of Roman law and of modern jurisprudence; and his *History of Roman Jurisprudence* traced the Romanist tradition from the Twelve Tables, through the scholastic and humanist interpreters, down to the time of Jean Domat and Claude de Ferrière.[6] As a form of wisdom and "true philosophy," law, as Heineccius recalled, citing the old formula of Ulpian, required a knowledge of things both divine and human, that is, historical as well as philosophical and theological matters. Heineccius himself wrote not only a survey of legal history from Justinian to the present (*ad nostra tempora novella*), German as well as Roman, but a history of philosophy, studies of Roman antiquities, including the Twelve Tables, and surveys of both natural law and the law of nations, which he called the "positive or secondary natural law" (*ius gentium positivum vel secondarium naturale*).[7] Some of his work continued to be published, translated, and taught well into the nineteenth century.

What is more, natural law itself was placed in historical perspective by post-Grotian scholars such as Martin Hübner and Adam Glafney, who traced the "history of the code of humanity" back to its ancient and pre-Christian sources, through its scholastic interpreters and adapters, down to its modern masters, including such "heretics of natural law" as Machiavelli, Hobbes, Bayle, and Mandeville. The history of natural law figured, too, in the contemporary histories of philosophy, including the classic work of Johann Brucker, published in the 1740s.[8] The law of nations also received historical treatment as an aspect of the history of civilization as idealized by Enlightenment scholars. In 1795 Robert Ward praised the "universality" of the *ius gentium* as he lamented its neglect. The history of mankind had been written, he admitted, but never so comprehensively as he proposed to do. "From the same collection of facts, one historian has drawn a history of man," he wrote; "another, of the progress of society; a third, of the effects of climate; a fourth, of military achievements; a fifth, of laws in general; a sixth, of a particular state. But," he concluded, "never yet has it been the fortune of the annals of the world . . . to produce from any commentator, A History of the Law of Nations."[9] And Ward went on to survey that aspect of human custom called the "secondary law of nations" from the beginning down to the age of Grotius.

By the eighteenth century the story of European law had been told many times from various points of view, and of course the continuous generation of interpretations and new customs contributed further to its elaboration. Indeed, it was the tradition of positive law that attracted the most considerable efforts of historical scholarship, since not the law of nature but only the interpretations thereof could possess a history—or reflect changes in terms of times, places, and cultural individuality. It was especially in the commentaries on European customs that historical and comparative interpretations were found to be essential and that the realm of Nomos could be preserved and extended.

The context of this interpretation was the massive cultural process which German scholars in particular have studied and celebrated as the "Reception" of Roman law. Like England and France, Germany long preserved a tradition of popular justice and procedures of "proof" for local customs, based on sworn testimony—the *Weistümer* being the German counterparts of the French *enquêtes par turbe*. Justice was largely in the hands of the "speakers of the law" (*Rechtssprecher*), who formed the institution of the *Schöffen*, which flourished in the later Middle Ages and survived in some places into the nineteenth century.[10] These *Rechtssprecher* were practical men who judged facts and did not hear arguments or speculate about the law.

During the fifteenth century this Germanic system was in large part supplanted by Romano-canonical procedures. The so-called "practical reception" of Roman law occurred officially in 1495 in the courts of the Holy Roman Empire, but of course earlier incursions had been made in the form of legal terminology, procedures, and devices in the courts, as well as Italian methods of education in the universities. The old Germanic law, for instance Eike von Reipgow's *Sachsenspiegel*, underwent extensive interpretation, systematization, and methodization at the hands of Romanists; and Lagus in particular applied his dual (philosophical-historical) "method"—*methodus, compendium,* and *speculum* were equivalents—to the reordering and in effect the Romanization of the medieval texts.[11] There was also talk of "reception" elsewhere in Europe—in England as well as France and Spain—but the conditions of such influence were limited largely to those parts of civil law locally acceptable as reasonable (the old formula of Roman law as *ratio scripta*). Even in Germany the "reception" concerned procedural rather than substantive law.

Nevertheless, the result was, as John P. Dawson has argued, a general triumph of learned law—that is, of italianate legal science and the corporate tradition of professional jurists, especially from the sixteenth to the eighteenth century. This was achieved officially not only through judgments of the imperial courts but also by the growing practice of sending cases to university scholars for advice (*Aktenversendung*) and interpretation. Benedict Carpzov—the Bartolus, as some have called him, of the *Juristenstand*—was only one scholar-judge who carried on the work of Romanization through judicial decisions. From the seventeenth century on, there was a veritable flood of publications—books of precedents and "praejudicia"—which defined and shaped German law, quite apart from the political and "state-building" initiatives of emperors and princes.

What finally emerged was a selective and interpretive use of Roman law which came to be called the "modern usage" of Roman sources (*usus modernus Pandectarum*) or "current customs" (*mores hodiernae*). In 1690 Samuel Stryk, in a book of this title, offered a comparative history of Germanic and Roman laws from Tacitus through the feudal period and the emergence of "doctors of law" down to the modern *receptio,* which was introduced in order to correct "irrational customs" and to promote the common good in the courts (*hodie ad publicae salutatis promotionem in foris Germaniae*).[12] Running through the German legal tradition, too, was the conventional distinction between academic and practical law (*jurisprudentia, jurisperitia*); and by the eighteenth century this had become accentuated and institutionalized, especially in the divergence between cameralist science and jurisprudence. In many ways the practical tradition, estranged from the natural law taught in the universities, inclined to more empirical and historical attitudes.

For several centuries, then, German jurists struggled with the conceptual and practical problems of reconciling ancient legal forms with modern social reality, and the result was a variety of methodological and ideological debates—Romanists against Germanists and both schools against jusnaturalists; champions of popular justice against champions of judicial initiative and both against apologists for executive interference and codification; and, as always, those inclined to legal philosophy and system—whether the rationalist defenders of natural law or the authoritarian "Pandectists"— against those inclined toward empirical and historical methods.[13]

Yet in a number of ways the study of history remained essential to legal science—to provide material for elementary legal education, for the understanding of contending legal systems, for practical judgments, and for legal reform. Even efforts of codification, although they often used the rhetoric of natural law, depended, as Justinian's had done, on the massive survey of legal literature; and as Thomasius lamented, there had been many more law books written in the four centuries since the four doctors than in the millennium before Justinian. "Our history is not our code," a revolutionary declared at the end of the eighteenth century.[14] But the reverse did not hold: "A Code is at once a history and a system," as Eugène Lerminier wrote a century later.[15] Indeed, Napoleon's legislative masterpiece drew heavily on the old legal tradition, as Justinian perforce had done, and so did the system of French legal education after as well as before the Restoration. If the form and much of the doctrine of the Code Napoléon was Roman, its substance was the customary law and "modern usage" of French tradition—as German critics would lament again and again.

Among the central topics of the legal tradition that of private property—extension or at least inseparable companion of individual liberty—was a most likely subject of historical investigation. The old conflict between Mine and Thine was an aspect of the law of nations discussed endlessly by medieval and modern jurists; and although the problem was often obscured by the technicalities of possessory and proprietary law, it also led to discussions of the emergence of human groups from a simple agrarian to a civilized and citified state. After the *ius naturale,* according to Alberico de Rosate, emerged the *ius gentium,* with its accommodations of the human (that is, a sinful) condition, including not only legal actions and obligations but also, he lamented, wars, conflicts, and other products of "those pronouns *meum et tuum.*"[16]

Property (*dominium*) was clearly enough defined in ancient Roman law, but medieval devices of possession and prescription vastly complicated the question. Yet jurists continued to debate the nature of dominion, private and well as public, and especially its "origins." In the context of natural law these debates tended to be highly theoretical, in the fashion of social-contract theories; but in the eighteenth century historical scholarship supplemented and corrected such speculations. Out of the legal controversies came modern theories of "stages"—three, four, or more—of human development, from agrarian to civic life, which followed for the most part the condition of the law of property.[17]

The distinction between a "primary" and a "secondary" nature continued to frame eighteenth-century disputes about the development of humanity. J. F. Finetti invoked this distinction in his attack on the godless naturalism of "Hobbes, Pufendorf, Thomasius, Wolf, and others"—"Protestants" or worse—and reminded his readers that "primary natural law" was the work of God, "secondary" of man only. Yet Finetti criticized the methods and conclusions of Vico (as well as Vico's disciple Emmanuele Duni and Rousseau) concerning the solitary and savage (*ferinus*) condition of man's primary nature as a disparagement of the "true" law of nations. By implication he also rejected Vico's and Duni's segregation of a sphere of "natural truth" (*Veri naturale*) from that of "human truth" (*Veri morale*), in which man in effect made himself—and made himself "social."[18]

The question of "sociability" indeed lay at the root of the debates over natural and human law—and more theoretically over the "social contract." In the wake of Hobbes, Pufendorf, and Rousseau the old confrontation of Nomos and Physis was resumed, in terms first of theological premises and finally of the "nature" of man, individually and collectively.[19] Was humanity—and its laws and its culture—an expression of an essentially animal nature (a suggestion which Ulpian had centuries before inserted into the law), or was it a wholly different, a "second" sort of nature which could only be understood in a diverse and changing social and cultural context? This was the fundamental question which the Historical School inherited from the Philosophical School. This was also the question faced by Vico, who was not only the most insistent and systematic critic of natural law— and champion of history—but virtually the only scholar to offer a comprehensive alternative to the vulgar naturalism of the age of Enlightenment. Vico's work has been studied from many anticipatory points of view, but he himself looked for wisdom in the cultural experience of the past, and his primary target was the Western legal tradition. What Vico's "new science" offered, in its first form, was an original philosophical (as distinguished from jurisprudential) synthesis of the legacy of civil science, the first modern expression of the world of Nomos, which drew, methodologically as well as substantively, upon history and philology as well as philosophy and legal science itself.

The New Science

Vico began as a champion of old-fashioned humanism—in the form of philology and rhetoric—and ended as a creator of a "new science," whose first formulation was "philology" and whose last incarnation was a grandiose philosophy of humanity.[20] At first Vico was fascinated by the natural law, but his attachment to earlier forms of learning, and especially to the older legal tradition, led him to extend his intellectual perspective. A "born glossator," as Frank Manuel called him, Vico was also one of the last of the Renaissance humanists; and it was his eclectic and encyclopedic purpose to combine the best of both—the logical analysis of medieval jurists (*giureconsulti medesimi,* he called the Bartolists) with the textual criticism of humanists (*interpetri eruditi*), "the pure historians of the Roman civil law"—and on this basis to give depth and substance to the modern "philosophers of natural equity."[21] "Why has philology been alienated from philosophy?" he asked, and he turned his efforts to restoring the "unity" between the letter and the spirit, the body and the soul, of the European legal tradition.

Although Vico was fascinated by the "new" scientific ideas of Descartes and Bacon, his humanistic inclinations soon led him to doubt the value of Cartesian skepticism. For Vico the *Cogito* led first not to metaphysics but to language, and the new "critical method" he expounded in his early discussion of "the study methods of our time" recommended concentration not on abstract disciplines such as geometry but on "topical knowledge" and the concrete arts of discourse. Wisdom was in the first instance practical rather than theoretical and was, in neo-Stoic fashion, to be identified with prudence. Rejecting the arguments of Descartes, Vico preserved an attachment to the Baconian progam of intellectual progress and joined to it the social ideas of Grotius, whom he called the "jurisconsult of the human race."[22] In this connection prudence soon came to imply juris-prudence.

For Vico legal science served as model for and entry into philosophy. This was already clear in his essay "On the ancient wisdom of the Romans taken from the origins of the Latin language," where he begins to develop not only his etymological method but also the dualist structure of his epistemology and social philosophy. In its early form Vico's "new science" was a meeting place for conceptual polarities long embedded in the law: authority and reason, letter and spirit, history and system. From such confrontations Vico derived his distinction between the "true" (*verum*), which is based on reason and demonstration and which constitutes "science" (*scienza*), and the merely "certain" (implying both the legal and the Cartesian concept of the *certum*), which is based on authority and history and which constitutes "consciousness" (*coscienza*).[23] The opposite of truth is falsehood, the opposite of certainty only (subjective) doubt. In jurisprudence the homologous concepts are primary (*prius*) and secondary (*posterius*) natural law—which is to say, in the tradition to which Vico often appealed, Physis and Nomos.

From the analogies of language and law, too, came Vico's famous "*verum-factum* principle": "the criterion of truth, the rule by which we may certainly know it, is to have made it."[24] And what we may certainly know is not nature—God's Creation—but the works of humanity, such as languages, laws, and other cultural artifacts. We understand language because it is based on human convention; we understand law (positive law, at least) because it is the product of human will, whether popular or princely. "Reason proceeds from the necessity of nature, authority from the wills of men," as Vico put it. "Philosophy studies the necessary causes of things, whereas history investigates individual wills." Medieval legal science, according to Baldus and others, fulfilled both of these requirements. It was the purpose of the "new science," building on these precedents, finally and more systematically to give historical as well as philosophical form to the world of man's making, including natural science (if not nature itself).

The crucial point of Vico's career—and indeed of his "new science"— was the founding of a system of philosophical jurisprudence, a transmuted form of civil law, which purported to be a modern restatement of the ancient ideal of wisdom. "To jurisprudence," as Vico pointed out in a seminal passage, "the Romans gave the same name as the Greeks had given to wisdom, 'the knowledge of things divine and human.'"[25] In Rome the "wise men" (*sapientes*) were the jurisconsults, who had combined the virtues of sophistry and philosophy, practice (which meant particular decisions, the *res judicatae*) and theory (the *principia iuris*); and initially Vico followed this same path in his first systematic effort to formulate a science of humanity—his treatise of 1720 on "universal law."

The essential thing about the *Diritto universale,* the first incarnation of Vico's "new science," is that it began by rejecting the natural-science model of thought and especially the mathematical approach of Descartes (and the rival "new science" of Galileo). This is evident not only in the anthropocentric form of Vico's book but also in its etymological methods and its terminology. The idea of "cause," for example, Vico understood not only in its "scientific" and explanatory but also in its juridical and custodial sense (from *cavere*). Thus—in contrast to the naturalistic conceptions of Hobbes, Pufendorf, and other Protestants and alleged atheists—utility and necessity represented only the "occasions" of society; the true "cause" of social gathering was moral (*honestas*). For Vico jurisprudence brought together not only reason and authority but also ethics and politics, and did so in a grand historical perspective.

Legal conceptions furnished the terminology, too, for Vico's ideas of the structure of human psychology and society. This structure he defined in terms of the fundamental triad of knowledge, will, and power (*nosse, velle, posse*)—to which corresponded the legal categories of property, liberty, and self-defense (*dominium, libertas, tutela*). What this signified, put simply, was the civilian assumptions that the human subject was defined in terms, first of all, of his "liberty" (being under one's own and not another's law— *suum iuris* and not *alienum iuris*); second, that the free person by nature acquired property (*dominium, proprietas*) for use and subsistence; and third, that he was permitted the right of self-defense, if necessary through violence (according to the old civilian maxim *vi vim repellere licet*). This trinity was also recapitulated on the political level, for as Vico added, "All republics are born out of lordship, liberty, and self-defense"—in particular, and respectively, the constitutional species of monarchy, democracy, and aristocracy (*regia, libera, optimatium*). Such was the first statement of what (by analogy with Cartesian metaphysics) might be called Vico's "metan-omics"—for a "system of universal law" was indeed one face of the "new science."[26]

In its conceptual reach, Vico's legal philosophy was as broad as it was deep, for not only did it try to plumb the depths of myth and prehistory, it also tried to cover the entire "world of nations." Vico's famous phrase derived, of course, from the "law of nations" of civilian tradition. The *ius gentium* defined the "intelligible field of study" for Vico's study of juris-prudence, and eventually his "new science," though as usual he gave the category his own characteristic twist. Again trying to fuse the authoritative and the rational, the positive and the natural, forms of law, Vico defined the arena of human collective behavior as the "natural law of nations" (*ius naturale gentium*)—an arena which, for the scholar, includes as well the whole range of "universal history," as it had for Bodin and other students of comparative law, whose work Vico well knew and abundantly cited.[27]

Like so many jurists before him, and Montesquieu (who was almost his contemporary and at least possessed his work), Vico sought above all the "spirit of the law"; and this old formula he once again interpreted according to a philologico-philosophical dualism which was at once original and conventional—recalling the discussion not only of Jacques de Révigny but also of Celsus, who likewise placed the spirit above the letter of the law. For Vico the *mens legum* represented its historical meaning, derived from human will and authority, while *ratio legum* referred to its rationality and truth. This, too, illustrates the distinction betwen the "certain" and the "true" (*certum ab authoritate, verum a ratione* is Vico's formula in this connection).[28]

The method of Vico's new science also depended heavily on the "art of interpretation" (*iuris interpretandi ars*), which Grotius (as Vico recalled) regarded as originating largely from rhetoric.[29] The legal study of the meaning of words (referring to the civilian—and canonist—rubric *De verborum significatione*) was actually "part of philosophy," Vico argued, especially when joined to a proper understanding of etymology and the genesis (*physis* in this sense) of words. In this way Vico identified his "new science" with philology (*Nova scientia tenatur*, the first chapter of the second part of his *Diritto universale*, "On the constancy of philology") and, by inference, with history (*historia verborum* and *historia rerum* being the two parts of *philologia*).

At this stage of his thought Vico's method was generally aimed at exploiting, adapting, and often reshaping some of the major features of civilian tradition. In characteristically radical—root-tracing—fashion Vico followed up the civilian interest in origins, especially the mythical sources of Roman law (the *fabulae* referred to by Justinian) and that "serious poem," the law

of the Twelve Tables, which was the model for the transition from unwritten, "heroic" custom to written law, pointing the way toward civilization
and, eventually, philosophy.[30] In the last sections of the *Diritto universale*
Vico turned directly to an examination, that is, an interpretation, of the
stages of human history as reflected in its legal institutions in order to
incorporate the temporal dimension of the "law of nations" into his new
science of humanity. Vico's impulse was to project legal themes back into
the *tempora obscura* of myth and violence played out in the religious phase
of the "law of nations"—not the *ius* but the *fas gentium*—and he projected
the "wisdom" of jurisprudence back to the poets (*prima sapientia poetarum*), who thus became the "first legislators." The origin of "feudal"
custom also became a universal pattern, applicable to early Roman as well
as German society, according to the old rule, which Vico duly invokes, that
"law originates in fact."[31] These attitudes—not only "historicist" but as it
were genetic—help to account for the extraordinary vogue of Vico in the
age of the Historical School and the "post-cursors" of the "new science."

In his *New Science* Vico assigned the origins of republics to institutions
of property and in particular to agrarian law, according to general patterns
of the "natural law of the gentes" (*ius naturale gentium*). This was his
interpretation, too, of Pomponius's remark that "when the institutions
themselves dictated it, kingdoms were founded"—the term "institutions"
(*res*) signifying property, either public or private (*Res publicae, res privatae*).
Vico recognized three stages of proprietary and "feudal" development—
plebeian tenants ("whom," he remarks, "Hotman is surprised to find called
vassals in the feudal law of the returned barbarism"), quiritary (or seig-
neurnial) domain, and "full property called civil ownership," from which
came the mercantile phase of civilization. "All the above history," he
concluded, "was preserved by the Greeks in the word *nomos,* signifying
both law and pasture."[32]

At all times, Vico continued his search for "principles" and indeed was
trying to assemble what was, in his own phrase, suggesting Newton as well
as Accursius, a "principia of legal science" (*legitimae scientiae principiae*).[33]
Like Bacon—but more like his juridical antecedents—Vico sought for a
union of the particular and the general, the contingent and the eternal; and
indeed his mature "new science" was, in one of its aspects, a "philosophy
of authority" ("authority" being derived both from "author" and from
autos, the self) and, in another, a "natural law of nations" (*diritto naturale
delle genti,* adapted from the earlier formulation, *ius naturale gentium*).
Like the great eighteenth-century codes, the *New Science* was both a philology and a philosophy, both a history and a system.

In its final form Vico's new science turned away from the legal, and the
Roman, form of human "wisdom" (*sapientia,* the "knowledge of things
divine and human" being the root of the idea of civilization), toward the

Greek, toward philological and philosophical tradition. This more familiar (though also more cryptic) Vico of heroes and giants, of *corsi* and *ricorsi,* cannot be considered here, although of course there are clear connections between the jurisprudential and the Homeric—in effect the Latin and the Greek incarnations of Vico's new science. In both cases his aim was to move from poetry (from the Twelve Tables and then Homer) to higher, more "civilized" forms of wisdom, and to infer the larger patterns of civilization and its *corsi*—and finally to construct an anthropocentric "science" of humanity on the basis of its own self-created, self-conscious, and self-reflective "nature" and creations.

Vico, too—with Grotius and against Machiavelli and Hobbes—believed that "man is by nature social" (*hominem esse natura socialem*), and in the final analysis the measure of his own history. "Humanity is its own work" (*che questo mondo civile egli certamente e stato fatto dagli uomini— L'humanité est son oeuvre à elle-même,* as Michelet liked to render the famous Vichian formula).[34] For Vico, as for the Greeks, custom was king (*lex regina* was Vico's rendering of the ancient Pindarean *nomos basileus*). Like the Sophists and the jurisconsults of ancient, medieval, and early modern tradition, in short, Vico was essentially a devotee not of Physis but of Nomos—although he aspired indeed to reconcile these ancient antagonists in a philological and philosophical, an encyclopedia and a metahistorical, science of humanity. His efforts were much appreciated and celebrated by critics of natural law who sought in history and in intellectual tradition a basis for such a human science—athough not before the passing of several generations of "enlightenment," a revolution, an empire, and the experience of total war and attendant social transformations.

Juristic Anthropology

The Historical School of Law was a post-revolutionary and in large part an anti-revolutionary phenomenon arising, to begin with, in German universities. The primary builder and moving spirit of this international establishment was Karl Friedrich von Savigny, Hegel's colleague and rival at the University of Berlin after 1810 and later minister for the reform of justice in Prussia; but its true founder was Gustav Hugo, a renowned member of the proto-"historicist" school of Göttingen. Savigny was the father of the *historische Rechtsschule,* but Hugo was its grandfather (*Altvater,* as Marx put it), and his work provides the most comprehensive critique of the kinds of rationalist jurisprudence grouped carelessly under the heading of "the Philosophical School."[35]

Yet the Historical School had much deeper roots, and Hugo himself was the spokesman for an older legal tradition. Founded in the year of the Glorious Revolution, the University of Göttingen was unusually open to

English and French influence (especially that of Hume, Shaftesbury, and Montesquieu), and since the late seventeenth century its law professors had been carrying on a continuing assault on natural law as construed by the "new scholasticism" of Wolf and his school. In 1754 J. J. Schmauss (1690–1757) published a "new system of the law of nature," emphasizing the irrational and animal (and in this sense "natural") side of humanity. The other side of this pursuit of a new idea of "nature" was the continuing search, following the work of Conring, for Germany's own legal tradition, which had been obscured by foreign influence. Writing in 1732, G. C. Gebauer (1690–1773) thought it absolutely clear (*sonnenklar*) that political science (*Staatslehre*) should be "illuminated not from Digest I, 2, *De origine juris,* or the last books of the Pandects or Code, but rather from German history." And as J. P. von Ludewig wrote two years later, "The German Reich has up to now forgotten itself, and German legal scholars [*Rechts-Gelehrten*] have built on the sands of Roman law."[36]

J. S. Pütter (1725–1809) pursued these aims during an extraordinarily long tenure in Göttingen, during which he wrote extensively on German legal and constitutional history as well as legal method. Pütter contrasted abstract systems with practical and "local" reason (*Lokalvernunft*) and the "voice of the people" embodied in home-grown Germanic customs with foreign importations. He especially deplored the intrusions of civil, canon, and feudal law and praised home-grown German *Gewohnheitsrecht,* which was "deeply rooted in its constitution, partly in its climate, and in everything that was common to Germany's situation." Hence Germany did not require written books of law. He also admitted that, after the interregnum of the thirteenth century, German law was in large part based on force: *Staatsrecht* was the product of *Faustrecht,* a proposition taken up later by Marx and other critics of the German legal tradition.[37]

Hugo, who was a student of Pütter, carried on the attack against the older Philosophical School and the search for a new conception of nature more in keeping with historical understanding, and of course he did so with a variety of new targets in mind—including the Revolution, the Code Napoléon, and German Idealism (though he also professed to be a critical Kantian). Hugo's textbook of natural law, which began to appear in 1789, undertook to redefine jurisprudence, to reform its canon, and in the process to comprehend in modern terms various questions of society, social change, and human nature in general. In this effort he was following the lead of the Göttingen tradition, represented by Pütter, J. F. Reitemeier, J. F. Flatt, and others who were offering "revisions" of natural law; but he was the one who first received credit for "recalling natural law from the heavens to the human world" (*ius naturae a coelo ad terram revocant*), as a later admirer put it, paraphrasing Cicero's famous remark about Socrates.[38] He was, so to speak, shifting emphasis from Physis to Nomos, or rather, trying to incorporate both in a single historical process.

Hugo was apparently unaware of Vico's work, but there are obvious parallels. Like Vico, Hugo at one point reflected on his own intellectual autobiography and sources of inspiration, which included not only Leibniz, Conring, and his German teachers Heineccius and Pütter, but also (among others) Montesquieu, Condillac, Bacon, Hume, and Gibbon (whose famous Chapter 44, on the "spirit" of Roman law, he translated).[39] Like Vico, too, Hugo was (as he thought fit to remark in his autobiographical reflections) "not a great mathematician" and preferred old-fashioned learning to abstract natural philosophy. And as Vico sought to combine learning with speculation, philology with philosophy, so Hugo hoped to assemble what he paradoxically and perhaps defiantly called a "philosophy of positive law, especially [as the subtitle continues] in private law." His aim was again, in a post-revolutionary age, to reconcile the old dualities—the things "divine" and "human" encompassed by legal wisdom, and especially the old rivals, Physis and Nomos.

For Hugo the "positive" or "realist" legal tradition had begun with the Greek notions of laws (*nomoi*), expressed by the Sophists and especially Plato (who provided values and goals for the laws), and had been developed by Roman and Christian interpretations; but it included also the modern contributions of Bodin and Montesquieu, who added "positive" considerations of culture and environment, and of Conring, who emphasized the essential dimension of history. It specifically did not include such "opponents of positive law" (*Gegner des positiven Rechts*) as "*les philosophes* (*die Aufklärer*)," "Physiocraten oder Economisten," and communists such as Rousseau, Diderot, Mably, and "many others."[40] From the heights of modern experience and critical philosophy, Hugo carried on his "encyclopedic" enterprise. Like Kant (but enriching and correcting "metaphysics" through history) he considered three fundamental questions: what legal right (*Rechtens*) is, whether it is in accord with reason, and what it is becoming—the questions, in other words, of dogma (what the "authorities" of the law declare), of philosophy (the rational basis of law according to conventional natural law), and of history (how and where law progresses). In these terms and through the successive editions of his seminal work Hugo reviewed the old legal themes of custom and law, of persons and things, of mine and thine (*Lehre vom Meum et Tuum oder Privatrecht*, as he put it), of interpretation and legislation, of legal history and legal system; but above all he was concerned with "fore-knowledge" (*Vorkenntnisse*, suggesting the legal notion of "prejudice" as well as Gadamer's and Heidegger's hermeneutical "fore-structure" of knowledge) as the basis for practical judgment and philosophizing. In this way Hugo was led to his "juristic anthropology"—the theoretical and academic prerequisites for legal expertise and understanding.

Like Kant, whom he admired in certain respects, Hugo was aroused from a conceptual stupor induced by the old, unexamined philosophy, in this case jusnaturalism. His conclusion that the foundations of jurisprudence ought to be "positive" and "historical," not rationalist and "metaphysical," was likewise encouraged by the skeptical views of Hume; and he noted in particular Hume's warning (*VorsichtsMassreglen*), which rejected the "metaphysical" aspirations of natural law in favor of "general opinion" as the proper position "in all questions with regard to morals, as well as criticism."[41] We should not, Hugo observed, expect others to behave in ways appropriate for "our" times and people. To illustrate this relativist attitude toward morals Hugo cited a remark by the historian Johannes von Müller regarding the excesses of Nero, that even aberrant sexual behavior might become "natural" (*sey uns durch Sitten zur Natur geworden*). Again the inference was that the proper arena of positive law and its philosophy was not primary but "second" nature.

Yet Hugo did hope, through "juristic anthropology," to connect the realms of Nomos and Physis. He recalled Aristotle's old formula that all intellectual matters were derived from sense experience (*nihil in intellectu quod non prius in sensu*) and applied it to the foundations of jurisprudence. Following Gaius's anthropocentric ordering, Hugo fashioned his philosophy of positive law from the center outward, or from the bottom up, beginning with the animal nature of humanity (*der Mensch als Thier*, adapting Ulpian's notorious definition of natural law as "what nature teaches all animals"), and proceeding to later, and higher, stages of consciousness, speech, and social organization.[42] All of this was preparatory to a rather more conventional survey of modern German jurisprudence, drawn from a variety of traditional sources, legal and extra-legal, and beginning especially with the fundamental—existential as well as economic—question posed on the frontiers between nature and society, which was the ancient, dual dilemma of liberty and property (*meum et tuum*), of self and what the self must acquire for subsistence. In the revolutionary and post-revolutionary age larger questions of social and political organization (*Verfassung*) turned on the theory and practice of property, and so in many ways did the fortunes of the Historical School.

What Hugo accomplished was, in modern and post-Enlightenment terms, to pose, if not to resolve, the questions of nature and history. This involved asking about the relationship both between instinct and civilization and between reason and practical judgment. The first represented the old Enlightenment question concerning a "natural" progress from savagery to civilization, the second the revolutionary solution to this question through a rational (and in this sense also "natural") creation of a civilized condition by planning and enforcement—symbolized especially by a code of laws. Hugo was not alone, but he was most systematic in seeing that both questions demanded not rationalist speculation but a "philosophy of positive law," which the Historical School of Law came to embody during the Restoration.

Historische Rechtsschule

It was on the basis of this historicist extension of the *Aufklärung,* but in a much more heated ideological context, that Savigny carried on the defense of positive and historical jurisprudence after the fall of Napoleon. Savigny's own campaign was waged on three fronts: a critique of contemporary legal science (his famous manifesto of 1814, "On the Vocation of this Age for Legislation and Jurisprudence"); the founding of the principal journal of his academic and professional reform program (*Zeitschrift für geschicht-liche Rechtswissenschaft*), and the assembling of a scholarly foundation (his monumental *History of Roman Law in the Middle Ages*).[43] Savigny had established his reputation a decade earlier with an equally controversial work on the law of possession, but it was the critique of 1814 that set him at the head of the Historical School. In this pamphlet, which spawned a vast critical literature from jurists of a more "philosophical" persuasion, Savigny opposed the new "historical spirit" to what a contemporary French jurist called the "spirit of codification," expressed especially in the Napoleonic Code of 1804 and the scholastic tradition which it had already begun to generate; and his argument held implications not only for scholarship and jurisprudence but also for the looming Social Questions of that age of restoration and renewed revolution.[44]

The great debate over codification was set off in 1814 by the pronouncement, anti-"philosophical" as well as anti-Bonapartist, made by A. W. Rehburg's "On the Code Napoléon and Its Influence in Germany" and by the more positive defense "Of the Necessity of a General Civil Code for Germany" published at almost the same time by A. F. T. Thibaut, among whose predecessors at the University of Heidelberg was that arch-jusnatur-alist, Samuel Pufendorf. For Thibaut a code would be the culmination both of German freedom (*Freiheit*) and of German unity (*wahre National-Ein-heit*). He acknowledged the assumptions of some jurists that law was an expression of the *Volksgeist;* but he argued that modern "civil" (*Bürger-liches—bourgeois*) law transcended the old local requirements, bound by time and place, that were demanded by Montesquieu and others. Such a German code would replace not only Roman law but also the old customs, which were often only corruptions of law (*Rechtsfaulheit*)—and which in any case were the work of lawyers, not the "people." Thibaut could not believe in Savigny's notion of "historical rebirth and salvation," and for another generation he complained about the "so-called Historical School of Law" (*sogennante historische Rechtsschule*) and its claims to special expertise and privileged access to national consciousness.[45]

It was to Thibaut's "philosophical" program that Savigny responded with his manifesto, and the *Kodifikationstreit* resounded in German periodicals, and in the republic of letters throughout Europe, for many years. The target at first was the Napoleonic Code. Based on a false theory of "positive" law as legislative fiat, which Hugo had long before opposed, this French construction had eaten like a "cancer" into German society, reinforcing the other imperial intrusions by Napoleon. Savigny took up the arguments against legislative presumption—and in effect social engineering, or (in Condorcet's phrase) "social mathematics"—where the juridical critics of Bonapartism had left them a decade earlier. He quoted in particular from the objections registered by the appellate court of Montpellier, which had lamented the defects, omissions, arbitrariness, and abstractness of the Code.[46] The notion of abolishing the old law, Roman or customary, was unhistorical, unprofessional, and—in Hugo's and Burke's sense—"unnatural." Legislation was intended "to come to the aid of custom," Savigny argued, not to supplant it; and in any case the redactors, including Portalis, had been so unprofessional and impractical that their creation was bound to fail. Nor, and this was Savigny's main point, could an age still dominated by a superficial or spurious "philosophy"—the "art of legislation," as philosophes had called it—hope to produce a practical system of positive law that would accommodate, as it must, both past legal tradition and present social reality.

One of Savigny's arguments hinged on the sensitive issue of "interpretation"—the "art of hermeneutics," as contemporary jurists, following Leibniz, called it—and indeed this was another issue separating him from Thibaut. Although they distrusted the practice of judicial construction of the texts of the law, the redactors had not been able to avoid acknowledging it. According to Portalis, there were five bases of interpretation—natural law or equity, Roman law, customs and decisions, "common law," and "general principles" (a philosophical rendering of the old maxims).[47] Unfortunately, they were unable to explain what these terms meant beyond judicial discretion—a practice frowned on by Savigny, who had as little respect for the learning of the contemporary judiciary, in France or Germany, as he did for that of Cambacérès, Portalis, and the other redactors. Nor could Savigny tolerate the superficial (grammatical and logical but unhistorical) "hermeneutics of law" proposed by his nemesis, Thibaut. His views were much closer to the Romantic hermeneutics associated with the theological and philosophical work of F. A. Wolf, Friedrich Ast, and Schleiermacher.

Savigny's position, like Hugo's, was considerably more complex than later critics would allow. He denied wanting to surrender to the "hegemony of the past" (*der Herrschaft der Vergangenheit*); and though a "Romanist," his concern was not with classical law but the "received" and modernized law of German legal tradition (*usus modernus Pandectarum; heutiges römisches Recht*).[48] Savigny displayed some admiration for the Prussian Code of 1792 because of the richness of its practical provisions and because the customs which it necessarily incorporated were those of the German *Volk*.

In general, he argued, law had a twofold life: "first, as part of the aggregate existence of the community, which it does not cease to be; and secondly, as a distinct branch of knowledge in the hands of the jurists." Not short-sighted *Gesetzgebung* but well-founded *Volksrecht* and *Juristenrecht* represented the true condition of jurisprudence, the object of its history, and the subject of its science.[49]

For Germany this meant especially the tradition of Roman law—as indeed it did for France, seeing that most of the Code, and especially the essential provisions concerning property and family, were based on this "common law." It also meant, however, local customs, which figured prominently in both the French and the Prussian codes; and this was the ground for Savigny's premise that law expressed the "spirit" of a people—not, in other words, the philosophical (Herderian and especially Hegelian) positing of a mystical *Volksgeist* but rather the standing of custom as a deposit, or residue, of local behavior. The proof of this, for Savigny, was the legal commonplace that the institutions of property and of possession were both of them partly fact and partly law—links in the chain of legalities, as it were, or stages in the process of legitimation.

The Historical School of Law was given an extraordinary impulse by advances in scholarship, the most sensational and symbolical of which was the discovery in 1816, by Savigny's friend Barthold Georg Niebuhr, of the manuscript of Gaius's *Institutes,* the only extant work of pre-Justinianian jurisprudence and the principal model for legal systematization. To Savigny the uncovering of this palimpsest was an epiphany. Of Gaius's famous definition of justice inserted in the Digest ("Justice is a steady and unwavering will to render unto everyone his right," D. I, 1, 3, 10), he exclaimed in a letter to Niebuhr at the end of that year, "Now this is without doubt from Gaius! . . . One hopes that more will be deciphered out of those pages."[50]

Like Gaius, Savigny believed that civil law demanded both history and system. Like Hugo (to put it another way), Savigny aspired to go beyond positive law to legal system—and indeed his massive *History of Roman Law in the Middle Ages* was intended in part as preparatory to his major work, the unfinished *System of Modern Roman Law,* which figured prominently in Germany's debate over its own Civil Code, achieved finally at the end of the century. In a sense Savigny was carrying on the old *Pandekten* tradition, but his aim was not a "dogmatic" or rational compendium; it was a historical Summa and synthesis of many of the polarities in the life of jurisprudence: custom and written law, Germanic and Roman law, scholasticism and humanism, tradition and novelty, legislation and jurisprudence, positive and natural law—and, as ever, Nomos and Physis.

The Historical School also had branches, or extensions, in other disciplines, including philology or linguistics (represented especially by Savigny's student Jakob Grimm), political economy, and in effect biblical criticism and religion. This illustrates Savigny's larger message, the fundamental historicity of all forms of human culture—which, like Hugo of course, he often expressed in the organic metaphors fashionable in the Romantic age. Savigny was not an authoritarian, nor did he dream of restoring a bygone age. The historical method did not involve "an exclusive admiration for the Roman law" or any established system: "On the contrary, its object was to trace every established system to its root, and thus discover an organic principle, whereby that which still has life may be separated from that which is lifeless and only belongs to history."[51]

For some later critics Savigny's historicist views constituted little more than ill-disguised "conservatism" and perhaps "irrationalism." This was in essense the charge made by Rudolph von Jhering, Hugo's successor at Heidelberg, and later repeated by Karl Mannheim and others, including probably a majority of the legal profession in the twentieth century. Mannheim also points out that Savigny did not actually employ the term "spirit of the people" (Volksgeist) until 1840, probably under the influence of G. F. Puchta; instead he wrote of the higher nature—perhaps, after Schelling, the "second nature" of the people—moving from instinct toward national consciousness.[52]

In any case it is obvious that Savigny's conception of jurisprudence was practical and "political" as well as scholarly, for he aspired to bring the insights of the "historical science of law" to bear upon legal reform. So did many of his students, in France as well as Germany. Savigny's notions of custom were drawn out more fully by disciples and colleagues such as Karl Friedrich Eichhorn, who shifted the focus to Germanic laws, and especially Puchta, who became the chief authority on customary law, its history, and its contemporary significance.[53] Once taught to a younger generation, historical jurisprudence would become, as Savigny had concluded in his manifesto, "a subject for living customary law—consequently, for real improvement." Only then could Roman law be transcended, or given a decent burial, and "a truly national law" be achieved. For Savigny and what we might call the left-wing Savignians, who hoped the Historical School would promote the social continuation of the Revolution, the past was not only usable, it was, if not perfectible, at least improvable; and it was historical wisdom, not philosophical speculation, that offered the key to a progressive and ameliorative "social science."

Law and the Social Question

In practical terms the war—at once Methodenstreit and Kulturkampf— seemed to be between the "Idealists" and the "Realists," the champions of Physis and the champions of Nomos; and it raged across three generations and throughout the first half of the nineteenth century. It was fought at the University of Berlin between the followers of Savigny and those of Hegel, especially Eduard Gans (and marginally Karl Marx). "The war is spectacular," wrote Eugène Lerminier, one of Savigny's French disciples. "In the historical school they fear philosophy . . . In the philosophical camp they look down with pity on the purely *historical* jurists."[54] The major issues had been explored long before by Hugo; but now they were debated in an intellectual context ignited by the appearance of what was coming to be called the Social Question, which revolved around the problem of property but came to center on that of class conflict and produced a "right-left" division between the followers of Savigny as well as between those of Hegel. That jurisprudence furnished the first conceptual framework of this question is a fact all too often forgotten by historians.

At the center of the dispute was a most unlikely and esoteric issue, the problem of the Roman law of possession, and a most pedantic and intellectually inaccessible publication, Savigny's *Das Recht des Besitzes* of 1803. Yet this first scholarly effort of Savigny went through eight editions and through Italian, French, and English translations; and it provoked dozens of scholarly replies, supplements, and corrections as well as popular extensions and digressive polemics—a vast scholasticism, pro and contra, which is still growing. According to John Austin, Savigny's book was "the most consummate and masterly and . . . the least alloyed with error and imperfection"; and Eugen Ehrlich regarded it as probably the most influential legal monograph of modern times—and passed this judgment without even noting that it was not only present at (and contributed to) the birth of Marxism but survived the death of the Historical School.[55]

From one point of view and in its own monographic terms, Savigny's *Besitz* reflected and recapitulated the whole tradition of civil law and illustrated the heuristic principle of the Historical School. The book carried the technical story of Roman *possessio* from classical origins through the interpretations of glossators and commentators (Azo, Odofredus), humanists (Alciato, Le Douaren, Cujas), and "systematists" (Doneau and many later jurists) down to Thibaut and other contemporaries. To modern readers it not only threw historical light on one people's solutions to the universal problem of "mine" and "thine" and illustrated the premises and methods of historical jurisprudence, but it also, in its later editions during the Restoration, fueled the fires of controversy raging around the "social science" claimed by both the Philosophical School and the Historical School.

How could a work of "pure scholarship" (*reine Wissenschaft*) do this? One reason, no doubt, is that Savigny's methods obviously contradicted the fashions of "pure reason" (*reine Vernunft*). Another is that the reactions to Savigny's work intersected with that most inflammatory post-revolutionary issue—the origins and provenance of private, "bourgeois" property, especially the idea of "absolute" property (derived from Roman law via the Old Regime jurist Pothier) in the Civil Code.[56] In historical terms— that is, in terms of the Roman model, which continued to be dominant in European social thought—it seemed to touch on all the incendiary questions formerly associated with the social contract.

One problem concerned the apparently contradictory statements in the Digest about *possessio* and *dominium*, latterly *proprietas*—the one deriving property from possession (*dominium rerum ex naturali possessione coepisse*, Digest, 41, 2, 1, 1), and the other holding that "possession and property have nothing in common" (*nihil commune habet proprietas cum possessione*, Digest, 21, 2, 12, 1). Savigny's own view emphasized the separation of possession and property; and his view received historical endorsement from the researches of his friend Niebuhr into the Roman "public land" (*ager publicus*), which alone was subject to *dominium*, as well as from the linguistic researches of his former student, Jakob Grimm, into the Indo-European background of the term.[57] On ancient authority Savigny also insisted that possession, "civil" as well as "natural," enjoyed the status both of fact and of law and, most important, that it depended not only on physical occupation but also on the "will" to maintain possession (*Besitzwille; animus possedendi*).

In Germany reactions accumulated during the next generation, and many jurists had their say—rivals such as Thibaut as well as disciples such as Puchta—but by the 1830s the polemics had shifted from scholarly to more general and philosophical grounds. The major critic was the Hegelian Eduard Gans, who had long objected to Savigny's Romanist and "external" ideas of legal development. Concerning the law of possession, he argued, the Romans had merely "practical sagacity," not "philosophical truth"; and to ground the law of possession in "nature," to make it only a "fact," was a contradiction. "Possession is a fact, a natural occurrence, and not law [*Recht*]," Gans sarcastically summed it up, "and yet the possessor, because he is a possessor, has rights [*Rechte*]."[58]

What struck Hegelian critics like Gans was the immoral and authoritarian implications of Savigny's position. According to A. Koeppe, coming to the assistance of Gans, the answer to the question of the origin, and thus the nature, of the law of possession (or law in general) lies not in the "sources" but only in reason and philosophy. Further politicizing the controversy, another "Prussian jurist" went on to complain of Savigny's emphasis on the factor of "will" (the arbitrary, characteristically Roman, *Willkür*), which would take reason out of history—and separate the collective Hegelian *Geist* from society. A state without a rational and organistic basis (*vernünftigen Organismus*), he added, has a unity grounded not on consciousness (*eine geistige Idee*) of itself but only of external factors, which makes it a *Polizeistaat*.[59] Here the debate between the Historical School and the Philosophical School expanded into the emerging contest between Romanists and Germanists—as well as "right" and "left" Hegelians.

In the post-Hegelian—and post-Savignian—generation the controversy passed beyond the boundaries of the legal profession. "What an awful book the *corpus juris* is, this Bible of selfishness," wrote Heinrich Heine. "Truly, we owe the theory of property, which was formerly a fact only, to these Roman thieves."[60] It was precisely in the conflict between historical "Realists" and philosophical "Idealists," too, that Karl Marx—a student of both Savigny and Gans as well as a "young Hegelian"—began to find his own historical and philosophical views. The notion that law originated in fact, that might made right, was abhorrent to him; and his first major published work (1842) attacked the Historical School on just these grounds—though he chose as his target not his former teacher, Savigny (recently appointed minister of justice), but Hugo, who had championed the same sort of immoral and authoritarian ideas under a "positive" façade and had founded that "school which legitimates the baseness of today by the baseness of yesterday." For Marx, Hugo's servile message seemed to be, "It is the holy duty of conscience to obey the authorities in whose hands power lies."[61]

In France many readers failed to see the relevance of Savigny's book. It might just as well have been written by a second-century Roman jurist (Gaius), complained one French critic, who warned as well against inquiries into the origins, and so the legitimacy, of property. "I shall go further," wrote this student of the law of possesssion: "not only was the idea of property born with the world, but it was first-born, and the idea of possession came afterwards."[62] Members of the "old" Philosophical School argued that property was "natural," if not "divine," in origin. "God forbid that I should think or write that property is a purely arbitrary institution!" exclaimed Frederic Taulier. "I have no hesitation in proclaiming that its source is divine and its origin eternal." And he added, in a more secular and legalistic mood, in the spirit of the Code, rejecting the anti-social and perhaps atheistic ideas of Grotius and Pufendorf: "Property is personality; it is liberty."[63] As Théodore Chavot wrote, in almost existential terms, "From the time that man has known his own individuality, he has known exterior objects, and has tried to appropriate them."[64]

This was of course to disregard Savigny's insistence that possession and property had "nothing in common," but in fact most German and French scholars made a historical connection based on the argument that, as Raymond Troplong wrote, "property is the law, possession the fact."[65] The easiest way to put it was that possession was the "cause" of property, and such indeed was the conclusion of the elder—the "right"—Proudhon. As Savigny's disciple and vulgarizer Edouard Laboulaye carelessly summed it up, "From the fact comes the law, and the law is property." One historian of possession argued, with reference to the Historical School, that property was neither natural nor absolute; it differed according to times, places, and social contexts, and it was still in process of evolution. And still another French student of possessory actions, J.-M. Carou, went on to associate this historicizing argument with a three-stage theory, according to which human society originated in "occupation" (the famous "first occupant"), advanced through a civilizing phase of "possession," and arrived at last at the human and rational state of "absolute" private property in a "free" society.[66]

The key to this process, and the central social dilemma of the Restoration, was the question of labor—"the property of those who possess neither land nor capital," as Prosper Barante put it, adding, "and this property is the most sacred of all."[67] Troplong refused to take seriously the natural-law idea of a human "time" without possession and property, but he subscribed to the historical thesis to the extent that he believed property to be "consecrated by time." He did not believe, as Grotius held, that property was based on mere prescription, and indeed he invoked Vico as well as Roman law to deny that time alone justified occupation. For Troplong possession was merely the "sign" of property, and property was tied to production and public utility. In the most fundamental sense property was the "daughter of labor" (*fille du travail*)—the theme underlying the Revolution of 1848.[68] The elder—the "right"—Proudhon, formerly a Bonapartist commentator on the Code, pointed to the "domain of property" as the focal point of the primary social question in Restoration France, which was the often violent struggle between the have's and the have-not's—the *propriétaires* and the *prolétaires*.[69]

In post-revolutionary France the tension, or confusion, between property and possession was intensified by the conflicts between "new" and "old" regime proprietors and the fact that, in practice, the disputes were carried out for the most part under the rubric not of the theoretical "absolute" private property of the Civil Code but rather of "possessory actions," which were handled by the new institution of the justices of the peace and the old customary law of seizin. As explained by Carou, following Troplong, the dilemma was the conflict between the "abstract" idea of property (defended especially by the *anciens propriétaires* and their theoretical, legalistic claims) and the useful and productive fact of possession: "One principle inert and idle, the other profitable to the state; decadence on the one hand, progress on the other." It is in this sense, Carou concluded, that "property has nothing in common with possession."[70]

It was this theme that Proudhon—the "other," the "left" Proudhon— took up; and he began indeed by reviewing the whole juridical tradition, its confusions and its hypocrisies, and ended with his paradox (and legalistic joke), that "property is theft" (that is, that under modern conditions *res privata* is *res furtiva*). The young Proudhon saw the same division as did his elder cousin; but he analyzed the problem differently, attributing the cause to the modern divorce between possession, hence production and "labor," and artificially titled and legalized "property"—and more generally between law and justice and, in a sense, convention and nature. Through this unnatural separation, Proudhon concluded, "the law has literally *created* a right outside its own province . . . It has sanctioned selfishness; it has endorsed monstrous pretensions."[71] Finally, he decided, following the same line of thought as Marx, that this separation toppled, or at least discredited, the whole structure of ancient jurisprudence.

Confronting the Social Question—arising from the problem of property, the economic predicament, and the class divisions stemming from it—the old jurisprudence reached an impasse in practical and political terms. For critics like Marx and Proudhon it was little more than an expression of Old Regime "ideology." In terms of social inquiry and interpretation, however (if not legal science), the Historical School had promoted the discussion of fundamental human questions; and by criticism and reaction (if not by adoption and extension), it had helped to provide the basis for a science of society in a new sort of "revolutionary" age, which went beyond the experience of the Historical School—and indeed that of the old legal tradition—altogether. Another phase in the story of Nomos had ended, or at least trailed off into neglect and irrelevance. On the frontiers of orthodox jurisprudence, however, several new paths were now opening up.

FOURTEEN

From Civil Science to the Human Sciences

Wer kann was Dummes, wer was Kluges denken,
Das nicht die Vorwelt schon gedacht?

Goethe, *Faust*, II, 2, i

Law Transcended by Philosophy

In the nineteenth century jurisprudence continued for a time to assert its imperial claims—continued, that is, to represent itself as "true philosophy," as the basis of the true science of society, and as the center of an intellectual system around which other disciplines deferentially circled. Since the mid-eighteenth century a continuous series of juristic "encyclopedias" had been published—from that of J. S. Pütter (1767) to those of Gustav Hugo (1792), A. F. J. Thibaut (1797), G. F. Puchta (1825), and many others—which were designed to illustrate these pretensions through Romanoid schemes of "Pandect law" (*Pandektenrecht*).[1] In general the juristic "encyclopedia" shared with formal philosophy, including Hegel's own notion of "encyclopedia," the impulse to system; but in significant contrast and perhaps to the detriment of its claims to be a "social science," the former preserved links with traditional learning, hence with traditional abuses and ideologies.

This is an extraordinary chapter in the history of social thought, which is only now being investigated. It includes many of the leading figures in the legal tradition. Savigny himself hoped to crown his historical efforts with an overarching "system" of modern Roman law (*System des heutigen römischen Rechts*), which would be valid not merely for the territories of Roman law but for all parts of European society. In this work, which began to appear in 1840 but was never completed, Savigny hoped to define "a scientific province . . . cultivated by the unbroken exertion of many centuries [and offering] a rich inheritance" for the present, thereby restoring the necessary connections between theory and practice, the individual and society, and the past and the present.[2]

For Savigny "positive law" was the product of history, and its "subject" was "the people." This position was not so sentimental or idealistic as it sounds. "It seems clearer now than it did then," John P. Dawson has written, "that the mystical conception of the Volksgeist—the slowly emerging collective mind that summed up the nation's experience—served as a protective fog, shrouding the continuities in the work the jurists were actually doing."[3] Fundamentally, the doctrine of the Historical School was a defense both of juristic supremacy against the pretensions of the sovereign and of legal learning and experience—"scientific law"—against abstract "philosophical" approaches to the law. The model of legal and of social science was not the likes of Aristotle, Aquinas, Hobbes, and Rousseau but rather of Gaius, Bartolus, Grotius, and Pothier—not, that is to say, of Kant and Hegel but rather of Savigny and Puchta.

Yet Savigny's professional agenda was obviously at odds with contemporary social and political thinking, especially the "Austinian" conception which defined law simply and directly as the command of the sovereign. Ideological forces, right and left, ranging from revolutionary socialism to conservative nationalism, rendered such a conservative and academic approach obsolete—and cut off from the movers and the shakers of social science. The Historical School of Law was at odds, too, with the new, equally professional conception of philosophy which in the post-Kantian age likewise claimed to be a "science" (and indeed the science of sciences), which looked to natural science for its conceptual model, and which subsumed all other disciplines, jurisprudence included, under its own imperial program.

The leading representative of this view was Savigny's great rival at the University of Berlin, Hegel, who was also drawing on the old notion that law was part of moral philosophy when he remarked that "the science of law is part of philosophy" (*die Rechtswissenschaft ist ein Teil der Philosophie*).[4] Joining practical reason and philosophical anthropology, Hegel's *Philosophy of Law* turned the tables on the jurists, who had long exploited the writings of philosophers and who claimed license to plunder the heritage of European jurisprudence as a part of the larger legacy of Western philosophy; and of course "younger Hegelians" of various persuasions followed suit.

What is perhaps most distinctive about Hegel's later philosophy is its unwavering awareness of social context and its determination to establish ties with all forms of human consciousness. This joining of the philosophical and the social is the primary import of his famous declaration: "What is rational is real and what is real is rational." Fascination with "the social" was characteristic of post-revolutionary thought in general, but never before Hegel (and Fichte) had there been such an intense and systematic effort to seek out the interconnections between *Geist* and *Gesellschaft*—between forms of thought and patterns of collective behavior. In part this was due to Hegel's extensive but insufficiently appreciated exposure to the Scottish Enlightenment (and specifically to Adam Smith, with whose work he was familiar at least by 1803) and its commonsense view of natural law, which had so profound an effect on the young Marx. "At its roots the *Philosophy of Right* is materialistic in approach," Herbert Marcuse has declared. "Hegel exposes in paragraph after paragraph the social and economic understructure of his philosophic concepts."[5] This aspect of Hegelian philosophy has usually been viewed, favorably or not, as an anticipation of Marxism. Yet in certain ways, and above all by shifting from a basis in jurisprudence to one in political economy, Marx departed from and even distorted Hegel's social philosophy by closing his eyes to ethical and anthropological concerns. This is another reason for trying to place Hegel's social thought in the perspective of the old legal tradition and more generally of moral philosophy.

In his *Philosophy of Law* (*Philosophy of Right* is the conventional but unsatisfactory English rendering) Hegel sets out quite deliberately on what seems to me an enterprise of interpretation, or translation, of the legal tradition (as he had already done for the tradition of Lutheran theology). In general, in form and in content, law is for him "positive" and must have a particularized historical aspect (as Montesquieu had understood), while "natural law" represents the classic "philosophical" point of view. Characteristically, Hegel proposes to establish a truly philosophical synthesis of (the mistakenly opposed) "positive" law and "natural" law; and he pursues this goal not only by application of his dynamic "logic" but also by analogy, or rather homology, with Roman jurisprudence in its modern as well as ancient form (as expounded by Heineccius, for example, as well as by Justinian's Institutes). To some degree, in other words, the Hegelian "philosophy of law" represented a sort of transmutation, or sublimation, of Roman "positive" law in terms of form and values as well as ideas and assumptions. Suggesting these relationships depends not so much on specific *Quellenforschung* (though there are abundant references in Hegel's book to the sources of and commentaries on Roman law) as on formal analysis and analogies—retracing, as it were, the rationale of Hegel's extrapolation from the orthodox legal tradition, its conventions, its vocabulary, and its structure.

Hegel begins with a severe critique of the methods of Roman law and of modern interpreters like Hugo, founder of the Historical School of Law (a bit ungraciously, in view of similar criticisms made by philosophical jurists like Heineccius, whom Hegel also cites). Roman lawyers were aware of the perils of arbitrary formulation—Hegel himself recalls the famous maxim from the Digest, "All definition is dangerous"—but in Hegel's view they were professionally trapped in a system of abstractions grounded neither in philosophy nor in history. It was foolish of Hugo, he thought, to celebrate the "rational" character of Roman law and especially to liken its categories and "trichotomies" to those of Kant.[6] Hegel is here setting out on a trail on which Marx would follow him almost a quarter of a century later, starting with the rejection of the notion, popularized by Hugo, that made "positive" law, whether custom or legislation, the basis of the legitimization of "natural" law. The lines in this struggle between the Philosophical School and the Historical School had already been drawn in the debate between Thibaut and Savigny. Hegel's contribution was to shift the grounds of the discussion from professional "jusnaturalism" to a truly philosophical formulation—namely, the establishment of the absolute idea of law.

Yet the basis of this dialectical formulation was in a sense already to be found in the structure of civil law, especially as arranged in the Digest and more especially the Institutes of Justinian. To begin with, civil law was fundamentally and incorrigibly anthropocentric: it was "person"-centered and so subjective. "The basis of law is above all conscious being," Hegel concludes (*Das Boden des Rechts ist überhaupt das Geistige*); and in general he followed the old "trichotomy" of Roman jurisprudence, that is, the distribution of law into the categories of person, thing, and action (*persona, res, actio*). "Personality" was defined legally in terms of liberty, implying both freedom of choice or action and responsibility for such action. Epistemologically crucial was the determination of intention—*mens* being the equivalent of "spirit" or "esprit" (and contributing at least to the connotations of "Geist") in the Hegelian usage. Hegel reinforces this line of argument, implicit in jurisprudence, by insisting on the force of "will" and "freedom of the will" in law and therefore in "right." The law itself has a "will" or spiritual meaning, and so do the subjects who are governed by it. These are the principal ingredients of Hegel's conception of law, or rather of the idea of law.[7]

The second member of the legal trinity is "thing"—"reality" (*res, realitas*)—which for Hegel, as for civilians, means the natural goal and necessary target of the free personality, the needy, and perhaps greedy, ego, which establishes the center of the world view of German idealists as it must for jurists. For philosophical consistency Hegel rejects the confusing legal convention of rights "in" persons and things (*ius ad personam, ad rem*) and locates individual right, and law in general, exclusively in the category of personality. Nevertheless, the subject of right, of law, required an object to fulfill—to "realize"—personal liberty; and the category of "reality" provided just this second defining characteristic of social being, which in Hegel's terms was the "external sphere" penetrated by the subject through the third member of the legal trinity, which was "action." (In civil law, too, rights were acquired, or preserved, by action, but this meant "action at law" and not social behavior in the more general sense.) Drawing in this way on the basic structure of law and reinterpreting it in a temporalized and dynamic form, Hegel established the first and most immediate stage of social action in terms of the most fundamental social unit, the self-determining person.

The social field designated by jurists as "reality" may be defined more concretely as the realm of property, or potential property, which is the object of individual and social, that is, of personal, occupancy.[8] A natural "thing" (*Sache*) becomes social property (*Eigentum*) through willful prehension by a free subject. Again Hegel refuses to be bound by legal conventions and technicalities, such as the distinction, insisted on by Savigny and the Historical School, between property (*dominium*) and civil possession or prescription. For Hegel, who was well aware of Savigny's work on the subject, possession (*Besitz*), established by intentional seizure (*Besitzgreifung*), was the first stage of property and prescription was simply the temporal expression of the intention—the "will"—to retain, which, along with need, was required for the social legitimization of property, as jurists also agreed. Historically, Hegel acknowledged, the evolution of private property had been a extraordinarily painful and bloody process. Whereas personal liberty had been the creation of Christian religion (which had been reinforced by Lutheranism), liberty of property had been achieved "only yesterday," as Hegel put it—referring mainly to the formulation of "absolute" private property by the French Revolution and its legislative extension in the Civil Code.

If freedom, for Hegel, was defined by that social joining of subject and object called property, so its social opposite was represented by another legal term given new meaning by Hegel—namely, "alienation."[9] In Roman law alienation signified the separation of a person from his goods—literally the disjunction between personality and reality. In modern terms—that is, in Hegelian terms—this alienation of an individual from the object of his desire and labor suggested also psychological disturbance, since self-consciousness depended upon fulfillment of the will through its object, which consisted of "goods" in some sense. It was this extended concept of alienation (*Entfremdung* or *Entäusserung*) that Marx seized upon in his critique—which in this connection was an elaboration—of Hegel's position. It was undeniable, of course, that the discussion of alienation by both men was associated with their reading of modern political economy; but in both cases too, it seems to me, their insights were informed and even inspired by the old tradition of civil law.

From the free, rights-bearing "person," human will expanded outward across concentric circles of human community—family, "civil society," and the nation-state—which represented the human and material expression of the Idea. Hegel accepted the ancient public-private distinction without question. The Nation encompassed and controlled the free individual and his belongings as, in civil law, the public sphere (*res publica*) encompassed and controlled (or at least regulated) the "person" and the private sphere (*res privata*). For Hegel, too, this social process recapitulated that of Nature, since "the system of right [that is, law] is the realm of Freedom made actual, the world of mind brought forth out of itself like a second nature."[10]

Hegel's critique of the Historical School of Law was developed later by Eduard Gans and still later by Gans's former student Marx. Essentially, the objection to Hugo and Savigny was that they attributed too much rationality to Roman law, thus confusing the question of will with that of reason—the question of origins with that of legitimation—and so giving positive law priority over philosophy. As Marx later wrote, Hugo had exaggerated the animal side of human nature; and in his celebration of "positive law" and the "authority" of the old legal tradition, he had in effect taught obedience to a corrupt political structure that had imposed itself upon the old legal tradition. By inference, then, Savigny's was a "school which legitimates the baseness of today by the baseness of yesterday," Marx charged, "a school to which history shows only its posterior" (punning on the crude empiricism, the *a posteriori* assumptions, of the historical school.)[11]

Yet in many ways Hegel indeed drew upon, and philosophically extended, the forms and the categories of the legal tradition, and detached them from their professional context. In this way he in effect reversed the process of the evolution of legal, moral, and political philosophy. "After all," he remarked in the preface of his *Philosophy of Law*, "the truth about [Law], Ethics, and the State is as old as its public recognition and formulation in the law of the land, in the morality of everyday life, and in religion." In his philosophical transmutation of human experience Hegel placed law in the service of a conceptual "encyclopedia" and system which pushed the imperial claims of philosophy into the world of social action and historical development and which, once again and perhaps for good, undercut the pretensions of jurisprudence to be the principal science of society. In any case, beyond the criticisms and pretensions offered by philosophy, other disciplines, new or "scientifically" improved, were already beginning to lay claim to such a position of authority in the kingdom of Nomos, beginning with the new field of inquiry that had most shaped Hegel's own thinking.

Law Subverted by Economics

The history of the relations between political economy and jurisprudence (and indeed of political economy itself in any comprehensive way) remains to be written. The fundamental connection is the premise of an autonomous, sub-political arena of "civil society," the primordial ground of private law. Beyond this premise, the story certainly must involve various rubrics of civil law, such as property, agrarian law, contract, and "interest" (*De eo quod interest*). Most directly, however, the theoretical foundations of economics were furnished by natural law (and the related school of the "second scholasticism"), which sought to redefine law more simply and

generally in terms of a uniform and calculable idea of human nature—an
"anthropology," which interpreted social behavior in terms of economic
motives and commercial relations. Such, for example, was the aim of Louis
Boullenois, who sought to join the legal conceptions of the "person" and
the "real" (in the sense of goods, *biens*) into a comprehensive definition of
the individual not as a "metaphysical" but as a social being (*in ordine ad
societatem*), as both subject and object.[12] Conceptually, this opened the
path from conventional jurisprudence to a universal science of social behavior which, in the seventeenth century, was already being called "political
economy" (the public as distinguished from the private *oeconomia*, or
household management), and later to be associated with the doctrines of
Physiocracy and the Scottish school.

    In eighteenth-century Germany natural law combined with cameralist
science (*Kameralwissenschaft*) to promote a shift from theoretical and legalistic to practical, economic, and statistical approaches to social and "state"
sciences (*Staatswissenschaften*) and what would later be called "national
economy" (*National-Ökonomik*). Georg Obrecht, professor of law at the
University of Strasbourg until his death in 1612, was one of the first jurists
to turn consciously from the conventions of jurisprudence to questions of
administration and the marshaling of economic and political forces for
state business, which as always focused on preparing for war.[13] But of
course practical administration was independent of the legal tradition, and
perhaps no less ancient. "The economic and cameral sciences are very old
in the world," wrote J. H. G. von Justi in the mid-eighteenth-century—
"older than one would have thought," added Blanqui. "The applications
of [political economy] occurred indeed at the moment property was introduced among men, and republics came into existence."[14] Retrospectively,
at least, cameralism constituted a rival tradition to jurisprudence, and Justi's
own work on the nature of the state (*Die Natur und das Wesen der Staaten*,
1760) was conceived as an "alternative treatise" to Montesquieu's work,
which, excellent as it was, erred in its lack of appreciation of the practical
function of laws.

    By that time "cameral science" was receiving further official recognition
in the form of journals and university chairs for the study of political
economy, which established as it were the auxiliary sciences of legislation,
and which marked further divergence or defection from an integrated view
of law and jurisprudence. In the Göttingen school of legal thought the
work of J. J. Schmauss illustrated this shift from legal to material considerations; and it was continued by the "older historical school of economics," in which Wilhelm Röscher, who was also a professor at Göttingen,
was a leading figure.[15] This school, which also included Bruno Hildebrand
and Karl Knies, and which was a branch of Savigny's Historical School of
Law, regarded "national economy" as in effect an analogue of customary

law, and likewise relative to national conditions and traditions. Röscher's great history of national economy did for modern economics what Savigny had done for the medieval sources of Roman law—namely, to establish its authoritative canon. In Germany, as in France, the influence of "Scot's knowledge," through James Steuart's *Inquiry into the Principles of Political Economy* (1767) and especially Adam Smith's *Wealth of Nations,* which was translated very soon after its publication in 1776, was extensive and decisive.

The modern discipline of economics was the creation to a very large degree of Scottish and English philosophy. This is a story that does not need telling here, except to the extent of suggesting a characteristic shift away from the conventional, conservative, and authoritarian traditions of jurisprudence. This again is most clearly illustrated in the work of Adam Smith himself, whose early lectures on jurisprudence—conceived, of course, within the broader field of moral philosophy, which he taught at the University of Edinburgh—anticipated his pioneering work in political economy. In this work Smith invoked civil as well as common law, but he exploited these sources in the context of rational and comparative analysis of the problems of property, contract, and modern commerce in terms especially of "natural rights" and of particular "stages" of social development. The ages respectively of hunters, shepherds, agriculture, and commerce were inferred from the metahistorical speculations of natural law—and secondarily, I would suggest, from the historical implications of civil law, especially as drawn out by the natural lawyers—and their function above all was to suggest the primary theme of Smithian jurisprudence, which was the inexorable extension of the domain of property and the field of commercial activities.

Smith pursued the theme of the "progress" of property, wealth, and power in his more famous work, which expanded "moral philosophy" into more technical areas of economic thought. *The Wealth of Nations* left behind distracting questions of law, custom, prescription, and their many variations in the world of nations, and seized directly on isolated questions of commercial behavior, treating them in the abstract and universalist style of natural law and indeed in accord with the presumptions of the Philosophical School of Law, which likewise aspired to a general theory of psychology as a basis for its explanations and legitimations.[16] The function of law through an independent judiciary (which Smith regarded as essential) was largely the negative one of making "every individual feel himself perfectly secure in the possession of every right which belongs to him." Although the pattern of history for Smith was an advance from primary to a socialized "second" nature, his theory of modern society, formulated by analogy to Newtonian science, would revert to a simplified conception of a fundamental, acquisitive human "nature," limited but not essentially transformed by the proprieties of trade and commerce, and operating in a uniform social system determined by market forces. Such at least was the "classical" caricature, disseminated in the next century, of what one nineteenth-century French critic called "metaphysical political economy." In any case Smith's masterwork set the stage for the battles of the nineteenth century over classical economics, including the famous *Methodenstreit* between liberalism and "historicism" in economic interpretation—another stage in the unending war between the Philosophical School and the Historical (in this case the Younger Historical) School.

Nineteenth-century French scholars noted the "turn" from the "speculative sciences" to political economy, which seemed to become a movement of "proselytism."[17] According to Henri Baudrillart, the "contest" between law and political economy had already been lost in 1789. Thereafter the experience of modern revolution tended to accentuate the division between older notions of law and newer ones of economic behavior—between Nomos and the new form taken by Physis in adaptations of social science to natural-science models. By Baudrillart's time the professionalization of political economy was complete, and for social science the motto of one of his colleagues (paraphrasing the requirement of geometry for the Platonic Academy) was, "Let no one enter who is not an economist."

The tendency to turn from the habits and values of the old legal tradition to the incisive and apparently "realistic" views of political economy became an increasingly common pattern among intellectuals (especially intellectuals denied access to power and legislative action) who were dreaming of a modern social science in which they could in other ways legislate and determine "laws" for humanity, as Smith had so instructively done. Thus Hegel, through his reading of the Scots during the decade of the French Revolution, "discovered the economy" and from then on framed his successive philosophical systems in a social context; thus the young Marx, student of the Hegelian Gans as well as of Savigny, dropped out of law school and, with the encouragement of Engels, prepared himself in Anglo-Scottish political economy on the way to his own conceptual (and revolutionary) systems of social science; thus the young Proudhon turned from his complaints against the old jurisprudence to a direct critique of the modern system of social "theft" that was property; thus the young Max Weber embarked on "a change of disciplines," from law to political economy, which (or rather, the two in combination) led him to his post-Marxist system of "sociology."[18]

Professional and academic jurisprudence was not unaware of the importance of political economy and of the inroads it had made on traditional conceptions of law. One of the most striking examples of the persistence of Old Regime law was the famous handbook for lawyers called *Profession d'avocat,* which was published first by A. G. Camus in 1770 and in its last (fifth) edition by A. A. J. Dupin in 1832.[19] The edition of 1804 added a section on "social economy" (recognized there as a "new word"), including statistics, as essential in the training of a modern lawyer. A year earlier a new journal had appeared, called *Bulletin de l'Institut de Jurisprudence et d'économie politique,* which celebrated both the old legal tradition (which had been "saved" by Placentinus of the University of Montpellier, in the so-called dark ages) and the new science of economics. About this time (1803) J. B. Say published his classic work on political economy, which rejected old mercantilist orthodoxies and popularized the views of Adam Smith; and in 1816 he taught the first course in France on the subject.

For Say the concept of property, which was the major (if not the only) subject of the Civil Code, provided the common ground for each of the disciplines which asserted its claim to be a science of society. "Speculative philosophy can busy itself with the search for the true foundations of the law of property," he wrote, with deliberate disregard for the legal niceties; "the jurist can establish the rules for the transmission of things possessed; political science can show the surest guarantees of this law; as for political economy, it considers property only as the most powerful encouragement for the increase of wealth" (*la multiplication des richesses*).[20]

Enthusiasm for the new discipline carried other scholars beyond the legal tradition. In 1823 the Swiss *Annales de législation et de jurisprudence,* featuring translations from Savigny as well as the work of Pietro Rossi and Sismondi, changed its title to *Annales de législation et d'économie politique;* and Rossi himself, devoted admirer of Savigny, accepted an invitation from Guizot to teach political economy at the College de France. Having earlier celebrated the Historical School as the basis of a new "social revolution," after 1830 Rossi praised this "high social science" of political economy as the proper basis for a "powerful synthesis of all moral science."[21] And as Villeneuve Bargement wrote in 1841, "We wish to declare that *political economy,* because of its important goal, may be considered to be *social science* par excellence."[22]

There were a few other areas of overlap between law and political economy, especially in the Older Historical School and the Younger Historical School of economics, which resisted the imposition of English doctrine—a sublimated form of British imperialism—on less advanced societies. This was most conspicuous in the famous methodological controversy (*Methodenstreit*) between Liberalism and Historicism in the 1880s. Another point of intersection occurred on the contested terrain of property and possession, which had been further complicated by revolutionary expropriations and indemnifications; and this continued to provide some common ground, if only as a battlefield, for law and economics. "Property" had been the common currency of European social and political thought, and its concomitant (also common to both law and economics) was the idea of individual "liberty." As Eugen Ehrlich has reminded us, however, property was the product of a legal fiction. By contrast, he declared, "the law of possession is the true law of the economic order and is most closely related to the living law of economics."[23]

This had been the insight of Marx, too, in his youthful turn to economics. "Political economy—like the real process," Marx wrote in his comments on the work of James Mill in 1843, "starts out from the *relation of man to man* as that of *property owner to property owner*." Property, or rather its expropriation, was also the original source of "alienation" in a legal sense, although Marx added to this the overtones of psychic distress emphasized by celebrators of Marxist "humanism." Marx further supported his interpretations with reference to Roman conceptions of property, especially in connection with the *ager publicus*, which was the original common land of the Romans and which seemed to illustrate a stage of "primitive communism," a thesis championed by both Marx and Engels in their revolutionary period.[24]

But the law had been Marx's point of departure as well as his chief target—along with its "ideological" comrade, organized religion. As a law student (of Savigny, among others) Marx had tried to devise his own legal system, following the model of the old Pandectologists; but he abandoned this work (of three hundred pages) when he came to realize, with the help of Hegelian philosophy, that conventional private law was in no way related to public law—that is, to the good of civil society or the state, which on the contrary was an apparatus to preserve the evil conventions of the legal tradition. So he rejected the "metaphysics of law" (a Kantian term), with its "tripartite divisions and tedious prolixity"; opened an attack, under the influence of Hegelianism, on the Historical School of Law; and, under the urging of Engels, took the direct route of political economy to a science of society, beginning with a study of Say, Smith, Ricardo, Mill, Bentham, and others, leading up to his critique of Hegel's *Philosophie des Rechts* and his own *Ökonomisch-Philosophische Manuskripte* of 1844.[25]

The young Marx was not alone in his disillusionment with conventional jurisprudence; for the young P. J. Proudhon, among others, made a very similar "turn" from law to economics and to the social questions of pre-1848 Europe—a turn, ultimately, from speculative philosophy to revolutionary action. Although Proudhon, too, had once hoped to erect a legal system, a replacement for the Civil Code which would achieve social justice, he, like Marx, gave up on the legal profession, so obviously in complicity with the Bourgeois Monarchy. Proudhon's answers to his notorious question "What is property?" were various and paradoxical: "It is everything"; "it is nothing"; "it is theft"; "it is the problem which is, after the fate of humanity, the greatest which reason can pose, the last which it can resolve." And for Proudhon, too, the answer to this "formidable question"—most fundamentally the relationship between "possession" and "property"—was to be found not in jurisprudence, which had hopelessly confused the two, as Proudhon argued at length, but only in political economy. And so to the next question: What is political economy? *"Political economy . . . is after all but the code, or immemorial routine, of property,"* he answered in his *Philosophy of Poverty*—but in his notebooks (1847) his answer was "revolution" (*La révolution, aujourd'hui, c'est l'économie politique*). And as for society, he added, "C'est la guerre."[26]

The targets of Prouhon's indignation, the lawyers, agreed about the value of this new discipline. In the Restoration the (likewise restored) legal profession in France, especially after 1848, had to come to terms with the new approach to social science; and in 1864 a chair of political economy, established a generation earlier (1819), was finally filled. In his first lecture Anselm Batbie was still celebrating jurists as "priests of the law," according to the ancient civilian formula, and "devoted to the cult of justice" and the welfare of the people (*salus populi*).[27] The problem of property was of course the major link between the two, and Batbie realized that the facts of political economy were often in conflict with the principles of the Civil Code. Batbie's successor, Henri Baudrillart, focused in particular on the terrible question of property, whose resolution (as well as origin) lay in the principle of labor.[28] What (repeating Proudhon's question) is property? It is a "battle-cry," he answered; but together, the sciences of economics and law, he hoped, would explain away this "mystery" and resolve the social problems it entailed. Together they also contributed to "social law" (*droit social*), which in the later nineteenth century was designed to mitigate the abuses and social costs of the free market and uncontrolled industrial expansion.

For its more imperialistic practitioners and champions, left and right, political economy was the key not only to understanding but also to controlling, or transforming, the world. For Say and Friedrich List (however they might disagree on the question of nationality) political economy was the science of survival, of wealth, and of progress; for Marx and Proudhon (however they might disagree on the question of revolution) political economy unmasked the pretensions and false consciousness and revealed the contradictions—the true "nature"—of modern industrial society. And for all of these the old jurisprudence had become practically as well as intellectually bankrupt because of its entanglements in old conventions, old methods, and old values. Political economy was jurisprudence demystified—and de-moralized (but not de-politicized). For the most part, however, the success story of economics in the past century (ideological differences aside) tipped the balance of human science even more in the direction of the unhistorical, nature-science models of social thought—and signaled another defeat of Nomos by the forces of Physis. Not that, in this triumphant march that has qualified practitioners of the "dismal science" for Nobel prizes, political economy has lacked for other rivals in the search for a newer and better science of society. Two of these disciplines remain to be considered, the first of them assuming a Greek name of modern coinage that had come, philosophically, to be identified with the "human measure"—that is, the modern field of anthropology.

Law Surpassed by Anthropology

Before achieving "scientific" status in the later nineteenth century, "anthropology" referred not to the various empirical traditions later drawn into the professional canon but to a branch of philosophy which inquired generally and theoretically into human nature. In modern times the term appeared first in the early sixteenth century in the title of a book by Magnus Hundt on the "dignity, nature, and properties of man" (*Anthropologium de hominis dignitate, natura et proprietatibus,* 1501), and by the eighteenth century the word had made its way into philosophical lexicons, and by the nineteenth, into the titles of scholarly journals.[29] Down at least to the idealist work of Carl Ludwig Michelet, *Anthropologie und Psychologie, oder die Philosophie des subjektiven Geistes* (1840), "anthropology" suggested the study of the human mind, whether the subjective or the physiological aspect of mentality. "Know thyself" was the first motto of the philosophical tradition, and (as Michelet recalled) anthropology sought this knowledge in the most direct, if largely speculative, fashion. So of course "anthropology" figured prominently in the great systems of German idealism, especially the Kantian and the Hegelian, and to the Kantian critiques J. F. Fries added an "anthropological critique of reason." There were some forty-seven works published on philosophical anthropology between 1800 and 1832, and the tradition still persists, especially in Germany.[30]

In the German universities of Marx's time anthropology was taught as a prerequisite for the study both of medicine and of law; and this was reflected as well in "encyclopedic" textbooks, such as that of Hugo (who invoked Kant's *Critique of Judgment* in this connection). At the University of Berlin in 1836 Marx took a course in "anthropology" with H. Steffans, for example, as part of his studies toward a law degree. In beginning with a systematic formulation of "juristic anthropology," Hugo's *Handbuch des Naturrechts* was simply presenting, in a more systematic way, the principles of law as set down in the first title of the Digest, that is, the identification of law with wisdom ("the knowledge of things divine and human"), the definition of law, especially natural law ("what nature teaches all animals"), and the notion of "natural reason." Hugo's "anthropology" also rehearsed the commonplace view of the potential and the "dignity" of man, which ranged from animal drives to subjective "spirit"—and subject to law in progressing states of cultural development.[31]

But if anthropology classically sought an irreducible "nature" in human behavior, it did not remain content with individual psychology; it attended also to collective and cultural patterns.[32] It treated, we might say, not only primary but also "second nature," and indeed the human—the free and responsible—"subject" of law was defined by various conventional and social as well as natural attributes. It was for this reason that jurists came increasingly to appreciate the benefits that might derive from closer ties between jurisprudence and anthropology (as from those between jurisprudence and political economy). The study of human "culture," as the larger context of social organization, was implicit in the work of Pufendorf and other natural lawyers (and the word itself occurred in an educational sense). Indeed the expansion of the *novum ius gentium* and the modernization of the old *ius naturale* had contributed to new anthropological perspectives in the legal tradition. In the nineteenth century these concerns, intensified by the premises of the Historical School, marked a convergence between the profession of law and the empirical investigations in many areas that went into the making of modern anthropology.[33]

What Carl Becker called the "new history" of the philosophes, itself reflecting the interests of the "new anthropology" of the Enlightenment, had an important effect on the old legal tradition. In a discourse of 1801 A. L. Jussieu, carrying on the celebration of "la science sociale" popular among jurists, acknowledged these expanding horizons in a historical way. "Social science studies the organization of the various colonies emanating from the Roman republic," he declared. "It examines the customary rights, the codes of the ancients, the laws favorable to marriage, the perhaps too limited control of mothers over children, the progress of the Athenian people in abrogating its laws; and always it seeks to take from the experience of preceding centuries lessons for the present generation." Anthropological enterprises, such as that of Baron Degérando to observe savage peoples, proposed to extend in space what these historical aspirations projected back in time; and both represented what Degérando expressed in the phrase of Pope (paraphrasing Pierre Charron), "the proper study of man."[34]

The "new anthropology" of the Enlightenment (as Georges Gusdorf has called it) sought self-knowledge on a number of levels—biological, psychological, social, and philological—and the extraordinary expansion of particular human (especially historical, economic, psychological, linguistic, and ethnographical) sciences had the effect both of undermining the authority of the old jurisprudence and of expanding its horizons and sense of relativism. These tendencies were heightened by the linguistic studies underlying the "oriental renaissance" of the late eighteenth and the nineteenth century, which projected cultural inquiries from a narrowly Western into a broader "Indo-European" arena and thus invited comparative scholarship.[35]

These phenomena had the effect, too, of causing defections from the old legal tradition to other fields, beginning especially with political economy but including ethnographical investigation as well. One of the most notable examples is J. J. Bachofen, who took the study of Roman law as the gateway to mythology and anthropology. "Roman law always appeared to me as a part of ancient, especially of Roman philology," remarked Bachofen in a sketch of his life written for Savigny, "hence as a section of a larger whole, embracing the study of classical antiquity in its entirety."[36] But new currents in philology opened up larger horizons for Bachofen, and from civil law he went into the more perilous terrain of myth and *Mutterrecht*.

In England the old jurisprudence played a major role in the emergence of "scientific" ethnology, and the key figure in this was Henry Sumner Maine, who taught Roman law both at the Inns of Court and as regius professor at Cambridge in the 1850s. Maine was an admirer not only of the Historical School but of the French legal tradition, and he remarked that "the book of Montesquieu, with all its defects, still proceeded on that Historical Method before which the Law of Nature has never maintained its footing for an instant."[37] Like Savigny, Maine was concerned fundamentally with reconciling, practically as well as intellectually, law and society; and he rejected the Benthamite and Austinian notion of law as simple command and obligation. This theory, like natural law, was irrelevant especially to earlier ages, when law appeared as custom and "habit" and was maintained in the custody of a privileged order and "juristical oligarchy."

For Maine the subject of his lectures on *Ancient Law* (1861) was important not only because "the European nations built the *debris* of Roman law into their walls" but also because Roman law "has the longest known history of any set of human institutions" and because, "from its commencement to its close, it was progressively modified for the better."[38] In other words, it was an ideal model both for historical understanding and for social improvement. Most important, in association with comparative jurisprudence and comparative mythology, Roman law afforded access to "the study of races in their primitive condition"—and in this sense a transition to anthropological inquiry. Maine pursued his quarry above all through the conventional rubrics of civil law, especially the family, succession, property, contract, and the development of equity and various "legal fictions" which were devised in written law. Yet he acknowledged that jurisprudence alone, aside from natural-law speculations, could not be expected to answer fundamental questions about the ultimate "origins" of society in general.

Like other alumni or admirers of the Historical School, Maine inclined to ideas of primitive communism, illustrated by the extreme antiquity of the village community and the belief that "ancient law . . . knows next to nothing of individuals," and indeed that the categories of "persons" and "things" were hardly distinguished. The key to ancient law, as (among others) Lewis Henry Morgan and John Ferguson McLennan (lawyers both) were also teaching, was not individual liberty but kinship; and for Maine the trajectory was traced generally "from status to contract." Maine "used Roman law to breathe new life into old truths," writes his most recent biographer.[39] Morgan likewise joined a "lawyer's inquiry," based especially on his reading of Blackstone (pertaining in particular to "degrees of consanguinity"), into an "ethnological object." According to his most recent biographer, Morgan's "vantage point for the description of Iroquois consanguinity is provided by canon law and Roman civil law as the foundation of the laws of civilized nations." This tendency to generalize from Roman experience, especially in the matter of "patriarchal theory" (extrapolated from the Roman *patria, potestas*) was later criticized by McLennan and others; but in his later lectures Morgan extended his horizons by employing the "new materials" of Hindu and Celtic legal history (the Laws of Manu and the Brehon laws) and also the work of Gustav von Maurer and Emile Laveleye on the primitive forms of property, which employed evidence from America, Russia, Japan, Java, and India as well as ancient Greece and Rome and modern Europe.[40]

Unlike the champions of natural law and of the new science of political economy, scholars who exploited ethnographical evidence tended to reject the notion of "absolute" property; and of course this view was intensified by contemporary evolutionary ideas, which were already enveloping the new fields of ethnology and anthropology. Reviewing the various theories of property, Emile de Laveleye rejected old ideas of first occupancy, the more plausible emphasis on labor made by political economists, a (counterfactual and unhistorical) contractual basis, the assumption of other economists that private property was identical with human nature, and the juristic convention (endorsed by the Historical School) that property rights were identical with law itself; and he turned back to the universalistic belief—reinforced by his investigations into comparative jurisprudence—that property was indeed a "natural right," tied both to the ancient notion of equality and to modern hopes for social justice.[41]

The old Marx was swept up by enthusiasm not only for Darwinian evolution but also for the new science of anthropology practiced by Maine, Morgan, McLennan, and others. Having as a young man been converted from the old jurisprudence to political economy, in his later years he expanded his views beyond the confines of European society. In his *Ethnological Notebooks* he began an assault on these authors, as forty years before he had studied the classics of British political economy, with an eye (it seems likely) to constructing an expanded theory of social development—based still on a form of dialectical materialism but taking into account historical experience beyond strictly Western patterns of feudalism, capitalism, and revolution.[42]

Marx rejected the work of Maine (as well as Austin) because of their projection of class divisions back into medieval times. To Marx, Maine seemed complacent, ethnocentric, narrow in perspective, elitist, and (in a word) *bourgeois*. Unaware of the work of Bachofen and Morgan, the "blockheaded" Maine resorted parochially to Roman legal history and especially to the principle of paternal power (*patria potestas*) to argue the case of masculine succession. The notorious formalism of Roman law celebrated by Maine ("als a lawyer") as a dramatization of the "origin of justice" appeared to Marx "rather Dramatization of how law disputes were becoming a source of fees profit to lawyers!" Like the "childish trivialities of Austin," Maine's arguments were not those of an anthropologist but (in Marx's polyglotist, notetaking jargon) of "either Jurist od. Ideolog."

To the legalistic speculations of Maine (the prime target of these late notebooks) Marx much preferred the views of Morgan, drawn as they were from "positive studies" and appreciation for technical and material factors—"the arts of subsistence"—in history. Though a lawyer, Morgan did not seek to base human science on legal formalisms. His assumption was expressed by Marx in this way: "The events of human progress embody themselves, independently of particular men, in a material record, which is crystallized in institutions, usages u. customs, u. preserved in inventions and discoveries." Concerning Morgan's important views on "the influence of property," Marx wrote: "It was the power [here crossing out the word "influence"] that brought the Aryan and Semitic nations out of barbarism into civilization"; and indeed "the passion for possession," spawned by that "property-making organization," the monogamous family, accounted for basic political as well as social patterns.[43]

Marx never finished the work on his post-*Kapital* system, which he published in a rather simplistic summary, but in his late (as in his early) efforts he illustrated the significance of the old legal tradition in both positive and negative ways. In a positive sense the Roman model of legal development, and especially the questions of property and kinship patterns (beyond the economic as well as legal analysis of class relationships), continued to shape the quasi-anthropological thinking of Marx and other contemporaries. In a negative and "critical" sense conventional jurisprudence served as a target for more "scientific" and wider-ranging inquiries into human history and social organization.

Marx continued to search for a material base for culture (as for society in a more restricted sense), but other roads to modern anthropology were broader and less predetermined. Among the anthropological offspring of (and defectors from) jurisprudence, the kingdom of Nomos was invaded by a new breed of explorers, and a new and wider basis for human science was fashioned. The governing abstractions of emergent anthropology guaranteed that human materials, if not a human measure, would be served. In Germany *Völkerpsychologie* began with the notion of a "popular spirit"

(*Volksgeist*), employed by Herder, Savigny, and others, who extended it into the speculative realm of social psychology. In England anthropology also avoided the reductionist tendencies of political economy and turned not to a rationally defined and mechanically determined "market" but to an eclectic and polyvalent abstraction, rendered by the term "culture" or "civilization," which Edward Tylor (in the "charter" he prepared for the discipline) defined as "that complex whole which includes knowledge, belief, art, morals, laws, customs, and any other capabilities and habits acquired by man as a member of society."[44] This was obviously still another way of saying "second nature."

Nevertheless, the lack of historical structure and the conceptual temptations of biologism, evolutionism, racism, psychologism, functionalism, structuralism, cross-cultural indexing, and other universalizing or systematizing ideas have often enticed anthropology, in its explanations if not in its field-work, beyond the familiar terrain of the kingdom of Nomos. Anthropology has always preserved interpretive and even philosophical (as well as literary) dimensions, but professionally the models of natural science have tended to prevail, and culture continues to be studied, normally, in the shadow of nature. This is even more the case with the last of the disciplines—of the offspring of and rebels from Nomos—to be considered here.

Law Overpowered by Sociology

"Sociology was born in a state of hostility to law," N. S. Timasheff declared, and there is some nominal truth to the statement.[45] "Sociology," the term if not the concept, was the brainchild of Auguste Comte and the capstone of the system of Positive Philosophy which he was preaching in the 1830s. Comte recognized predecessors—Condorcet, Montesquieu, and even Aristotle—but the recognition was honorific; and in general his inclination was to claim originality in his "new philosophy" and to suppress other influences (most notably, that of Saint-Simon). He dismissed Vico (though without naming him) as the fabricator of "vague and chimerical conceptions of oscillating or circular movements," and of the works of the jurists he seems quite innocent. His revised classification of sciences, ranging from mathematics and natural science to "social physics," moral science, and secular religion shows an unquestioning devotion to the tradition of Physis. Comte assumed that law and the vagaries of Nomos, "the vague and turbulent discussion of right," would disappear altogether in the wake of Positive Philosophy.[46]

The inclination to simplistic scientism was given further encouragement by two other motives. One was the fascination of sociologists, especially in France and England, with the explanatory power of Darwinism; and the other was the growing anxiety of sociologists to assert a scientific status for their discipline. Like jurists in ages past and legislators more recently, sociologists have aspired to measure and to master society directly; and their imperialistic dreams (again, like those of jurists in a pre-scientific age) have helped to shape—or to misshape—not only their self-image but also their historical perspective. According to a sort of Higher Whiggery which emphasizes the connections with natural science and philosophy, Positivism and Marxism have been placed at center stage, with the brighter side of the Enlightenment providing illumination and the earlier and less sharply doctrinaire approaches being relegated to a vague background, along with selected figures from the formal philosophical tradition since Plato and Aristotle, all playing out a drama of the triumph of reason and modernity.[47]

Yet on closer examination this seems to be a narrow and unhistorical way of looking at the question. A much more comprehensive and convincing view was suggested by Albion Small, a founder of the discipline in America, in his pioneering survey of the history of sociology. "Sociology is not a comet as popularly pictured, viz., a body coming from nowhere and bound nowhere," he declared. "Its lineage is as old as man's efforts to understand the human lot." He did not try to trace the entire lineage, but he did offer an extraordinarily broad perspective on the immediate antecedents of this branch of social science, including not only various schools of economic thought but also historical scholarship. Small began not with Marx, Comte, or even the Scottish moralists but rather with the debate between Savigny and Thibaut over the suitability for German society of a code of laws. The issue separating these two jurists was the fundamental question of rationality and social change—"the nexus between antecedents and consequents in human experience"—and modern sociologists, according to Small, inherited the same set of questions.[48]

Some historians of social thought, such as Robert Nisbet, have taken a similarly broad perspective on the "sociological tradition"; and Montesquieu in particular has long been recognized—by Durkheim, Eugen Ehrlich, Werner Stark, and Raymond Aron, among others—as at least a precursor of sociology.[49] The German tradition, too, has preserved ties with legal thought, as suggested, most notably, by the work of Lorenz von Stein, Fernand Tönnies, Georg Simmel, Rudolf von Jhering, Otto Gierke, and Max Weber.[50] Nor, as Nisbet argues, could the thought of these men be merely the product of "logico-empirical analysis," no matter what their rhetorical strategies. Nisbet himself chooses to follow his insight through Lovejovian analysis of "unit-ideas" (community, authority, status, the sacred, and alienation), but such ideas also represent legal categories which are familiar to all of these scholars and are of course embedded in the ordinary language which they sought to transform into more scientific terminology. What is more, they encourage us to focus on—and to try to recover some appreciation of—the significance of the legal tradition in the development of such concepts and attendant attitudes and methods.

As anthropologists took "culture," so sociologists took "society" as their master abstraction. In general their aim has been to apprehend directly the patterns and structures of "society," to find what Lester Ward called its "real laws," and to do so without much regard for content, or at least for the significance of variability, change, and "local knowledge." This tendency can be seen in the history of the "social movement" in France by Lorenz von Stein, who began his career as a lawyer but, like Marx, Proudhon, and others, came to believe in the primacy of the economic order, and especially of property. Following Hegel's lead and setting apart the "common will" which was the State, Stein sought "the concept of society and its dynamic laws."[51] The residual influence of law is evident in some areas, most notably in Gierke's corporation theory and Tönnies's ideas of community and association; but Gierke also inclined toward a scholastic sort of social "realism," as Tönnies turned back to the categories of the old natural lawyers. The most extreme example of "sociologism" is the formalist theory of Georg Simmel, who directed his attention to generalized "societal forms"; but even Weber and his followers have, despite respect for "empirical" research, shared this anti-historical tendency toward formalism.[52]

Like the old jurisprudence in its most imperialistic and naturalistic stages, sociology aspired to "scientific" status on the basis of its claims to universality, concern with questions of cause and effect, and systematic character. Similarly, from Romantic corporation theory to the social phenomenology of Alfred Schutz, sociology has created a remarkable scholasticism alienated both from legal tradition and, despite commitments to empiricism, from historical perspective. In a sense sociology may be seen as a sort of sublimation of the old dogmatic juridical "encyclopedias" (which indeed were still being issued in the later nineteenth century), preserving some of their forms and language but discarding their premises and scholarly baggage and turning toward new kinds of abstract and naturalistic universalism.[53] As Clifford Geertz has remarked, "The only thing that links Freud, Piaget, von Neumann and Chomsky (to say nothing of Carl Jung and B. F. Skinner) is the conviction that the mechanics of human thinking is invariable across time, space, culture, and circumstance, and that they know what it is."[54] This critique applies no less appropriately, it seems to me, to the "forerunners and founders" of classical sociology (with the qualified exception of Max Weber), and the neo-scholastic tradition generated by them, especially in this country.

The necessary condition of modern sociology is the basic distinction between the political and the social—the abstractions which are the state and civil (or "bourgeois") society. "Society" itself has been a controversial construct, torn between the economic and social ("socialist," in a general sense, and derivatively "sociological") conceptions—between market and community. This ambivalence was expressed formally in the famous distinction drawn by Henry Sumner Maine between status and contract and in Tönnies's equally famous distinction between community and association (*Gemeinschaft* and *Gesellschaft*), which transformed legal conventions into general sociological categories. That they did so specifically and self-consciously, is evident from his main example, which was that possession was characteristic of community, as property was of association.[55] In general Tönnies took as his point of departure a critique of the extremes of the legal tradition—on the one hand the abstract jusnaturalism of Hobbes and on the other hand the reactionary views of the Historical School. Yet Tönnies himself joined his theories to a generalized version of the Historical School's concept of custom as an expression of popular (and "tacit") will— "social will itself," in Tönnies's formulation, "distilled from habit, usage, and practice."[56]

Despite the heritage of French Positivism, Emile Durkheim preserved a certain respect for the forces of Nomos in the general sense that he refused to borrow, for sociological use, materials from other "positive sciences." According to Durkheim's "rules of sociological method," the empirical units and categories of his discipline, though analogous to natural science, were distinctive of social science. For him collective human behavior had to be understood in terms not of physical determinism or psychological motivation but rather of "social facts" which found meaning only in the context of society; only on this basis could sociological inferences be drawn and sociological "laws" be inferred. Methodologically (or perhaps axiomatically), Durkheim acknowledged the Nomos in the form of "social solidarity" (scientific successor to Comtean and Saint-Simonian "harmony"), which was itself, unfortunately, so often lacking in a modern existence increasingly afflicted by a state of disorder and "lawlessness" (*anomie*). Nevertheless, Durkheim's idea of community, expressed in terms of various social functions and institutions, represented a sort of sublimated—metaphysical, or rather metanomical—form of the categories of traditional law, which indeed, as Durkheim said, was a principal form or primary expression of "social solidarity."[57]

Max Weber, trained in the law and concerned centrally with the field of the sociology of law (*Rechtssoziologie*), tried even more directly to replicate the structures of legal thought in his systematic sociology—and in fact one may regard his intellectual efforts as in a sense continuations of the social thought of the tradition of "legal honoratiores," which he transformed from a Roman professional class into a social category. For Weber, as for Durkheim (but also for the old Romanist system-builders and the modern "pandectologists"), meaning was a function of a social system; and this applied in particular to human actions, to questions of value, and to means of legitimation. In Weber's fragmentary and "modernist" analysis law was severed from moral philosophy, and the legal tradition was relegated to one "unscientific" category of social conduct. In general it was the corrosive and dissolving effect of political economy on jurisprudence that turned Weber toward more systematic and "value-free" inquiries into the social condition of humankind. Weberian sociology represented a sort of synthesis of legal conventions and economic analysis, reinforced by materials drawn from the widest range of comparative and "general" history (including frequent citations from Roman and Germanic law) and attentive to questions of legitimacy as well as structure and "power."[58]

In a sense, what Durkheim did for the idea of "community," to extricate it from conventional social and historical thinking and turn it into a socio-logical abstraction, Weber did for the idea of authority, through his famous threefold classification—rational-legal, charismatic, and traditional. As usual with Weber, such categories were derived not merely from empirical investigations but from historical conventions and examples or from legal topics. Thus "charismatic authority" was exemplified by, if not derived from, the old (especially Germanic) notion of divine-right kingship, though as usual the idea was reinforced by illustrations from the whole range of world history. As for the other two forms of authority, they constitute the *termini a quo* and *ad quem* of the process of legal history, though characteristically Weber began with an abstract and universalizing formulation. "In the pure type of traditional authority it is impossible for law or administrative rules to be deliberately created by legislation," Weber wrote. "Rules which in part are innovations can be legitimized only by claims that they have been 'valid of yore,' but have only now been recognized by means of 'Wisdom' [the *Weistum* of ancient Germanic law]. Legal decisions of finding the law (*Rechtsfindung*) can refer only to documents of tradition, namely to precedents and earlier decisions."[59] And of course the "pure type" of rational-legal authority refers to a later period of codification, rational organization, and bureaucratic consolidation characteristic of modern industrial states and the eclipse of traditional jurisprudence by political economy and social engineering.

In the capitalist society interpreted by Weber the flight path of the owl of Minerva had become more complicated, and Hegelian and Marxist consciousness of social context had led to a new level of critical thinking associated with the new sub-field of the "sociology of knowledge." The connections between *Wissensoziologie* and legal thought were slight, but two points might be mentioned, one (as usual) on the positive and the other on the negative side. First, the old legal tradition did serve as an exemplar of "social meaning," in which terms and concepts had to be understood within a legal system; and more concretely and locally, the notion of custom was related to particular social and cultural contexts and above all to special "interests." It was such a conception of the "spirit of the laws" that gave Montesquieu a retrospective place in the canon of the sociology of knowledge. On the negative side, law could be seen as a locus classicus of "ideology," or juridical false consciousness, and as such it became a favorite target of critics of the political implications of established legal tradition.[60]

This negative dimension may remind us that sociology, at least in its more activist forms, is (as Jürgen Habermas has said) "the science of crisis *par excellence*." To this extent it marks a break with the social thought associated with the old legal tradition, which has always taken stabililty and stasis, or at least gradualist change, as its object. In this "critical," often Marxist, mode sociology has been marked by the "decline of the subject"—of "homocentrism," as one recent observer puts it in his study *Sociology and the Twilight of Man*—and the rise of "value-free" social science on the model of economics and ultimately of natural science.[61] In France this has been illustrated by Durkheimian sociology and later by structuralism. In Germany a generational gap between social scientists (those born roughly before and after 1855) has widened this break with a consensus approach to social science: on the one hand, the generation of Schmoller (leader of the Younger Historical School of Economics), mostly tenured faculty opposed to university reform, politically conservative, and committed to the State and its research priorities; on the other hand, the generation of Weber (severe critic of the historical schools), mostly "extraordinary" faculty in favor of reform, liberal or radical, and devoted to theory and to "independent research." This circumstance, too, has contributed to the autonomy of sociology.

Yet links between sociology and law have been preserved and, though often covert, have become visible at certain points. One has been the movement of "social law" (*droit social*—the term applied by Gabriel Le Bras to the canonist tradition) in France, which paralleled and in some ways reinforced the "social solidarity" pursued more naturalistically by Durkheim. Léon Duguit emphasized the social function of law, and consequently of institutions such as property, which had been neglected by liberal economists and by most commentators on the Civil Code. The "metaphysical and individualist system of order" established by the Code, Duguit argued, should be replaced by a "juridically realist and socialist system of order."[62]

The connections between law and social thought were also apparent in the emergence of another sub-discipline (already encountered in Weber's work), which was "sociological jurisprudence." The occasion, as Timasheff put it, was a "discovery of sociology in jurisprudence," accompanied by a somewhat larger perspective on the history of social thought.[63] Georges

Gurvitch looked back to Aristotle as a founder; however, it was to the Aristotle not of the *Politics* but of the *Nicomachean Ethics,* where the meaning of justice is first established in terms of civil society—that is, in terms of "the different sorts of positive law, in their relation to the *Nomos* (the really efficient social order) the *Filia* (sociality or social solidarity), and the particular groups (*koinoniai*), of which the State is but the crown." And, Gurvitch concluded, "all law, whether established by human will or independent of human will (and in this sense 'natural') is, according to Aristotle, only the rational formulation of the requirements of the *Nomos . . .* the living and spontaneous body of rules governing social conduct."[64] In this way Gurvitch utilized philosophy in order to rationalize, to legitimize, and to universalize the conceptual core of the legal tradition and to appropriate it for the canon of modern sociology.

These suggestions are surely insufficient to illustrate the richness and depth of the achievements of these magisterial sociologists—as well as the troubles of what Ernst Becker called "the lost science of man"—but they may indicate some of the concealed links, substantial as well as formal, with the old legal tradition made through the medium of ordinary language if not specific professional convention. In many ways law formed the conceptual archetype and even substratum of sociological thought, and furnished much of its vocabulary. The distinctive language of sociology was created through a sort of distillation from social and legal conventions at hand—beginning with the obvious designations of personality, property, action, inheritance, custom, contract, domination, sacred and civil law, public and private law, law-making and law-finding, codification and administration, and other commonplaces of the old Gaian system. Much the same (more inferentially) might be said about shared formal qualities and structures (inaccessible as these may be to intellectual historians). Suffice it to suggest in the present, long (all-too-long) perspective, that if, as Comte remarked, metaphysics was the ghost of dead theology, sociology was in a similar way the ghost of jurisprudence past.

· FIFTEEN ·

Conclusion: The Legacy of Nomos

Well, as you say, we live for small horizons:
We move in crowds, we flow and talk together,
Seeing so many eyes and hands and faces,
So many mouths, and all with secret meanings,—
Yet know so little of them; only seeing
The small bright circle of our consciousness,
Beyond which lies the dark.

Conrad Aiken, *Palimpsest*

•

Social Scientism

The dialectic of nature and culture is still with us, in our language and in our intellectual habits if not in our intellectual preferences. The duality has been expressed by Richard Rorty as a difference of mental sets, or communities of discourse. Human beings give sense to their lives in two major ways, he writes. "The first is by telling the story of their contribution to the community, [whether] the actual historical one in which they live, or another actual one, distant in time and place, or a quite imaginary one, consisting perhaps of a dozen heroes and heroines selected from history or fiction or both. The second way is by describing themselves as standing in immediate relation to a nonhuman reality."[1] The first group Rorty calls the pragmatists, "who work within small horizons and the limits of the human condition" (the *Lebenswelt,* as Husserl would say); the second are the "realists," remote descendants of Plato, whose thought (or rhetoric) is "natural and not local." In effect I have been telling the story of the first community, the representatives of practical philosophy, if not of the "pragmatist" canon in Rorty's sense.

The struggles between Nomos and Physis have been carried on over some two and a half millennia of Western history. "Naturalism and historicism are the two great intellectual creations of the modern world," Ernst Troeltsch wrote, with specific reference to the opposition of Vico to Descartes—though to be sure one can trace the distinction between the "natural" and "moral" sciences back into medieval and even (in the distinction between theoretical and practical science) ancient thought.[2] Troeltsch's own immediate purpose was to deplore the ascendancy of *Naturalismus,* in the form of "positivism," and the more general intellectual and skeptical malaise of the Weimar period called the "crisis of historicism." Certain problems in the fields of economics and religion, both under assault by humanizing and "historicizing" forces in the later nineteenth century, were calling into question reason as well as revelation; and Troeltsch pursued his own critique along historical and sociological lines.

By then, however, and indeed beginning in the time of Kant, the conflict had shifted increasingly to the grounds of philosophy and in particular "neo-critical" transcendental idealism. The opposition between Physis and Nomos continued, especially in the efforts of neo-Kantians such as Wilhelm Windelband, Heinrich Rickert, and Wilhelm Dilthey, to establish boundaries between the natural and the human sciences (*Naturwissenschaften* and *Kultur-* or *Geisteswissenschaften*—the German rendering, incidentally, of J. S. Mill's "moral sciences").[3] Apart from Dilthey's historical studies, however, these discussions were carried on very far from the "lifeworld" of human society, culture, and jurisprudence. Rickert's concept of cultural and individualizing ("idiographic") sciences as distinct from natural and generalizing ("nomothetic") sciences hardly corresponded to what either natural or social scientists were about (their "rhetoric" to the contrary notwithstanding), and the diremption of *Wissenschaft* in terms of "value" was hardly more satisfactory, relying as it did on objectivist conceptions of natural science and even then being discredited.

Formerly, jurisprudence had transcended this diremption, claiming to be the habitat both of Nomos and of Physis and featuring various confrontations and interactions, especially the pyrotechnics produced by the exchanges between the Historical School and the Philosophical School in the later eighteenth and early nineteenth centuries, which resounded throughout all of the newer human disciplines, beginning with economics and sociology. By the end of the nineteenth century, however, jurisprudence, which had once boasted of being a bridge between nature and culture, played an increasingly minor role in these debates. In his discussion of the "contest of faculties" Kant had cast doubt on the claim of the law to constitute a rational science, arguing that jurists, in contrast to the philosophers, look to the Code rather than to reason. Kant was referring to professional and "dogmatic" jurisprudence, especially to *Pandectenrecht,* rather than to the legal tradition more broadly viewed; and it is perhaps unfortunate (as Weber's colleague Georg Jellinek remarked) that Kant never produced a critique of legal judgment which would have clarified his conceptions of jurisprudence.[4]

Yet Kant's perfunctory remarks do serve to criticize the unexamined and "unenlightened" attachment of jurists to the authority, prejudice, and contingencies of history, and to reinforce, from his aprioristic standpoint, the major complaints of the Philosophical against the Historical School of Law, that it was bound to an a posteriori method in the worst sense. Kant's invidious judgment also presages the intellectual fall from grace experienced by the study of law in the next century—in the otherwise irreconcilable views of Liberals, Marxists, and Positivists alike. Hans-Georg Gadamer has recently resurrected Kant's conception, arguing that "legal hermeneutics has become separated from understanding as a whole because it has a dogmatic purpose."[5] Yet Gadamer himself points to problems of "authority" and "prejudice," discredited by Enlightenment conceptions of rationality but essential to hermeneutical understanding in a larger sense. What is more, legal hermeneutics escapes from the fundamental charge against philosophical hermeneutics (registered by Habermas, among others), that it is divorced from social "reality" and in effect a species of idealism.

If philosophers, following Kant's line, have generally denied "scientific" status to the law, the new social sciences have refused to acknowledge that jurists had any true understanding of social reality, either. This was the implication, too, of jurists such as Hans Kelsen and the Austro-Marxist Karl Renner, who have insisted, though on very different grounds, on the disjunction between law and social order.[6] In general, jurisprudence was itself part of the cultural crisis perceived and lamented by philosophers and social scientists in the early decades of this century. Not that the legal profession itself had been weakened, but for the serious study of society and culture there were other disciplines with better claims for a "scientific" status, derivative as they were of "legal science." Jurisprudence has been fragmented into positivist, idealist, formalist, sociological, socialist, and "pure" sectors with little in common, hardly even a professional memory; and in the wake of relativism and the "crisis of historicism" natural law has experienced a revival throughout Europe. Indeed the same "crisis" out of which modern sociolology was born and from which all of the sciences suffered (as Husserl lamented)[7] left jurisprudence in conceptual and moral disarray—as an abstract doctrine, a bankrupt "legalism," or, worse, an expression of an antiquated "ideology." The history of law has been carried on by scholars, but it has been largely detached from the study of the human sciences and even from history itself.

There have been more recent attempts to establish ties between law and other disciplines, including economics, anthropology, rhetoric, and even literary criticism (often in their most fashionable forms). Yet the aim has been technical or ideological rather than historical or anthropological, and it has been based on a concern for the legal profession rather than for human understanding in any broad sense. The Economics and Law movement has been an effort to accommodate law to the assumptions of the free market; and even Critical Legal Studies, which adapts "critical theory" and restores social values to the law, tends to turn its back on history as limited to "nostalgia," apologetics for Progress, or a façade for "timeless discourse."[8]

Most of the "scientific" concerns of traditional legal science have in fact passed on to, or been appropriated by, other disciplines; and these have also been indifferent to historical perspective, if not always to "local knowledge." Questions of property and commerce, linked irrevocably to production and finance, were reformulated by political economy, in which the market replaced the juristic "encyclopedia" as the intelligible field of investigation.[9] Sociology arose in part in reaction to the anti-social tendencies of economic analysis, but substituted its own anti-historical abstractions; and its structural-functionalist, behaviorist, and sociobiological excesses have reduced the human dimension.[10] Anthropology took a broader view of the human condition, but its commitments to evolutionism, cross-cultural analysis, and structuralism continue to incline it toward naturalistic and universalistic models of interpretation. In general the deviations from these models—institutional economics, "interpretive" sociology and anthropology, and philosophical anthropology—have been marginal in this century; and intellectual (including economic and institutional) forces and neglect of historical perspective have tended to increase this marginality.

There is of course a political dimension to the public eclipse of the tradition of prudence and practical philosophy at the expense of scientism, for the universalizing of Science continues to represent—on the right and on the left—power and control on the largest scale. Prudence, including jurisprudence, suggests "prejudices," norms, and goals originating from centers of authority critical of the powers that be, and perhaps obstacles to the exigencies of control and modernization. This is an aspect of the story of Nomos that has, I hope, been at least implicit here.

The Human Measure

Yet Physis, in the form of positivism and mathematical methods, while it may be institutionally victorious, has not emerged intellectually unscathed. Among the resistances to the imperialist thrusts of Physis in this century, three in particular deserve attention. One is the *verstehende Soziologie* of Weber, which had roots both in law and in political economy, and which has been carried on by Talcott Parsons and some of his disciples in this country; the second is the "philosophical anthropology" pursued by followers of Dilthey such as Erich Rothacker, Michael Landmann, and certain "new anthropologists" in Germany; and the third, closely related, is the cultural turn given to modern hermeneutics, especially by Gadamer, who emphasizes "the exemplary significance of legal hermeneutics" for the human sciences.[11] For Gadamer this significance lies in the fact that the jurist has to combine historical understanding and legal doctrine, to give meaning to legal texts embedded in tradition through application to present circumstances, and thus to create that "fusion of horizons" essential to understanding and judgment. Nor, for Gadamer, was Habermas's objection, that the "extra-linguistic modes of experience" are neglected, to the point, since the function of language is to open up the world (the *Lebenswelt*) of experience, judgment, communication, action, and interaction with both the natural and the social aspects.

To these should be added more recent critiques of natural-science models of explanation tied not only to antiquated conceptions of scientific method but also to the seventeenth-century "metaphysical foundations" thereof. "Modernism" (presumably the intellectual end product of "moderniza- tion") has been defined as "the program of Descartes, regnant in philosophy since the seventeenth century, to build knowledge on a foundation of radical doubt"—the "modern project to rigor," which culminated in, though it did not end with, Nietzsche.[12] It suggests a kind of vulgar scientism which is implicit in the assumptions, if not always in the formal declarations, of much of modern natural and social science. It involves a "flight from ambiguity" and a predilection for "methodologies" that privilege the syl- logism and the experiment (the bottom lines of naive Cartesian and Bacon- ian methods), rejecting "prejudice" and prizing "prediction," skirting ques- tions of value and embracing devices of control, and scorning "local knowledge" except as it serves larger schemes.

Modernism is the beneficiary of two aspects of the Cartesian heritage— both the rationalism and the doubt—and the ambivalence has led at once to the exaltation and to the denigration of individual reason. To the prog- ress of scientific and philosophical reason there seems no limit, but to the single agent, the lay target of scientific analysis, the field of thought and choice has been reduced correspondingly. The human object of Ricardo's economics, of Durkheim's sociology, and of structuralist (or, to take an extreme example, Marvin Harris's physiological) anthropology is no longer the free and responsible "person" of the law, but rather the—non-human— factor in quantitative analysis. The drive to be rid of the illusions of ideology and "prejudice" has led not only to allegations of the "death of the author" but also to the abolishing of the human agent, as implied variously by Foucault, Heidegger, and deconstructionist criticism. These are some of the later conditions of the obsolescence of jurisprudence as a viable "social science." Despite the radical inferences that have been drawn by some champions of natural law, the legal tradition never lost its anthropocentric and voluntarist assumptions and, if for no other reason, was unable itself to follow the road to scientific modernism and the "project to rigor."

A central question of the human sciences has always been the subject— Psyche, the *persona,* the individual, the author. "Individualism" is not just a product of bourgeois society, for in a longer perspective the legal tradition has been the main lodging of this sustaining feature of Western thought and especially of "moral science." In modern times the fortunes of the old legal tradition and the free, thinking, and responsible subject have in many ways been parallel, and intellectually both have been approaching bankruptcy. "The 'subject,'" as Nietzsche put it, "is a fiction."[13] Nineteenth-century social thought still took psychology—and rationalism—seriously, and even Marx recognized a psychological dimension to the basically legal and economic concept of "alienation." But inroads were made by social psychology (especially *Völkerpsychologie* and mass psychology); and (despite residual notions of "mentality" preserved by anthropologists such as Lucien Levy-Bruhl) economic analysis, right and left, and sociology, Durkheimian and structuralist, not to speak of neo-cameralist statistics, have found it possible to dispense with psychology entirely.

For collective behavior such assumptions may well be necessary, but the reductionism often accompanying such attitudes can be an impediment to understanding. Recently there have been a few more voices raised against the "regnant" philosophy of modernism. Clifford Geertz and James Boone have campaigned for "local knowledge"; Richard H. Brown has thrown down a challenge to the "paradigm imperialists" in the form of a metaphorics and a "poetic of sociology"; Donald McCloskey has suggested that economics has a powerful and essential "rhetoric" as well as scientific methods; and Charles Taylor, among others, has written in defense of the human "agent" and interpretive social science.[14] What these critics have in common, indeed, is a renewed appreciation for rhetoric and literary categories; for as Geertz has reminded us, what practitioners of the human sciences really "do" in their theory and practice is to "write," often in the "first person," and what they write about is often the writings of others. In the human sciences, at least, the author lives, and so do the scholastic and "subjective" habits of authorship.[15]

What Physis, like the Cartesian *Cogito,* seems to require is a loss of memory. The Enlightenment, or its excesses, has turned us away from the communities of intellectual endeavor and, according to Alasdair MacIntyre, has made us blind to "a conception of rational enquiry as embodied in a tradition, a conception according to which the standards of rational justification themselves emerge from and are part of a history in which they are vindicated by the way in which they transcend the limitations of and provide for the defects of their predecessors within the history of that same tradition." I do not quite share MacIntyre's view of "rationality" or exclusive deference to the tradition of school philosophy (Aristotle, Augustine, Aquinas, and all that), but I do endorse his notion of tradition as "an argument extended through time in which certain fundamental agreements are defined and redefined"—debates, that is, with those outside the tradition, as well as "those internal debates through which the meaning and rationale of the fundamental agreements come to be expressed and by whose progress a tradition is constituted."[16] I would only add that the tradition can best be understood in terms of language rather than of doctrine, certainly in the case of Nomos.

If there is a moral to the story of Nomos, it is that self-knowledge in the social and cultural spheres does not come easily, or "naturally." The forces of Physis are intimidating. Across the ages natural science has affected to tear off the cultural masks hiding "reality," but beneath there is always another disguise, another *persona* (which signifies a mask as well as a human subject); though "put to the question," as Bacon thought, "nature will lie to the very end." In the investigation of human "nature" in historical context, in other words, there is no end to myth—no "last" myth to be deciphered.[17] The strength of social thought in the "nomical" mode is that it accepts the limits of human insight, and rejects the "abuses of reason" that perennially recur in the effort to reduce human experience to a manageable code from which all answers may be derived. The problem is that the questions themselves change from generation to generation, and so must the myths—or, what may be the same thing, the meanings—which are sought in particular social, cultural, or political contexts.

What Nomos requires is awareness of the ultimate constraints of the human condition—the "horizon-structure of experience" and the tedious sequence of chronology that make up human and historical "space-time." It requires, too, attention to the ways of coping and "acting" in this predicament, which are gathered under the rubric of "practical wisdom." It requires, finally, taking seriously the thinking, that is, the free and responsible, "subject"—though not ignoring the social construction, shaping, and distorting of this subject.[18] In all of these conditions Nomos, as to a large extent the legal tradition in which it was expressed, resembles human languages, certainly the Western languages presiding over our cultural horizons, and shares their anthropocentric premises and structure.

What may be implied is a Copernican Counter-Revolution, in which the "person" is indeed, in terms of experience, at the center of the cosmos; in which the sun indeed rises, sets, and "moves," and the individual basks, or burns, in the middle; in which social and moral choices are made; and in which human meanings are permitted to take shape. ("The earth is still the center of the metaphysical world" is Hegel's way of putting it.) This anthropocentric myth not only is embedded in language; but it corresponds to our emotional and social state, perhaps even to our "natural" reason, though we have learned to think, and occasionally to talk, differently. From other perspectives, of course, this putative "self" may disappear; but these perspectives must themselves be attached to mythical structures remote from practical reason and so irrelevant to many questions of practical judgment and action. Finding an Archimedean point is a useful hypothesis for mechanics, but we cannot stand—and we certainly cannot understand from—there.

Nor, finally, can we unlearn the lessons of modern science, but we can place them in proper and useful perspective. Proverbially, man's central position in the world has been undermined by various intellectual revolutions—the Copernican, the Darwinian, and the Freudian (and one might add, the Feminist)—but he, she, cannot act socially from those grand perspectives. Humankind can appreciate, but barely experience, the post-Copernican cosmos; understand, but not devolve into, the animal side of human nature; investigate, but not choose and act in terms of, the unconscious—and therefore must live "as if" the felt and perceived human condition indeed prevails. We continue to live anthropocentrically, to judge anthropomorphically, to live within the confines of "the small bright circle of our consciousness." And in this human world, for good or for ill, however modified by demography, technology, genetics, and psychotherapy, and whatever we may suppose or pretend, King Nomos still rules.

Notes

Preface

1. Pascal, *Pensées*, Eng. tr. (New York, 1958), no. 454.2.
2. Ibid., no. 159; cf. no. 93.
3. Cf. Nietzsche, *Twilight of the Idols*, tr. R. Hollingdale (New York, 1968), 40.
4. *Suidae lexicon, graecae et latinae* (Halle, 1953), "Nomos." On classical usage see the entry in Pauly-Wissowa, *Real-Encyclopädie der classischen Altertumswissenschaft*.
5. Paul Ricoeur, *Interpretation Theory* (Ft. Worth, 1976), 25.
6. Nietzsche, *The Will to Power*, tr. W. Kaufmann and R. J. Hollingdale (New York, 1967), 239.
7. See Chs. 3, 12.
8. See, e.g., Donald N. McCloskey, *The Rhetoric of Economics* (Madison, Wis., 1987), 11, defining "Modernism" in terms of scientism, behaviorism, operationalism, positive economics, quantitative enthusiasm, etc.; and Peter T. Manicas, *A History and Philosophy of the Social Sciences* (Oxford, 1987), 281: "The divorce of history from social science was in some ways the most devastating development in the Americanization of social science."
9. Hans Blumenberg, *Work on Myth*, tr. Robert M. Wallace (Cambridge, Mass., 1985).
10. For my views on this in a more historical mode, see my *Beginning of Ideology* (Cambridge, Eng., 1981, 1984).

1 · Introduction

1. R. G. Collingwood, *The Idea of Nature* (Oxford, 1945).
2. See Clarence J. Glacken, *Traces on the Rhodian Shore: Nature and Culture in Western Thought from Ancient Times to the End of the Eighteenth Century* (Berkeley, 1967); Hans Kelsen, *Society and Nature: A Sociological Inquiry* (Chicago, 1943); and Georges Gusdorf, *Les Sciences humaines et la pensée occidentale* (14 vols., Paris, 1966–88). See also Ch. 15.
3. Almost none of the standard histories of sociology and anthropology (see Ch. 14), which cleave generally to the old canons of philosophy or political thought, are of much value for the present enterprise, nor for the most part are general

surveys of legal and political thought, such as those of Fassò and the Carlyles, except as guides to sources.

4. Wilhelm Nestle, *Vom Mythos zum Logos* (Stuttgart, 1942); and Gusdorf, II, 98.

5. Henri Frankfort, *Before Philosophy* (Chicago, 1946), 12.

6. Richard Broxton Onians, *The Origins of European Thought* (Cambridge, Eng., 1951).

7. See Ch. 2 at n. 44.

8. Pico della Mirandola, "Oration on the Dignity of Man." On the rise and fall of this view see the controversial work of Martin Bernal, *Black Athena: The Afroasiatic Roots of Classical Civilization,* I (Brunswick, N.J., 1987).

9. Joyce O. Herzler, *The Social Thought of Ancient Civilizations* (New York, 1936), 89; cf. Paul Vinogradoff, *Outlines of Historical Jurisprudence* (Oxford, 1920), I; A. S. Diamond, *Primitive Law, Past and Present* (London, 1977). Also suggestive in this connection is the work of Georges Dumézil.

10. Calvert Watkins, "Studies in Indo-European Legal Language, Institutions, and Mythology," in *Indo-European and Indo-Europeans,* ed. G. Cardone et al. (Philadelphia, 1970), 345.

11. G. S. Kirk, *Myth: Its Meaning and Function in Greek and Other Cultures* (Cambridge, Eng., 1970), 172, and 152ff, discussing the dualism of *physis* and *nomos.*

12. Stephen Toulmin, *Human Understanding: The Collective Use and Evolution of Concepts* (Princeton, 1972), 86–87.

13. G. A. di Gennaro, *Respublica jurisconsultorum* (Naples, 1752). Cf. Max Weber, *On Law in Economy and Society,* tr. Edward Shils and Max Rheinstein (New York, 1967), 198 and 332, giving a sociological extension into modern times of the ancient Roman professional function of the *honoratiores.* See also Ch. 14.

14. Hans Blumenberg, *Work on Myth,* tr. Robert M. Wallace (Cambridge, Mass., 1985), 627.

15. A. C. Crombie, *From Augustine to Galileo* (London, 1952), I, 1.

16. Thomas Kuhn, *The Essential Tension* (Chicago, 1977), 151; and Antonio de Gennaro, *Introduzione alla storia del pensiero giuridico* (Turin, 1979).

17. Marshall Claggett, *The Science of Mechanics in the Middle Ages* (Madison, Wis., 1959), xix.

18. Frankfort, 12. Cf. Gunther Buck, "The Structure of Hermeneutical Experience and the Problem of Tradition," *New Literary History,* 10 (1978), 31–47.

19. Eugen Ehrlich, *Fundamental Principles of the Sociology of Law,* tr. Walter L. Moll (Cambridge, Mass., 1936), 98. Cf. C. Reinhold Noyes, *The Institution of Property* (New York, 1936), 49.

20. Ralph Waldo Emerson, "Ode" (inscribed to W. H. Channing).

21. See Ch. 14.

22. Emile Beneveniste, "De la subjectivité dans le langage," in *Problèmes de linguistique générale* (Paris, 1966), 258–66.

23. Hans-Georg Gadamer, *Philosophical Hermeneutics,* tr. David Linge (Berkeley, 1976), 71.

24. Ehrlich, 251.

25. See Ch. 13.
26. Ernst Robert Curtius, *European Literature and the Latin Middle Ages*, tr. W. Trask (New York, 1953); and Hans Blumenberg, *Die Lesbarkeit der Welt* (Frankfurt, 1981).
27. Walter Ullmann, *The Medieval Idea of Law as Represented by Lucas de Penna* (London, 1946), 163.
28. D. R. Kelley, "Hermes, Clio, Themis: Historical Interpretation and Legal Hermeneutics," *Journal of Modern History*, 55 (1983), 350–67 (reprinted in my *History, Law, and the Human Sciences* [London, 1984]).
29. Paul Ricoeur, *Freud and Philosophy: An Essay on Interpretation*, tr. Dennis Savage (New Haven, 1970), 4.
30. Pindar, *Nemean Odes*, IV, 346.

2 · Greek Roots

1. In general see Werner Jaeger, *Paideia*, tr. Gilbert Highet (3 vols., Oxford, 1939–45); W. K. C. Guthrie, *A History of Greek Philosophy* (6 vols., Cambridge, Eng., 1962–79); E. R. Dodds, *The Greeks and the Irrational* (Berkeley, 1951); Eric Havelock, *The Greek Concept of Justice: From its Shadow in Homer to Its Substance in Plato* (Cambridge, Mass., 1978); Bruno Snell, *The Greek Origins of European Thought* (New York, 1960); Richard Broxton Onians, *The Origin of European Thought about the Body, the Mind, the Soul, the World, Time, and Fate* (Cambridge, Eng., 1951); David B. Claus, *Toward the Soul* (New Haven, 1981); Friedrich Solmsen, "Plato and the Concept of the Soul (Psyche)," *Journal of the History of Ideas*, 44 (1983), 355–67; Ignace Meyerson, ed., *Problèmes de la personne* (Paris, 1973), articles by J.-P. Vernant, M. Détienne, and G. Le Bras; also the classic work by Nietzsche's friend Erwin Rohde, *Psyche: The Cult of Souls and Belief in Immortality among the Greeks*, tr. W. B. Hollis (New York, 1966); and finally Emile Benveniste, *Le Vocabulaire des institutions indo-européennes* (2 vols., Paris, 1969).
2. Heraclitus, Fr. 45, in Kathleen Freeman, *The Pre-Socratic Philosophers* (Oxford, 1946), 27; Jonathan Barnes, *The Presocratic Philosophers* (London, 1986), 473; and G. S. Kirk and J. E. Raven, *The Presocratic Philosophers* (Cambridge, Eng., 1971). All three works are based on H. Diels and W. Kranz, *Die Fragmente der Vorsokratiker* (Berlin, 1960).
3. Dodds, 15; and see Onians, 95.
4. Gustav Glotz, *La Solidarité de la famille dans le droit criminel* (Paris, 1904); and W. K. Lacey, *The Family in Classical Greece* (Ithaca, 1968). See also Durkheim's comments on Glotz's thesis in Stephen Lukes, *Emile Durkheim* (New York, 1972), 624; and also Ch. 14.
5. Dodds, 17.
6. James M. Redfield, *Nature and Culture in the Iliad* (Chicago, 1975), 116.
7. Brian Vickers, *Towards Greek Tragedy: Drama, Myth, Society* (London, 1973), 3.
8. Kathleen Freeman, *The Work and Life of Solon* (Cardiff, 1926), 208.
9. Havelock, 233.
10. Plato, *Cratylus*, 408. See Ch. 1, n. 10.

11. Rudolf Pfeiffer, *History of Classical Scholarship* (Oxford, 1968). See Ch. 8.
12. Mario Untersteiner, *The Sophists*, tr. K. Freeman (Oxford, 1954), 62.
13. In general see Wilhelm Nestle, *Vom Mythos zum Logos* (Stuttgart, 1942); Walter Burkert, *Structure and History in Greek Mythology and Ritual* (Berkeley, 1979); F. M. Cornford, *From Religion to Philosophy* (New York, 1957); William Green, *Moira: Fate, Good, and Evil in Greek Thought* (Cambridge, Mass., 1944); Werner Jaeger, *The Theology of the Early Greek Philosophers* (Oxford, 1947); G. S. Kirk, *Myth: Its Meaning and Function in Greek and Other Cultures* (Cambridge, Eng., 1970); Hugh Lloyd-Jones, *The Justice of Zeus* (Berkeley, 1971); Martin Persson Nilsson, *Greek Piety*, tr. H. J. Rose (Oxford, 1948); Jean-Pierre Vernant, *Myth and Society in Ancient Greece*, tr. Janet Lloyd (Atlantic Highlands, N.J., 1980), and *Mythe et pensée chez les Grecs* (Paris, 1965–74); M. L. West, *Early Greek Philosophy and the Orient* (Oxford, 1971); and Ernst Cassirer, *Logos, Dike, Kosmos in der Entwicklung der griechische Philosophie* (Göteborg, 1941).
14. Marcel Détienne and J.-P. Vernant, *Cunning Intelligence in Greek Culture and Society*, tr. Janet Lloyd (Hassocks, Sussex, 1978).
15. Hesiod, *Theogony*, tr. H. Evelyn-White (London, 1926), 144; and *Homeric Hymns*, 432.
16. Jane Ellen Harrison, *Themis* (New York, 1962), 485; and Rudolf Hirzel, *Themis, Dike, und Verwantes* (Leipzig, 1907).
17. Hesiod, *Works and Days*, tr. H. Evelyn-White (Cambridge, Mass., 1970), 20.
18. Homer, *Iliad*, XVIII, 580; and see Benveniste, II, 99–110.
19. Pindar, *Nemean Odes*, IV, 10; and Herodotus, VII, 104. Plato, *Gorgias*, 484b; and see Marcello Gigante, *Nomos Basileus* (Naples, 1956).
20. Emmanuel La Roche, *Histoire de la racine NEM- en grec ancien* (Paris, 1949). All translations are mine unless otherwise indicated.
21. Heraclitus, Fr. 32, in Freeman, *Pre-Socratic Philosophers*, 27; Xenophon, *Memorabilia*, 4.3.16.
22. Heraclitus, Fr. 44, in Freeman, *Pre-Socratic Philosophers*, 27; cf. Xenophon, *Memorabilia*, 4.3.16, cited by Guthrie, III, 227.
23. Freeman, *Solon*, 216.
24. Heraclitus, Fr. 53, in Freeman *Pre-Socratic Philosophers*, 28. See Erik Wolf, *Griechisches Rechtsdenken* (Frankfurt, 1950); also Erich Berneker, ed., *Zur Griechischen Rechtsgeschichte* (Darmstadt, 1968); Victor Ehrenberg, *Die Rechtsidee im frühen Greichtum* (Leipzig, 1921); Richard Garner, *Law and Society in Classical Athens* (New York, 1987); Glotz, *Études sociales et juridiques sur l'antiquité grecque* (Paris, 1906); J. Walter Jones, *The Law and Legal Theory of the Greeks* (Oxford, 1956); Douglas M. MacDowell, *The Law in Classical Greece* (Ithaca, 1978); Michael Gagarin, *Early Greek Law* (Berkeley, 1986); Martin Ostwald, *Nomos and the Beginnings of Athenian Democracy* (Oxford, 1969), and *From Popular Sovereignty to the Sovereignty of Law* (Berkeley, 1986); P. J. Rhodes, *The Athenian Boule* (Oxford, 1972); Jacqueline de Romilly, *La Loi dans la pensée grecque* (Paris, 1971); also S. H. Humphreys, "Law as Discourse," *History and Anthropology*, 1 (1985), 241–64, and "The Discourse of Law," *History and Law Review*, 6 (1988), 465–93.

25. Isocrates, *Areopagiticus*, 40; Tacitus, *Annals*, 3, 27.
26. Jaeger, *Paideia*, I, 103.
27. M. I. Finley, *The Ancient Greeks* (London, 1963), 36.
28. Romilly, 24.
29. Jones, 99.
30. Besides the classic work of Fustel de Coulanges, *The Ancient City*, see A. R. W. Harrison, *The Law of Athens: The Family and Property* (Oxford, 1968); and above, n. 4.
31. Plutarch's life of Solon.
32. Freeman, *Solon*, 209; cf. Victor Ehrenberg, *From Solon to Socrates* (London, 1968), 52.
33. *Demosthenes*, tr. J. H. Vince (Cambridge, Mass., 1964), vol. III.
34. La Roche, 183; and Ostwald, *Nomos*, 20ff.
35. MacDowell, 47.
36. Friedrich Solmsen, *Intellectual Experiments of the Greek Enlightenment* (Princeton, 1975); cf. Nietzsche, *the Will to Power*, tr. W. Kaufmann and R. J. Hollingdale (New York, 1967), 239.
37. In general, Guthrie, I, 55; Jones, 20; Ehrenberg, *From Solon to Socrates*, 334; G. E. R. Lloyd, *Polarity and Analogy: Two Types of Argumentation in Early Greek Thought* (Cambridge, Eng., 1966); and especially Felix Heinemann, *Nomos und Physis* (Basel, 1945).
38. Guthrie, III, 63, 141, referring also to the "historicist theory" of the Sophists; and see below, n. 66.
39. Nietzsche, "The Greek State," tr. M. Mügge, in *The Works*, ed. O. Levy (New York, 1924), II, 7.
40. Untersteiner, *The Sophists*, 121, 140.
41. Cited by Guthrie, I, 113.
42. Charles H. Kahn, *The Art and Thought of Heraclitus: An Edition of the Fragments with Translation and Commentary* (Cambridge, Mass., 1979), 260–61 and 335 (on the difference between *ethos*, "character," and *ethos*, "habit"). Cf. Martin Heidegger, "Letter on Humanism," *Basic Writings*, ed. D. Krell (New York, 1977), 233; and J. Salis and K. Maly, eds., *Heraclitean Fragments: A Companion Volume to the Heidegger-Fink Seminar on Heraclitus* (University, Ala., 1980).
43. See Ch. 6, n. 47; Ch. 11, nn. 17, 63; Ch. 12, n. 27.
44. Aristotle, *On the Soul*, tr. W. S. Hett (Cambridge, Mass., 1975), 304, and *De memoria*, II (451b13); cf. Richard Sorabji, *Aristotle on Memory* (London, 1972), 54. See also Aristotle, *Rhetoric*, I. 11 (1370a3), and *Nicomachean Ethics*, tr. H. Rackham (Cambridge, Mass., 1926), VII. 10 (1152b29–33), "for every habit is hard to change because it is a sort of nature."
45. Plato, *Cratylus*, 433.
46. The use of etymological arguments in Western (historical, social, and cultural) thought is badly in need of further study.
47. Aristotle, *Nicomachaean Ethics*, V, 7 (1134b18–21), and also VIII, 13 (1162b21).
48. Plato, *The Laws*, tr. Thomas L. Pangle (New York, 1980), 18 (638e).
49. Snell, 40.

50. Diogenes Laertius, *Lives of Eminent Philosophers*, tr. R. D. Hicks (London, 1925), IX, 61.
51. Guthrie, I, 108. Of course the locus classicus of the notion of justice as conventional and arbitrary is given by Glaucon in Plato's *Republic*, 357c. See Ch. 12, n. 28.
52. Louis Gernet, *The Anthropology of Ancient Greece*, tr. J. Hamilton and B. Nagy (Baltimore, 1981), 234.
53. Guthrie, I, 164.
54. Diogenes Laertius, IX, 61.
55. Jaeger, *Theology*, 185. In general see Untersteiner; Guthrie, I, 176ff; Carl Joachim Classen, ed., *Sophistik* (Darmstadt, 1976); George Kennedy, *The Art of Persuasion in Greece* (Princeton, 1963); Ehrenberg, *From Solon to Socrates*, 330; Rosamond Kent Sprague, *The Older Sophists* (Columbia, S.C., 1972), translating from Diels-Kranz; and especially Brian Vickers, *In Defense of Rhetoric* (Oxford, 1988).
56. Aristotle, *Politics*, III, 5 (1280b8).
57. Sprague, 79; cf. *Aristides*, tr. C. A. Behr (Cambridge, Mass., 1973), "To Plato: In Defense of Oratory."
58. Plato, *Protagoras*, tr. W. Lamb (Cambridge, Mass., 1967), 128.
59. Sprague, 291.
60. Besides Vickers, see Ch. Perelmen and L. Olbrechts-Tyteca, *The New Rhetoric*, tr. J. Wilkinson and P. Weaver (Notre Dame, 1969); John Nelson, Allan Megill, and Donald N. McCloskey, eds., *The Rhetoric of the Human Sciences* (Madison, Wis., 1987).
61. Diogenes Laertius, IX, 51; cf. Untersteiner, 19.
62. Sprague, 99.
63. Kurt Von Fritz, *The Theory of the Mixed Constitution in Classical Antiquity* (New York, 1954).
64. Isocrates, *Against the Sophists*, tr. George Norton (Cambridge, Mass., 1968).
65. Jaeger, *Paideia*, I, 143.
66. Sprague, 80. On the "Homomensurasatz" cf. (in a vast literature) Barnes, 541; Ehrenberg, *From Solon to Socrates*, 330; and Cynthia Farrar, *The Origins of Democratic Thinking* (Cambridge, Eng., 1988), 49ff. In general see Gernet; S. H. Humphreys, *Anthropology and the Greeks* (London, 1978); Thomas Cole, *Democritus and the Sources of Greek Anthropology*, Philosophical Monographs, vol. XXV (Philadelphia, 1967); and especially Clarence J. Glacken, *Traces on the Rhodian Shore: Nature and Culture in Western Thought from Ancient Times to the End of the Eighteenth Century* (Berkeley, 1967).
67. Plato, *Protagoras*, 124 (320).
68. Sprague, 90, 279.
69. Guthrie, I, 135.
70. Antiphon, *On Truth*, II, 22.
71. Glacken, 116ff.
72. E. R. Dodds, *The Ancient Concept of Progress* (Oxford, 1973), 19.
73. See François Hartog, *The Mirror of Herodotus* (Berkeley, 1988), on his "representation of the other."

3 · Roman Foundations

1. See in general Jean Bayet, *Histoire politique et psychologique de la religion romaine* (Paris, 1957); Raymond Bloch, *The Origins of Rome* (New York, 1960); Georges Cornil, *Ancient Droit romain: le problème des origines* (Paris, 1930); Georges Dumézil, *Jupiter, Mars, Quirinus* (Paris, 1941), *Naissance de Rome* (Paris, 1944), and *Archaic Roman Religion*, tr. P. Krapp (Chicago, 1970); Frederick C. Grant, ed., *Ancient Roman Religion* (New York, 1957); H. W. G. Liebeschuetz, *Continuity and Change in Roman Religion* (Oxford, 1979); Joachim Marquardt, *Römische Staatsverwaltung: Das Sacralwesen* (Leipzig, 1885); Pierre Noailles, *Du Droit sacré au droit civil* (Paris, 1949); H. J. Rose, *Primitive Culture in Italy* (London, 1926); and Emile Benveniste, *Le Vocabulaire des institutions indo-européennes* (2 vols., Paris, 1969). Reference is always made to the Mommsen-Krueger edition of the *Corpus Juris Justiniani*, Digest, Code, and Institutes (abbreviated D, C, and I), photoreproduced with facing translation by Alan Watson (Philadelphia, 1986).
2. Cornil, 27. Cf. Johannes Stroux, *Summum Ius Summa Iniuria: Ein Kapitel aus der Geschichte der Interpretatio Iuris* (Leipzig, 1926); and Carlo Alberto Maschi, *Studi sull'interpretazione dei legati* (Milan, 1938).
3. Cicero, *De oratore*, I, xlvi. Recall that "prudence" (*phronesis*), along with courage, temperance, and justice, was one of the four Stoic virtues and indeed, according to Zeno, the first one.
4. Bloch, 57.
5. Henry Sumner Maine, *Ancient Law* (London, 1861), 1.
6. Livy, *Ab urbe condita*, III, xxxiii; D. 1, 2, 2.
7. See Bayet, and especially the works of Dumézil; also Hans Ankum, "Towards a Rehabilitation of Pomponius," *Daube Noster*, ed. A. Watson (Edinburgh, 1974), 1–13.
8. Liebeschuetz, 51; Marquardt, 27; Dumézil, *Archaic Roman Religion*, II, 367.
9. Fustel de Coulanges, *The Ancient City*, Eng. tr. (New York, 1955), 112.
10. Bloch, 51.
11. Ibid., 124.
12. Ovid, *Fasti*, II, 641; cf. Grant, 11.
13. Noailles, 1; and R. Orestano, "Dal ius al fas," *Bullettino dell'Istituto di diritto romana*, 46 (1940), 194–273.
14. In general see Hildegard Temporini, ed., *Aufstieg und Niedergang der römischen Welt* (New York, 1972), including several articles on the law; Eberhard Bruch, *Uber römisches Recht im Rahmen der Kulturgeschichte* (Berlin, 1954); John Crook, *Law and Life of Rome* (Ithaca, 1967); Einar Gjerstad, *Early Rome*, vol. V, *The Written Sources* (Lund, 1973); Paul Krueger, *Geschichte der Quellen und Literatur des römischen Rechts* (Munich, 1912); Wolfgang Kunkel, *An Introduction to Roman Legal and Constitutional History* (Oxford, 1973); Fritz Schulz, *History of Roman Legal Science* (Oxford, 1953), and *Principles of Roman Law*, tr. M. Wolff (Oxford, 1936), the latter based on the classic work of Rudolf von Jhering, *Der Geist des römischen Rechts* (3 vols., Leipzig, 1852–65); Leopold Wenger, *Die Quellen des römischen Rechts*

(Vienna, 1953); C. W. Westrup, *Introduction to Early Roman Law: Comparative Sociological Studies* (4 vols., Copenhagen, 1944–50); Hans Julius Wolff, *Roman Law* (Norman, Okla., 1951), 16.

15. Gjerstad, 309; Michele Ducos, *L'Influence grecque sur la loi des douze tables* (Paris, 1978).

16. D. I, 1.

17. D. I, 2, 2.

18. Westrup, vols. II and III; cf. Jane Chance Nitzsche, *The Genius Figure in Antiquity and the Middle Ages* (New York, 1975).

19. Liebeschuetz, 51.

20. Gjerstad, 113; Westrup, II, 15; and see Bruce W. Frier, *Landlords and Tenants in Imperial Rome* (Princeton, 1980), 196ff.

21. Dumézil, *Jupiter, Mars, Quirinus*.

22. Cicero, *De republica*, tr. C. W. Keyes (New York, 1928), II, 1.

23. In general see A. S. Schiller, *Roman Law: Mechanisms of Development* (The Hague, 1978); Alan Watson, *Roman Private Law around 200 B.C.* (Edinburgh, 1971); and especially Schulz, *Roman Legal Science*.

24. Max Weber, *On Law and Society*, tr. E. Shils, ed. M. Rheinstein (New York, 1967), 214; and see Bruce W. Frier, *The Rise of the Roman Jurists* (Princeton, 1985).

25. Schulz, *Roman Legal Science*.

26. *Codex Theodosianus*, ed. Mommsen (Berlin, 1904), tr. J. C. Rolfe (Cambridge, Mass., 1967–84), I, 4, 3.

27. Aulus Gellius, *Noctes atticae*, XX, 1; and see Leofranc Holford-Strevens, *Aulus Gellius* (Chapel Hill, 1988), 218–23.

28. Cicero, *De legibus*, I, 6.

29. Crook, 138.

30. See Ch. 12.

31. D. I, 1, 1.

32. See in general E. Vernon Arnold, *Roman Stoicism* (London, 1958); Max Käser, *Roman Private Law*, tr. R. Dannenburg (Durban, 1965); Fabio Lanfranchi, *Il diritto nei retori romani* (Milan, 1938); Carol Alberto Maschi, *La concezione naturalistica del diritto degli istituti giuridici romani* (Milan, 1937); Dieter Nörr, *Divisio und Partitio* (Berlin, 1972), and *Rechtskritik in der römischen Antike* (Munich, 1974); Peter Stein, *Regulae Iuris* (Edinburgh, 1966); Uwe Wesel, *Rhetorische Statuslehre und Gesetzauslegung der römischen Juristen* (Cologne, 1967); Franz Wieacker, *Textstufen Klassischen Jurisen* (Göttingen, 1960); and again Schulz, *Roman Legal Science*.

33. Quintilian, *Institutiones oratoriae*, I, 1; and Pliny, *Naturalis historia*, XXVI, 6; also Varro, *De linguae latinae*, VIII, 27; Aulus Gellius, *Noctes atticae*, XII, 13, 29; and Sextus Empiricus, *Outlines of Pyrrhonism*, in J. Annas and J. Barnes, *The Modes of Skepticism* (Cambridge, Eng., 1985). Besides modern dictionaries, see Henri Estienne, *Thesaurus linguae latinae* and *Thesaurus linguae graecae; Suidae lexicon;* Thomas Cooper, *Thesaurus linguae graecae et brittanicae;* and Du Cange, *Glossarium mediae et infimae latinitatis*.

34. See Ch. 7 at n. 5.

35. Cicero, *De republica*, iv, 12.

36. Emmanuel La Roche, *Histoire de la racine NEM- en grec ancien* (Paris, 1949).
37. D. I, 1, 1.
38. D. I, 2, 2 ("De origine juris").
39. Schulz, *Roman Legal Science*, 62–69.
40. D. L, 17; see Stein, *Regulae Iuris;* and Ch. 12 at n. 21.
41. D. L, 17, 202.
42. I. 1, 3; cf. Peter Stein, "The Relations between Grammar and Law in the Early Principate: The Beginnings of Analogy," *La critica del testo,* 2 (1971), 757–69; also Vincenzo Scarano Ussani, *Valori e storia nella cultura giuridica fra Nerva e Adriano* (Naples, 1979); and J. Hellegouarc'h, *Le Vocabulaire latine des relations et des partis politiques dans la République* (Paris, 1972).
43. Schulz, *Roman Legal Science*, 62–69; and Marcia Colish, *The Stoic Tradition from Antiquity to the Early Middle Ages* (Leiden, 1985), I, 31ff.
44. D. I, 2, 3, 2 (Marcianus): "Sed ut philosophus summae stoicae sapientiae Chrysippus sic incipit libro, quem fecit *peri nomou: ho nomos panton esti basileus theuon te kan anthropinon pragmaton*" (translated in part as "The *nomos* is the ruler of all divine and human things"). See Ch. 11, epigraph, and Ch. 13 at n. 37.
45. In general see A. M. Honoré, *Gaius* (Oxford, 1962); also Richard Gregor Bohm, ed., *Gaius Studien* (Freiburg, 1968–); F. Bova, ed., *Prospettive sistematiche nel diritto romano* (Turin, 1976); *Gaio nel suo tempo: atti del simposio romanistico* (Naples, 1967); and Bernardo Santalucia, *L'Opera di Gaio "ad edictum praetoris urbani"* (Milan, 1975).
46. Schulz, *Roman Legal Science*, 94.
47. D. I, 5, 3; and Gaius, *Institutiones,* I, 8.
48. Henry Goudy, *Trichotomy in Roman Law* (Oxford, 1910).
49. Burkhard Schmiedel, *Consuetudo im klassischen und nachklassischen Recht* (Graz, 1966).
50. See Ch. 11 at nn. 18 and 23, and Ch. 12 at n. 36.
51. P. W. Duff, *Personality in Roman Private Law* (Cambridge, Eng., 1938); Paolo Zatti, *Persona giuridica et soggettività* (Padua, 1975); Heinz Hübner, "Subjektivismus in der Entwicklung des Privatrechts," in *Festschrift fur Max Käser* (Munich, 1976), 715–42; Peter Garnsey, *Social Status and Legal Privilege in the Roman Empire* (Oxford, 1970); Jhering, I, 3; and *Quaderni fiorentini per la storia del diritto,* 11–12 (1982–83), issue devoted to "Itinerari moderni della persona giuridica."
52. See Ch. 12, n. 56.
53. Carlo Maiorca, *La cosa in senso giuridico* (Turin, 1937); Frier, *Landlords and Tenants;* also Riccardo Orestano, "Gaio e le 'res incorporeales,'" in *Diritto, incontri, e scontri* (Bologna, 1981); Giovanni Pugliese, "'Res corporeales,' 'res incorporeales,' e il problema del diritto soggetivo," in *Studi in onore di Vincenzo Arangio-Ruiz* (Naples, 1953), III, 223–60; and Pierpaolo Zamorani, "Gaio e la distizione 'res corporeales' 'res incorporeales,'" *Labeo,* 20 (1974), 362–69, and also his *Possessio e animus* (Milan, 1977).
54. C. Reinold Noyes, *The Institution of Property* (New York, 1936), 49. See Ch. 13, n. 25.

55. Ernst Immanuel Bekker, *Die Aktionen des römischen Privatrechts* (Berlin, 1871).
56. See Weber, *On Law and Society.*
57. Gunther Buck, "The Structure of Hermeneutica Experience and the Problem of Tradition," *New Literary History,* 10 (1978), 31–47. See Max Käser, "'Ius publicum' et 'ius privatum,'" *Zeitschrift der Savigny-Stiftung fur Rechtsgeschichte,* Röm. Abt., 103 (1986), 1–101; Hans Mullejan, *Publicus und Privatus im römischen Recht und im alteren kanonischen Recht* (Munich, 1961); and Gianetto Longo, "Utilitas publica," *Labeo,* 18 (1972), 7–71.
58. Westrup, vol. II; also Vincenzo Mannino, *L'"auctoritas patrum"* (Milan, 1979).
59. D. I, 1, 1; and see Ch. 11, n. 32.

4 · Byzantine Canon

1. François Baudouin, *Commentarius de legib. XII. tab.,* in *Tractatus universi iuris* (Venice, 1584), I, 226. See in general, besides the bibliographies for Chapter 3, A. M. Honoré, *Tribonian* (Ithaca, 1978); Paul Collinet, *Etudes historiques sur le droit de Justinien* (Paris, 1912); Gerhart Ladner, "Justinian's Theory of Law and the Renewal Ideology of the *Leges Barbarorum,*" in *Images and Ideas in the Middle Ages* (Rome, 1983), II, 609–28; H. F. Jolowicz, *Roman Foundations of Modern Law* (Oxford, 1957); Max Käser, *Roman Private Law,* tr. Rolf Dannenburg (Durban, 1965); and Adolf Berger, *Encyclopedic Dictionary of Roman Law* (Philadelphia, 1953).
2. Constitution *Omnem,* prefacing Digest: ". . . quae omnia optinere sancimus in omne aeuum."
3. C. N. Cochrane, *Christianity and Classical Culture* (Oxford, 1940), 318–57.
4. Ibid., 180.
5. Honoré, *Tribonian,* 242ff.
6. Eugène Lerminier, *Philosophie du droit* (Paris, 1831), 311.
7. D. I, 1, 2, 2; and see Donald R. Kelley, "The Rise of Legal History in the Renaissance," *History and Theory,* 9 (1970), 174–94 (reprinted in *History, Law, and the Human Sciences*).
8. D. I, 1, 1; I, 2, 2; and constitutions *Omnem* and *Deo auctore;* also F. Pringsheim, "Justinian's Prohibition of Commentaries to the Digest," in his *Gesammelte Abhandlungen* (Heidelberg, 1961), 86–106. See Ch. 8, n. 16.
9. Accursius, *ad tit.*
10. Constitution *Omnem:* ". . . multas etenim formas edere natura novas deproperat."
11. See Ch. 11 at n. 21.
12. D. I, 1, 1, 1: ". . . veram nisi fallor philosophiam, non simulatam affectantes," which Accursius glosses: "Civilis sapientia vera philosophia dicitur, id est amor sapientiae." And D. I, 1, 10, 2, "Iuris prudentia est divinarum atque humanarum rerum notitia, iusti atque iniusti scientia."
13. See Eugene Rice, *The Renaissance Idea of Wisdom* (Cambridge, Mass., 1957).
14. D. I, 1, 3.
15. D. I, 1, 9.

16. D. I, 1, 3, 35, and 37. See Ch. 4, n. 16; Ch. 6, nn. 9, 47; and Ch. 8, n. 20.

17. D. L, 16 and 17. See Ch. 8, n. 16.

18. A. M. Honoré, *Gaius* (Oxford, 1962); and see Donald R. Kelley, "Gaius Noster: Substructures of Western Social Thought," *American Historical Review*, 84 (1979), 619–48 (reprinted in *History, Law, and the Human Sciences*), and the literature there cited.

19. D. I, 4, 1, and *Deo auctore*.

20. See Ch. 13 at n. 20.

21. Robert Villers, *Rome et le droit privé* (Paris, 1977), 286ff.

22. See Ch. 13, n. 56, and Ch. 14, n. 24.

23. The bibliography of the history of the *ius gentium* must be approached through that of natural law (see Ch. 12, n. 17).

24. See Ch. 11 at n. 23.

25. H. Wagner, *Studien zur allgemeinen Rechtslehre des Gaius* (Zutphen, 1978); and the article in Pauly-Wissowa, *Real-Encyclopädie der classischen Altertumswissenschaft*.

26. See Ch. 12 at n. 28.

27. Peter Stein, "The Development of the Notion of *Naturalis Ratio*," *Daube Noster*, ed. A. Watson (Edinburgh, 1974), 315.

28. D. I, 12, 1, 13; XLII, 22, 7, 15; L, 1, 33. See Fritz Schulz, *Principles of Roman Law*, tr. M. Wolff (Oxford, 1936), 109ff, which sums up the classic work by Rudolf von Jhering, *Der Geist des römischen Rechts*.

29. Ernest Levy, *West Roman Vulgar Law: The Law of Property* (Philadelphia, 1951), 7.

30. Edward Pickman, *The Mind of Latin Christendom* (Oxford, 1937), 8.

31. For what follows see Adolph Berger, *Encyclopedic Dictionary of Roman Law*, as well as modern lexicons such as those of Brisson and Calvinus (and see Ch. 12 at n. 7).

5 · Christian Tradition

1. In general see Boaz Cohen, *Law and Tradition in Judaism* (New York, 1969); W. E. Ball, *St. Paul and the Roman Law* (Edinburgh, 1901); Edward Carpenter, *Pagan and Christian Creeds* (New York, 1920); Henry Chadwick, *Early Christian Thought and the Classical Tradition* (New York, 1966); Charles Norris Cochrane, *Christianity and Classical Culture* (Oxford, 1940); Jean Dauvillier, *Histoire du droit et des institutions de l'église en Occident*, vol. II, *Les Temps apostoliques* (Paris, 1970); J. Duncan M. Derrett, *Law in the New Testament* (London, 1970); E. O. James, *The Worship of the Sky-God* (London, 1963); Werner Jaeger, *Early Christianity and Greek Paideia* (Cambridge, Mass., 1961); Jaroslav Pelikan, *The Christian Tradition* (5 vols., Chicago, 1971–89), vol. I; and A. N. Sherwin-White, *Roman Society and Roman Law in the New Testament* (Oxford, 1963). The most useful guide to patristic literature is Johannes Quasten, *Patrology* (3 vols., Utrecht, 1950–60), completed by vol. IV, tr. R. Solari from the Italian volume by several scholars (Westminster, Md., 1986). Louis Duchesne, *Early History of the Church* (London, 1909), I, 112, remarks: "It is strange that no one has attempted to draw a distinction between

nature and morality, and to trace them to two distinct sources. This is of course the result of biblical education. Given the Bible, there is no possibility of separating the Creator from the Lawgiver."

2. Chadwick, 23 (as Paul, Origen thought, had read Heraclitus).

3. M. Hyamson, ed., *Mosaicarum et Romanarum legum collatio* (London, 1913), 81, remarking that "a constitution of the Emperor Theodosius followed to the full the spirit *(mens)* of the Mosaic law."

4. A. Cancrini, *Syneidesis* (Rome, 1970); J. Stelzenberger, *Syneidesis, Conscientia, Gewissen* (Paderborn, 1963); and C. A. Pierce, *Conscience and the New Testament* (Chicago, 1955).

5. Harry Wolfson, *Philo* (Cambridge, Mass., 1962), 183 and 194, comparing the "Laws" of Moses and Plato.

6. Tertullian, *Apology,* tr. S. Thelwall (Buffalo, 1885), 21: "If your law has gone wrong, it is of human origins, I think; it has not fallen from heaven. Did not the Lacedemonians amend the law of Lycurgus himself? . . . Are you not yourselves every day, in your efforts to illumine the darkness of antiquity, cutting and hewing with the new axes of imperial rescripts, that whole ancient and rugged forest of your laws?" In general see Yves M. J. Congar, *Tradition and Traditions,* tr. M. Nasby and T. Ramborough (New York, 1966); August Deneffe, *Traditionsbegriff* (Münster, 1931); R. P. C. Hanson, *Origen's Doctrine of Tradition* (London, 1954); and Gerard E. Caspary, *Politics and Exegesis: Origen and the Two Swords* (Berkeley, 1979).

7. See Ch. 7, n. 32.

8. Gal. 3:13; and see Thomas S. Kepler, ed., *Contemporary Thinking about Paul* (New York, 1950).

9. Paul, Rom. 2:14.

10. Paul, Acts 17:28; cf. E. K. Rand, *Founders of the Middle Ages* (Cambridge, Mass., 1929).

11. Paul, Gal. 3:28; Eph. 4:5; I Tim. 1:9.

12. Tertullian, *Adversos Judaeos,* 3. 8; cf. Justin, *Dialogue with Trypho,* 18. 3 (Pelikan, I, 35).

13. Pelikan, I, 72ff.

14. Ibid., 76.

15. Caspary, 21; cf. Macklin Smith, *Prudentius's Psychomachia* (Princeton, 1976), esp. 127.

16. In general see Pelikan; Hanson; L. W. Barnard, *Justin Martyr: His Life and Thought* (Cambridge, Eng., 1967); J. Hefele-H. Leclercq, *Histoire des conciles,* vol. I (Paris, 1907); Pierre de Labriolle, *History and Literature of Christianity from Tertullian to Boethius,* tr. H. Wilson (New York, 1925); Gerhard Ladner, *The Idea of Reform: Its Impact on Christian Thought in the Age of the Fathers* (Cambridge, Mass., 1959; New York, 1925); R. A. Markus, *History and Society in the Theology of St. Augustine* (Cambridge, Eng., 1970); E. M. Pickman, *The Mind of Latin Christendom* (Oxford, 1937); and Harry Wolfson, *The Philosophy of the Church Fathers: Faith, Trinity, Incarnation* (Cambridge, Mass., 1956).

17. Irenaeus, *Against Heresies,* in *The Ante-Nicene Fathers,* ed. A. Roberts and J. Donaldson, I (Buffalo, 1885), 23, 2.

18. Hippolytus, *The Treatise on the Apostolic Tradition,* ed. G. Dix (London, 1968), 2ff.
19. Hanson, 174.
20. Origen, *Song of Songs,* tr. R. Lawson (London, 1957), 218.
21. Irenaeus, *Against Heresies,* I, 10, 2; cf. Congar, 31–37, with further references.
22. Ladner, 301.
23. Ibid., 302; cf. Matt. 11:27.
24. Eusebius *Praeparatio evangelium;* Vincent of Lerins, *Commontory,* tr. R. Morris, in *The Fathers of the Church* (New York, 1949); and see n. 18 above.
25. See Congar and Deneffe.
26. "Letter to Diognetus," tr. Cyril Richardson, in *Early Christian Fathers* (Philadelphia, 1953), 216.
27. Tertullian, *The Prescription against Heretics,* in *The Ante-Nicene Fathers,* vol. III, ed. A. Roberts and J. Donaldson (Buffalo, 1885), 243; cf. Tertullian, *Apology* and *Ad Nationes,* ibid., 21, 109.
28. J. DuQuesnay Adams, *The Populus of Augustine and Jerome* (New Haven, 1971). Cf. George Boas, *Vox Populi* (Baltimore, 1969); and Michael Hoeflich, "The Concept of Utilitas Populi in Early Ecclesiastical Law and Government," *Zeitschrift der Savigny-Stiftung für Rechtsgeschichte,* Kan. Abt., 67 (1981), 36–74.
29. John 14:6, quoted by various authors from Tertullian to Gregory VII (and later Luther). See Ladner, 138; Gerd Tellenbach, *Church, State, and Christian Society at the Time of the Investiture Contest,* tr. R. F. Bennett (Oxford, 1940), 164; and René Wehrlé, *De la coutume dans le droit canonique* (Paris, 1928), 47.
30. Augustine, *Contra Julianum Pelagium* (Patrilogia Latina, XLIV, 816); Jerome, *Epistolae,* XCVIII, 3; and Clement, *Exhortation to the Greeks.*
31. Eberhard F. Bruck, *Kirchenvater und soziales Erbrecht: Wanderungen religiöser Ideen durch die Rechte des östlichen und westlichen Welt* (Berlin, 1952). See Ch. 9 at n. 11.
32. Irenaeus, *Against Heresies,* 3.3.1.
33. Guy Swanson, *Religion and Regime* (Ann Arbor, 1967).
34. Gabriel Le Bras, *Institutions ecclésiastiques de la chrétienté médiévale* (Paris, 1959); and J. Flach in *Mélanges Fitting,* I, 383–421. In general see R. W. and A. J. Carlyle, *A History of Medieval Political Theory in the West* (6 vols., London, 1903–36); Stanley Chodorow, *Christian Political Theory and Church Politics in the Mid-Twelfth Century: The Ecclesiology of Gratian's Decretum* (Berkeley, 1972); Jean Gaudemet, *La Formation du droit séculier et du droit de l'église au IV et V siècles* (Paris, 1957), and *Eglise et société en Occident en moyen âge* (London, 1984); Pierre Legendre, *La Pénétration du droit romain dans le droit canonique classique de Gratien à Innocent IV* (Paris, 1961); Gabriel Le Bras, "Le Droit romain au service de la domination pontificale," *Revue historique de droit français et étranger,* 27 (1949), 377–98; J. Westbury-Jones, *Roman and Christian Imperialism* (New York, 1939); Tellenbach; and the works of Walter Ullmann, especially *The Growth of Papal Government in the Middle Ages* (New York, 1956).

35. Salvian, *The Governance of God,* tr. J. F. O'Sullivan (Washington, D.C., 1962), 113.
36. See Ball, 5, 17, 39.
37. See John T. McNeil and Helen M. Gerner, *Medieval Handbooks of Penance* (New York, 1938); and Oscar D. Watkin, *A History of Penance* (New York, 1920).
38. Eusebius, *Theophania,* 3.2 (cf. *Praise of Constantine,* 16.4), cited by T. E. Mommsen, *Medieval and Renaissance Studies,* ed. E. Rice (Ithaca, 1959), 283.
39. See above n. 6. Duchesne remarks that Christianity had been declared *crimen laesae religionis romanae.*
40. Isidore, *Etymologiae,* V.
41. Ullman, *Growth of Papal Government.*
42. In general see John S. Dunne, *The City of the Gods* (New York, 1965); Kenneth Setton, *Christian Attitudes toward the Empire in the Fourth Century* (New York, 1941); and n. 34 above.
43. Lactantius, *The Divine Institutes,* tr. M. MacDonald (Washington, D.C.), 338ff.
44. Rand, 16. Cf. Jaeger; Labriolle; and Cochrane.
45. Augustine, *Civitas Dei,* III, 25. Cf. R. A. Markus, *Saeculum: History and Society in the Theology of St. Augustine* (Cambridge, Eng., 1970); and H. Arquillière, *L'Augustinisme politique* (Paris, 1955).
46. Cf. Ullmann, *Growth of Papal Government,* 18.
47. P. A. van den Baar, *Die kirchliche Lehre der Translatio Imperii Romani bis zur mitte des 13 Jahrhunderts* (Rome, 1956); Werner Goez, *Translatio Imperii* (Tübingen, 1958); Percy Ernst Schramm, *Kaiser, Rom, und Renovatio* (Berlin, 1929); and Walter Ullmann, *Medieval Papalism* (London, 1949), Ch. 6.
48. Tellenbach, vii. The "battle-cry" of the Gregorian reformers furnishes the original title of this book: *Libertas Ecclesiae: Kirche und Weltordnung im Zeitalter des Investitursreites* (Stuttgart, 1936).
49. Ullmann, *Growth of Papal Government,* 359; and Ernst Kantorowicz, *The King's Two Bodies: A Study in Mediaeval Political Theology* (Princeton, 1957).
50. Ullmann, *Growth of Papal Government,* Ch. 12.
51. See Walter Ullmann, *Law and Politics in the Middle Ages* (Ithaca, 1975); Harold Berman, *Law and Revolution: The Formation of the Western Legal Tradition* (Cambridge, Mass., 1983); Charles Duggan, *Twelfth-century Decretal Collections* (London, 1963); H. E. Feine, *Kirchliche Rechtsgeschichte* (Weimar, 1955), Vol. I; Stephan Kuttner, *Kanonistische Schuldlehre von Gratian bis auf die Dekretalen Gregors IX* (Rome, 1935), and *Harmony from Dissonance* (Latrobe, Pa., 1960); Friedrich Maasen, *Geschichte der Quellen und der Literatur des canonischen Rechts* (Graz, 1870); R. C. Mortimer, *Western Canon Law* (Berkeley, 1953); Paolo Silli, *Mito e realita dell'"aequitas christiana"* (Milan, 1980); Eugen Wohlhaupter, *Aequitas canonica* (Paderborn, 1937); Wehrlé; and *The Cambridge History of Medieval Political Thought,* ed. J. H. Burns (Cambridge, Eng., 1988), esp Ch. 15, "Law," by Kenneth Pennington and J. P. Canning.
52. Vincent of Lerins, *Commontory,* 309.
53. Salvian, *The Governance of God,* tr. J. O'Sullivan (Washington, 1962), 164;

and Gregory I, *Homiliarum in Ezechielem*, 2.6, cited by Gustav Schnürer, *Church and Culture in the Middle Ages*, tr. G. Undreiner (Paterson, N.J., 1956), I, 225.

54. Patrice Cousin, *Précis d'histoire monastique*. (Paris, 1956); and see Ch. 6 at n. 10.
55. P. Fournier and G. Le Bras, *Histoire des collections canoniques en occident*. (Paris, 1931–32); and Ullmann, *Law and Politics*, with further references.
56. Domenico Maffei, *La Donazione di Costantino nei giuristi medievali* (Milan, 1964); and on canonist detection of forgeries, R. L. Poole, *Lectures on the History of the Papal Chancery down to the Time of Innocent III* (Cambridge, Eng., 1915); and Ullmann, *Law and Politics*, 128–31.
57. *The Correspondence of Pope Gregory VII*, tr. E. Emerton (New York, 1932), 194; see also Chodorow, 107, and Duggan, 14.
58. Joseph Gilchrist, ed., *The Collection in Seventy-Four Titles: A Canon Law Manual of the Gregorian Reform* (Toronto, 1980).
59. Cf. Ullmann, *Growth of Papal Government*, 169.
60. Reference is always to Emil Friedberg, ed., *Corpus Iuris Canonici* (Graz, 1959); and see Ch. 8, n. 26.

6 · Germanic Intrusions

1. Isidore of Seville, *Etymologiae*, V, 2, cited by Gratian, *Decretum*, I, d. 1. In general see Gerhard Funke, *Gewohnheit* (Bonn, 1958); Siegfried Brie, *Die Lehre vom Gewohnheitsrecht* (Breslau, 1899); Auguste Lebrun, *La Coutume* (Paris, 1932); Burkhard Schmiedel, *Consuetudo in klassischen und nachklassischen römischen Recht* (Graz, 1966); Enrico Besta, *Introduzione al diritto commune* (Milan, 1938); Francesco Calasso, *Medeo evo del diritto*, vol. I (Milan, 1954); Filippo Gallo, *Interpretazione e formazione consuetudinaria del diritto* (Turin, 1971); Eugen Ehrlich, *Fundamental Principles of the Sociology of Law*, tr. W. Moll (Cambridge, Mass., 1936); R. W. and A. J. Carlyle, *A History of Medieval Political Theory in the West* (6 vols., London, 1903–36), II, 50–67, III, 41–51, IV, 45–50, VI, 17–25, 150–53; and Walter Ullmann, *Principles of Government and Politics in the Middle Ages* (London, 1961).
2. Luigi Prosdocimi, "Ex facto ius oritur," *Studi senesi*, 66–67 (1954–55), 808–19; and Ennio Cortese, *La Norma giuridica* (Milan, 1962–64), II, 150.
3. Patrice Cousin, *Précis d'histoire monastique* (Tournai, 1956), with bibliography of monastic *consuetudines*.
4. Digest I, 3, 40; and cf. I, 3, 32, and 35; also Code, VII, 52; and in general, Adolph Berger. *Encyclopedic Dictionary of Roman Law* (Philadelphia, 1953).
5. See Ch. 3 at n. 43.
6. E.g., Cicero, *De finibus*, V, 74; Quintilian, *Institutiones oratoriae*, I, 1; Pliny, *Naturalis historia*, VII, 78; Varro, *De linguae latinae*, VIII, 27; and Aulus Gellius, *Noctes atticae*, XII, 13, 29.
7. See Andrea Alciato, *Opera omnia* (Venice, 1553), IV, 935; and Jean Coras, *De iuris arte libellus* (Lyon, 1560), 259.
8. René Wehrlé, *De la coutume dans le droit canonique* (Paris, 1928); and *Dictionnaire du droit canonique*, ed. R. Naz (Paris, 1935–65), article "Coutume."

9. D. I, 3, 37. See Ch. 4, n. 16; n. 49 in this chapter; and Ch. 8, n. 20.

10. Of the immense literature see especially J.-M. Clement, *Lexique des anciennes règles monastiques*, vol. I (A–M) (Steenbrigis, 1978), article, "Consuetudo"; Bede K. Lackner, *The Eleventh-Century Background of Cîteaux* (Washington, D.C., 1972); David Knowles, *The Monastic Order in England* (Cambridge, Eng., 1950); and Richard Yeo, *The Structure and Content of the Monastic Profession* (Rome, 1982). See also Anthony Black, *Guilds and Civil Society in European Political Thought from the Twelfth Century to the Present* (Ithaca, 1984).

11. Simeon L. Guterman, *From Personal to Territorial Law* (Metuchen, N.J., 1972); and cf. Ehrlich, 436ff.

12. Hostiensis, *In primum librum Decretalium commentaria* (Lyon, 1537); and Azo, *In ius civile summa* (Lyon, 1564), v.

13. See Peter of Ravenna (A.D. 1508), *De Consuetudine*, in *Tractatus universi juris*, II, fol. 384v, and fol. 388r on *desuetudo*. See also *Corpus juris canonici, per regulas digestas* (Cologne, 1738), I, 79.

14. Andrea de Isernia, *In usus feudorum commentaria* (Frankfurt, 1598), 1.

15. *Proverbia sententiaque Latinitatis medii aevi*, ed. Hans Walther (Göttingen, 1963), II, 377, and also 3227a.

16. Pierre de Fontaines, *Le Conseil à un ami*, ed. A. J. Marnier (Paris, 1846), 492. Cf. Aristotle, *On the Soul*, tr. W. S. Hett (Cambridge, Mass., 1975), 304; and Richard Sorabji, *Aristotle on Memory* (London, 1972), 56. See also Ch. 2, n. 44.

17. See Ernest Levy, *West Roman Vulgar Law* (Philadelphia, 1951); Fritz Kern, *Kingship and Law in the Middle Ages*, tr. S. B. Chrimes (Oxford, 1948); Ferdinand Lot, *Les Invasions germaniques* (Paris, 1945); E. A. Thomson, *The Early Germans* (Oxford, 1965); P. D. King, *Law and Society in the Visigothic Kingdom* (Cambridge, Eng., 1972); Gerhart B. Ladner, "Justinian's Theory of Law and the Renewal Ideology of the *Leges Barbarorum*," in his *Images and Ideas in the Middle Ages* (Rome, 1983), II, 609–28; and Rosamond M. McKittrick, *The Carolingians and the Written Word* (Cambridge, Eng., 1989). See also Franz Wieacker, *Privatrechtsgeschichte der Neuzeit* (Göttingen, 1967); and Adriano Cavanna, *Storia del diritto moderno in Europa* (Milan, 1982); as well as the various manuals of national law: especially Hermann Conrad and Heinrich Brunner for Germany; Paul Viollet, Jean Brissaud, Emile Chenon, and François Olivier-Martin for France; A. Pertile, Carlo Calisse, and Bruno Paradisi for Italy; Alfonso Garcia-Gallo and E. N. Van Kleffens for Spain; and Pollock and Maitland, William Holdsworth, and T. F. T. Plucknett for England.

18. *Las Siete partidas*, ed. G. Lopez (Paris, 1851), 24; and *Leyes del Fuero-Juzgo* (Madrid, 1792), 1. Cf. *Leges Visigothorum*, ed. K. Zeuner, in *Monumenta Germaniae Historica: Leges*, I (Hannover, 1902), 38ff; and L. Stouff, "L'Interpretatio de la loi romaine des Wisigothes dans les formules et les chartes du VIe au XIe siècle," *Mélanges Fitting* (Montpellier, 1908), II, 167–88.

19. *Leges Burgundiorum*, ed L. Salis, in *Monumenta Germaniae Historica: Leges*, II (1) (Hannover, 1892), 29. Cf. Katherine Fisher Drew, *The Burgundian Code* (Philadelphia, 1949).

20. *Lex Salica, 100 Titel Text,* ed. K. Eckhardt (Weimar, 1953).

21. Erwin Hölzle, *Die Idee einer altgermanischen Freiheit vor Montesquieu* (Munich, 1925).

22. Lot, 246, citing a cartulary of 757.

23. Kern, 151; and see Rolf Sprandel, "Über das Problem neueren Rechts in früheren Mittelalter, *Zeitschrift der Savigny-Stiftung fur Rechtsgeschichte,* Kan. Abt., 48 (1962), 117–37.

24. See Louis Halphen, *Charlemagne et l'empire carolingienne* (Paris, 1947); Werner Goez, *Translatio Imperii* (Tübingen, 1958); Luitpold Wallach, *Alcuin and Charlemagne* (Ithaca, 1959); H. R. Loyne, ed., *The Reign of Charlemegne* (London, 1975); Robert Folz, *Le Souvenir et la légende de Charlemagne dans l'Empire germanique médiévale. (Paris, 1950);* McKittrick; and Walter Ullmann, *The Carolingian Renaissance and the Idea of Kingship* (London, 1969).

25. Marc Bloch, *La Société féodale* (Paris, 1939), I, 177; cf. François Olivier-Martin, *Histoire de la coutume de la prévôté et vicomté de Paris,* I (Paris, 1922), 6–7.

26. Besides Bloch, *La Société féodale,* see F. L. Ganshof, *Feudalism,* tr. P. Grierson (London, 1952); and Boutruche, *Seigneurie et féodalité,* vol. I (Paris, 1959). See also K. J. Hollyman, *Le Développement du vocabulaire féodale en France pendant le haut moyen âge* (Paris, 1957); Ernst Adolph Laspeyres, *Ueber die Entstehung und älteste Bearbeitung der Libri Feudorum* (Berlin, 1830); Karl Lehmann, *Das Langobardisches Lehnrecht* (Göttingen, 1896); Marie-Louise Carlin, *La Pénétration du droit romain dans les actes de la practique provencale, XIe–XIIIe siècle* (Paris, 1967); J. S. Critchley, *Feudalism* (London, 1978); Claudio Sanchez-Albornoz y Mendina, *En torno a los origines del feudalismo,* vol. III (Mendoza, 1942); and Ch. 11, n. 31.

27. E. Meynial, "Notes sur la formation de la théorie du domaine divisé (domaine directe et domaine utile) du XIIe au XIVe siècle chez les romanistes," *Mélanges Fitting,* II, 409–61; cf. Antoine Loisel, *Institutes coutumières* (Paris, 1607), II, 2, 1.

28. See Ch. 11 at n. 42.

29. Ugo Gualazzini, "I 'Libri Feudorum' e il contributo di Accursio alla sistemazione e alla loro 'glossa,'" *Atti del convegno internazionali di studi accursiani,* ed. G. Rossi (Milan, 1965), II, 579–96.

30. See D. R. Kelley, "De Origine Feudorum: The Beginnings of an Historical Problem," *Speculum,* 39 (1964), 207–28 (reprinted in *History, Law, and the Human Sciences*).

31. Henri Beaune, *Introduction historique à l'etude historique du Droit coutumier français* (Paris, 1880); Robert Besnier, *La Coutume de Normandie* (Paris, 1935); Marc Bloch, *French Rural History,* tr. J. Sondheimer (Berkeley, 1966); Gaston Roupnel, *Histoire de la campagne française* (Paris, 1932); Emile Champeaux, "Coutumes de Bourgogne et coutumes du duché de Bourgogne," *Mémoires de la Société pour l'histoire du droit et des institutions des anciens pays bouguignons [MSHDB],* 2 (1935), 47–76; M. Petitjean, "La Coutume de Bourgogne: des coutumes officieux à la coutume officielle," *MSHDB,* 42 (1985), 13–20; Paul Viollet, "Les Coutumes de Normandie," *Histoire littéraire*

de la France, 33 (Paris, 1906), 41–190; and Jean Yver, "Les caractères originaux du groupe de coutumes de l'Ouest de la France," *Revue historique de droit français et étranger*, 30 (1952), 5–36.

32. John Cowell, *The Interpreter* (Cambridge, Eng., 1607), "Custom."

33. Emily Zack Tabuteau, *Transfers of Property in Eleventh-Century Normandy* (Chapel Hill, 1988), 2, 226.

34. Jacques d'Ableiges, *Le Grand Coustumier de France*, ed. L. Le Caron (Paris, 1598), 102; Jean Bouteiller, *Somme rurale* (Paris, 1603), 5.

35. Gilles Fortin, *Conference de la coustume de Paris, avec les autres coustumes de France* (Paris, 1605), "Epitre"; cf. Guy Coquille, *Commentaires sur les coustumes de Nivernois*, in *Les Oeuvres* (Paris, 1646), 2.

36. M. T. Clanchy, *From Memory to Written Record: England, 1066–1307* (London, 1979); and J. P. Dawson, *A History of Lay Judges* (Cambridge, Mass., 1960).

37. Olivier-Martin; and in general see the listings in Andre Gouron and Odile Terrin, *Bibliographie des coutumes de France* (Geneva, 1975), and in Jean Caswell and Ivan Sipkov, *The Customs of France in the Library of Congress* (Washington, D.C., 1977).

38. E. N. Van Kleffens, *Hispanic Law until the End of the Middle Ages* (Edinburgh, 1968), 39ff.

39. J. P. Dawson, *Oracles of the Law* (Ann Arbor, 1968), 154.

40. See Erik Wolf, *Grosse Rechtsdenker* (Tübingen, 1963), 1–27; and Hermann Conrad, *Deutsche Rechtsgeschichte*, I (Karlsruhe, 1954), 476.

41. R. C. Van Caenegem, *Royal Writs in England from the Conquest to Glanville* (London, 1959); Fredric Cheyette, "Custom, Case Law, and Medieval 'Constitutionalism': A Reconsideration," *Political Science Quarterly*, 88 (1963), 362–90; and see Ch. 10, n. 7.

42. H. Pissard, *Essai su la conaissance et la preuve des coutumes* (Paris, 1910); *La Preuve: Recueil de la Société Jean Bodin pour l'histoire comparative des institutions* (4 vols., Brussels, 1963–65); and Piero Craveri, *Ricerche sulla formazione del diritto consuetudinario in Francia (sec. XIII–XVI)* (Milan, 1969).

43. Cited by Aubépin, "De l'influence de Dumoulin sur la législation française," *Revue de législation et de jurisprudence*, 6 (1855), 77.

44. *Très ancien Coutumier de Normandie*, ed. E. J. Tardif (Paris, 1896), 2. See the works cited above in notes 1 and 30; and also Olivier Guillot, "Consuetudines, consuetudo," *MSHDB*, 40 (1983), 21–48; and Paul Guilhiermoz, "La Persistance du caractère oral dans la procédure civile française," *Nouvelle Revue historique de droit français et étranger*, 13 (1889), 21–65.

45. Bouteiller, 6.

46. Beaumanoir, *Coutumes de Beauvaisis*, ed. A. Salmon (Paris, 1889), I, 3.

47. See Ch. 1, n. 2, and Ch. 11, n. 63.

48. Loisel, I, 1, 3, and II, 5, 1; also *Coutume de Paris*, art. 318. And on *Rex non moritur* see the classic study of Ernst Kantorowicz, *The King's Two Bodies* (Princeton, 1957), 408.

49. Odofredus, *Lectura super Codice* (Lyon, 1552), fol. 3r; cf. Vicarius, cited by Paul Vinogradoff, *Roman Law in Medieval Europe* (Oxford, 1949), 57.

50. A. Esmein, "Decem faciunt populum," *Mélanges P. F. Girard* (Paris, 1912), I,

457–73; cf. Jeremy Duquesnay Adams, *The* Populus *of Augustine and Jerome* (New Haven, 1971).
51. Azo, *In ius civile summa* (Lyon, 1564), fol. 233v; and Odofredus, *Lectura super Digesto veteri* (Lyon, 1550), fol. 14r; cf. Digest I, 3, 37.
52. Gaines Post, *Studies in Medieval Legal and Political Thought* (Princeton, 1964).
53. See Ch. 10 at n. 72; cf. Daniel Boorstin, *The Mysterious Science of Law* (Cambridge, Mass., 1941).
54. See Ch. 11 at n. 41.
55. Montesquieu, *De l'esprit des loix*, L. XXVII, ch. 45.
56. Bloch, *French Rural History*, 46.
57. Beaumanoir, *Coutumes de Beauvaisis*, I, 436. Cf. Loisel, 46; and Roland and Boyer, *Locutions latines et adages du droit français contemporain* (Lyon, 1978), I, 118.
58. Bloch, *French Rural History*, 70 and 59 (citing Laurière).

7 · *Medieval Reconstruction*

1. See, besides the works cited in the previous chapter—and especially Helmut Coing, ed., *Handbuch der Quellen und Literatur der neueren europäischen Privatrechtsgeschichte* (Munich, 1973), vol. I, with extensive bibliography—C. H. Haskins, *The Renaissance of the Twelfth Century* (Cambridge, Mass., 1927); Hastings Rashdall, *The Universities of Europe in the Middle Ages* (Oxford, 1936); Paul Koschaker, *Europa und das römische Recht* (Munich, 1953); Walter Ullmann, *Law and Politics in the Middle Ages* (Ithaca, 1975); Paul Vinogradoff, *Roman Law in Medieval Europe* (Oxford, 1927); Eduard Meijers, *Etudes d'histoire du droit* (4 vols., Leiden, 1956–66); and Stephan Kuttner, "The Revival of Jurisprudence"; as well as Knut Wolfgang Norr, "Institutional Foundations of the New Jurisprudence," in *Renaissance and Renewal in the Twelfth Century*, ed. R. Benson and G. Constable (Cambridge, Mass., 1982), 299–338; James A. Brundage, "The Medieval Advocate's Profession," *Law and History Review*, 6 (1988), 439–93; and *The Cambridge History of Medieval Political Thought* (Cambridge, Eng., 1988), esp. ch. 15.
2. Chrétien de Troyes, *Cligés*, lines 35–38.
3. Alexander of Roes, *De translatione imperii*, tr. in Ewart Lewis, *Medieval Political Ideas* (New York, 1954), II, 466.
4. *Summa Lipsiensis*, cited by Sergio Mochy Onory, *Fonti canonistiche dell'idea moderno dello stato* (Milan, 1951), 174.
5. Odofredus, *Super Digesto veteri* (Lyon, 1550), fol. 2r; cf. Azo, *Digestum vetus, ad tit.*; Baldus, *Super Digesto veteri* (n.p., 1535), fol. 3r; and Pierre Rebuffi, *De privilegiis scholasticorum tractatus varii* (Lyon, 1581), 500; and see Ch. 8 at n. 47.
6. See Charles Radding, *The Origins of Medieval Jurisprudence: Paris and Bologna, 850–1150* (New Haven, 1988), even though his arguments for the priority of Lombard over Bolognese jurisprudence have not been well received.
7. Haskins, 201: "Bulgarus os aureum,/ Martinus copia legum,/ Mens legum est Ugo,/ Jacobus id quod ego."

8. *Monumenta Germaniae Historica: Constitutiones*, I, ed. L. Weiland (Hannover, 1893), 249; and see Ch. 8 at n. 16.
9. Henri d'Andeli, *The Battle of the Seven Arts*, tr. L. Paetow (Berkeley, 1914), 43.
10. Otto of Freising, *The Deeds of Frederick Barbarossa*, tr. C. Mierow (New York, 1952), 61.
11. G. A. di Gennaro, *Respublica jurisconsultorum* (Naples, 1752).
12. Karl O. Apel, *Transformation der Philosophie* (Frankfurt, 1976), II, 178–221; Max Weber, *On Law in Economy and Society*, tr. E. Shils and M. Rheinstein (Cambridge, Mass., 1954), 198–223; and see Johannes Fried, *Die Entstehung des Juristenstandes im 12. Jahrhundert* (Cologne, 1974).
13. Collected texts are in: S. Caprioli et al., eds., *Glosse preaccursiane alle istitutione* (Rome, 1984); Ugo Nicolini, ed., *Per lo studio dell'ordinamento giuridico nel commune medievale* (Milan, 1972); and Rudolph Weigand, *Die Naturrechtslehre der Legisten und Dekretisten von Irnerius bis Accursius und von Gratian bis Johannes Teutonicus* (Munich, 1967). In general see Woldemar Engelmann, *Die Wiedergeburt der Rechtskultur in Italien durch der wissenschaftliche Lehre* (Leipzig, 1939); Winfried Trusen, *Anfänge des gelehrten Rechts in Deutschland* (Wiesbaden, 1962; Riccardo Orestano, *Introduzione allo studio del diritto romano* (Bologna, 1987), 26–36, "Scienza giuridico europea"; Francesco Calasso, *I glossatori e la teoria della sovranità* (Milan, 1951); Gerhard Otte, *Dialektik und Jurisprudenz* (Frankfurt, 1971); Theodor Vieweg, *Topik und Jurisprudenz* (Munich, 1974); Ennio Cortese, *La norma giuridica* (2 vols., Milan, 1962–64); Ernst Kantorowicz, *The King's Two Bodies* (Princeton, 1957); Gaines Post, *Studies in Medieval Legal and Political Thought* (Princeton, 1964); R. W. and A. J. Carlyle, *A History of Medieval Political Theory in the West* (6 vols.), London, 1903–36), vol. II; Eugenio Dupre Theseider, *L'Idea imperiale di Roma nella tradizione del medioevo* (Milan, 1942); *Atti del convegno internazionali di studi accursiani*, ed. G. Rossi (3 vols., Milan, 1968); and especially *Ius Romanum Medii Aevi* (Milan, 1961–), a work in 24 parts by various experts, with a European-wide scope.
14. Fritz Schulz, *History of Roman Legal Science* (Oxford, 1953), 279. Cf. Luigi Prosdocimi, "'Ius vetus' accursiano e 'ius novum' postaccursiano," in *Atti*, III, 947–51.
15. Hermann Kantorowicz, "Note on the Development of the Gloss to the Justinian and the Canon Law," in B. Smalley, *The Study of the Bible in the Middle Ages* (Oxford, 1952), 52–55, and "A Medieval Grammarian on the Sources of the Law," *Tijdschrift voor Rechtsgeschiedenis*, 15 (1937), 25–47; also Hugolinus, cited by K. F. von Savigny, *Geschichte des römischen Rechts im Mittelalter* (6 vols., Heidelberg, 1815–31), III, 553. See also Edwin A. Quain, "The Medieval Accessus ad Auctores," *Traditio*, 3 (1945), 215–64; Carlo Alberto Maschi, "Accursio, precursore del metodo storico-critico nello studio del'corpur iuris civilis," in *Atti*, II, 599–618; and J. A. C. Smith, *Medieval Law Teachers and Writers* (Ottawa, 1975).
16. *Quaestiones de iuris subtilitatibus*, ed. G. Zanetti (Florence, 1958); also Nicolini, *Per lo studio dell'ordinamento giuridico* and *Aspetti dell'insegnamento giuridico nella universita medievali* (Reggio Calabria, 1974).

17. Digest L, 17, 207, gloss.
18. *Dissensiones dominorum sive controversiae veterum iuris romani interpretum qui glossatores vocantur,* ed. G. Haenel (Leipzig, 1834), 151–52; cf. J. P. Dawson, *Oracles of the Law* (Ann Arbor, 1968), 129–30; and more generally, Hermann Krause, "Dauer und Vergänglichkeit im mittelalterlichen Recht," *Zeitschrift der Savigny-Stiftung für Rechtsgeschichte,* Ger. Abt., 75 (1958), 206–51.
19. See, e.g., Baldus, *Super Digesto veteri* (n.p., 1535), fol. 211; and Andrea de Isernia, *In usus feudorum commentaria* (Frankfurt, 1598), 4. See also Cortese, I, 184; and Ch. 8 at n. 37.
20. Adriano Cavanna, *Storia del diritto moderna in Europa,* I (Milan, 1982), 353. See also Otte, 62; and D. R. Kelley, "Gaius Noster," *American Historical Review,* 84 (1979), 619–48 (reprinted in *History, Law, and the Human Sciences*).
21. Weigand, 51.
22. Ibid., 155.
23. Paolo Grossi, *Le situazioni reali nell'esperanza giuridica medievale* (Padua, 1968); Wilhelm Endemann, *Studien in der römisch-kanonistischen Wirthschafts- und Rechtslehre* (Berlin, 1874–83); C. Karsten, *Die Lehre von Vertrag bei den italienischen Juristen der Mittelalters* (Rostok, 1882); and C. Lefebvre, *Juges et savants en Europe du XIIIe au XVIe siècle* (Rome, 1965).
24. See Ch. 8 at n. 40.
25. Pierre Michaud-Quantin, *Universitas: expression du mouvement communitaire dans le moyen-âge latin* (Paris, 1970), and *Études sur le vocabulaire philosophique du moyen âge* (Rome, 1970); and also Pietro Costa, *Iurisdictio: semantica del potere politico nella pubblicistica medievale, 1100–1433* (Milan, 1969).
26. Emil Friedberg, ed., *Corpus Iuris Canonici* (Graz, 1959); and see G. Lebras, *Histoire du droit at des institutions de l'Église en Occident,* I, *Prolegomènes,* and, with C. Lefebvre and J. Rambaud, VII, *L'Age classique, 1140–1378* (Paris, 1965). See also Stephan Kuttner, *Harmony from Dissonance* (Latrobe, Pa., 1960), and his many articles collected in *Gratian and the Schools of Law, 1140–1234* (London, 1983), *Medieval Councils, Decretals, and Collections of Canon Law* (London, 1980), and *The History of Ideas and Doctrines of Canon Law in the Middle Ages* (London, 1980); Harold Berman, *Law and Revolution: The Formation of the Western Legal Tradition* (Cambridge, Mass., 1983); and, further, Lefebvre, *Juges et savants,* and *Les Pouvoirs du juge en droit canonique* (Paris, 1938); P. A. Van den Baar, *Die kirchliche Lehre der Translatio Imperii Romani* (Rome, 1956); Stanley Chodorow, *Christian Political Theory and Church Politics in the Mid-Twelfth Century: The Ecclesiology of Gratian's Decretum* (Berkeley, 1972); Charles Duggan, *Twelfth-Century Decretal Collections* (London, 1963); Mochy Onory; and R. G. G. Knox, "Rufinus and Stephan on Church Judgment" (Ph. D. diss., Yale University, 1976).
27. Glenn Olsen, "The Idea of the Ecclesias Primitiva in the Writings of the Twelfth-Century Canonists," *Traditio,* 25 (1969), 61–86.
28. Kantorowicz, *King's Two Bodies;* Pierre Gillet, *La Personnalité juridique en droit ecclésiastique* (Mainz, 1927); Paolo Grossi, "'Unanimitas,' alle origine del concetto di persona giuridica nel diritto canonico," *Annali di storia del*

diritto, 2 (1958), 229–331; Melchiore Roberti, "Il corpus mysticum nella storia della persona giuridica," in *Studi di storia e diritto in onore di Enrico Besta* (Milan, 1939), IV, 37–82; and R. E. Giesey, "The French Estates and the Corpus Mysticum Regni," *Album Maude Cam* (Louvain, 1960), 155–71; also Walter Ullmann, *Principles of Government and Politics in the Middle Ages* (London, 1961).

29. See Charles Lefebvre, "Le Droit canonique dans les additions à la glose du Code de Justinian: le ius commune," *Studia Gratiani,* 12 (1967), 331–58; and E. F. Vodola, "Fides et Culpa: The Use of Roman Law in Ecclesiastical Ideology," in *Authority and Power,* ed. B. Tierney and P. Linehan (Cambridge, Eng., 1980), 83–97.

30. R. C. Mortimer, *Western Canon Law* (Berkeley, 1953); Oswald J. Reichel, *A Complete Manual of Canon Law* (London, 1896); Stephan Kuttner, *Kanonistische Schuldlehre* (Rome, 1935); Clarence Gallagher, *Canon Law and the Christian Community* (Rome, 1978), on Hostiensis; J. Gilchrist, *The Church and Economic Activity in the Middle Ages* (New York, 1969); Frederick W. Russell, *The Just War in the Middle Ages* (Cambridge, Eng., 1975); and Berman, 218ff.

31. Friedrich Maasen, *Geschichte der Quellen und der Literatur des canonischen Rechts* (Graz, 1870); Joh. Friedrich von Schulte, *Die Geschichte der Quellen und Literatur des canonischen Rechts* (Stuttgart, 1880); and Vodola.

32. See, e.g., Albericus de Rosate, *Commentariorum . . . super Digesto veteri* (Lyon, 1545), fol. 11r, "Natura naturans est Deus: natura autem naturata est homo;" cf. Hostiensis, *Summa* (Lyon, 1537), fol. 2v; and Reginaldo Pizzorini, *Il diritto naturali delle origini a s. Tommaso d'Aquino* (Rome, 1978). See also Brian Tierney, "Natura id est Deus: A Case of Juristic Pantheism?" *Journal of the History of Ideas,* 24 (1963), 307–22.

33. John Baldwin, "Critics of the Legal Profession: Peter the Chanter and His Circle," *Proceedings of the Second International Congress of Medieval Canon Law* (Rome, 1965), 249–59.

34. Azo, *In ius civile summa* (Venice, 1566), fol. 233v; Odofredus, *Lectura super Digesto veter.* (Lyon, 1550), fol. 14v, following Digest I, 3, 37.

35. Fritz Schulz, *Principles of Roman Law,* tr. M. Wolff (Oxford, 1936), 109.

36. Hermann Krause, *Kaiserrecht und Rezeption* (Heidelberg, 1952); Percy Ernst Schramm, *Der König von Frankreich* (Weimar, 1960); Kantorowicz, *King's Two Bodies,* ch. 7; and Mochi Onory, 96ff.

37. See Ch. 8 at n. 16.

38. Arthur Duck, *De usu et autoritate juris civilis Romanorum per dominia principum christianorum* (London, 1653).

39. Karl Lehmann, *Das langobardische Lehnrecht* (Göttingen, 1896); E. A. Laspeyres, *Ueber die Entstehung und älteste Bearbeitung der libri feudorum* (Berlin, 1830); and Ugo Gualazzini, "I 'Libri feudorum' e il contributo di Accursio alla loro sistemazione e alla loro 'glossa,'" in *Atti,* II, 579–96.

40. William Durandus, *Speculum* (Lyon, 1547), fols. 117r–124v; and Accursius, *Digestum vetus, ad tit.,* "nam civilis sapientia vera philosophia dicitur et est amor sapientiae." Cf. Andrea de Isernia, 5.

41. Thea Buyken, *Das römische Recht in den Constitutionem von Melfi* (Cologne, 1960); and *The Liber Augustalis,* tr. James Powell (Syracuse, 1971).

42. Jacob Burckhardt, *Civilization of the Renaissance in Italy,* tr. S. G. C. Middlemore (London, 1950), 2.
43. See Ch. 13 at n. 12.
44. Duck, *de usu,* 235.
45. See Ch. 8 at n. 21.
46. See Ch. 6 at n. 46, and Ch. 11; also André Gouron, "Die Entstehung der französischen Rechtsschule: Summa Iustiniani est in hoc opere and Tübinger Rechtsbuch," *Zeitschrift der Savigny-Stiftung für Rechtsgeschichte,* Röm. Abt., 93 (1976), 138–60.
47. L. Waelkens, *La Théorie de la coutume chez Jacques de Révigny* (Leiden, 1984), with edition of MS texts; and Cortese, index.
48. See especially F. W. Maitland, ed., *Selected Passages from the Works of Bracton and Azo* (London, 1895); and H. G. Richardson, *Bracton: The Problem of His Text* (London, 1965).
49. Albericus de Rosate, *In Primam ff. [Digesti] Veter. Part. Commentarii* (Venice, 1585), fol. 46; and cf. Giason del Maino, *In Primam Digesti Veteris Partem Commentarii* (Venice, 1589), *Praefatiuncula.* See also James Muldoon, *Popes, Lawyers, and Infidels* (Philadelphia, 1979); and Steven Rowan, *Ulrich Zasius* (Frankfurt, 1987), 44.
50. See Ch. 12 at n. 42.

8 · Jurisprudence Italian Style

1. Most useful (in a massive technical literature on jurisprudence) are Helmut Coing, ed., *Handbuch der Quellen und Literatur der neueren europäischen Privatrechtsgeschichte* (2 vols., Munich, 1973–77); Adriano Cavanna, *Storia del diritto moderno in Europa,* vol. I (Milan, 1982); Walter Ullmann, *Law and Politics in the Middle Ages* (Ithaca, 1975); Ennio Cortese, *La norma giuridica* (2 vols., Milan, 1962–64); Enrico Besta, *Introduzione al diritto commune* (Milan, 1938); Riccardo Orestano, *Introduzione alla studia storica del diritto romano* (Turin, 1963); Woldemar Engelmann, *Die Wiedergeburt der Rechtskultur in Italien durch die wissenschaftliche Lehre* (Leipzig, 1939); E. M. Meijers, *Etudes d'histoire du droit* (4 vols., Leiden, 1956–66); Ernst Kantorowicz, *The King's Two Bodies* (Princeton, 1957); Pietro Costa, *Iurisdictio: semantica del potere publico nella pubblistica medievale, 1100–1400* (Milan, 1969); Vincenzo Piano Mortari, *Dogmatica e interpretazione* (Naples, 1976); and *La formazione storica del diritto moderno in Europa,* Atti del III congresso internazionale del diritto moderno in Europa (3 vols., Florence, 1977); also D. R. Kelley, "Civil Science in the Renaissance: Jurisprudence Italian Style," *Historical Journal,* 22 (1979), 777–94, and "Vera Philosophia: The Philosophical Significance of Renaissance Jurisprudence," *Journal of the History of Philosophy,* 14 (1976), 267–79 (both reprinted in my *History, Law, and the Human Sciences*); and the literature on individual jurists as noted below.
2. Nicolas Reusner, ed., *CHEIRAGOGIA, sive cynosura iuris* (Spires, 1588), appendix; also in Guido Kisch, *Studien zur humanistischen Jurisprudenz* (Berlin, 1972), 46.
3. Accursius, *Digestum vetus, ad tit.;* cf. Chasseneuz, *Catalogue gloriae mundi* (Frankfurt, 1586), fol. 207r.

4. Baldus, *Lectura in Codicem* (Paris, 1528), *ad tit.;* and see G. Monti, *Cino da Pistoia giurista* (Citta di Castello, 1924); G. Zaccagnini, *Cino da Pistoia* (Pistoia, 1918); the collaborative volume, *Cino da Pistoia nei VI centenario della morte* (Pistoia, 1937); Engelmann, 204; and William Bowsky, "A New Consilium of Cino of Pistoia (1324): Citizenship, Residence, and Taxation," *Speculum,* 42 (1967), 431–41. Baldus is quoted from *L'Opera di Baldo, per cura dell'Università di Perugia nel V centenario della morte del grande giureconsulto* (Perugia, 1901), 78. See Norbert Horn, *Aequitas in den Lehren des Baldus* (Cologne, 1968); and especially Joseph Canning, *Baldus de Ubaldis* (Cambridge, Eng., 1987).

5. See, e.g., Bartolus, *In primam ff.* [*Digesti*] *veteris partem commentaria* (Turin, 1574), fol. 13v; Baldus, *Super Digesto veteri commentarii* (n.p., 1535), fol. 12r, and *In praelectiones ad Codicem* (Lyon, 1556), fol. 5r; Placentinus, *Summa Codicis* (Mainz, 1536), 17; and Odofredus, *Lectura super Codice* (Lyon, 1522), fol. 3r; also Emilio Albertario, "Hodie," in *Studi di diritto romano,* VI (Milan, 1953), 125–42; Cortese, I, 81; Calasso, *I glossatori e la teoria della sovranità* (Milan, 1951), 38; and Ullmann, *The Medieval Idea of Law as Represented by Lucas de Penna* (London, 1946), 49.

6. Belleperche, *In aliquot Cod. leges* (Frankfurt, 1571), 8 (a passage which, according to Baldus, Bartolus published as his own—see *Dictionnaire de biographie française*); Baldus, *Super Digesto veteri,* fol. 12r, and *Repetitio super lege cunctos populos (C. 1.1.1),* ed. E. Meijers (Haarlem, 1939); Albericus de Rosate, *Commentariorum . . . super Codice* (Lyon, 1545), fol. 7r; and Giason del Maino, *In primam Codicis partem commentaria* (Venice, 1589), fol. 2v.

7. See the classic work, C. N. S. Woolf, *Bartolus of Sassoferrato* (Cambridge, Eng., 1913); the collection *Bartolo da Sassoferrato: studi e documenti per il VI. centenario* (Milan, 1962); and Y. Sasaki, "Ius gentium in der Lehre des Bartolus," in *Satura Roberto Feenstra,* ed. J. A. Ankum et al. (Freiburg, 1985), 421–36.

8. Cortese, I, 86; Horn, 74; Besta, 43; and Ullmann, *Lucas de Penna,* 107.

9. Alciato, *De verborum significatione,* in *Opera omnia* (Milan, 1617), I, 461; and Luigi Palazzini Finetti, *Storia della ricerca della interpolazioni nel corpus iuris giustinianeo* (Milan, 1953), 21. Cf. P. C. Brederode, *Thesaurus dictionum et sententiarum ex Bartoli a Saxoferrato operibus* (Frankfurt, 1660).

10. Baldus, *Super Digesto,* fol. 4r.

11. R. Stintzing, *Das Sprichwort "Juristen böse Christen"* (Bonn, 1875); and C. Kenny, "Bonus Jurista, Malus Christa," *Law Quarterly Review,* 19 (1903), 326ff.

12. Coing, *Handbuch,* I, 39–128, II, 3–102.

13. John P. Dawson, *A History of Lay Judges* (Cambridge, Mass., 1960), 69.

14. Roberto Weiss, *The Dawn of Humanism in Italy* (London, 1947), 5.

15. See Ch. 3 at n. 25.

16. Johann Oldendorp, *Interpretatio privilegii duplicis* (n.p., 1543), and Justinian's constitution *Omnem.* See also Cortese; Piano Mortari, *Dogmatica;* Orestano, 51–131; Mario Sbriccoli, *L'Interpretazione dello statuto* (Milan, 1969); and D. R. Kelley, "Civil Science in the Renaissance: The Problem of Interpretation," in *The Languages of Political Theory in Early-Modern Europe,* ed. Anthony

Pagden (Cambridge, Eng., 1987), 57–78, with further references; and Ch. 11 at n. 6.

17. P. Gammaro, *De extensionibus*, in *Tractatus universi iuris* (10 vols., Venice, 1583), XVIII, 248, "Nam ista interpretatio est pars ipsius iuris."

18. Digest 1, 3, 17.

19. Baldus, *Super Digesto veteri*, fol. 4v; and Bartolus, *Commentaria*, fols. 16 and (on the *regulae antiqui iuris*) 248; see also Vincenzo Piano Mortari, *Richerche sulla teoria dell' interpretazione del diritto nel secolo XVI* (Milan, 1956), 68ff; and Engelmann, 152ff.

20. Odofredus, *Lectura super Digesto veteri* (Lyon, 1550), fol. 14r; cf. Azo, *In ius civile summa* (Lyon, 1564), fol. 233v; Digest, I, 3, 37; and see Ch. 4, n. 16.

21. Révigny, *Lectura super Codice* (Paris, n.d.), on Code I, 14, 5; Belleperche, *In libros Institutionum . . . commentarii* (n.p., n.d.), on Institutes I, 1, 3; cf. also E. Meijers, III, 59, 95; and W. M. Gordon, "Cinus and Pierre de Belleperche," *Daube Noster*, ed. A. Watson (Edinburgh, 1974), 105–17.

22. Norbert Bobbio, *L'Analogia nella logica del diritto* (Turin, 1938).

23. Digest L, 17, 202.

24. Ullmann, *Lucas de Penna*, 111ff.

25. Bartolus, *Commentaria*, fol. 21r.

26. Baldus, *Super Digesto veteri*, fol. 10r; and cf. C. Karsten, *Die Lehre von Vertrage bei den italienischen Juristen des Mittelalters* (Rostok, 1881), on contractual actions.

27. Bartolus, fol. 22v. See also Pierre Rebuffi, *Explicatio ad quartuor primos Pandectarum libros* (Lyon, 1589), 1; and Jacques de Révigny, cited by Cortese, II, 32.

28. Claude de Seyssel, *Speculum feudorum* (Basel, 1566), 11.

29. Albericus de Rosate, in *Tractatus des statutis, diversorum autorum et j. c. in Europea praestantissimorum* (Frankfurt, 1608), 10. See also P. C. Brederode, *Thesaurus dictionum et sententiarum ex Bartoli a Saxoferrato operibus* (Frankfurt, 1660): "Interpretatio extensiva non habet locum in statutis," "interpretatio probabilis non est necessaria," "Statutorum interpretatio fieri debet per conditores," "Verborum interpretatio fieri debet secundum communem usum loquendi," etc.

30. Dante dal Re, *I precursori italiani di una nuova scuola di diritto romano nel secolo XV* (Rome, 1878), 31.

31. D. R. Kelley, *Foundations of Modern Historical Scholarship* (New York, 1970), 37ff. Valla's attack on Bartolus appears in his letter to Pier Candido Decembrio in *Opera omnia* (Turin, 1962), I, 633.

32. Andrea Alciato, *De verborum significatione* (Lyon, 1536), 86, and also 92 (*extensio de similibus ad similia*), 91 (*legis correctio*), and 90 ("Qua propter qui hodie est communis usus, olim fuisse non praesumitur"). See Hans Troje, "Alciats Methode der Kommentierung des "corpus iuris civilis," in A. Buck and O. Herding, eds., *Der Kommentar in der Renaissance* (Godesburg, 1975); Guido Kisch, *Erasmus und die Jurisprudenz seiner Zeit* (Basel, 1960); and *La critico del testo* (Florence, 1971), on the history of law.

33. Alciato, 13, 202.

34. See above, n. 1.

35. Cited by Calasso, *Medio evo del diritto* (Milan, 1954), 571. And see D. R. Kelley, "The Prehistory of Sociology: Montesquieu, Vico, and the Legal Tradition," *Journal of the History of the Behavioral Sciences,* 16 (1980), 133–44 (reprinted in *History, Law, and the Human Sciences*). Cf. Alciato, 20.

36. Giason del Maino, *In Primam Digesti Veteris Partem Commentaria* (Venice, 1589), on D. 1, 1, 9; see also Baldus, *Super Digesto veteri,* fol. 3r; also Cortese, 184ff; and A. London Fell, *The Origins of Legislative Sovereignty* (3 vols., Königstein, 1983–87). See more generally Robert Merton, *Social Causation* (Boston, 1942); and H. L. A. Hart and A. M. Honoré, *Causation in the Law* (Oxford, 1959).

37. André Tiragueau, *Tractatus Varii* (Lyon, 1574); cf. Jacques Brejon, *André Tiraqueau, 1488–1558* (Paris, 1937); and Cortese, index.

38. Chasseneux, *Catalogus gloriae mundi,* fol. 209v; A. Favre, *Institutiones Papinianiae scientia* (Cologne, 1631), 8; and Jean Coras, *De iure arte libellus* (Lyon, 1560).

39. See Ch. 12, n. 24.

40. See J. P. Canning, "Law," in *The Cambridge History of Medieval Political Theory,* 461; and Horn, 28.

41. Cino da Pistoia, *Super Codice et Digesto veteri lectura* (Lyon, 1517), fol. 2r; Albericus de Rosate, *Commentariorum . . . super Digesto veteri* (Lyon, 1545), fol. 11r; and others (see Cortese, I, 45, 56–58); also Ch. 7 at n. 31.

42. Azo, *Summa* (Venice, 1566), vol. 29; Placentinus, cited by Orestano, 189; and Révigny, cited by Cortese, I, 301, 375; and see Ch. 4.

43. Paolo Grossi, *Le Situazione reali nell'esperienza giuridica medievale* (Bologna, 1968); and Ch. 13, n. 52.

44. Odofredus, *Lectura super Codice,* fol. 3r; Placentinus, *Summa Codicis* (Mainz, 1536), 17; and see D. R. Kelley, "Clio and the Lawyers: Forms of Historical Consciousness in Medieval Jurisprudence," *Medievalia et Humanistica,* n.s. 5 (1974), 25–49 (reprinted in *History, Law, and the Human Sciences*).

45. Baldus, *Commentarii,* fol. 6; cf. Cortese, II, 5ff; and *L'Opera di Baldo,* 433, 435; cf. Ullmann, *Lucas de Penna,* 41.

46. Cina da Pistoia, *In Digesti veteris . . . commentaria* (Lyon, 1547), fol. 1.

47. Baldus, *Opus aureum . . . super feudis* (Venice, 1516), fol. 2r; Andrea, *In usu feudorum epitome* (Lyon, 1556), 3; and see D. K. Kelley, "De Origine Feudorum," *Speculum,* 39 (1964), 207–28 (reprinted in *History, Law, and the Human Sciences*).

48. Albericus de Rosate, *In primam ff. [Digest] ceter. part. commentarii* (Venice, 1585), fol. 44v; and cf. Ullmann, *Lucas de Penna,* 57; also *Quaderni fiorentini,* 11–12 (1982–83), issue devoted to "Itinerari moderni della persona giuridica."

49. See Ch. 9 at n. 19, and Ch. 12.

50. Baldus, cited in *L'Opera del Baldo,* 435.

51. Lorenzo Valla, *Elegantia linguae latinae,* Bk. I, "prefatio," and *Antidoti in Poggium,* in *Opera Omnia,* I, 3, 295. See F. Ercole, *Da Bartolo all'Althusio* (Florence, 1932); Gaines Post, *Studies in Medieval Political and Legal Thought* (Princeton, 1964); Peter Riesenberg, "Civism and Roman Law in Eighteenth-Century Italian Society," *Explorations in Economic History,* 7 (1960–70), 237–54; Julius Kirshner, "*Civitas sibi facit civem:* Bartolus de Sassoferrato's

Doctrine on the Making of a Citizen," *Speculum,* 48 (1973), 694, as well as "*Ars imitatur naturam:* A Consilium of Baldus on Naturalization in Florence," *Viator,* 5 (1974), 289, and "Between Nature and Culture: An Opinion of Baldus of Perugia on Venetian Citizenship as Second Nature," *Journal of Medieval and Renaissance Studies,* 9 (1979), 179–208; and especially Canning, *Baldus.*

52. Rabelais, *Pantagruel,* Ch. 5. See Enzo Nardi, *Rabelais e il diritto romano* (Milan, 1962); and Robert Marichal, "Rabelais et la réforme de la justice," *Bibliothèque d'humanisme et renaissance,* 14 (1952), 176–92.

53. Coluccio Salutati, *De nobilitate legum et medicinae,* ed. E. Garin (Florence, 1947).

54. Claude de Seyssel, *Commentaria in sex partes Digestorum et Codicis* (n.p., 1508); and see D. R. Kelley, "Vera Philosophia: The Philosophical Significance of Renaissance Jurisprudence," *Journal of the History of Philosophy,* 145 (1976), 267–79 (reprinted in *History, Law, and the Human Sciences*). For Trapezuntius, "civilis scientia" was rhetoric (G. Cotroneo, *I Trattatisti dell'"Ars Historica"* [Naples, 1971], 40).

55. I am referring especially to Hans Baron, *The Crisis of the Early Italian Renaissance* (Princeton, 1966), as well as his last statements, *In Search of Florentine Civic Humanism* (Princeton, 1988); and to J. G. A. Pocock, *The Machiavellian Moment* (Princeton, 1975), and the works inspired by both of them. See also note 47 above; Iulio Tarducci in *L'Opera di Baldo,* 409–66; and Lauro Martines, *Lawyers and Statecraft in Renaissance Florence* (Princeton, 1968). The phrase "political humanism" is used by Werner Jaeger (*Paideia,* I, 436), who was Baron's teacher and model, as well as by Walter Ullmann, *Medieval Foundations of Renaissance Humanism* (London, 1977), 118.

56. Kantorowicz, *King's Two Bodies,* 277.

57. Alciato, *De verborum significatione,* 20: "verba debent civiliter et secundum ius interpretari," etc.

58. See Kirschner, "Between Nature and Culture"; cf. Randolph Starn, *Contrary Commonwealth: The Theme of Exile in Medieval and Renaissance Italy* (Berkeley, 1982).

59. Baldus, *Commentaria,* fol. 16r; and cf. Ullmann, "De Bartoli sententia: concilium repraesentat mentem populi," in the collection *Bartolo da Sassoferrato,* II, 707–33.

9 · Tradition and Reform

1. See Ernst Kantorowicz, *King's Two Bodies* (Princeton, 1957); Walter Ullmann, *Principles of Government and Politics in the Middle Ages* (London, 1961), and *Medieval Foundations of Renaissance Humanism* (London, 1977); Brian Tierney, *Foundations of the Conciliar Theory* (Cambridge, Eng., 1955); Gaines Post, *Studies in Medieval Legal Thought* (Princeton, 1964); A. J. Carlyle, *History of Political Theory in the West* (London, 1936), VI; Congar, *Tradition and Traditions,* tr. M. Naseby and T. Rainborough (New York, 1967); *Dictionnaire du droit canonique,* tr. R. Naz (Paris, 1936–66); and other works cited in Ch. 5, n. 51, and Ch. 7, n. 25.

2. Gabriel Le Bras, *Histoire du droit et des institutions de l'Église en Occident,* I, *Prolégomènes* (Paris, 1955), 25.
3. Pier Giovanni Caron, "'Aequitas et interpretatio' dans la doctrine canonique aux XIIIe et XIVe siècles," *Proceedings of the Third International Congress of Medieval Canon Law,* ed. S. Kuttner (Paris, 1971); Eugen Wohlhaupter, *Aequitas Canonica* (Paderborn, 1931); Felix Grat, *Etude sur le motu proprio* (Melun, 1945); and J. Muldoon, "Extra Ecclesiam non est Imperium," *Studia Gratiana,* 9 (1966), 553–80.
4. Sergio Mochi Onory, *Fonti canonistiche dell'idea moderno dello stato* (Milan, 1951); Victor Martin, *Les Origines du gallicanisme* (Paris, 1939); Gustav Mollat, "Les Origines du gallicanisme parlementaire aux XIVe et XVe siècles," *Revue d'histoire ecclésiastique,* 43 (1948), 90–147; Joseph Lecler, "Qu'est-ce que les libertés de l'église gallicane?" *Recherches de science religieuse,* 23 (1933), 385–410; and P. A. van den Baar, *Die kirchliche Lehre der Translatio Imperii Romani bis zur Mitte des 13. Jahrunderts* (Rome, 1956). On the modern and derivative notion of "secularization" see Hans Blumenberg, *The Legitimacy of the Modern Age,* tr. R. Wallace (Cambridge, Mass., 1983); and Franco Todescan, *Le radici teologiche del giusnaturalismo laico,* I (Milan, 1983), 1–18.
5. Cited by Brian Tierney, *Medieval Poor Law* (Berkeley, 1959), 32–33.
6. Kantorowicz; Otto von Gierke, *Das deutsche Genossenschaftsrecht* (Berlin, 1868); Pierre Gillet, *La Personnalité juridique en droit ecclésiastique* (Malines, 1927); Paul Sigmund, *Nicolas of Cusa and Medieval Political Thought* (Cambridge, Mass., 1963); Walter Ullmann, *The Medieval Idea of Law as Represented by Lucas de Penna* (London, 1946), 163; and R. E. Giesey, "The French Estates and the Corpus Mysticum Regni," *Album Helen Maud Cam* (Louvain, 1960), 155–71.
7. Pierre Michaud-Quantin, *Universitas: expression du mouvement communitaire dans le moyen-âge latin* (Paris, 1970), and *Etudes sur le vocabulaire philosophique du moyen âge* (Rome, 1970); and Paul Ourliac, "Science politique et droit canonique au XVe siècle," in *La Storia del diritto nel quadro delle scienze storiche,* Atti de primo congresso internazionale della società italiana di storia del diritto (Florence, 1966), 497–521, and "La Notion de loi fondamentale dans le droit canonique des XIVe et XVe siècles," in *Théorie et practique politique à la Renaissance* (Paris, 1977), 121–31.
8. Peter Riesenberg, *Inalienability of Sovereignty in Medieval Political Thought* (New York, 1956).
9. Paolo Grossi, "'Unanimitas': alle origine del concetto di persona giuridica nel diritto canonico," *Annali di storia del diritto,* 2 (1958), 229–331.
10. Ullmann, *Lucas de Penna,* 163; and cf. Pierre Legendre, "L'Histoire du droit canonique et la science des cultures," in *Proceedings of the Second International Congress of Medieval Canon Law* (Rome, 1965), 281–94.
11. Harold Berman, *Law and Revolution* (Cambridge, Mass., 1983); Le Bras; Hans Erich Feine, *Kirchliche Rechtsgeschichte* (Weimar, 1955), I; Geoffrey Barraclough, *Papal Provisions* (Oxford, 1935); F. Kempf, *The Church in the Age of Feudalism,* Vol. III of *Handbook of Church History,* ed. H. Jedin et al. (New York, 1969); James A. Watt, *The Theory of Papal Monarchy in the*

Thirteenth Century (New York, 1965); Tierney, *Origins of Papal Infallibility, 1150–1350* (Leiden, 1972); Kuttner, *Kanonistisches Schuldlehre von Gratian bis auf die Dekretalen Gregors IX* (Rome, 1935); Oswald J. Reichel, *A Complete Manual of Canon Law* (London, 1896); R. C. Mortimer, *Western Canon Law* (Berkeley, 1953); also Richard Potz, *Die Geltung kirchenrechtlicher Normen* (Vienna, 1978); and Helmuth Pree, *Die evolutive Integration der Rechtsnorm in kanonischen Recht* (Vienna, 1980).

12. Cited by R. G. G. Knox, *Rufinus and Stephen on Church Judgment* (Ph.D. diss., Yale University, 1976); cf. Gillet.

13. Reichel; John T. Noonan, "Marital Affection in the Canonists," *Studia Gratiana,* 12 (1967), 481–509; Tierney, *Medieval Poor Law;* Richard Trexler, *Synodal Law in Florence and Fiesole, 1306–1518* (Rome, 1971); Wilhelm Endemann, *Studien in der romanisch-kanonistischen Wirthschafts- und Rechtslehre* (2 vols., Berlin, 1874–83); and James A. Brundage, *Law, Sex, and Christian Society in Medieval Europe* (Chicago, 1987).

14. René Wehrlé, *De la coutume dans le droit canonique* (Paris, 1928); John P. Dawson, *A History of Lay Judges* (Cambridge, Mass., 1960); *La norma en el derecho canónico,* Actas del III congreso internacional de derecho canónico (Pamplona, 1979); Martin Hechel, "Säkularisierung: Staatskirchliche Aspekte eines umstrittenden Kategorie," *Zeitschrift der Savigny-Stiftung für Rechtsgeschichte,* Kan. Abt., 66 (1980), 1–163; also Damian van den Eyde, "The Terms 'ius positivum' and 'signum positivum' in Twelfth-Century Scholasticism," *Franciscan Studies,* 9 (1949), 41–49; and Stephan Kuttner, "Sur les origines du terme 'droit positif,' " *Revue historique de droit français et étranger,* 4th ser., 15 (1936), 728–40, reprinted in his *History of Ideas and Doctrines of Canon Law in the Middle Ages* (London, 1980).

15. Abbo of Fleury (d. 1004), *Collectio canonum* (*Patrilogia latinae,* 139, col. 481), cited by Jean-Marie Salgado, "La Méthode d'interprétation du droit en usage chez les canonistes," *Revue de l'Université d'Ottawa,* 21 (1951), 209. See also Kuttner, "Urban II and the Doctrine of Interpretation: A Turning Point?" *Studia Gratiana,* 15 (1972), 55–86, reprinted in his *History of Ideas;* and Le Bras, *Histoire du droit,* 116, and "Les Problèmes du temps dans l'histoire du droit canon," *Revue historique de droit français et étranger,* 4th ser., 30 (1952), 487–513; and Mortimer, 46ff.

16. Hostiensis, *Summa,* cited by Caron, 133, and on Hostiensis, Clarence Gallagher, *Canon Law and the Christian Community* (Rome, 1978). See also C. Lefebvre, *Les Pouvoirs du juge en droit canonique* (Paris, 1938); Wohlhaupter, 68ff; and F. W. Maitland, *Roman Canon Law in the Church of England* (London, 1898).

17. Kenneth Pennington, "Law," in *Cambridge History of Medieval Political Thought,* ed. J. H. Burns (Cambridge, Eng., 1988), 428.

18. J. T. McNeil and Helen M. Garne, *Medieval Handbooks of Penance* (New York, 1938); and see H. Appel, *Die Lehre der Scholastiker von der Synteresis* (Rostok, 1891); J. Stelzenberger, *Syneidesis, Conscientia, Gewissen* (Paderborn, 1963); and A. Cancrini, *Syneidesis* (Rome, 1970).

19. J. Gilchrist, *The Church and Economic Activity in the Middle Ages* (New York, 1969); Philippe Godding, "La Notion de possession du droit romano-canonique dans les principalités belges aux 12e et 13e siècles," *Studia Gratiana,* 19

(1976), 315–35; Benjamin N. Nelson, *The Idea of Usury: From Tribal Brotherhood to Universal Otherhood* (Princeton, 1949). On the significance of canon law for codification, see Sten Gagnér, *Studien zur Ideengeschichte der Gesetzgebung* (Stockholm, 1960).

20. A useful guide is Patrice Cousin, *Précis d'histoire monastique* (Paris, 1956); and see Ch. 6 at n. 10.

21. James Muldoon, *Popes, Lawyers, and Infidels* (Philadelphia, 1979); Joan D. Tooke, *The Just War in Aquinas and Grotius* (London, 1965).

22. Joseph Hefele (-Leclercq), *Histoire des conciles* (11 vols., Paris, 1907–49); Tierney; Anthony J. Black, *Monarchy and Community: Political Ideas in the Later Conciliar Controversy* (Cambridge, Eng., 1970); Hubert Jedin, *A History of the Council of Trent*, Vol. II, tr. E. Graf (Edinburgh, 1961).

23. Henry of Langenstein, *A Letter on Behalf of a Council of Peace*, and Dietrich of Niem, *Ways of Uniting and Reforming the Church*, both in *Advocates of Reform*, ed. M. Spinka (Philadelphia, 1953); and cf. Post, 163–240. The "QOT" formula became a "rule" of canon law, on the analogy of the civilian *regulae antiqui juris*: see, eg., J. C. Dantoine, *Les Règles du droit canon* (Liège, 1775), 181, "Quod omnes tangit . . . Le consentement de tous les intéressés est requis dans une affaire commune entre plusieurs personnes."

24. Anthony J. Black, *Council and Commune: The Conciliar Movement and the Fifteenth-Century Heritage* (London, 1979).

25. See Jean Pierre Royer, *L'Église et le royaume de France au XIVe siècle d'après le "Songe du Vergier" et la jurisprudence du Parlement* (Paris, 1969); Georges de Lagarde, "Le 'Songe du verger' et les origines du gallicanisme," extracted from *Revue des sciences religieuses* (Paris, 1934); and works cited above, n. 4.

26. See *La seconda scolastica nella formazione del diritto privato moderno*, ed. P. Grossi (Florence, 1973); Joseph Soder, *Francesco Suarez und die Völkerrecht* (Frankfurt, 1973); Michel Villey, "La Promotion de la loi et du droit subjectif dans la seconde scolastique," *Quaderni fiorentini*, 1 (1972), 23–52; José Fernande-Santamaria, *The State, War, and Peace: Spanish Political Thought in the Renaissance, 1516–1559* (Cambridge, Eng., 1977); also Paolo Prodi, *Il sovrano pontifice* (Bologna, 1982); Eng. tr. by Susan Haskins (Cambridge, Eng., 1987); and Ch. 12.

27. See E. N. Van Kleffens, *Hispanic Law* (Edinburgh, 1968), 183, 291.

28. Robert Feenstra, "L'Influence de la scolastique espanole sur Grotius en droit privé, *Quaderni fiorentini*, 1 (1973) 377–402.

29. In general see Y. Congar, *Tradition and Traditions*, tr. M. Naseby and T. Ramborough (New York, 1966); August Deneffe, *Der Traditionsbegriff* (Münster, 1931); and Jaroslav Pelikan, *The Christian Tradition* (Chicago, 1971).

30. Alberto Pincherle, "Graziano e Lutero," *Studia Gratiana*, 3 (1953), 453–81. See Gordon Rupp, *The Righteousness of God* (London, 1963), on Luther and *justitia*. (In general, I refrain from referring to the huge literature on Luther's view of "law.")

31. "Why the Books of the Pope and his Disciples Were Burned by Doctor Martin Luther," tr. L. Spitz [Sr.], in *Luther's Works*, XXXI, ed. H. Grimm (Philadelphia, 1957), 383–95.

32. Domenico Maffei, *La Donazione di Costantino nei giuristi medievali* (Milan, 1964).
33. Luther, "Why the Books Were Burned."
34. Philip Melanchthon, "Oratio de legibus" (1523–25), ed. Guido Kisch, *Melanchthons Rechts- und Soziallehre* (Berlin, 1967), 189–209.
35. Jean Calvin, *Institutes de la religion chrétienne*, esp. II, vii; and, also in a large literature, see Josef Bohatec, *Calvin und das Recht* (Feudingen, 1934).
36. François Hotman, *De statu primitivae ecclesiae* (Geneva, 1553); and see D. R. Kelley, *François Hotman: A Revolutionary's Ordeal* (Princeton, 1973).
37. Charles Dumoulin, *Annotationes ad jus canonicum,* in *Opera omnia* (Paris, 1681), IV; and in general René Metz, "La Contribution de la France à l'étude du décret de Gratien depuis le XVIe siècle jusqu'à nos jours," *Studia Gratiana,* 2 (1954), 495–518; Michel Reulos, "Le Décret de Gratien chez les humanistes, les Gallicans, et les réformés français du XVIe siècle," *Studia Gratiana,* 2 (1954), 679–96; and J. F. von Schulte, *Die Geschichte der Quellen und Literatur des canonischen Rechts von der Mitte des 16. Jahrhunderts bis zu Gegenwart* (Stuttgart, 1880).
38. Dumoulin, *Annotationes,* 176, and also 121 (referring to "stulta praxis canonistarum") and 156 (concerning their method, "falsum et Judaicum").
39. D. R. Kelley, "Fides Historiae: Charles Dumoulin and the Gallican View of History," *Traditio,* 22 (1966), 347–402; and see J. L. Thireau, *Charles Dumoulin, 1500–1566* (Geneva, 1980).
40. Richard Hooker, *Of the Laws of Ecclesiastical Polity,* I, ed. G. Edelen (Cambridge, Mass., 1977), dedicated "To Men that seeke (as they terme it) the reformation of Lawes, and orders Ecclesiastical, in the church of England," with a discussion of "*Primarie* and *Secondarie* lawes" (see 108).

10 · *English Developments*

1. Bracton, *De legibus et consuetudinibus Angliae,* ed. and tr. Samuel Thorne (Cambridge, Mass., 1968), I, 19. In general see W. S. Holdsworth, *A History of English Law* (London, 1923–66), and *Sources and Literature of English Law* (London, 1925); F. Pollack and F. W. Maitland, *The History of English Law before the Time of Edward I* (2 vols., Cambridge, Eng., 1898); T. F. T. Plucknett, *A Concise History of the Common Law* (London, 1956), and *Early English Legal Literature* (Cambridge, Eng., 1958); H. G. Richardson and G. O. Sayles, *Law and Legislation from Aethelbert to Magna Carta* (Edinburgh, 1966); J. P. Dawson, *The Oracles of the Law* (Ann Arbor, 1968), and *A History of Lay Judges* (Cambridge, Mass., 1967); S. F. C. Milsom, *The Legal Framework of English Feudalism* (Cambridge, Eng., 1976); and Arthur R. Hogue, *Origins of the Common Law* (Indianapolis, 1966).
2. Henri Levy-Ullman, *The English Legal Tradition: Its Sources and History,* tr. M. Mitchell (London, 1935), 23.
3. L. J. Downer, ed., *Leges Henrici Primi* (Oxford, 1972), 80.
4. See Ch. 6, n. 40.
5. M. T. Clanchy, *From Memory to Written Record: England, 1066–1307* (London, 1979); Paul Brand, "The Origin of the English Legal Profession," *Law*

and History Review, 5 (1987), 31–50; and James A. Brundage, "The Medieval Advocate's Profession," *Law and History Review,* 6 (1988), 439–64; V. H. Galbraith, *Studies in the Public Records* (London, 1948); and L. W. Abbott, *Law Reporting in England, 1485–1585* (London, 1973).

6. J. W. Gough, *Fundamental Law in English Constitutional History* (Oxford, 1955); Charles Gray, "Reason, Authority, and Imagination: The Jurisprudence of Sir Edward Coke," in *Culture and Politics from Puritanism to the Enlightenment,* ed. P. Zagorin (Berkeley, 1980); Stephen D. White, *Sir Edward Coke and "The Grievances of the Commonwealth," 1621–1628* (Chapel Hill, 1979).

7. R. C. Van Caenegem, *Royal Writs in England from the Conquest to Glanvill* (London, 1959); and Robert Palmer, "The Origin of Property in England," *Law and History Review,* 3 (1985), 1–50 (and cf. 375–96).

8. Samuel Thorne, ed., *Bracton on the Laws and Customs of England* (Cambridge, Mass., 1968).

9. Gaines Post, *Studies in Medieval Legal and Political Thought* (Princeton, 1964), 163–240 (esp. 189).

10. C. H. McIlwain, *The High Court of Parliament and Its Supremacy* (New Haven, 1934).

11. T. F. T. Plucknett, *Statutes and their Interpretation in the First Half of the Fourteenth Century* (Cambridge, Eng., 1922).

12. David Jenkins, cited by John Dykstra Eusden, *Puritans, Lawyers, and Politics in Early Seventeenth-Century England* (New Haven, 1958), 46.

13. John Fortescue, *De laudibus legum Anglie,* ed. and tr. S. B. Chrimes (Cambridge, Eng., 1949), 16. See in general Lawrence Manley, *Convention, 1500–1700* (Cambridge, Mass., 1980), 106; J. G. A. Pocock, *The Ancient Constitution and the Feudal Law,* 2nd ed. (Cambridge, Eng., 1987), 16, 34; Samuel Kliger, *The Goths in England* (Cambridge, Mass., 1952); Donald W. Henson, *From Kingdom to Commonwealth* (Cambridge, Mass., 1970); G. R. Elton, "The Rule of Law in Sixteenth-Century England," in his *Studies in Tudor and Stuart Politics and Government* (Cambridge, Eng., 1974), I, 260–84; E. W. Ives, *The Common Lawyers of Pre-Reformation England* (Cambridge, Eng., 1983); Wilfrid Prest, *The Inns of Court under Elizabeth and the Early Stuarts* (Totowa, N.J., 1972); Wilfrid Prest, ed., *Lawyers in Early Modern Europe and America* (New York, 1981), esp. Prest, "The English Bar, 1550–1700," 65–85, J. H. Baker, "The English Legal Profession, 1450–1550," 16–41, and C. W. Brooke, "The Common Lawyers in England, c. 1558–1642," 42–64; J. H. Baker, "The Dark Age of English Legal History, 1500–1700," *Legal History Studies, 1972,* ed. D. Jenkins (Cardiff, 1975), 1–27; C. W. Brooke, "Litigants and Attorneys in the King's Bench and Common Pleas, 1560–1640," in *Legal Records and the Historian,* ed. J. H. Baker (London, 1978); Johann P. Sommerville, *Politics and Ideology in England, 1603–1640* (London, 1986), and "The Norman Conquest in Early Stuart Political Thought," *Political Studies,* 34 (1986), 249–61.

14. Pollock and Maitland, I, 58–65; and R. F. Jones, *The Triumph of the English Language* (Stanford, 1953).

15. Fortescue, 15ff; cf. Daniel Boorstin, *The Mysterious Science of Law* (Cambridge, Mass., 1941).

16. Charles Gray, *Copyhold, Equity, and the Common Law* (Cambridge, Mass., 1963).
17. Coke, *The Reports* (13 vols., London, 1738), vol. X, fol. xvii; and cf. François Hotman, *De feudis commentatio tripertita,* in *Operum* (Lyon, 1599–1600), vol. II, col. 913.
18. Christopher St. German, *Doctor and Student,* ed. T. F. T. Plucknett and J. Barton (London, 1974), chs. 6–11; John A. Guy, *Christopher St. German on Chancery and Statute* (London, 1985); W. J. Jones, *The Elizabethan Court of Chancery* (London, 1967); Stuart Prall, "The Development of Equity in Tudor England," *Journal of Legal History,* 8 (1964), 1–19; and John A. Guy, "Law, Equity, and Conscience in Henrician Juristic Thought," in *Reassessing the Henrician Age,* ed. A. Fox and John A. Guy (London, 1986), 179–98; also Maitland, *Equity,* revised by J. Brunyate (Cambridge, Eng., 1936).
19. St. German, 57.
20. Fortescue, ch. 39.
21. St. German, xlvi (editor's preface).
22. William Blackstone, *Commentaries on the Laws of England in Four Books,* ed. G. Sharswood (2 vols., Philadelphia, 1862), bk. II, ch. 9 (#145).
23. Richard Hooker, *Of the Laws of Ecclesiastical Polity,* I, ed. George Edelen (Cambridge, Mass., 1977), 108; cf. Manley, 90; and Arthur Ferguson, *Clio Unbound* (Durham, N.C., 1979), 329–45.
24. Burke, cited in James K. Chandler, *Wordsworth's Second Nature: A Study of Poetry and Politics* (Chicago, 1984), 71.
25. Coke, II, preface; and cf. Pocock, *The Ancient Constitution;* Herbert Butterfield, *The Englishman and His History* (Cambridge, Eng., 1944); and John W. McKenna, "How God Became an Englishman," in *Tudor Rule and Revolution,* ed. D. Guth and John McKenna (Cambridge, Eng., 1982), 25–44.
26. Coke, III, preface; and on *judex lex loquens* see Karel Menzo Schönfeld, *Montesquieu en "la bouche de la loi"* (Leiden, 1979), 42, etc.
27. William Lambarde, *Archeion, or a Discourse upon the High Courts of Justice in England,* ed. C. McIlwain and P. Ward (Cambridge, Mass., 1959), 126; and cf. *William Lambarde and Local Government,* ed. C. Reed (Ithaca, 1962); and Wilbur Dunkel, *William Lambarde: Elizabethan Jurist, 1536–1601* (New Brunswick, N.J., 1965). Cf. Thomas Phaer, *A newe boke of presidentes* (London, 1543); and Rupert Cross, *Precedents in English Law* (Oxford, 1961). Cf. also *Magna Carta,* c. 39; and *Libri Feudorum,* V, 1.
28. Henry Finch, *Nomotechnia, Cest a scavoir, un description del cannon leyes dangleterre solonque les Rules del Art Parallelees oue les Prerogatives le Roy* (London, 1613; and cf. Wilfred R. Prest, "The Art of Law and the Law of God: Sir Henry Finch, 1558–1625," in *Puritans and Revolutionaries* (Oxford, 1978), 95–117.
29. Coke, VII, preface; and Fortescue, 21. John Bridall, *Speculum juris anglicana* (London, 1673), 49, defines custom as a reasonable act done once, growing to perfection, and good for the people.
30. Oliver Wendell Holmes, Jr., *The Common Law* (Boston, 1881), 1.
31. Duck, *De usu et autoritate juris civilis Romanorum per dominia principum christianorum* (London, 1653); *Ius Romani Medii Aevi* (Milan, 1961–), 24

vols. by various authors; Holdsworth, *History of English Law,* IV; Eleanor
Rathbone, "Roman Law in the Anglo-Norman Realm," *Studia Gratiana,* 11
(1967), 255–71; Ralph V. Turner, "Roman Law in England before the Time
of Bracton," *Journal of British Studies,* 15 (1975), 1–25; H. Coing, "Das
Schrifttum der englischen Civilians und die kontinentale Rechtsliteratur in dere
Zeit zwischen 1550 und 1800," *Ius Commune,* 5 (1975), 1–55; Walter Ull-
mann, "Bartolus and English Jurisprudence," *Jurisprudence in the Middle Ages*
(London, 1980), 18 (remarking on Gentili's phrase "Bartolus Noster"); Brian
P. Levack, *The Civil Laws in England* (Oxford, 1973), "The English Civilians,
1500–1700," in Prest, ed., *Lawyers,* 108–28, "Law and Ideology: The Civil
Law and Theories of Absolutism in Elizabethan and Jacobean England," in
The Historical Renaissance, ed. R. Strier and H. Dubrow (Chicago, 1988), and
*The Formation of the English State: England, Scotland, and the Union, 1603–
1707* (Oxford, 1987). See also Maitland, *English Law and the Renaissance*
(Cambridge, Eng., 1901), and the corrective article of the same title by Samuel
Thorne in *La storia del diritto nel quadro delle scienze storiche* (Florence,
1966), 437–45; and W. S. Holdsworth, "Reception of Roman Law in the
Sixteenth Century," *Law Quarterly Review,* 27 (1911), 387–98, and *Essays in
Law and History,* ed. A. L. Goodhart and H. G. Hanbury (Oxford, 1946),
188; Daniel R. Coquillette, "Legal Ideology and Incorporation: I, The English
Civilian Writers, 1523–1607," *Boston University Law Review,* 61 (1981), 1–
89; Louis Knafla, "The Influence of Continental Humanism on English Com-
mon Law in the Renaissance," in *Acta Conventus Neo-Latini Bononiensis,* ed.
R. J. Schoeck (Binghamton, N.Y., 1985); and D. R. Kelley, "History, English
Law, and the Renaissance," *Past and Present,* 65 (1974), 24–51 (reprinted in
History, Law, and the Human Sciences) and 72 (1976), 143–46.

32. R. Crompton, *L'Authorité et iurisdiction des courts de la maiesté de la royne*
    (London, 1637).
33. Hooker, preface; cf. Cosin, *An Apologie of, and for, sundrie proceedings by
    Iurisdiction Ecclesiasticall* (London, 1591).
34. Cambridge University Library, Baker MS 37, fols. 212r–220v, "D. Thomas
    Smith Doctoris LL. et Regii apud Cantabrigiensis Professoris, Oratio prima,
    de suis auditoribus, et de ratione studii juris civilis."
35. Alberico Gentili, *De iuris interpretibus* (London, 1582); and see Guido Astuti,
    *Mos italicus e mos gallicus nei dialoghi "de iuris interpretibus" de Alberico
    Gentili* (Bologna, 1937); and Diego Panizza, *Alberico Gentili: giurista ideolgico
    nell'Inghliterra elizabettiana* (Padua, 1981).
36. *Opus epistolarum Des. Erasmi,* ed. P. S. Allen, IV (Oxford, 1922), 17.
37. Robert Wiseman, *The Law of Laws: or the Excellency of the Civil Law, above
    all other humane laws whatsoever* (London, 1656).
38. Cited by Dunkel, 33.
39. Coke, X, preface.
40. Fortescue, 42.
41. *Acts of the Privy Council of England,* ed. J. R. Dasent (London, 1890), II, 49.
42. Thomas Smith, *De Republica Anglorum,* ed. Mary Dewar (Cambridge, Eng.,
    1982), 89 and 96, remarking that in civil law, after establishing the truth, "the
    advocats doe dispute of the lawe to make of it what they can: saying, *ex facto
    jus oritur.*"

43. John Aylmer, *An Harborovve for faithful and trewe subiectes* (Strasbourg, [1559]), sig. K4v, Q2v.

44. John Rastel, *Expositiones terminorum legum anglorum* (n.p., 1527), "prohemium."

45. John Doderidge, *The English Lawyer* (London, 1631), a reprinting of the anonymous *The Lawyers Light*.

46. Edward Hake, *Epieikeia: A Dialogue on Equity in Three Parts*, ed. D. E. C. Yale (New Haven, 1953), 33.

47. *The Political Works of James I*, ed. C. McIlwain (Cambridge, Mass., 1918), 310.

48. [Anon.], *Englands Monarch* (London, 1644), opposing Gentili's *Regales disputationes tres* (London, 1604); and cf. John Cowell, *The Interpreter* (Cambridge, Eng., 1607).

49. Wiseman, 19; and Etienne Pasquier, *L'Interprétation des Institutes de Justinian*, ed. M. le duc Pasquier (Paris, 1847), I, 26; cf. Roger Twysden, *Certain Considerations upon the Government of England*, ed. J. M. Kemble (Cambridge, Eng., 1849), 84–85.

50. William Fulbeke, *A Parallele or Conference of the Civil Law, the Canon Law, and the Common Law of this Realme of England* (London, 1618), preface; and cf. his *Pandectes of the Law of Nations* (London, 1602), to the reader: "I likewise wandering in my thoughts through the paradise of learning, amongst many delightful apparitions espied four excellent lawes: the first was canon-law, to which for the gravity I bowed: the second Civil, which for the wisdom I admired: the third the Common Law, to which I did my homage: the fourth the law of Nations, which I submissively reverenced."

51. See Ch. 13 at n. 2.

52. John Selden, "Notes on Sir John Fortescue's *De laudibus . . . in Opera omnia* (London, 1725), vol. III, col. 1892; and see Paul Christianson, "John Selden, the Five Knights' Case, and Discretionary Imprisonment," *Criminal Justice History*, 6 (1985), 65–87; and Richard Tuck, *Natural Rights Theories: Their Origin and Development* (Cambridge, Eng., 1979), ch. 4.

53. *English Works of Sir H. Spelman* (London, 1723), II, 100.

54. British Library, Sloane MS 3828, "A Discourse on the First 4 Chapters of the Digest to Shew the Excellence and usefullnesse of the Civill Law," by George Mackenzie (dictated just before his death, 8 May 1691), and Harleian MS 6850, "Proposals for publishing the body of the Civil Law with annotations."

55. Francis Bacon, *The Elements of the Common Lawes* (London, 1617), dedicated to Queen Elizabeth, in *The Letters and the Life of Francis Bacon*, ed. James Spedding (London, 1874), VII, 358, and *Works*, ed. Spedding, (Boston, 1861), XV, 317; and William Phillips, *Studii Legalis Ratio* (London, 1675), 70. See also Barbara Shapiro, "Codification of Laws in Seventeenth-Century England," *Wisconsin Law Review* (1974), 428–65; and Roger T. Simonds, "Bacon's Legal Learning: Its Influence on His Philosophical Ideas," *Acta Conventus Neo-Latini Sanctadreani*, ed. I. D. McFarlane (Binghamton, N.Y., 1986).

56. William Noy, *The Compleat Lawyer, or a treatise concerning tenures and estates* (London, 1670); and see Holdsworth, *History of English Law*, VI, 683–94.

57. William Dugdale, *Origines juridicales*, 2nd ed. (London, 1671), 3.

58. See above, n. 13.
59. Thomas Hobbes, *The Elements of Law, Natural and Politic,* ed. F. Tönnies (Cambridge, Eng., 1928),51; and see also Stuart E. Prall, *The Agitation for Law Reform during the Puritan Revolution* (The Hague, 1966).
60. Thomas Hobbes, *A Dialogue between a Philosopher and a Student of the Common Laws of England,* ed. J. Cropsey (Chicago, 1971), 55ff.
61. Matthew Hale's "Criticisms on Hobbes's Dialogue of the Common Laws" (British Library, Harleian MS 711, fols. 418–39), in Holdsworth, *History of English Law,* V, 499–513; and cf. Hale, *The History of the Common Law of England,* ed. C. Gray (Chicago, 1971).
62. Hale's "Criticisms," in Holdsworth, V, 512.
63. John Bowle, *Hobbes and His Critics* (London, 1951); Samuel Mintz, *The Hunting of Leviathan* (Cambridge, Eng., 1962); and Corinne Comstock Weston and Janille Renfrom Greenberg, *Subject and Sovereign: The Grand Controversy on Legal Sovereignty in Stuart England* (Cambridge, Eng., 1981).
64. William Petyt, *The Antient Right of the Commons of England Asserted* (London, 1680). Cf. William Atwood, *Jus Anglorum ab Antiquo* (London, 1688), and Robert Brady, *An Introduction to the English History* (n.p., n.d.), the latter including tracts against Petyt and the treatise *Argumentum Antinormanicum,* and a history of succession to the crown. See also J. G. A. Pocock, "Robert Brady," *Cambridge Historical Journal,* 10 (1950–52), 186–204.
65. John Tyrrell, *Biblioteca politica, or a discourse By way of dialogue whether Monarchy be jure divino* (London, 1694).
66. Blackstone, 16; cf. Luc Henry Dunoyer, *Blackstone et Pothier* (Paris, 1927); Robert Chambers, *A Course of Lectures on the English Law, 1767–73* (Madison, 1986); Boorstin; and now David Lieberman, *The Province of Legislation Determined: Legal Theory in Eighteenth-Century Britain* (Cambridge, 1989).
67. Richard B. Sher, *Church and University in the Scottish Enlightenment* (Princeton, 1985), 315–18, on the "dramatic shift" from clerics to lawyers," See in general Stair Society, ed., *Introduction to Scottish Legal History* (Edinburgh, 1958), and *An Introductory Survey of the Sources and Literature of Scots Law* (Edinburgh, 1936); D. M. Walker, *The Scottish Jurists* (Edinburgh, 1985); R. H. Campbell and Andrew Skinner, eds., *The Origins and Nature of the Scottish Enlightenment* (Edinburgh, 1982); Anand C. Chitnis, *The Scottish Enlightenment: A Social History* (Totowa, N.J., 1976), ch. 4, and *The Scottish Enlightenment and Early Victorian Society* (London, 1986); Jane Rendall, *The Origins of the Scottish Enlightenment* (London, 1978); Peter Stein, "Law and Society in Eighteenth-Century Scottish Thought," *Essays in Scottish History in the Eighteenth Century,* ed. N. T. Phillipson and R. Mitchison (Edinburgh, 1970), 148–68; I. Hont and M. Ignatieff, eds., *Wealth and Virtue* (Cambridge, Eng., 1983); and Ronald Meek, *Social Science and the Ignoble Savage* (Cambridge, Eng., 1976), and his other works.
68. James Dalrymple, Viscount Stair, *The Institutions of the Law of Scotland* [1681, 1693], ed. D. Walker (Edinburgh, 1981); and see William M. Gordon, "Stairs's Use of Roman Law," *Law-Making and Law-Makers in British History,* ed. A. Harding (London, 1980).

69. James Moore and Michael Silverthorne, "Gershom Carmichael and the Natural Jurisprudence Tradition in Eighteenth-Century Scotland," and J. G. A. Pocock, "Cambridge Paradigms: A Study of the Relations between Civic Humanism and the Civil Jurisprudence Interpretations of Eighteenth-Century Social Thought," in *Wealth and Virtue*, 235–52.

70. Henry Home, Lord Kames, *Historical Law Tracts* (Edinburgh, 1761), 22; and see William C. Lehman, *Henry Home, Lord Kames, and the Scottish Enlightenment* (The Hague, 1971); and David Lieberman, "The Legal Needs of a Commercial Society: The Jurisprudence of Lord Kames," in *Wealth and Virtue*, 203–34.

71. See Ch. 14 at n. 16.

72. A. Y. Goguet, *The Origin of Laws, Arts and Sciences and their Progress among the Most Ancient Nations* (Edinburgh, 1775).

73. *The Works of James Wilson*, ed. R. G. McCloskey (Cambridge, Mass., 1967), lectures on law (1790–91), I, 70; and see Geoffrey Seed, *James Wilson* (Millwood, N.Y., 1978); also H. Trevor Coulborn, *The Lamp of Experience: Whig History and the Origins of the American Revolution* (Chapel Hill, 1965).

74. *The Earliest Diary of John Adams*, ed. L. H. Butterfield (Cambridge, Mass., 1966), 55, 76; and *Diary and Autobiography of John Adams*, ed. Butterfield (Cambridge, Mass., 1962), II, 375, III, 271, IV, 200; and see Gilbert Chinard, *Honest John Adams* (Boston, 1933).

75. Thomas Jefferson, *The Writings*, ed. Paul Leicester Ford (New York, 1898), IX, 480, XVIII, 1 ("The Batture at New Orleans"), XV, 207; and see Merrill D. Peterson, *Thomas Jefferson and the New Nation* (New York, 1970); and Karl Lehman, *Thomas Jefferson: American Humanist* (New York, 1947).

11 · *Jurisprudence in the French Manner*

1. Nicolas Reusner, *CHEIRAGOGIA, sive Cynosura iuris* (Speier, 1588), appendix. In general and for further references, see D. R. Kelley, *Foundations of Modern Historical Scholarship* (New York, 1970), and "Civil Science in the Renaissance: Jurisprudence in the French Manner," *History of European Ideas*, 2 (1981), 261–76 (reprinted in *History, Law, and the Human Sciences*); various works by Vincenzo Piano Mortari, including *Diritto romano e diritto nazionale in Francia nel secolo XVI* (Milan, 1962), *Diritto logica metodo nel secolo XVI* (Naples, 1978), and *Gli Inizi del diritto moderno en Europa* (Naples, 1980); and also Hans Erich Troje, *Graeca Leguntur* (Cologne, 1971), and his sections in Helmut Coing, *Handbuch der Quellen und Literatur der neueren europäischen Privatrechts geschichte*, II (1) (Munich, 1977), 615–795.

2. De juris interpretibus dialogi sex (London, 1582), 4; and see Ch. 8 at n. 51. Cf. G. C. J. J. van der Bergh, "Auctoritas Poetarum: The Fortunes of a Legal Argument," in *Daube Noster*, ed. A. Watson (Edinburgh, 1974), 105–17, as well as "A Note on Humanist Philology and Legal Scholarship," *Satura Roberto Feenstra* (Freiburg, 1985), 523–32, and *Themis en de Muzen* (Haarlem, 1964).

3. "Epistola Francisci Duareni ad Andream Guillartum . . . De ratione docendi discendique Iuris conscripta," *Opera omnia* (Geneva, 1608), 288–93; and

Equinaire Baron, "De ratione docendi, discendique iuris civilis, Ad iuventutum," in his *Opera omnia*, ed. F. Baudouin (Paris, 1562), 1; both are reprinted in Reusner, 11–37, 37–40. See E. Durtelle Saint-Sauveur, "Eguiner Baron et l'École de Bourges avant Cujas," *Travaux juridiques et canoniques de l'Université de Rennes*, 15 (1936), 69–114; and W. Vogt, *Franciscus Duarenus, 1509–1559* (Stuttgart, 1970).

4. Jacques Flach, *Cujas, les glossateurs, et les bartolistes* (Paris, 1883); and Pierre Mesnard, "La Place de Cujas dans la querelle de l'humanisme juridique," *Revue historique de droit français et étranger*, 4th ser., 28 (1950), 521–37.

5. David Quint, *Origins and Originality in Renaissance Literature* (New Haven, 1983).

6. Anthony Grafton, *Joseph Scaliger* (London, 1984), I; John D'Amico, *Theory and Practice in Renaissance Textual Criticism: Beatus Rhenanus between Conjecture and History* (Berkeley, 1988); and William McCuaig, *Carlo Sigonio: The Changing World of the Late Renaissance* (Princeton, 1989), on the Italian, French, and German styles of textual criticism; and see Ch. 8 at n. 31.

7. See D. R. Kelley, "Civil Science in the Renaissance: The Problem of Interpretation," in *The Languages of Political Theory in Early-Modern Europe*, ed. A. Pagden, (Cambridge, Eng., 1987), 57–78; and Ch. 12 at n. 7.

8. François Baudouin, *De institutione historiae universae et eius cum jurisprudentia coniunctione* [1561] (Strasbourg, 1608); and see M. Erbe, *François Bauduin* (Gutersloh, 1978); D. R. Kelley, "The Rise of Legal History in the Renaissance," *History and Theory*, 9 (1970), 174–94 (reprinted in *History, Law, and the Human Sciences*), and *François Hotman: A Revolutionary's Ordeal* (Princeton, 1973); and A. Eyssel, *Doneau, sa vie et ses ouvrages* (Dijon, 1860).

9. See this chapter at n. 41.

10. Baron, *Opera*, I, 29; and Hugues Doneau, *Opera omnia* (Lucca, 1762), vol. I, col. 48.

11. See Jean Moreau-Reibel, *Jean Bodin et le droit public comparé dans ses rapports avec la philosophie de l'histoire* (Paris, 1933); also Jacques Brejon, *André Tiraqueau, 1488–1558* (Paris, 1937); and A. J. Carlyle, *A History of Medieval Political Theory in the West*, VI, (Cambridge, Eng., 1936).

12. Leonardo Bruni, *Humanistisch-Philosophische Schriften*, ed. H. Baron (Leipzig, 1928), 88–96, tr. in G. Griffiths et al., *The Humanism of Leonardo Bruni: Selected Texts* (Binghamton, N.Y., 1987); and on Budé, David O. MacNeill, *Guillaume Budé and Humanism in the Reign of Francis I* (Geneva, 1975); and D. R. Kelley, *Foundations of Modern Historical Scholarship*, ch. 3; but see also the criticisms by Douglas Osler in *Ius Commune*, 13 (1985), 195–212.

13. Baron, "Commentary on the Digest," in *Opera*, I, 27, 38; and his *Institutionum civilium ab Iustiniano Caesare editarum libri quattuor, bipartito commentario illustrati* (Poitou, 1546).

14. Baron, *Opera*, I, 164.

15. Ibid., 67. For Baron (I, 49), *consuetudo* was either *observata* or *antiquata*.

16. François Connan, *Commentarii iuris civilis libri X* (Paris, 1553), fols. 39v–44v; and see Christoph Bergfeld, *Franciscus Connanus, 1508–1551* (Cologne, 1551).

17. Connan, fol. 43.
18. Ibid., fols. 44, 40.
19. Pierre Ayrault, *Rerum ab omni antiquitate iudicarum Pandectae* (Paris, 1573), sig. a2, "Res iudicatae, prima pars iuris, aut sola, aut praecipua," and sig. a4, "Et Constitutio quid aliud est, quam quod ex multis iudiciis et opinionibus item variis aliorum exemplis definiri atque constituti placuit?"
20. Jean Bodin, *Methodus ad facilem historiarum cognitionem*, in *Oeuvres philosophiques*, ed. Pierre Mesnard (Paris, 1951), 109. In the vast literature on Bodin see especially Horst Denzer, ed., *Jean Bodin: Verhandlungen der Internationalen Bodin Tagung (Munich, 1973);* and J. P. Mayer, ed., *Fundamental Studies on Jean Bodin* (New York, 1979), reprinting the classic works by Bezold, Feist, Hauser, Mesnard, and others.
21. See in general Troje, *Graeca Leguntur*; Cesare Vasoli, *La dialettica e la retorica dell'umanesimo* (Milan, 1968); Otto Ritschl, *System und systematische Methode in der Geschichte der wissenschaftlichen Sprachgebrauchs und der philosophischen Methodologie* (Bonn, 1906); Guido Kisch, *Studien zur humanistische Jurisprudenz* (Basel, 1972), and *Humanismus und Jurisprudenz* (Basel, 1955); and see Ch. 12.
22. Joanna Artelle, "Le Thème de l'utilité publique dans la polémique anti-nobiliaire en France dans la deuxième moitié du XVI siècle," in *Théorie et Practice*, ed. P. Ourliac.
23. See Ch. 7 at n. 47.
24. Doneau, *Opera*, I, 75.
25. François Hotman, *Dialecticae Institutiones* (Geneva, 1573); and cf. his *Partitiones iuris civilis elementariae* (Basel, 1560).
26. Jean Coras, *De iuris arte libellus* (Lyon, 1560), *In titulum Pandectarum de Iustitia et Iure* (Lyon, 1568), and *De Iure civile, in artem redigendo*, in *Tractatus universi juris* (Venice, 1584), vol. I, fol. 59ff; and see A. London Fell, *Origins of Legislative Sovereignty and the Legislative State* (3 vols., Königstein, 1983–87).
27. Connan, fol. 8v.
28. Doneau, vol. I, col. 47.
29. Gregory of Toulouse, *Syntagma iuris universi, atque legum pene omnium gentium et rerum publicarum praecipuarum* (Frankfurt, 1591), and *De Republica* (Frankfurt, 1609); and see Claude Collot, *L'École doctrinale de droit public de Pont-à-Mousson (Pierre Grégoire de Toulouse et Guillaume Barclay)* (Paris, 1965); and Luigi Gambino, *Il De Republica de Pierre Grégoire* (Milan, 1975).
30. See Ch. 3 at n. 60.
31. See Auguste Lebrun, *La Coutume, ses sources—son autorité en droit privé* (Paris, 1932); Piero Craveri, *Ricerche sulla formazione del diritto consuetudinario in Francia (sec. XIII–XVI)* (Milan, 1969); François Olivier-Martin, *Histoire de la coutume de la prévôté et vicomté de Paris* (Paris, 1922); Henri Beaune, *Introduction à l'étude historique du droit coutumier français* (Paris, 1880); Yvonne Bongert, *Recherches sur les cours laïques du Xe au XIIIe siècle* (Paris, 1949); René Filhol, *Le Premier Président Christofle de Thou et la Réformation des Coutumes* (Paris, 1937); John P. Dawson, *Oracles of the Law*

(Ann Arbor, 1968), and "The Codification of the French Customs," *Michigan Law Review,* 30 (1940), 765–800; Paul Viollet, "Les Coutumes de Normandie," in *Histoire littéraire de France,* XXXIII (Paris, 1906), 41–190; and Robert Besnier, *La Coutume de Normandie* (Paris, 1935).

32. Louis Le Caron, *Peithanon, seu verisimilium libri tres priores* (Paris, 1553), and *La Claire, ou de la prudence du droit* (Paris, 1554); cf. Baudouin, *Commentarius in quatuor libros institutionum iuris civilis* (Paris, 1554), *in tit.*; see also D. R. Kelley, "Louis Le Caron Philosophe," in *Philosophy and Humanism: Renaissance Essays in Honor of Paul Oskar Kristeller,* ed. E. Mahoney (Leiden, 1976), reprinted in *History, Law, and the Human Sciences*; and Madeleine Foisil, "'La Loi et la Monarchie absolue selon les Pandectes ou Digestes du droit français de Louis Charondas Le Caron (XVI siècle)," in *La Formazione storica del diritto moderno en Europa* (Florence, 1977), I, 221–36.

33. Louis Le Caron, *La Philosophie* (Paris, 1555), f. 12, discussing the Apollonian precept, "Cognoi toi-mesme."

34. Louis Le Caron, *Panegyrique, ou Oraison de louange au Roy Charles VIII* (Paris, 1566), sig. Dii.

35. Louis Le Caron, *Pandectes, ou Digestes du droict françois* (Paris, 1587), I, 3.

36. Etienne Pasquier, *L'Interprétation des Institutes de Justinian, avec la conférence de chasque paragraphe aux ordonnances royaux, arretz de Parlement at coustumes générales de la France,* ed. M. le duc Pasquier (Paris, 1847); and Guy Coquille, *Institution au droict françois,* in *Oeuvres* (3 vols., Paris, 1646), II.

37. Antoine Loisel, *Institutes coutumières,* ed. Michel Reulos (Paris, 1935); and Michel Reulos, *Etude sur l'esprit, les sources, et la méthode des Institutes coutumières d'Antoine Loisel* (Paris, 1935). See also François de Launay, *Commentaire sur les Institutes Coutumières de M. Antoine Loisel* (Paris, 1688); Pierre L'Hommeau, *Maximes generales du droict françois* (Paris, 1665); and Claude Pocquet de Livonnière, *Regles du droit françois* (Paris, 1761).

38. François Hotman, *Antitribonian* (Paris, 1603). See the law thesis by A. H. Saint-Charmaran (Paris, Law Faculty, 1973); and Kelley, *François Hotman,* 192–97.

39. Etienne Pasquier, *Les Lettres* (Paris, 1619), bk. 19, letters 8–14; and *Épitre d'Antoine Loisel à son Ami Etienne Pasquier,* ed. A. Sorel (Arras, n.d.); and see Dorothy Thickett, *Estienne Pasquier, 1529–1615: The Versatile Barrister of Sixteenth-Century France* (London, 1979). These letters are not in Thickett's critical editions.

40. Loisel, *Pasquier, ou dialogue des avocats du parlement de Paris,* ed. A. Dupin (Paris, 1844).

41. Montesquieu, *De l'esprit des lois,* XXVIII, 45. In general see François Olivier-Martin and Vincenzo Piano Mortari, "Potere regio e consuetudine redatta nella Francia del cinquecento," *Quaderni Fiorentini,* 1 (1972), 131–75; also Elie Carcassonne, *Montesquieu et le problème de la constitution français au XVIIIe siècle* (Paris, 1927).

42. Jacques Godefroy, *Commentaires sur la coustume reformee du pays et duché de Normandie* (Rouen, 1626), 1. See in general John Glisson, *Introduction historique au droit* (Brussells, 1979); Hippolyte Pissard, *Essai sur la connaissance et la preuve des coutumes* (Paris, 1910); Paul Ourliac, *Etudes du droit*

mediéval (Paris, 1979); J.-Fr. Poudret, "Réflexions sur la preuve de la coutume devant les jurisdictions royales françaises aux XIIIe et XIVe siècles: le rôle de l'enquête par turbe," *Revue historique du droit français et étranger*, 65 (1987), 71–86; *La Preuve: Recueils de la Société Jean Bodin pour l'histoire comparative des institutions* (4 vols., Brussels, 1963–65). See especially André Gouron and Odile Terrin, *Bibliographie des coutumes de France* (Geneva, 1975); and Jean Caswell and Ivan Sipkov, *The Coutumes of France in the Library of Congress* (Washington, D.C., 1977).

43. Laurent Bouchel, *Les Coustumes de bailliages de Senlis . . .* (Paris, 1615), 3.
44. Philippe Bugnyon, *Traicté des lois abrogees et enusitees en toutes less cours du royaume* (Lyon, 1563).
45. Pierre Angleberme, *Commentarius in Aurelianas consuetudines* (n.p., n.d.), fol. clxxxvi. And see Paul Guilhiermoz, "La Persistance du caractère oral dans la procedure civile française," *Nouvelle revue historique de droit français et étranger*, 13 (1889), 21–65.
46. Filhol, 115.
47. Ibid., 67.
48. *Commentaires generales et locales . . . de Bourbonnais*, ed. M. A. des Pommiers (Paris, 1732), iii; and cf. Coquille, *Commentaires sur les coustumes de Nivernois*, in *Oeuvres*, I, 2.
49. Bernard Automne, *La Conference du droict françois avec le droict romain, civil et canon* (Paris, 1610), preface.
50. Edme Billon, *Coutume du Comté et Bailliage d'Auxerre (Paris, 1693)*, preface.
51. Coquille, *Coustumes de Nivernois*, I, 2.
52. Charles Dumoulin, *Prima pars Commentariorum in Consuetudines Parisiensis* (Paris, 1539), and *Oratio de concordia et unione consuetudinem Franciae* (Paris, 1546). See D. R. Kelley, "Fides Historiae: Charles Dumoulin and the Gallican View of History," *Traditio*, 22 (1966), 347–402; Jean-Louis Thireau, *Charles Dumoulin, 1500–1566* (Geneva, 1980); also Pierre Laborderie-Boulou, *Quelques réflexions sur l'influence de Dumoulin dans l'histoire du droit français* (Paris, 1908); Ph. Meylan, "Les Statutes réels et personnels dans la doctrine de Du Moulin," *Mélanges Paul Fournier* (Paris, 1929), 511–26; Aubépin, "De l'influence de Dumoulin sur la législation française," *Revue critique de législation et de jurisprudence*, 3 (1853), 603–25.
53. Claude de Seyssel, *The Monarchy of France*, ed. D. R. Kelley, tr. J. H. Hexter (New Haven, 1981), I, x.
54. Julien Brodeau, *Commentaire sur la coustume de la Prevosté et Vicomté de Paris* (Paris, 1658), 3.
55. Claude de Ferrière, *Commentaire sur la coutume de la prevoté et vicomté de Paris* (n.p., n.d.), 1. Cf. François Bourjon, *Le Droit commun de la France et la coutume de Paris reduits en principes* (Paris, 1747), preface, "Le droit commun du Royaume est l'exact explication de la Coutume"; and see Renée Martinage-Baranger, *Bourjon at le Code Civil* (Paris, 1971); also Jacques Vanderlinden, *Le Concept de Code en Europe* (Brussels, 1967), appendix.
56. Launay, xxxiii.
57. Claude Berroyer and Eusèbe de Laurière, eds., *Bibliotheque des coutumes* (Paris, 1699), "avec des Conjectures sur l'origine du Droit François"; and see

the fundamental collection by Charles A. Bourdot de Richebourg, *Nouveau coutumier general* (Paris, 1724).

58. Paul Challine, *Methode generale pour intelligence des coustumes de France* (Paris, 1666); cf. Coquille, I, 1; and René Choppin, *Commentaires sur la Coustume d'Aniou* (Paris, 1612).

59. Claude de Ferrière, *Nouvelle Institution coutumiere* (Paris, 1692), 14. Cf. Christiane Chêne, *L'Enseignement du droit français en pays de droit écrit, 1679–1793* (Geneva, 1982); Alfred de Curzon, *L'Enseignement du droit français dans les universités de France aux XVIIe et XVIIIe siècles* (Paris, 1920); and G. Péries, *La Faculté de droit dans l'ancienne Université de Paris* (Paris, 1890); also Jean Gaudemet, "Les Tendances à l'unification du droit en France dans les derniers siècles de l'ancien regime (XVIe-XVIIe)," in *La formazione storica del diritto moderno in Europa* (Florence, 1977), I, 157–94; André-Jean Arnaud, *Les Origines doctrinales du Code civil français* (Paris, 1969).

60. Jean Bouhier, *Oeuvres de jurisprudence* (Dijon, 1787), 353ff ("Observations sur la coutume de Bourgogne"), and 396; and see J. Bart, "Les Préoccupations du président Bouhier pendant les derniers années de sa vie," *Mémoires de la Société pour l'Histoire du Droit et des Institutions des anciens pays bouguignons, comtois et romands,* 28 (1967), 141–72; and A. Lombard, *L'Abbé Du Bos, un initiateur de la pensée moderne, 1670–1742* (Paris, 1913).

61. Pierre Grosely, *Recherches pour servir à l'histoire du droit françois* (Paris, 1752), 122ff.

62. Hans Blumenberg, *Work on Myth,* tr. R. Wallace (Cambridge, Mass. 1985); see also Erwin Hölzle, *Die Idee einer altgermanischen Freiheit vor Montesquieu* (Berlin, 1925); and above, 42.

63. Ferrière, 2.

64. Angleberme, fol. clxxxvi.

65. [P. G. Michaux], *Les Coutumes considerees comme loix de la nation dans son origine et dans son etat actuel* (Paris, 1783), 2, 10, 108, 30.

12 · *The Philosophical School*

1. In general see Rodolf Stintzing, *Geschichte der deutschen Rechtswissenschaft,* I (Munich, 1880); Neal Ward Gilbert, *Concepts of Method in the Renaissance* (New York, 1960); Cesare Vasoli, *La dialettica e la retorica dell'umanesimo* (Milan, 1968), and "La dialettica umanistica e la metodologia giuridica nel secolo XVI," in *La formazione storica del diritto moderno in Europa* (3 vols., Florence, 1977), I, 237–79; Theodor Vieweg, *Topik und Jurisprudenz* (Munich, 1969); Klaus Luig, "Institutionen-Lehrbuchen des nationalen Rechts in 17. und 18. Jahrhundert," *Ius Commune,* 3 (1970), 64–97; J. Blühdorn and J. Ritter, eds., *Philosophie und Rechtswissenschaft* (Frankfurt, 1969); Norbert Bobbio, *L'Analogia nella logica del diritto* (Turin, 1938); Gerhard Otte, *Dialektik und Jurisprudenz* (Frankfurt, 1971); Hans Erich Troje, "Arbeitshypothesen zum Thema 'humanistische Jurisprudenz,'" *Tijdschrift voor Rechtsgeschiedenis,* 38 (1970), 519–63; Friedrich Ebrard, "Über Methoden, Systeme, Dogmen in der Geschichte des Privatrechts," *Zeitschrift fur sweizerisches Recht,* 67 (1948), 95–136; Georges Kalinowski, "La Logique et son histoire," *Archives de phil-*

osophie du droit, 27 (1982), 275–89; Aldo Mazzacane, *Scienza, logica, e ideologia nella giurisprudenza tedesca del sec. XVI* (Milan, 1971), and "Umanesimo e sistematiche giuridiche in Germania alla fine del cinquecento: 'equita' e 'giurisprudenza' nella opere di Hermann Vultejus," *Annali di storia del diritto,* 12–13 (1968–69), 257–319; and D. R. Kelley, "Law," in *Cambridge History of Political Thought, 1450–1700* (Cambridge, Eng., [1990]).

2. Many of these treatises are preserved in Reusner, *CHEIRAGOGIA* (Speier, 1588), and in *Variorum opuscula ad cultiorem jurisprudentiam adsequandam pertinentia* (Pisa, 1769); see also D. R. Kelley, "Civil Science in the Renaissance: The Problem of Interpretation," in *The Languages of Political Theory in Early-Modern Europe,* ed. A. Pagden (Cambridge, Eng., 1987), 57–78; and Vincenzo Piano Mortari, *Ricerche sulla teoria dell'interpretazione del diritto nel secolo XVI* (Milan, 1956).

3. *Methodica dialectices ratio ad iurisprudentiam accommodata,* in Claudius Cantiuncula, *Topica legalia* (Basel, 1545), 111; and see Guido Kisch, *Claudius Cantiuncula: Ein Basler Jurist und Humanist des 16. Jahrhunderts* (Basel, 1970). On *ius in arten redigendo,* see Quintilian, XII, 3, 10, and Aulus Gellius, I, 22, 7.

4. For example, a Latin version of part of Pierre Droit de Gaillard's *Methode qu'on doit tenir en la lecture de l'histoire* (Paris, 1579) is referred to as "deprompta ex suis institutionibus historicis" in his preface to B. Fulgosias, *Factorum dictorumque memorabilem libri IX* (Pais, 1578).

5. Leibniz, *Nova Methodus discendae docendaeque jurisprudentiae* (1667), in *Sammtliche Schriften und Briefe,* ed. Preussische Akademie der Wissenschaften, VI (1) (Berlin, 1923), 338; and see below, n. 18.

6. Johannes Oldendorp, *De duplici verborum et rerum significatione* (Venice, 1557), fol. 7r. Cf. Pietro Andrea Gammaro, *De veritate ac excellentia legum scientiae,* in *Tractatus universi juris* (11 vols., Venice, 1583), I, fol. 249: "Finis iuris civilis est reipublicae gubernatio."

7. Barnabé Brisson, *De verborum significatione* (Halle, 1743), preface; see Jacob Spiegel, *Lexicon juris civilis* (Basel, 1539); Oldendorp, *De copia verborum et rerum in iure civili* (Lyon, 1546); François Hotman, *Novus commentarius de verbis iuris* (Basel, 1563); see also P. Brederode, *Thesaurus dictionum et sententiarum ex Bartoli a Saxoferrato operibus* (Frankfurt, 1660); and Guido Kisch, "Juridical Lexicography and the Reception of Roman Law," in his *Forschungen zur Rechts- und Sozialgeschichte des Mittelalters* (Simaringen, 1980).

8. Stephanus de Federicus, *De interpretatione legum,* in *Tractus universi juris,* I, fol. 210; cf. Gammaro, *De veritate,* fol. 132.

9. Bartolommeo Cepolla, *De interpretatione legis extensiva* (Venice, 1557), fol. 7.

10. Christopher Hegendorf, *Dialecticae legalis libri quinque* (Lyon, 1534), 71.

11. Oldendorp, *De duplici verorum et rerum significatione,* 13–32 ("Regulae aliquot de significatione"); and see Peter Macke, *Die Rechts- und Staatsdenken des Johannes Oldendorp* (Cologne, 1966); and Erik Wolf, *Grosse Rechtsdenker der deutschen Geistesgeschichte* (Tübingen, 1963), 138–76.

12. Conrad Lagus, *Methodica iuris utriusque traditio* (Lyon, 1566), 2.

13. Matteo Gribaldi, *De methodo ac ratione studiendi libri tres* (Lyon, 1556); and see Guido Kisch, *Melanchthons Rechts- und Soziallehre* (Basel, 1967).
14. Frannçois Hotman, *Jurisconsultus* (Basel, 1559), 11. On the distinction between *ius naturale primaevum* and *secondarium* see also Antoine Faber, *Iurisprudentia Papinianae scientia* (Lyon, 1607), 35.
15. Gammaro, *De extensionibus*, in *Tractatus universi juris*, vol. XVIII, fol. 248.
16. Cantiuncula, *Topica legalia,* first "topic," and p. 10: "Non est tamen eorum interpretatio firmum et necessarium praejudicium: sed probabile."
17. Claude de Seyssel, *In VI. fforum [Digesti] partes et primam C[odicis]* (n.p., n.d.), 11. In general see *Althusius-Bibliographie,* ed. H. U. Scupin et al. (Berlin, 1973); Otto Gierke, *Natural Law and the Theory of Society,* tr. Ernest Barker (Cambridge, Eng., 1934); Carl von Kaltenborn, *Die Vorläufer des Hugo Grotius* (Leipzig, 1848); Francesco Ercole, *Da Bartolo all'Althusio* (Florence, 1932); Otto Wilhelm Krause, *Naturrechtler des sechzehnten Jahrhunderts* (Frankfurt, 1982); Hans Medick, *Naturzustand und Naturgeschichte der bürgerlichen Gesellschaft* (Göttingen, 1973); Ernst Reibstein, *Volkerrecht: Eine Geschichte seiner Idee in Lehre und Paxis* (Munich, 1957); G. Solari, *Studi storici di filosofia del diritto* (Turin, 1949); Michael Stolleis, ed., *Staatsdenker im 17. und 18. Jahrhundert* (Frankfurt, 1977); Richard Tuck, *Natural Rights Theories* (Cambridge, Eng., 1979), and "The 'Modern' Theory of Natural law," in *The Languages of Political Theory,* 99–122; Michel Villey, "Les Fondateurs de l'école du droit naturel moderne au XVIIe siècle," *Archives de philosophie du droit,* 6 (1961), 73–105; Hans Welzel, *Naturrecht und materiale Gerechtigkeit* (Göttingen, 1962). See also Erik Wolf, *Da Problem der Naturrechtlehre* (Karlsruhe, 1964); Marcelino Rodriguez Molinero, *Derecho natural e historia en el pensamiento europeo contemporaneo* (Madrid, 1973); and Franco Todescan, *Le radici teologiche del giusnaturalismo* (2 vols., Milan, 1983–87), on "the problem of secularization" in Grotius (vol. I) and in Domat (vol. II). A number of valuable papers were delivered at an international conference on natural law in Göttingen in June 1989.
18. Leibniz, *Nova Methodus,* 233; and see Hans-Peter Schneider, *Justitia Universalis* (Frankfurt, 1967); Kurt Dickerhof, *Leibniz' Bedeutung für die Gesetzgebung* (Freiburg, 1941); Klaus Luig, "Die Rolle des deutschen Rechts in Leibniz' Kodificationsplan," *Ius Commune,* 5 (1975), 56–70; Hansjakob Stehle, *Der Rechtsgedanke im politischen Weltbild von Leibniz* (Frankfurt, 1950); Fritz Sturm, *Das römische Recht in der Sicht von Gottfried Wilhelm Leibniz* (Tübingen, 1968); Vasoli, "Encyclopedismo, pansofia, e riforma 'metodica' del diritto nella 'Nova Methodus' di Leibniz," *Quaderni fiorentini per la storia del pensiero giuridico moderno,* 2 (1973), 37ff; also Ch. H. Eckhard, *Hermeneutica iuris,* ed. C. W. Walch (Leipzig, 1802).
19. Peter Peterson, *Geschichte der aristotelischen Philosophie im Protestantischen Deutschland* (Leipzig, 1921); H. Drietzel, *Protestantisches Aristotelismus und absolutes Staat: die Politica des H. Arnisaeus* (Wiesbaden, 1970); H. Rommen, *Die ewige Wiederkehr des Naturrechts* (Munich, 1947); M. Stolleis, *Geschichte des offentlichen Rechts in Deutschland,* I (Munich, 1988); and Ch. 9, n. 25. A classic Ramist scheme is given by Althusius, *Iurisprudentiae Romanae libri: Ad leges Methodi Rameae conformati* (Basel, 1589).

20. Ulrich Gottfried Leinsle, *Das Ding und die Method* (Augsburg, 1985); and *RES, Lessico intellettuale europeo*, vol. 26, ed. M. Fattori and M. Bianchi (Rome, 1982); see also Hans-Georg Gadamer, *Philosophical Hermeneutics*, tr. D. Linge (Berkeley, 1976), 69–81.

21. Digest, L, 17; and see Peter Stein, *Regulae Juris* (Edinburgh, 1966). See also Henri Roland and Laurent Boyer, *Locutions latines et adages du droit français contemporain* (Paris, 1978); M. A. Screech, "Commonplaces of Law, Proverbial Wisdom, and Philosophy," in *Classical Influences on European Culture, A.D. 1500–1700*, ed. R. R. Bolgar (Cambridge, Eng., 1976), 127–34; Ferdinand Elsener, "Regula iuris, Brocardum, Sprichwort," *Studien und Mitteilungen zur Geschichte des Benediktinerordens und seiner Zweige*, 73 (1962), 177–218, with further bibliography.

22. Digest, L, 17.

23. Leibniz, *Textes inédites*, ed. Gaston Grua (2 vols., Paris, 1948), II, 649. Jean Domat, *Les Loix civiles dans leur ordre naturel* (2 vols., Luxembourg, 1702), I, 6; and see Nicola Matteucci, *Jean Domat, un magistrato giansenista* (Bologna, 1959); Franco Todesca, "Domat et les sources du droit, *Archives de philosophie du droit*, 27 (1980), 55–66; René-Frederic Voeltzel, *Jean Domat, (1625–1969)* (Paris, 1936); Carmine Ventimiglia, *Società, politica, diritto: il christiano e il mondo in Pascal e Domat* (Parma, 1983).

24. François Bourjon, *Le Droit commun de la France et la coutume de Paris reduits en principes* (Paris, 1747); and Pierre Merville, *La Coutume de Normandie reduite en maximes* (Paris, 1707).

25. Louis Boullenois, *Dissertations sur des questions qui naissent de la contrarieté des loix et des coutumes* (Paris, 1732), xiv.

26. Leibniz, *Textes inédites*, II, 649, 703, and *Die philosophischen Schriften*, ed. G. J. Gerhardt (Berlin, 1875), I, 159. See also Horst Denzer, *Moralphilosophie und Naturrecht bei Samuel Pufendorf* (Munich, 1972); Leonard Krieger, *The Politics of Discretion: Pufendorf and the Acceptance of Natural Law* (Chicago, 1965); Istvan Hont, "The Language of Sociability and Commerce: Samuel Pufendorf and the Theoretical Foundations of the 'Four-Stages Theory,'" in *The Languages of Political Theory*, 253–76; Bernard Gagnebin, *Burlamaqui et le droit naturel* (Geneva, 1944); Ph. Meylan, *Jean Barberac, 1674–1744, et les débuts d l'enseignement du droit dans l'ancienne académie de Lausanne* (Lausanne, 1937); Ricardo Orestano, "Institution, Barbeyrac, e l'anagrafe di un significato," *Quaderni fiorentini*, 11–12 (1982–83), I, 169–78; Siegelinde Othmer, *Berlin und die Verbreitung des Naturrechts in Europa: Kultur und sozialgeschichtliche Studien zu Jean Barbeyracs Pufendorf-Übersetzungen und eine Analyse seiner Leserschaft* (Berlin, 1970); and Fiametta Palladini, ed., *Discussioni seicentesche su Samuel Pufendorf: scritti latini, 1663–1700* (Bologna, 1978).

27. Cepolla, *De interpretatione legis*, fol. 27r, "extensio interpretiva introducta fuit iure naturali secundario"; [Schneidewein], *In quatuor institutionum imperialium commentarii* (Turin, 1660), 7: "Doctores dividunt ius naturali in primaevum, et secundarium. Primaevum appellant, quod homines cum brutis commune habent . . . Secondarium vero ius naturale dicitur, quod solus hominibus convenit, quod in sola naturali ratione conquiescit . . ."; J. W. Textor,

Synopsis juris gentium (Washington, D.C., 1916), 8, referring to Aristotle: "It is a common doctrine of the doctors, especially of the early ones, that the Law of Nations is divided into the Primordial and the Secondary, the former of these consisting of material dictated by Reason, right away from the beginnings of institutions, while the latter sprang up later in usage and the necessities of human life"; and cf. Emmerich de Vattel, *The Law of Nations,* tr. J. Chitty (London, 1834), preface. Also see Ch. 9, no. 10; and J. C. Heineccius, *Opera omnia* (Geneva, 1744), I, 10.

28. Grotius, *De jure belli ac pacis* (1625), Proleg. 5, and *De Iure Praedae Commentarius* (Oxford, 1950), 6; and cf. Leibniz, *The Political Writings,* tr. P. Riley (Cambridge, Eng., 1972), 45: "whether justice and goodness are arbitrary or whether they belong to the necessary and eternal truths about the nature of things, as do number and proportion." In general see Robert Feenstra, "L'Influence de la scolastique espanole sur Grotius en droit privé," *Quaderni fiorentini,* 1 (1973), 377–402; and Robert Feenstra with C. J. D. Waal, *Seventeenth-Century Leiden Law Professors and Their Influence on the Development of the Civil Law* (Amsterdam, 1975); Peter Pavel Remec, *The Position of the Individual in International Law according to Grotius and Vattel* (The Hague, 1960); and L. Rosa, "Grozio fra il giusnaturalismo scolastico e il giusnaturalismo moderno," *Miscellanea Adriano Gazzana,* II (Milan, 1960); also Grotius, *The Jurisprudence of Holland* (Oxford, 1953), 6. And see Gesina van der Molem, *Alberico Gentili and the Development of International Law* (Leiden, 1968); and C. Van Vollenhoven, *Les Trois Phases du droit des gens* (The Hague, 1919).

29. Domat, I, 6; cf. Laurens Bouchel, *La Bibliotheque ou thresor du droict françoise* (Paris, 1615), 120: "Le droict civil soit muable et changeable par civile raison: le naturel estably par la divine providence soit constant et stable."

30. Ian Hacking, *The Emergence of Probability* (Cambridge, Eng., 1975), 86.

31. Georges Gurvitch's *L'Idée du droit social* (Paris, 1932), 175.

32. Samuel Rachel, *De Jure Naturae et Gentium Dissertationes* (1676) (Washington, D.C., 1916).

33. Textor, ch. 1, and esp. p. 6: "It may be gathered that the Law of Nations was not developed out of hand by one or two operations, but over a long period and by continued usage. So Grotius also holds . . ."

34. Heineccius, *Opera omnia* (Geneva, 1744), I, 190, and IV, 37.

35. Henry Sumner Maine, *Ancient Law,* 24th ed. (London, 1924), 52.

36. Digest, I, 3, 17; cf. *SPIRITUS, Lessico intellectuale europeo,* vol. 32, ed. M. Fattori and M. Bianchi (Rome, 1984); and Giovanni Tarello, *Le ideologie della codificazione nel secolo XVIII* (Geneva, 1976), 145.

37. Domat, I, i–xxxi ("Traité des lois"), esp. p. xvi.

38. Ibid., I, 1; and see Ch. 3, n. 51.

39. Montesquieu, *De l'esprit des lois;* and see Edouard Laboulaye, *Histoire du droit de propriété foncière en occident* (Paris, 1839), 13; also Raymond Aron, *Main Currents in Sociological Thought* (New York, 1968), I, 14; Eugen Ehrlich, "Montesquieu and Sociological Jurisprudence," *Harvard Law Review,* 29 (1915–16), 582–600; Etienne Fournol, *Bodin prédécesseur de Montesquieu* (Paris, 1896); Mark Huilling, *Montesquieu and the Old Regime* (Berkeley,

1976); Mark H. Waddicor, *Montesquieu and the Philosophy of Natural Law* (The Hague, 1970); and Simone Goyard-Fabre, *La Philosophie du droit de Montesquieu* (Paris, 1973). Montesquieu had at least seen Vico's *Scienza nuova,* according to Roger Mercier, *Le Réhabilitation de la nature humaine, 1700–1750* (Villemomble, 1960), 189.

40. Montesquieu, *De l'esprit des lois,* bk. XXVI, chs. 1, 29, 38. Iris Cox, *Montesquieu and the History of French Laws* (Oxford, 1983).

41. Ibid., bk. XXVIII, ch. 34.

42. In general see Sten Gagnér, *Ideengeschichte der Gesetzgebung* (Stockholm, 1960); André-Jean Arnaud, *Les Origines doctrinales du Code civil français* (Paris, 1969); Giovanni Tarello, *Storia della cultura giuridica moderna* (Bologna, 1976), and *Le ideologie della codificazione;* J. Van Kan, *Les Efforts de codification en France* (Paris, 1929); Walter Wilhem, "Gesetzgebung und Kodification im 17. und 18. Jahrhundert," *Ius Commune,* 1 (1967), 241–70; Marcel Thomann, "Histoire de l'idéologie juridique au XVIIIe siècle, ou: 'le droit prisonnier des mots,'" *Archives de philosophie du droit,* 19 (1974), 127–49; and *Rechtsphilosophie der Aufklärung,* ed. Reinhard Brandt (Berlin, 1981).

43. M. Duchet, *Anthropologie et histoire au siècle des lumières* (Paris, 1971), 373; and cf. Morelly, *Code de la nature,* ed. G. Chinard (n.p., 1950).

44. Rabaut Saint-Etienne, *Considerations sur les interets du tiers-etat addresses au peuple des provinces* (Paris, 1788), 13, cited by Keith Baker, "Memory and Practice: Politics and the Representation of the Past in Eighteenth-Century France," *Representations,* no. 11 (1985), 159.

45. Charles Dumoulin, *Oratio de concordia et unione consuetudinarium Franciae,* in his *Tractatus commerciorum* (Paris, 1546), 807; and see Ch. 11, n. 52.

46. Rodolfo Batiza, *Domat, Pothier, and the Code Napoléon* (n.p., 1973).

47. Samuel Cocceij, *Code Frederic, ou corps de droit pour les etats de sa majesté le Roi de Prusse,* tr. from the German (Halle, 1751), xxiii, xviii; Cocceij remarked also that "l'Homme est ne pour la Societé," and that "les Loix de la Societé Civile" organized in this new "Systeme de droit" followed the plan of Justinian.

48. See Ch. 10 at n. 60.

49. Jeremy Bentham, *Handbook of Political Fallacies,* ed. H. Larrabee (Baltimore, 1953), 34, 43, and *Of Laws in General,* ed. H. L. A. Hart (London, 1960), 194; and see Elie Halevy, *The Growth of Philosophical Radicalism,* tr. M. Moriss (London, 1928); and Gerald J. Postrema, *Bentham and the Common Law Tradition* (Oxford, 1986).

50. *Codification Proposal Addressed by Jeremy Bentham to All Nations Professing Liberal Opinions* (London, 1822). And cf. H. F. Jolowicz, "Was Bentham a Lawyer?" in *Jeremy Bentham and the Law,* ed. G. Keeton and G. Schwarzenberger (London, 1948), 1–19.

51. John Austin, *Lectures on Jurisprudence, or The Philosophy of Positive Law,* ed. R. Campbell (London, 1874); and see W. L. Morison, *John Austin* (Stanford, 1982); and Andreas Schwarz, "John Austin and the German Jurisprudence of His Time," *Politica,* 1 (1934), 178–99.

52. See, e.g., *L'Esprit de legislation,* "traduit de l'allemand" (London, 1768); and Gaetano Filangieri, *La Science de legislation* (Paris, 1786).

53. L. Cahen and R. Guyot, eds., *L'Oeuvre législative de la révolution* (Paris, 1913), and *Archives parlementaires* ed. J. Mavidal and E. Laurent (82 vols., Paris, 1862), X, 717ff. In general see Raoul Aubin, *L'Organisation judiciaire d'après les Cahiers de 1789* (Paris, 1928); and Guy Chaussinand-Nogaret, *The French Nobility in the Eighteenth Century,* tr. W. Doyle (Cambridge, Eng., 1985), showing from the *cahiers* that more than three quarters of the nobility wanted a reform of civil law; Edmond Seligman, *La Justice de France pendant la révolution, 1789–1792* (Paris, 1901); A. Mater, *L'Histoire juridique de la révolution* (Besançon, 1919); C. D. A. Valette, *De le durée persistante de l'ensemble du droit civil français pendant et depuis la révolution de 1789* (Paris, 1892); also J. C. Q. Mackreel, *The Attack on "Feudalism" in Eighteenth-Century France* (London, 1973); Philippe Sagnac, *La Législation civile de la révolution française, 1789–1804: Essai d'histoire sociale* (Paris, 1898); Philippe Sagnac and P. Caron eds., *Les Comités des droits féodaux et de législation et d'abolition du régime seigneurial, 1789–1793* (Paris, 1907); and the fine collection, *La Révolution et l'ordre juridique privé: rationalité ou scandale?* Actes du colloque d'Orléans (Orléans, 1988).
54. *Archives parlementaires,* XII, 570; and see Michael Fitzsimmons, *Dissolution and Disillusionment: The Parisian Order of Barristers, 1789–1815* (Cambridge, Mass., 1987).
55. Jeremy Bentham, *Draught of a new plan for the organisation of the Judicial Establishment in France* (n.p., 21 Dec. 1789).
56. P. A. Fenet, *Recueil complet des travaux préparatoires du Code Civil* (15 vols., Paris, 1827), I, 1; and see F. Papillard, *Cambacérès* (Paris, 1961).
57. Fenet, VI, 169.
58. See especially Sergio Moravia, *Il pensiero degli Idéologues: scienza e filosofia in Francia, 1780–1815* (Florence, 1974), 746; Georges Gusdorf, *Les Sciences humaines et la pensée occidentale,* VIII, *La Conscience révolutionnaire: Les Idéologues* (Paris, 1978), 401; and Maxime Leroy, *Histoire des idées sociales en France,* II (Paris, 1950). And on the connections between law and "la science social" see also A. L. Jussieu, *Discours, Corps Législatif: Conseil des Cinqcents* (Paris, An 7; BN.Le.43.3603.), 3.
59. A. Esmein, "L'Originalité du Code Civil," *Le Code Civil: livre du centenaire* (Paris, 1904), I, 17; and see Claude Journès, *La Coutume et la loi: études d'un conflit* (Lyon, 1986).
60. J. B. D. Riffé-Caubray, *Les Pandectes françaises, ou recueil complet de toutes les lois en vigueur* (Paris, 1803), 5; and in general see D. R. Kelley, *Historians and the Law in Postrevolutionary France* (Princeton, 1984).

13 · The Historical School

1. Digest I, 2, 2. In general see (R. Stintzing-) E. Landsberg, *Geschichte der deutschen Rechtswissenschaft,* III (Berlin, 1898); Notker Hammerstein, *Jus und Historie: Ein Beitrag zur Geschichte des historischen Denkens an deutschen Universitäten im späten 17. und im 18. Jahrhundert* (Göttingen, 1973); Peter Stein, *Legal Evolution: The Story of an Idea* (Cambridge, Eng.,

1980); Alan Watson, *Sources of Law, Legal Change, and Ambiguity* (Philadelphia, 1984); D. R. Kelley, "The Rise of Legal History in the Renaissance," *History and Theory,* 9 (1970), 174–94 (reprinted in *History, Law, and the Human Sciences*), and "Ancient Verses on New Ideas: Legal Tradition and the French Historical School," *History and Theory,* 26 (1987), 319–38; Hans Thieme, "Die Zeit der späten Naturrechts," *Zeitschrift der Savigny-Stiftung für Rechtsgeschichte,* Ger. Abt., 56 (1936), 202–63; and see Ch. 12 at n. 17. See also Riccardo Orestano, *Introduzione allo studio del diritto romano* (Bologna, 1987), esp. 221–306; and James Whitman, *Roman Civilization and the German Rule of Law* (Princeton, 1990).

2. Norbert Horn, "Römisches Recht als gemeinschaftliches Recht bei Arthur Duck," *Studien zur europäischen Rechtsgeschichte,* ed. Walter Wilhelm (Frankfurt, 1972), 170–80; M. Stolleis, ed., *Hermann Conring, 1600–1681* (Berlin, 1983); Karl Kossert, *Hermann Conrings Rechtsgeschichtlicher Verdienst* (Cologne, 1939); and Ernst von Moeller, *Hermann Conring: Der Vorkämpfer der deutschen Rechts, 1601–1681* (Hannover, 1915).

3. Conrad Lagus, *Methodica iuris utriusque traditio* (Lyon, 1556), 2; Jean Barbeyrac, *Oratio inauguralis de dignitate et utilitate juris achistoriarum et utriusque disciplinae amica coniunctione* (Amsterdam, 1711), 20, citing Dionysius of Halicarnassus's "philosophy teaching by example"; Johann Eisenart, *De fide historica commentarii accessit Oratio de conjugendis jurisprudentiae et historiarum studiis,* cited in Hammerstein, 107; and see Ch. 11, n. 21.

4. See Ch. 4, n. 16.

5. Montesquieu, *De l'esprit des lois,* XXXI, 2.

6. André Terrasson, *Histoire de la jurisprudence romaine* (Paris, 1750), vii. Cf. C. G. Biener, *Commentarii de origine et progressu legum iuriumque Germanicorum* (Leipzig, 1787); Carlo Ghisalberti, *Gian Vincenzo Gravina* (Milan, 1962); and Michael Steinberg, "The Twelve Tables and Their Origins: An Eighteenth-Century Debate," *Journal of the History of Ideas,* 43 (1982), 379–96.

7. J. G. Heineccius, *Opera omnia* (Geneva, 1771), I, 10 ("Elementa Iuris Naturae et Gentium"); and cf. L. J. F. Höpfner, *Theoretisches-practisches Commentarii über die heineccischen Institutionen* (Frankfurt, 1803).

8. Franciscus Buddeus, *Selecta iuris naturae et gentium* (Halle, 1717), "Historia Iuris Naturalis"; Adam Friedrich Glafney, *Vollstandige Geschichte des Rechts der Vernunft* (Leipzig, 1739); [Martin Hübner], *Essai sur l'histoire du droit naturel* (London, 1757); L. J. F. Höpfner, *Naturrecht der einzelnen Menschen der Gesellschaft und der Volker* (Frankfurt, 1790); J. J. Brucker, *Historia critica de philosophia* (Leipzig, 1741–42); Diethelm Klippel, *Politische Freiheit im deutschen Naturrecht des 18. Jahrhunderts* (Paderborn, 1976); and also T. J. Hochstrasser, *The Natural Law Tradition and the Historiography of Moral Philosophy in the Enlightenment* (D. Phil. diss., Cambridge University, 1989).

9. Robert Ward, *An Enquiry into the Foundation and History of the Law of Nations in Europe* (London, 1795), xx.

10. See John P. Dawson, *Oracles of the Law* (Ann Arbor, 1968); and also Ch. 6 at n. 32.

11. Gerhard Theuerkauf, *Lex, Speculum, Compendium: Rechtsaufzeichnung und*

Rechtsbewusstsein in Norddeutschland von 8. bis zum 16. Jahrhundert (Cologne, 1968).

12. Samuel Stryk, *Specimen usus moderni pandectarum* (Halle, 1730). A critique of Roman influence as the source of foreign ideas of "reason of state" is given by "Hippolithus a Lapide" (Martin Chemnitz), *Dissertatio de Ratio Status* (n.p., 1640), with a paraphrase of the Tacitean formula, "in corruptissima Respl. plurimae leges; plurimae legistae." In general see Stintzing-Landsberg; Helmut Coing, *Die Rezeption des römischen Rechts in Frankfurt am Main* (Frankfurt, 1939); Georg Dahm, "On the Reception of Roman and Italian Law in Germany," in *Pre-Reformation Germany*, ed. G. Strauss (New York, 1972); Giovanni Pugliese, "I Pandettisti tra tradizione romanistica e moderna scienza del diritto," in *La formazione storica del diritto moderno in Europa* (3 vols., Florence, 1977), I, 29–72; Hermann Krause, *Kaiserrecht und Rezeption* (Heidelberg, 1952); Winfried Trusen, *Anfänge des gelehrten Rechts in Deutschland* (Wiesbaden, 1962); Rudolph Hoke, "Die Emanzipation der deutschen Rechtswissenschaft von der Zivilistik in 17. Jahrhundert," *Der Staat*, 15 (1976), 211–40; and Alfred Söllner, "Zu den Literatur-typen des deutschen *Usus modernus*," *Ius Commune*, 1 (1975), 167–86.

13. On this point see above all the compendious work of Paolo Cappellini, *Systema iuris*, published in *Quaderni fiorentini*, 17 and 19 (Milan, 1984–85), I. *Genesi del sistema e nascita della "scienza" delle pandette*, and II. *Dalla sistema alla teoria generale;* and also Gabriella Valera, "Dalla scienza generale alla enciclopedia giuridica tedesca nella seconda metà dell '700" (MS provided by the author). See also Andreas B. Schwarz, "Zur Entstehung des modernen Pandektensystems," *Zeitschrift der Savigny-Stiftung für Rechtsgeschichte*, Röm. Abt., 42 (1921), 578–610; and for the older literature, Robert von Mohl, *Die Geschichte und Literatur der Staatswissenschaften* (Erlangen, 1855), 113ff.

14. Rabaut Saint-Etienne, cited in Georges Gusdorf, *Les Sciences humaines et la pensée occidentale* (13 vols., Paris, 1966–88), VIII, 122.

15. Eugène Lerminier, *La Philosophie du droit* (Paris, 1831), II, 311.

16. Albericus de Rosate, *Commentariorum . . . super Digesto veteri* (Lyon, 1545), fol. 14v.

17. See especially Ronald Meek, *Smith, Marx, and After* (London, 1977); and Stein.

18. J. F. Finetti, *De principiis juris naturae, et gentium, adversus Hobbsium, Pufendorfium, Thomasium, Wolfium et alios* (Venice, 1764), I, 122, 146.

19. Georges Gurvitch, *L'Idée du droit social* (Paris, 1932); and Ernst Troeltsch, "The Idea of Natural Law and Humanity in World Politics," in Otto Gierke, *Natural Law and the Theory of Society, 1500 to 1800*, tr. Ernest Barker (Boston, 1957), 201–23.

20. Giambattista Vico, *Diritto universale*, ed. P. Cristofolini (Florence, 1974), consisting of *De universi iuris uno principio et fine uno* and *De constantia jurisprudentiae*, the latter part translated by C. Henri and J. Schlefer in *Origines de la poesie et du droit* (Cafe, 1983). In general see D. R. Kelley, "Vico's Road: From Philology to Jurisprudence and Back," in *Giambattista Vico's Science of Humanity*, ed. G. Tagliacozzo and D. P. Verene (Baltimore, 1976), 15–29 (reprinted in *History, Law, and the Human Sciences*), with further bibliogra-

phy; also Luigi Bellofiore, *La dottrina del diritto naturale in Vico* (Milan, 1954); Gaetano Catalino, *Tra storia e diritto* (Soveria, 1982); Armelo D'Amato, *Il mito di Vico e la filosofia della storia in Francia nella prima meta dell'ottocento* (Naples, 1977); Mario Donzelli, "La Conception de l'histoire de J. B. Vico et son interprétation par J. Michelet," *Archives historiques de la Révolution française*, 53 (1981), 633–58; A. C. 't Hart, *Recht en Staat in het Denken van Giambattista Vico* (Alphen, 1979); Benvenuto Donati, *Nuovi studi sulla filosofia civile di G. B. Vico* (Florence, 1936), on Domat; Dino Pasini, *Diritto e stato in Vico* (Naples, 1970); Andrea Battistini, "Vico e l'etimologia mitopoetica," *Lingua e stile*, 9 (1974), 31–66; Max H. Fisch, "Vico and Roman Law," *Essays Presented to George H. Sabine*, ed. M. Konvitz and A. Murphy (Ithaca, 1948), 62–88; Michael Mooney, *Vico in the Tradition of Rhetoric* (Princeton, 1985); Isaiah Berlin, *Vico and Herder* (London, 1976); and the whole issue of *Rivista internazionale di filosofia del diritto*, 5 (1925).

21. Vico, though a man of "erudition immense," was criticized for his "esprit de système" by more than one scholar, beginning at least with Dubignon, *Histoire critique du gouvernement romain* (Paris, 1765), who added (xxxv) that "ce n'est que par le continu historique qu'on les [historiens] refutes, qu'il respecter la suite des faits, et y assujettir ses idees particulieres." And see Frank Manuel, *The Eighteenth Century Confronts the Gods* (Cambridge, Mass., 1959), 150.

22. Vico, *Diritto universale*, 97; cf. Vico, *Autobiografia*, ed. B. Croce and F. Nicolini, in *Opere*, V (Bari, 1929), 7ff; and see Guido Fassò, *Vico e Grozio* (Naples, 1971).

23. Vico, *Diritto universale*, 35.

24. Ibid., 101; and Vico, *De Antiquissima Italorum sapientia*, ed. F. Nicolini (Bari, 1914), 62.

25. Vico, *De studio ratione*, *Opere*, I, 101, and *Diritto universale*, 5. The term and idea of *principia*, associated with Newtonian science, was of course an ancient convention of legal science: see one of the seventeenth-century commentators on the *regulae juris* of civil and canon law, Jacques Godefroy, *Aphorismes du droit*, tr. M. Caillau (Paris, 1809), "Le partie la plus importante de chaque chose est son principe," citing Pomponius (Digest I, 2, 1).

26. Vico, *Diritto universale*, 33, 75, for example.

27. Ibid., 163; cf. Vico, *La scienza nuova seconda*, ed. F. Nicolini, in *Opere*, IV (Bari, 1953, 31, 154, 394; and also Vico, "Sul diritto naturale delle genti," in *Opere*, VII, 25–31.

28. *Diritto universale*, 31, 99.

29. Ibid., 25.

30. Ibid., 259.

31. Ibid., 111ff.

32. Ibid., 485.

33. Ibid., 53.

34. Ibid., 133.

35. In general see Landsberg; Hammerstein; Hans Erich Bödeker, ed., *Aufklärung und Geschichte* (Göttingen, 1986); Peter Hanns Reill, *The German Enlightenment and the Rise of Historicism* (Berkeley, 1975); Giuliano Marini, *I Maestri della Germania: Göttingen 1770–1820* (Turin, 1975); Hans-Ulrich Stuhle,

Die Diskussion um die Erneuerung der Rechtswissenschaft von 1780–1815
(Berlin, 1978); Bödeker, "The University of Göttingen and the Natural Law
Tradition" (MS provided by the author); Pierangelo Schiera, *Dall 'Arte di
governo alle scienze dello stato: il cameralismo e l'assolutismo tedesco* (Milan,
1968); and Whitman. And see Marx's "Das philosophische Manifest der historischen Rechtsschule," *Marx-Engels Gesamtausgabe*, I (1), 251–59; and
below, n. 43.

36. J. J. Schmauss, *Neues Systema des Rechts der Natur* (Göttingen, 1754); and
see Reill, 56–59. Gebauer and Ludewig are cited by Hammerstein, 336 and
180.

37. J. S. Pütter, *Neuer Versuch einer Juristischen Enzyclopädie und Methodologie*
(Göttingen, 1767); cf. Reill, 184; and Wilhelm Ebel, *Der Göttinger Professor
Johann Stephan Pütter aus Iserlohn* (Göttingen, 1975). The term *Lokalvernunft*
is that of Justus Moser—see Gusdorf, VI, 478.

38. K. S. Zachariae, cited by Giuliano Marini, *Savigny e il methodo della scienza
giuridica* (Milan, 1966), 156; and J. F. Reitemeier, *Encyclopädie und Geschichte des Rechts in Deutschland* (Göttingen, 1785). In general see Cappellini
and Valera; also Arno Buschmann, *Ursprung und Grundlagen der geschicht-
lichen Rechtswissenschaft und Interpretationen zur Rechtslehre Gustav Hugos*
(Krefeld, 1963); F. Eichengrün, *Die Rechtsphilosophie Gustav Hugos* (The
Hague, 1935); Ernst-Jurgen Trojan, *Über Justus Moser, Johann Gottfried
Herder, und Gustav Hugo zur Grundlagung der historischen Schule* (Bonn,
1971); and Jurgen Blühdorn, "Naturrechtskritik und 'Philosophie des positiven
Rechts,' zu Begründung der Jurisprudenz als positiven Fachtswissenschaft
durch Gustav Hugo," *Tijdschrift voor Rechtsgeschiedenis*, 16 (1973), 3–17.

39. Gustav Hugo, *Beiträge zur civilistischen Bucherkenntniss der letzen vierzig
Jahre* (Berlin, 1828), 15ff, 130.

40. Hugo, *Lehrbuch des Naturrechts* (Berlin, 1819; photoreproduced 1971), with
an introduction by Theodor Vieweg; this constitutes vol. II of Hugo's *Lehrbuch
eines civilistisches Cursus*, 7th ed. (Berlin, 1823) (see esp. 104). Cf. L. A.
Warnkönig, *Rechtsphilosophie als Naturlehre des Rechts* (Freiburg, 1839); and
F. J. Stahl, *Die Philosophie des Rechts nach geschichtlicher Ansicht* (Heidelberg,
1830); also A. T. Woeniger, *Die Rechtsphilosophie Stahl's und die historische
Juristenschule* (Berlin, 1841).

41. Hugo, *Lehrbuch*, 45.

42. Ibid., 53.

43. Marini; Aldo Mazzacane, *Savigny e la storiografia giuridica tra storica e sistema*
(Naples, 1976); Hermann Kantorowicz, "Savigny and the Historical School of
Law," *Law Quarterly Review*, 53 (1937), 326–43, reprinted in *Rechtshisto-
rische Schriften* (Karlsruhe, 1970), 419–34; Alfred Manigk, *Savigny und der
Modernismus im Recht* (Berlin, 1914); Olivier Motte, *Savigny et la France*
(Berne, 1983); Hedwig Vonessen, *Friedrich Karl von Savigny und Jakob Grimm*
(Cologne, 1958); Edouard Laboulaye, *Essai sur la vie et les doctrines de
Frédéric Charles de Savigny* (Paris, 1842); the collection *Su Federico Carlo di
Savigny*, in *Quaderni fiorentini*, 9 (1980); and the bibliography compiled by
Klaus Luig and Barbara Dolemayr in *Quaderni fiorentini*, 8 (1979), 501–59;
also Sten Gagnér, *Ideengeschichte der Gesetzgebung* (Stockholm, 1960), 20.

44. von Savigny, *Vom Beruf unsrer Zeit für Gesetzgebung und Rechtswissenschaft* (Heidelberg, 1814), reproduced with other material relating to the quarrel with Thibaut in J. Stern, *Thibaut und Savigny* (Darmstadt, 1959), English tr.; also Reinhart Kosselleck, *Preussen zwischen Reform und Revolution* (Stuttgart, 1967); Werner Schubert, *Französisches Recht in Deutschland zu Beginn des 19. Jahrhunderts* (Cologne, 1977); and on the political context of the *Kodifikationsstreit* see Michael John, *Politics and Law in Late Nineteenth-Century Germany* (Oxford, 1989).
45. A. F. T. Thibaut, *Ueber die Nothwendigkeit einer allgemeinen bürgerlichen Rechts für Deutschland* (Heidelberg, 1814), and his "Über die sogenannte historische und nicht-historische Schule," *Hallische Jahrbuch*, 76–78 (1839), 611ff; and cf. Thibaut's "Antikritik" of Savigny in *Heidelbergische Jahrbücher des Litteraturs*, no. 59 (1814), 202.
46. Savigny, *Beruf*, in Stern, 255—tr. into English by A. Hayward as *On the Vocation of Our Age for Legislation and Jurisprudence* (London, 1831), 185.
47. Savigny, *Vocation*, 91; and cf. Thibaut, *Théorie de l'interprétation logigue*, tr. G. de Sandt and A. Mailher de Chassat (Paris, 1811).
48. Savigny, *System des heutigen römischen Rechts* (Berlin, 1940), I, xiv, 45, 206; and see Savigny, *Das Obligationsrecht* (Berlin, 1851).
49. Savigny, *Vocation*, 28.
50. Adolph Stoll, *Friedrich Karl von Savigny*, II (Berlin, 1929), 213 (to B. G. Niebuhr, 5 Dec. 1816).
51. Savigny, *System*, preface.
52. See the discussion by Karl Mannheim, *Conservatism: A Contribution to the Sociology of Knowledge*, ed. D. Kettler, V. Meja, and N. Stehr (London, 1986), 153ff.
53. See especially Georg Friedrich Puchta, *Die Gewohnheitsrecht* (Erlangen, 1828; reprinted Darmstadt, 1965); and see Joachim Bohnert, *Über die Rechtslehre Georg Friedrich Puchtas, 1798–1846* (Karlsruhe, 1975); Bruno Montanari, *Arbitrio normativo e sapere giuridico a partire da G. F. Puchta* (Milan, 1984); and Georg Beseler, *Volksrecht und Juristenrecht* (Leipzig, 1843).
54. Eugène Lerminier, *Introduction générale à l'histoire du droit* (Paris, 1831), 270. In general see above, note 43; also Alfred Dufour, "Droit et langage dans l'école historique du Droit," *Archives de philosophie du droit*, 19 (1974), 151–80, and "La Théorie des sources du Droit dans l'école du Droit historique," ibid., 27 (1982), 85–119; and also G. Solari, *Storicismo e diritto privato*, II (Turin, 1940).
55. Savigny, *Das Recht des Besitzes* [1803], ed. A. Rudorff, 7th ed. (Berlin, 1865), with a full listing of treatises on *possessio;* and see L. A. Warnkonig, *Analysis of Savigny's Treatise on the Law of Possession* (Edinburgh, 1839). Cf. Eugen Ehrlich, *Fundamental Principles of the Sociology of Law*, tr. W. Moll (New York, 1962), 320; and John Austin, *Lectures on Jurisprudence*, 4th ed. (London, 1873), I, 53 (the subtitle, "The Philosophy of Positive Law," was borrowed from Hugo's work). Lerminier, Savigny's first disciple in France, wrote his thesis on the question: *De possessione analytica Savignianae doctrinae expositio* (Paris, 1827).
56. Discussed in further detail in D. R. Kelley and Bonnie Smith, "What Was

Property? Legal Dimensions of the Social Question in France, 1789–1848," *Proceedings of the American Philosophical Society*, 128 (1984), 200–30.

57. Jakob Grimm, "Das Wort des Besitzes," in his *Reden und Abhandlungen* (Berlin, 1864), 113–44 (written in 1850 for the 50th anniversary of Savigny's doctorate); and cf. Grimm "Von der Poesie im Recht," *Zeitschrift für geschichtliche Rechtswissenschaft*, 2 (1816), 25–99.

58. Eduard Gans, *Ueber die Grundlage des Besitzes: Eine Duplik* (Berlin, 1839), 11, opposed by Friedrich Schaff, *Gans' Kritik gegen Hern von Savigny die Grundlage des Besitzes betreffend* (Berlin, 1839); and see Manfred Riedel, "Eduard Gans als Schüler Hegels: Zur politischen Auslegung der Rechtsphilosophie," *Rivista di filosofia*, 68 (1977), 234–68.

59. A. Koeppe, *Zur Lehre vom Besitz* (Berlin, 1839); and [ein prussischer Jurist], *Darstellung der Lehre vom Besitz als Kritik der v. Savigny'schen Buches* (Berlin, 1840), 28. There is a vast literature on this still controversial question—e.g., Rudolf Jhering, *Ueber den Grund des Bestizschutzes* (Jena, 1869), and *Der Besitzwille* (Jena, 1889); and Geoffrey MacCormick, "The Role of Animus and the Classical Law of Possession," *Zeitschrift der Savigny-Stiftung für Rechtsgeschichte*, Rom. Abt., 68 (1973), 105–45.

60. Cited in Max Brod, *Heine* (New York, 1956), 77.

61. "Zur kritik der Hegel'schen Rechtsphilosophie: Einleitung," *Marx-Engels Ausgabe*, I (1) (Berlin, 1927), 609; and in general see D. R. Kelley, "The Metaphysics of Law: An Essay on the Very Young Marx," *American Historical Review*, 83 (1978), 350–67 (reprinted in *History, Law, and the Human Sciences*); Christoph Schefold, *Die Rechtsphilosophie der jungen Marx von 1842* (Munich, 1970); Hasso Jaeger, "Savigny et Marx," *Archives de philosophie du droit*, 12 (1967), 65–89 (the whole issue devoted to "Marx et le droit moderne"); Peter Landau, "Marx und die Rechtsgeschichte," *Tijdschrift voor Rechtsgeschedenis*, 41 (1973), 361–71; Heinz Lubasz, "Marx's Initial Problematic: the Problem of Poverty," *Political Studies*, 24 (1976), 24–42; Riccardo Guastini, *Marx dalla filosofia del diritto alla scienza della societa: il lessico giuridico marxisno, 1842–1851* (Bologna, 1974). For Marx on the problem of possession (from the *Grundrisse*) see Michael Cain and Alan Hunt, eds., *Marx and Engels on Law* (London, 1979), 139. And see Ch. 14, n. 24.

62. W. Belime, *Traité du droit de possession* (Paris, 1842), viii; see D. R. Kelley, *Historians and the Law in Postrevolutionary France* (Princeton, 1984), ch. 11, and (with Bonnie Smith), "What Was Property?"

63. Frederic Taulier, *Théorie raisonnée du Code Civil* (Grenoble, 1840), 205.

64. Cf. Théodore Chavot, *Traité de la propriété moilière suivant le Code Civil* (Paris, 1839), 217.

65. Raymond Troplong, *De la Prescription* (Paris, 1835), I, 383, with reference to Vico as well as Savigny; and Edouard Laboulaye, *Histoire du droit de propriété foncière en occident* (Paris, 1839), 59.

66. J.-M. Carou, *Traité théorétique et practique des Actions possessoires* (Paris, 1841), 71.

67. Prosper Barante, *Etudes littéraires et historiques* (Paris, 1858), 441.

68. Raymond Troplong, *De la propriété d'après le code civil* (Paris, 1848), 15.

69. J. B. V. Proudhon, *Traité du domain de propriété* (Dijon, 1839), 51, on which

see Paolo Grossi, *An Alternative to Private Property: Collective Property in the Juridical Consciousness of the Nineteenth Century*, tr. L. Cochrane (Chicago, 1981).

70. Carou, 17.

71. P. J. Proudhon, *Qu'est-ce que la propriété?* (Paris, 1966), which badly needs reassessment in the light of the legal tradition, which fascinated and repelled Proudhon—and which was the principal target of his book. Like Marx, Proudhon once planned a legal system, to decide "ce qu'il y a bon dans les codes ou dans l'un des codes," but he gave up this ambition to concern himself with more urgent "social" questions; see *Carnets de Proudhon,* ed. S. Henneguy and J. Faure-Fremet (Paris, 1960), 64 (*année 1844–45*).

14 · *From Civil Science to the Human Sciences*

1. Paolo Cappellini, *Systema iuris,* published in *Quaderni fiorentini,* 17 and 19 (Milan, 1984–85); Peter Stein, *Legal Evolution: The Story of an Idea* (Cambridge, Eng., 1980); Giuliano Marini, *I Maestri della Germania: Göttingen 1770–1820* (Turin, 1975); D. R. Kelley, "Ancient Versus on New Ideas: Legal Tradition and the French Historical School," *History and Theory,* 26 (1987), 319–38; Riccardo Orestano, *Introduzione allo studio del diritto romano. (Bologna, 1987);* and James Whitman, *Roman Civilization and the German Rule of Law* (Princeton, 1989). Other early juristic encyclopedias are those of A. F. Schott (1772), J. F. Gildemeister (1883), J. F. Reitemeier (1785), W. G. Tafinger (1789), T. Schmalz (1790), and K. S. Zachariae (1795). For a useful survey see Cornelis Anne Den Tex, *Encyclopaedia Jurisprudentiae* (Amsterdam, 1835); and more generally, U. Dierse, *Enzyklopaedie: Zur Geschichte eines philosophischen und wissenschaftstheoretischen Begriff* (Bonn, 1977).

2. K. F. von Savigny, *System des heutigen römischen Rechts* (Berlin, 1840), I, ix.

3. John P. Dawson, *Oracles of the Law* (Ann Arbor, 1968), 453.

4. Hegel, *Philosophie des Rechts,* intro., 2, tr. T. M. Knox as *Philosophy of Right* (Oxford, 1952); cf. Hegel, *Philosophy of Subjective Spirit,* tr. M. J. Perry (Dordrecht, 1978), II, "Anthropology," and also *Vorlesung über Rechtsphilosophie,* ed. K. H. Itting (Stuttgart, 1973).

5. Herbert Marcuse, *Reason and Revolution: Hegel and the Rise of Social Theory* (Boston, 1960). In the massive literature on Hegel's legal and social philosophy see also V. S. Harris, *Hegel's Development toward the Sunlight, 1770–1801* (Oxford, 1972); Lawrence Dickey, *Religion, Economics, and the Politics of Spirit, 1770–1807* (Cambridge, Eng., 1987); Norbert Waswek, *The Scottish Enlightenment and Hegel's Account of "Civil Society"* (Dordrecht, 1988), on translations of works on economics (but not on law); Aldo Schiavone, *Alle origini del diritto borghese: Hegel contro Savigny* (Rome, 1984); John Edward Toews, *Hegelianism: The Path toward Dialectical Humanism, 1805–1841* (Cambridge, Eng., 1986); Hans-Christian Lucas and Otto Pöggler, eds., *Hegels Rechtsphilosophie im Zussamenhang der europäischen Verfassungsgeschichte* (Stuttgart, 1986), esp. 221–56, Walter Jaeschke, "Die Vernünftigkeit des Gesetzes"; and Dieter Henrich and Rolf-Peter Horstmann, eds., *Hegels Philosophie des Rechts: Die Theorie der Rechtsformen und ihre Logik* (Stuttgart, 1982).

See also Guido Fassò, *Storia della filosofia del diritto,* III (Bologna, 1984), with further bibliography.

6. Hegel, *Philosophy of Right,* introduction, 3.
7. Ibid., 4ff.
8. Ibid., I, 41ff. Cf. Ch. 13, n. 55.
9. On the legal conception of *alienatio* see D. R. Kelley, "The Metaphysics of Law: An Essay on the Very Young Marx," *American Historical Review,* 83 (1978), 350–67 (reprinted in *History, Law, and the Human Sciences).* This is an aspect specifically not treated by Bertell Ollman, *Alienation: Marx's Conception of Man in Capitalist Society* (Cambridge, Eng., 1971), or Joachim Israel, *Alienation: From Marx to Modern Sociology* (Boston, 1971); see also this chapter at n. 25.
10. Hegel, *Philosophy of Right,* introduction, 4.
11. Marx, "Zur Kritik der Hegel'schen Rechtsphilosophie," in *Marx-Engels Ausgabe,* I (1) (Berlin, 1929), 609—*Collected Works,* III (New York, 1975), 177—but especially Marx, "Das philosophischen Manifest der historische Rechtsschule," *Marx-Engels Ausgabe,* I (1), 251–59—*Collected Works,* I (New York, 1975), 203–10.
12. Louis Bouillenois, *Dissertations sur des questions qui naissent de la contrariété des loix et des coutumes* (Paris, 1732), xiv; and see Ch. 9 at n. 26. In general see Joseph Schumpeter, *A History of Economic Analysis* (New York, 1968), and "Some Questions of Principle," ed. Loring Allen, in *Research in the History of Economic Theory and Analysis,* 5 (1987), 93–116; on which see Mark Perlman, "Schumpeter as a Historian of Economic Thought," in *Research in Economic Thought and Analysis,* 1 (1983). Also Villeneuve Bargemont, *Histoire de l'écon. politique* (Paris, 1841); Wilhelm Röscher, *Geschichte der National-Oekonomie in Deutschland* (Munich, 1874); Charles Gide, *Histoire des doctrines économiques,* 2nd ed. (Paris, 1913); Luigi Cossa, *Introduzione alla economia politica,* 3rd ed. (Milan, 1892); and Karl Pibram, *A History of Economic Reasoning* (Baltimore, 1983). For a critique of "the poverty of economic modernism" see Donald N. McCloskey, *The Rhetoric of Economics* (Madison, 1985).
13. Albion Small, *The Cameralists: The Pioneers of German Social Theory* (Chicago, 1909); and *Aufklarung und Geschichte: Studien zur deutschen Geschichtswissenschaft im 18. Jahrhundert,* ed. H. Bödeker (Gottingen, 1986), esp. 119–43, Gabriella Valera, "Statistik, Staatengeschichte, Geschichte im 18. Jahrhundert," and 144–68, Pasquale Pasquino, "Politisches und historische Interesse: Statistik und historische Staatslehre bei Gottfried Achenwall, 1719–1772"; also Anthony Oberschall, *Empirical Social Research in Germany, 1848–1914* (The Hague, 1965); and Pierangelo Schiera, *Dall'Arte di governo alle scienze dello Stato: il cameralismo e l'assolutismo tedesco* (Milan, 1960).
14. J. H. G. von Justi, cited by Small, 294; and cf. A. J. Blanqui, *Histoire de l'économie politique* (Paris, 1882), I.
15. See Ch. 13 at n. 35, and, on the Historical School of Economics, Röscher's classic work; Joseph Schumpeter, *History of Economic Analysis;* and Gerhard Titzel, *Schmoller versus Menger: Ein Analyse des Methodenstreits in Hinblick auf den Historismus in der Nationalökonomie* (Basel, 1950).

16. Adam Smith, *Lectures on Jurisprudence,* ed. R. L. Meek, D. D. Raphael, and P. G. Stein (Oxford, 1978), 14; Smith, *The Wealth of Nations,* V, 1, ii. See ch. 10, n. 67, and also Peter Stein, "Adam Smith's Theory of Law and Society," *Classical Influences on Western Thought, A.D. 1650–1820,* ed. R. R. Bolgar (Cambridge, Eng., 1978), 263–73.

17. C. Louandre, "Du Travail et des classes laboreuses dans l'ancienne France," *Revue des deux mondes,* 8, no. 4 (1850), 833, and 820 ("Nul n'entre ici qui n'est économiste"); see also A. C.-T., "Des plus récents travaux en économie politique," *Revue des deux mondes,* 1, no. 1 (1839), 705–37, "L'économie est en verve de prosélytisme."

18. Wilhelm Hennis, "A Science of Man: Max Weber and the Political Economy of the Historical School," in *Max Weber and His Contemporaries,* ed. Wolfgang Mommsen and Jurgen Osterhammel (London, 1987), 28; and, on Weber's "change of discipline," Walther Wegener, *Die Quellen der Wissenschaftsauffassung Max Webers und die Problematik der Werturteilsfreiheit des Nationalökonomie* (Berlin, 1962); and see below, n. 58.

19. *Profession d'avocat* (Paris, 1832), I, 359–67, "Sur l'étude des principes de l'économie sociale," by A. G. Camus, author of the original (1770) version of this handbook.

20. J. B. Say, *Traité d'économie politique,* 6th ed. (Paris, 1841), 132–33.

21. Pietro Rossi, *Cours d'économie politique* (Paris, 1840), and *Mélanges d'économie politique, d'histoire, et de philosophie* (Paris, 1857); and see D. R. Kelley, *Historians and the Law in Postrevolutionary France* (Princeton, 1984), 124.

22. Bargement, 8.

23. Eugen Ehrlich, *Fundamental Principles of the Sociology of Law,* tr. W. Moll (Cambridge, Mass., 1936), 98; Paul Cauwès, *Précis du cours d'économie politique* (Paris, 1881).

24. Marx-Engels, *Collected Works,* III, 217 and 218, on "the loss or surrender of private property [*Entäusserung oder Entfremdung des Privateigentums*]" (*Marx-Engels Gesamtausgabe,* I, pt. 3, 531); also, on the ancient Roman examples, from the *Grundrisse,* now in *Collected Works,* XXVIII (New York, 1986), 404ff.

25. Letter to Heinrich Marx, in *Collected Works,* I (New York, 1975), 10–21; *Economic and Philosophic Manuscripts,* in *Collected Works,* III, 229–346; see also n. 9 above and Ch. 13, n. 61. "Metaphysik des Rechts" is used by Kant in the "Vorrede" of his "Metaphysische Anfangsgrunde der Rechtslehre," in *Metaphysik der Sitten.*

26. P. J. Proudhon, *Carnets,* ed. S. Henneguy and J. Faure-Fremet (Paris, 1960), II, 66, and 139 ("La phénoménologie de l'esprit, c'est l'économie politique"); also Proudhon, *System of Economic Contradictions, or The Philosophy of Misery,* tr. B. Tucker (Boston, 1888), *Qu'est-ce que la propriété?,* and *Théorie de la propriété,* II, 158; and see Ch. 13, n. 70.

27. Anselm Batbie, *Nouveau cours d'économie politique* (Paris, 1866); and see Henri Baudrillart, "Un Jurisconsulte Économiste: M. Charles Renouard," *Revue des deux mondes,* 50, no. 4 (1880), 802–28, and "Le Nouvel Experiment de l'économie politique dans les facultés de droit," *Revue des deux mondes,*

55, no. 3 (1885), 158–85; and Alfred Jourdan, "L'Enseignement de l'économie politique," *Revue d'économie politique,* 1 (1887), 3–31.

28. Henri Baudrillart, *Du principe de propriété* (Paris, 1855), 10, and *La Propriété* (Paris, 1867).

29. Michelle Duchet, *Anthropologie et histoire au siècle des lumières* (Paris, 1971); René Hubert, *Les Sciences sociales dans l'Encyclopédie* (Lille, 1923); Georges Gusdorf, *Les Sciences humaines et la pensée occidentale,* VII (Paris, 1976), on the "new anthropology"; and cf. Gusdorf, II (2) (Paris, 1969), 178ff; Anthony Pagden, *The Fall of Natural Man: The American Indian and the Origins of Comparative Ethnology* (Cambridge, Eng., 1982). More general treatments include Annemarie de Waal Malefijt, *Images of Man: A History of Anthropological Thought* (New York, 1974); Murray J. Leaf, *Man, Mind, and Science: A History of Anthropology* (New York, 1979); and the anthologies collected by Burton Feldman and Robert D. Richardson, *The Rise of Modern Anthropology* (Bloomington, Ind., 1972); and also V. F. Calverton, ed., *The Making of Man: An Outline of Anthropology* (New York, 1930).

30. Odo Marquard, "Zur Geschichte des philosophischen Begriffs 'Anthropologie' seit dem Ende des 18. Jahrhunderts," in *Collegium Philosophicum* (Berlin, 1965); see also Michael Landmann, *Philosophical Anthropology,* tr. D. Parent (Philadelphia, 1974), 11, and *De Homine: Der Mensch im Spiegel seines Gedankens* (Munich, 1962); and H. G. Gadamer and Paul Vogler, eds., *Neue Anthropologie,* IV, *Kulturanthropologie* (Stuttgart, 1972), 225, on *Rechtssystem.*

31. D. R. Kelley, "The Science of Anthropology: An Essay on the Very Old Marx," *Journal of the History of Ideas,* 40 (1984), 245–62.

32. For background see Joseph Niedermann, *Kultur: Werden und Wandlungen des Begriffs und seines Ersatzbegriffe von Cicero bis Herder* (Florence, 1941); and for contrast the article "Culture" in the *International Encyclopedia of Social Science;* also Stephen Horigan, *Nature and Culture in Western Discourse* (London, 1988); as well as Leo Strauss's tendentious attack on "conventionalism" and "historicism," *Natural Right and History* (Chicago, 1953).

33. See, e.g., J. O. Brew, ed., *One Hundred Years of Anthropology* (Cambridge, Mass., 1968); T. K. Penniman, *A Hundred Years of Anthropology* (New York, 1974); Robert H. Lowie, *The History of Ethnological Theory* (New York, 1937); and George W. Stocking, Jr., *Race, Culture, and Evolution* (New York, 1968), and *Victorian Anthropology* (New York, 1987).

34. A. L. Jussieu, *Discours: Corps Législatif, Conseil des Cinq-cents* (Paris, An. 7; BN Le.43.3603). Cf. Baron Degérando, *The Observation of Savage Peoples,* tr. F. C. T. Moore (Berkeley, 1969), preface by E. E. Evans-Pritchard.

35. Raymond Schwab, *The Oriental Renaissance,* tr. G. Patterson and A. Reinking (New York, 1984); and Martin Bernal, *Black Athena: The Afroasiatic Roots of Classical Civilization,* I (New Brunswick, N.J., 1987); cf. Gusdorf, V, 355.

36. J. J. Bachofen, *Myth, Religion, and Mother Right,* tr. Ralph Manheim (Princeton, 1967), 3.

37. Henry Sumner Maine, *Ancient Law,* 10th ed. (London, 1924), 91; also Maine, *Lectures on the Early History of Institutions* (New York, 1975), and *Dissertations on Early Law and Customs* (New York, 1886). See also J. W. Burrow,

Evolution and Society: A Study of Victorian Social Theory (Cambridge, Eng., 1966), 137–79; George Feaver, *From Status to Contract: A Biography of Sir Henry Sumner Maine, 1827–1888* (London, 1969); and R. C. J. Cocks, *Sir Henry Maine: A Study in Victorian Jurisprudence* (Cambridge, Eng., 1988).

38. Maine, *Ancient Law*, 43, 271. Cf. John Ferguson McLennan, *The Patriarchal Theory* (London, 1885); Lewis Henry Morgan, *Ancient Society*, ed. Leslie A. White (Cambridge, Mass., 1964); Edward Tylor, *Researches into the Early History of Mankind* (London, 1870), and *Anthropology* (London, 1904); and especially Paolo Grossi, *An Alternative to Private Property: Collective Property in the Juridical Consciousness of the Nineteenth Century*, tr. L. Cochrane (Chicago, 1981).

39. Feaver, 24.

40. Thomas R. Trautmann, *Lewis Henry Morgan and the Invention of Kinship* (Berkeley, 1987), 54.

41. Emile de Laveleye, *Primitive Property*, tr. G. Marriott (London, 1878).

42. *The Ethnological Notebooks of Karl Marx*, ed. Lawrence Krader (Assen, 1972), 324ff; and see Kelley, "The Science of Anthropology," with further citations.

43. *Ethnological Notebooks*, 112, 224. It was on the basis of Marx's notes that Engels produced his *Origin of the Family, Private Property, and the State*, tr. Eleanor Burke Leacock (New York, 1972).

44. Edward Tylor, *Primitive Culture* (London, 1871), and *Main Trends of Research in the Social and Human Sciences*, ed. J. Havet (The Hague, 1978), II, pt. 1, 18; cf. Ivan Kalvar, "The *Völkerpsychologie* of Lazarus and Steinthal and the Modern Concept of Culture," *Journal of the History of Ideas*, 48 (1987), 671–90.

45. N. S. Timasheff, *An Introduction to the Sociology of Law* (Cambridge, Mass., 1939). The large literature on the history of sociology is mainly superficial (except for commentary on major figures) and has little to do with the law. Detailed surveys include: Ronald Fletcher, *The Making of Sociology* (New York, 1971); Alberto Izzo, ed., *Storia del pensiero sociologico* (Bologna, 1974–77); and Raymond Aron, *Main Currents in Sociological Thought* (New York, 1965). Of more theoretical interest are Peter T. Manicas, *A History and Philosophy of the Social Sciences* (Oxford, 1987), on the "Americanization of social science"; Geoffrey Hawthorne, *Enlightenment and Despair: A History of Social Theory*, 2nd ed. (Cambridge, Eng., 1987), with up-to-date bibliography; and Philip Abrams, "The Sense of the Past and the Origin of Sociology," *Past and Present*, 35 (1972), 18–32.

46. Auguste Comte, *Cours de philosophie positive*, ed. J. P. Enthoven (Paris, 1975), II, *Physique sociale*, 88.

47. Stefan Collini, Donald Winch, and John Burrow, *That Noble Science of Politics* (Cambridge, Eng., 1983).

48. Albion Small, *Origins of Sociology* (Chicago, 1924); see also Ernst Becker, *The Lost Science of Man* (New York, 1971); and D. R. Kelley, "The Prehistory of Sociology: Montesquieu, Vico, and the Legal Tradition," *Journal of the History of the Behavioral Sciences*, 16 (1980), 133–44 (reprinted in *History, Law, and the Human Sciences*). Yet Small's progeny have cut themselves off from the roots he traced; see two recent books, both entitled *The Chicago School of*

Sociology, by Martin Bulmer (Chicago, 1984), and by Dennis Smith (New York, 1988), who both quite neglect Becker on "the tragic paradox of Albion Small."

49. Robert Nisbet, *The Sociological Tradition* (New York, 1966); and see especially Emile Durkheim, *Montesquieu and Rousseau: Forerunners of Sociology,* tr. R. Manheim (Ann Arbor, 1960); Werner Stark, *Montesquieu: Pioneer of the Sociology of Knowledge* (London, 1960); and Eugen Ehrlich, "Montesquieu and Sociological Jurisprudence," *Harvard Law Review,* 29 (1916), 516.

50. Arthur Mitzman, *Sociology and Estrangement: Three Sociologists of Imperial Germany* (New York, 1973), on Tönnies, Sombart, and Michels; Harry Liebersohn, *Fate and Utopia in German Sociology, 1870–1923* (Cambridge, Mass., 1988), on Tönnies, Troeltsch, Weber, Simmel, and Lukacs; Raymond Aron, *La Sociologie allemande contemporaine* (Paris, 1936), on Simmel, Weber, Oppenheimer, and others; and the essays by M. Rainer Lepsius, Kurt Lenk, and Jurgen Kocka in *Modern German Sociology,* ed. Volker Meja, Dieter Misgeld, and Nico Stehr (New York, 1987), 37–111. Of particular significance for the legal connection are Otto Gierke, *Die Genossenschaftstheorie* (Berlin, 1887); John D. Lewis, *The Genossenschaft-Theory of Otto von Gierke* (Madison, Wis., 1935); and A. Schaffle, *Bau und Leben des socialen Körpers* (Tübingen, 1875), beginning with "Allgemeine Sociologie"; and also Timasheff and Gurvitch, *L'Idée du droit sociale* (Paris, 1932).

51. Lorenz von Stein, *The History of the Social Movement in France, 1789–1850,* tr. K. Mengelberg (Totowa, N.J., 1964), 43.

52. *The Sociology of Georg Simmel,* ed. Kurt H. Wolff (New York, 1950); and see Peter Lawrence, *Georg Simmel, Sociologist and European* (New York, 1976).

53. See, e.g., Franz von Holtzendorf, *Encyclopädie der Rechtswissenschaft* (Leipzig, 1870); and Henri Ahrens, *Encyclopédie juridique ou exposition organisé de la science du droit privé,* tr. A. Chauffard (Paris, 1880) from first German ed. (1855).

54. Clifford Geertz, *Local Knowledge* (New York, 1983), 150.

55. Fernand Tönnies, *Community and Association,* tr. C. P. Loomis (London, 1955); cf. Tönnies, *On Sociology: Pure, Applied, and Empirical,* tr. W. Cahnman and R. Heberle (Chicago, 1971), *Custom: An Essay on Social Codes,* tr. A. Borenstein (New York, 1961), and *On Social Ideas and Ideologies,* tr. E. G. Jacoby (New York, 1974); and cf. Feaver.

56. Tönnies, *On Sociology,* 199.

57. Emile Durkheim, *Les Règles de la méthode sociologique* (Paris, 1981); Durkheim, *Textes* (Paris, 1975), I. *Eléments d'une théorie sociale,* and III. *Fonctions sociales et institutions; Durkheim and the Law,* ed. Steven Lukes and Andrew Scull (New York, 1983); and see especially Lukes, *Emile Durkheim: His Life and Work* (New York, 1972). And on the background of the Durkheimian conception, see Marco Orrù, "Anomy and Reason in the English Renaissance," *Journal of the History of Ideas,* 47 (1986), 177–96.

58. Max Weber, *Economy and Society,* ed. G. Roth and C. Wittich (New York, 1968), esp. II, 641ff (*Rechtssoziologie*), and *On the Methodology of the Social Sciences,* tr. E. Shils and H. Finch (Glencoe, Ill., 1945); on the juridical aspects

of Weberian sociology see Anthony T. Kronen, *Max Weber* (London, 1983); also, in a large and growing literature, Brian Turner, *For Weber: Essays in the Sociology of Fate* (Boston, 1981), 318–51; Arthur Mitzman, *The Iron Cage: An Historical Interpretation of Max Weber* (New York, 1970); Wolfgang Mommsen, *The Political and Social Thought of Max Weber* (Chicago, 1989); and Mommsen and Osterhammel, eds., *Max Weber and His Contemporaries*.

59. Weber, *Economy and Society*, I, 227; and see Ch. 6 at n. 34.
60. Mannheim, *Ideology and Utopia: An Introduction to the Sociology of Knowledge*, tr. L. Wirth and E. Shils (New York, 1952), and *Essays on the Sociology of Knowledge*, tr. P. Kecskemeti (New York, 1952); cf. Colin Loader, *The Intellectual Development of Karl Mannheim* (Cambridge, Eng., 1985); Volker Meja and Nico Stehr, eds., *Der Streit uber die Wissensoziologie* (Frankfurt, 1981); and Georges Gurvitch, *The Social Framework of Knowledge*, tr. M. and K. Thompson (Oxford, 1971).
61. Jürgen Habermas, *The Theory of Communicative Action*, tr. T. McCarthy (Boston, 1981), I, 4. See Lawrence A. Scaff, "Culture, Philosophy, and Politics: The Formation of the Socio-cultural Sciences in Germany," *History of the Human Sciences*, 1 (1988), 237; and cf. Charles Lemert, *Sociology and the Twilight of Man: Homocentrism and Discourse in Social Theory* (Carbondale, Ill., 1979).
62. Léon Duguit, *Les Transformations générales du droit privé depuis le Code Napoléon* (Paris, 1912), and *Le Droit social, le droit individuel, et la transformation de l'état* (Paris, 1908); also Fassò, III, 164; and William Logue, *From Philosophy to Sociology: The Evolution of French Liberalism, 1870–1914* (Dekalb, Ill., 1983). In 1891 Duguit gave a seminar on sociology, which, however, was not attended by Durkheim—see Terry Clark, *Prophets and Patrons: The French University and the Emergence of the Social Sciences* (Cambridge, Mass., 1973), 182.
63. Timasheff, 49. See especially Ehrlich, *Fundamental Principles of the Sociology of Law*; Georges Gurvitch, *Sociology of Law* (New York, 1942); René Worms, *La Sociologie et le droit* (Paris, 1895), and *Sociology of Law*, ed. V. Aubert (New York, 1969); Paul Vinogradoff, *Outlines of Historical Jurisprudence* (London, 1920), vol. I; and Julien Bonnecase, *La Pensée juridique française* (Bordeaux, 1933).
64. Gurvitch, *Sociology of Law*, 69.

15 · Conclusion

1. Richard Rorty, "Solidarity or Objectivity?" in *Relativism: Interpretation and Confrontation*, ed. Michael Kranz (Notre Dame, 1989), 35.
2. Ernst Troeltsch, *Der Historismus und seine Probleme* (Tübingen, 1922), 102–10, "Naturalismus und Historismus." In a vast literature, see Franco Bianco, ed., *Il dibatto sullo storicismo* (Bologna, 1978).
3. See especially Heinrich Rickert, *Kulturwissenschaft und Naturwissenschaft* (Freiburg, 1899), and *The Limits of Concept Formation in Natural Science*, tr. G. Oakes (Cambridge, Eng., 1986). Cf., in another large literature, Michael Ermath, *Wilhelm Dilthey: The Critique of Historical Reason* (Chicago, 1978),

186ff, on the discussion after Windelband's rectoral address of 1894 on "Geschichte und Naturwissenschaft"; and Troeltsch, 30, n. 15.

4. Kant, *Der Streit der Fakultäten,* tr. by M. Gregor as *The Conflict of the Faculties* (New York, 1979), 141. Jellinek is cited by Paul Honigsheim, *On Max Weber,* tr. J. Rytina (New York, 1968), 68.

5. H. G. Gadamer, *Truth and Method,* tr. G. Barden and J. Cumming (New York, 1975), 290.

6. Karl Renner, *The Institutions of Private Law and Their Social Function,* tr. A. Schwarzschild (London, 1949); and Hans Kelsen, *The Pure Theory of Law* (Berkeley, 1967). On recent attempts of the law to come to terms with modern thought, see Peter Goodrich, *Legal Discourse: Studies in Linguistics, Rhetoric, and Legal Analysis* (New York, 1987); S. H. Humphreys, "Law, Anthropology, and History," *History and Anthropology,* 1 (1984), 241–64; Sanford Levinson and Steven Mailloux, eds., *Interpreting Law and Literature: A Hermeneutical Reader* (Evanston, Ill., 1988); Ronald Dworkin, "Law as Interpretation," *The Politics of Interpretation,* ed. W. J. T. Mitchell (Chicago, 1985); and Robert Gordon, "Historicism in Legal Scholarship," *Yale Law Journal,* 90 (1981), 1017–56.

7. Edmund Husserl, *Gesammelte Werke,* IV, *Der Krisis der europäischen Wissenschaften und die tranzendentale Phänomenologie* (The Hague, 1954); cf. Jürgen Habermas, *The Theory of Communicative Action,* tr. Thomas McCarthy (2 vols., Boston, 1981–87), I, 4; Judith Shklar, *Legalism* (Cambridge, Mass., 1964); and Erik Wolf, *Das Problem der Naturrechtslehre: Versuch einer Orientierung* (Karlsruhe, 1955).

8. See, most recently, Mark Kelman, *A Guide to Critical Legal Studies* (Cambridge, Mass., 1987).

9. See Ch. 14, n. 1.

10. See, e.g., Ernest Becker, *The Lost Science of Man* (New York, 1971); Charles Lemert, *Sociology and the Twilight of Man* (Carbondale, Ill., 1979); but cf. David Thomas, *Naturalism and Social Science: A Post-Empiricist Philosophy of Social Science* (Cambridge, Eng., 1979). Karl W. Deutsch, *Advances in the Social Sciences, 1900–1980* (Cambridge, Mass., 1986), 356, distinguishes between "two basic styles of social science," "the hermeneutical-literary or the empirical and mathematical." On the other hand, A. J. Arnaud, *Dictionnaire encyclopédique de théorie et de sociologie de droit* (Paris, 1988), speaks of the "vulgarisation, balkanisation, et babélisation" of the discipline.

11. Gadamer, *Truth and Method,* 289, 495; and see Giuseppe Zaccaria, *Ermeneutica e giurisprudenza: i fondamenti filosofici nella teoria di Hans Georg Gadamer* (Milan, 1982).

12. Donald N. McCloskey, *The Rhetoric of Economics* (Madison, Wis., 1985), 5; and Patrick Madigan, *The Modern Project to Rigor: Descartes to Nietzsche* (Lanham, Md., 1986).

13. Nietzsche, *The Will to Power,* 199.

14. Donald McCloskey, *The Rhetoric of Economics;* Clifford Geertz, *Local Knowledge* (New York, 1983); James Boone, *Other Tribes, Other Scribes* (Cambridge, Eng., 1982); George E. Marcus and Michael M. J. Fischer, *Anthropology as Cultural Critique* (Chicago, 1986); Richard H. Brown, *A Poetic for*

Sociology (Chicago, 1977); Charles Taylor, *Philosophical Papers,* vol. I, *Human Agency and Language,* and vol. II, *Philosophy and the Human Sciences* (Cambridge, Eng., 1985). See also Richard Bernstein, *The Restructuring of Social and Political Theory* (Philadelphia, 1978), and *Beyond Objectivism and Relativism* (Philadelphia, 1983); *The Rhetoric of the Human Sciences,* ed. John S. Nelson, Allan Megill, and Donald N. McCloskey (Madison, Wis., 1987), and the exchange with Peter Munz in *Journal of the History of Ideas,* 51 (1990), 121–47; Richard Rorty, *Philosophy and the Mirror of Nature* (Princeton, 1979); Donald N. Levine, *The Flight from Ambiguity* (Chicago, 1985); and Paul Ricoeur, *Hermeneutics and the Human Sciences,* tr. John B. Thompson (Cambridge, Eng., 1981).

15. Clifford Geertz, *Works and Lives: The Anthropologist as Author* (Stanford, 1988).

16. Alasdair MacIntyre, *Whose Justice? Which Rationality?* (Notre Dame, 1988), 7.

17. Hans Blumenberg, *Work on Myth,* tr. R. Wallace (Cambridge, Mass., 1985), 263.

18. See, e.g., Thomas Heller, Morton Sosna, and David E. Wellbery, eds., *Reconstructing Individualism: Autonomy, Individuality, and the Self in Western Thought* (Stanford, 1986) and now Charles Taylor, *Sources of the Self: The Making of the Modern Identity* (Cambridge, Mass., 1989).

Index

Ius canonicum, 82–88, 126, 174, 178, 191
Ius civile, 39, 40–47, 49, 91, 126, 167,
 174–80, 186, 190, 191, 194, 195, 197,
 216, 228, 266
Ius commune, 62, 87, 96, 100, 182, 216
Ius feudale, 96–99, 122, 123, 139, 168,
 178, 190, 204, 221, 238
Ius gentium, 47, 57, 61–64, 82, 116, 121–
 27, 130, 139, 157, 160, 184, 190–96,
 218, 230, 231, 233, 237, 238, 265
Ius naturale, 47, 61, 62, 88, 127, 139, 143,
 150, 160, 185, 194, 208, 211, 213, 216,
 217, 221, 224, 230, 233, 234, 237–42,
 253, 264, 265, 266
Ius proprium, 57, 62, 96, 121, 129, 167,
 169, 182, 191, 216, 217
Ius respondendi, 42, 56
Ivo of Chartres, 87, 88

Jacobins, 227
Jacobus, 111
Jacqueminot, 227
Jaeger, Werner, 20, 28, 29, 31
James I, 177
Jefferson, Thomas, 186
Jellinek, Georg, 277
Jenkins, David, 168
Jerome (St.), 48, 73, 74, 79, 84, 106
Jesus, 68
Jhering, Rudolph, 246, 270
Johannes Teutonicus, 118, 149, 150
John of Salisbury, 151, 160
Judex est lex loquens, 173
Julian (Emperor), 78, 79
Jung, Carl Gustav, 271
Jupiter, 37, 40
Jusnaturalism, 213–19, 232
Jussieu, A. L., 265
Justi, J. H. G. von, 258
Justin Martyr, 71
Justinian, 4, 45, 46, 48, 53–66, 76, 78, 79,
 80, 82, 93, 109–13, 118, 120, 122, 123,
 125, 130, 132, 133, 136, 140, 141, 142,
 149, 170, 172, 177, 178, 186, 190, 191,
 193, 196, 198, 200, 203, 210, 222, 223,
 224, 225, 227, 230, 233, 237, 254, 255

Kames, Lord, 184
Kant, Immanuel, 1, 240, 241, 253, 254,
 262, 264, 277, 278
Kantorowicz, Ernst, 81, 146, 150
Kelsen, Hans, 278
Kirk, G. S., 4, 24
Knies, Karl, 258

Knowles, David, 91
Koeppe, A., 248
Kuhn, Thomas, 7, 225

L'Hôpital, Michel de, 223
Laboulaye, Edouard, 249
Lactantius, 79
Lagus, Conrad, 209, 211, 212, 229, 231
Lambarde, William, 172, 173, 175, 180
Landmann, Michael, 279
Launay, Francois de, 205
Laurentius Hispanus, 155
Laurière, Eusebe, 108, 205
Laveleye, Emile, 267
Le Caron, Louis, 199, 200, 204, 213, 221
Le Douaren, François, 187, 188, 190, 196,
 214, 247
Lebras, Gabriel, 148, 160, 274
Leges barbarorum, 93–96
Leges actiones, 39, 49, 103, 166
Leibniz, G. W., 2, 132, 143, 209, 210, 213,
 214, 215, 216, 217, 241, 244
Leo I (Pope), 84
Lerminier, Eugène, 233, 247
Levy, Ernest, 63
Levy-Bruhl, Lucien, 281
Lex ex facto oritur, 9, 89, 176, 238, 249
Lex regia, 82, 175, 177, 227
Lex Salica, 94, 95
Lexicography, 189, 211
Liber Augustalis, 123, 124, 223
Liberty, 50, 81, 118, 145, 161, 167, 193,
 214, 236
Libri Carolini, 159
Libri Feudorum, 99, 101, 122, 123, 135,
 142, 160, 173, 191, 220
List, Friedrich, 263
Littleton, 170, 172
Livius, Titus, 36
Lizet, Pierre, 204, 206
Locus regit actum, 105
Logos, 3, 14, 25, 27, 29, 30, 31, 32, 33,
 54, 67, 69, 70, 71, 72, 74, 75, 76, 81,
 82, 86, 87, 89, 120, 150, 155, 156, 161
Loisel, Antoine, 200, 201, 202, 204, 205
Lokalvernunft, 11, 240
Louis IX, 98, 103, 104, 221
Louis XI, 223
Louis XIV, 205, 224
Lovejoy, Arthur O., 270
Lucas de Penna, 128, 134, 141, 142, 151
Ludewig, J. P. von, 240
Luitprand (king of the Lombards), 94
Luther, 72, 131, 148, 159, 161–63, 225,
 254, 256